NEW EXPLORATIONS IN THEOLOGY

JONATHAN EDWARDS AND DEIFICATION

RECONCILING *THEOSIS* AND THE REFORMED TRADITION

JAMES R. SALLADIN

An imprint of InterVarsity Press
Downers Grove, Illinois

InterVarsity Press
P.O. Box 1400, Downers Grove, IL 60515-1426
ivpress.com
email@ivpress.com

©2022 by James Salladin

All rights reserved. No part of this book may be reproduced in any form without written permission from InterVarsity Press.

InterVarsity Press® is the book-publishing division of InterVarsity Christian Fellowship/USA®, a movement of students and faculty active on campus at hundreds of universities, colleges, and schools of nursing in the United States of America, and a member movement of the International Fellowship of Evangelical Students. For information about local and regional activities, visit intervarsity.org.

Scripture quotations, unless otherwise noted, are from The Holy Bible, English Standard Version, copyright © 2001 by Crossway Bibles, a division of Good News Publishers. Used by permission. All rights reserved.

An earlier version of chapter 1 was originally published as "Essence and Fullness: Evaluating the Creator-Creature Distinction in Jonathan Edwards." Scottish Journal of Theology 70/4 (2017), 427-444. Reprinted with permission.

The publisher cannot verify the accuracy or functionality of website URLs used in this book beyond the date of publication.

Cover design: Cindy Kiple
Interior design: Beth McGill

ISBN 978-1-5140-0046-5 (print)
ISBN 978-1-5140-0047-2 (digital)

Printed in the United States of America ∞

InterVarsity Press is committed to ecological stewardship and to the conservation of natural resources in all our operations. This book was printed using sustainably sourced paper.

Library of Congress Cataloging-in-Publication Data

Names: Salladin, James R., 1977- author.
Title: Jonathan Edwards and deification : reconciling theosis and the Reformed tradition / James R. Salladin.
Description: Downers Grove, IL : IVP Academic, [2022] | Series: New explorations in theology | Includes bibliographical references and index.
Identifiers: LCCN 2021042645 (print) | LCCN 2021042646 (ebook) | ISBN 9781514000465 (print) | ISBN 9781514000472 (digital)
Subjects: LCSH: Edwards, Jonathan, 1703-1758. | Salvation—Christianity—History of doctrines. | Deification (Christianity)—History of doctrines. | Reformed Church—Doctrines.
Classification: LCC BX7260.E3 S35 2022 (print) | LCC BX7260.E3 (ebook) | DDC 230/.58—dc23
LC record available at https://lccn.loc.gov/2021042645
LC ebook record available at https://lccn.loc.gov/2021042646

"Divinization, theosis, participation, and synonymous concepts are engaging scholars of Christian thought, particularly those who consider the eighteenth-century British-American theologian Jonathan Edwards. While saintly participation in God is usually associated with Eastern Orthodoxy, Jim Salladin recommends Edwards as an intentionally Reformed thinker whose formulation of deification involved a supernatural communication of divine grace and fullness to the regenerate, a union of natures that maintained the Creator-creature distinction. Here, Edwards emerges not only as a significant historical figure but also as a resource for contemporary consideration."

Kenneth P. Minkema, Jonathan Edwards Center at Yale University

"God, in the infinite plenitude of his self-delight, opens his life to pour forth his fullness to his own. Salladin unpacks and develops this theme in Edwards's writings, revealing the overarching impulse of Edwards's doctrines of grace, participation, and deification. This is a substantial contribution to the field and an important retrieval for the ongoing conversation about these themes in modern theology."

Kyle Strobel, associate professor at Talbot School of Theology and author of *Jonathan Edwards's Theology: A Reinterpretation*

"Does God save us by working outside of us and helping us accept that external work? Or does he save by drawing us into his very being so that we participate in his inner life? James Salladin argues that Jonathan Edwards taught a version of the latter and so is one of the great theologians teaching what the Eastern Orthodox call *theosis*. All Christians and scholars interested in divinization and its relation to the Reformed tradition will want to read this clear and engaging study."

Gerald McDermott, retired Anglican Chair of Divinity at Beeson Divinity School, Samford University, and coauthor of *The Theology of Jonathan Edwards*

"Reformed theology must embrace divinization. Such is Jim Salladin's conviction, grounded in his extensive study of Jonathan Edwards. Salladin persuasively argues that the Northampton pastor saw all of creation as participating in the being of God, while divinization fills us with the fulness of God. Perhaps the most intriguing aspect of Salladin's proposal is that Edwards's embrace of theosis left his Calvinism intact. *Jonathan Edwards and Deification* is a significant contribution to the ongoing debate on Edwards's Reformed credentials."

Hans Boersma, Saint Benedict Servants of Christ Chair in Ascetical Theology at Nashotah House and author of *Five Things Theologians Wish Biblical Scholars Knew*

"James Salladin's elegantly written and convincing argument distinguishes itself within the expanding discipline of Edwardsian studies by way of a comprehensive understanding of secondary literature and a mastery of Jonathan Edwards's own written corpus. Salladin's close reading of Edwards allows the Northampton pastor to speak for himself regarding matters of deification as 'participation in divine fullness.' This noteworthy contribution substantiates a significant reality: Edwards articulates his philosophical and theological creativity from within a Reformed theological heritage, even as it relates to the concept of theosis. Jonathan Edwards is first and foremost a theologian of the lineage of Calvin, Perkins, and Stoddard, yet it is a line with an expansive understanding of sanctification that envelopes 'God's end in creation' within the elect themselves."

John J. Bombaro, associate director of Eurasia, Lutheran Church Missouri Synod, and author of *Jonathan Edwards's Vision of Reality*

"An outstanding study of Edwards's theology of deification, which highlights the coherence of his theological vision."

Alister McGrath, Andreas Idreos Professor of Science and Religion and director of the Ian Ramsey Centre for Science and Religion, Oxford University

"Jim Salladin's work on deification in Jonathan Edwards is a welcome addition to Edwardsian scholarship on the important matter of salvation as participation in the divine life. It builds on previous work in this area but gives significant clarity to some of the key issues involved in a Reformational appropriation of this doctrine of deification. In so doing, Jim has served to enhance ecumenical dialogue in soteriological matters and to remind the Reformed tradition that it comes within the wider theologically catholic tradition of the church, while preserving the distinctly Reformed contribution to it. As Jim has acknowledged, even if Edwards did not deploy the word *deification*, he did 'espouse a concept of grace that delivers its substance.' Edwards has perhaps preeminently, in the older Reformed tradition, centered salvation in participation in the life of God: it is centered on matters filial and ontological as the grounding of matters forensic or juridical. Jim vindicates Edwards in his doctrine of special saving grace so formative in evangelical life, as well as in his keeping the Creator-creature distinction clear. This book does not merely contribute academically, however. It will edify and inspire all Christians to press in to the life of the triune God."

W. Ross Hastings, Sangwoo Youtong Chee Professor of Theology at Regent College and author of *Total Atonement: Participation in the Reconciliation of Humanity and Creation*

"This erudite book is exactly what we need to continue advancing the ecumenical conversation about deification in the Christian tradition. Jim Salladin provides a careful and compelling study of how Jonathan Edwards develops a vision of deification by going deeper into his own Reformed tradition. Rather than borrowing from the East or anachronistically reading doctrines into older authors, Salladin shows how Edwards creatively draws on the categories of his own tradition to offer a distinctively Reformed understanding of deification. A model study."

Jared Ortiz, associate professor of religion at Hope College and editor of *Deification in the Latin Patristic Tradition*

"One of the most important contributions Jonathan Edwards made to Christian theology was his claim that fallen human beings are destined to become partakers of the divine nature on a journey into God that is everlasting. But what does Edwards mean by this puzzling idea? Drawing on the wealth of recent research in this area, James Salladin provides his readers with an answer that is both intellectually satisfying and heartwarming."

Oliver D. Crisp, professor of analytic theology and director of the Logos Institute for Analytic and Exegetical Theology, University of St. Andrews

To the parishioners of St. John's, St. James's, and Emmanuel

May you be filled with the fullness of

the God who is his best gift.

Ephesians 3:14-21

Contents

Acknowledgments — ix

Abbreviations — xi

Introduction — 1

   1 Grace and Fullness — 19

   2 Grace and Nature — 65

   3 Grace and God — 96

   4 Grace and Creation — 145

   5 Grace and Fulfillment — 196

Conclusion — 238

Bibliography — 251

Name Index — 259

Subject Index — 260

Scripture Index — 266

Acknowledgments

IF GOD IS HIS OWN BEST GIFT, then it would appear that his second-best gift is the community of saints who point us to him. That is true on the grand scale of salvation and redemption, but it is also true on the much smaller scale of academics. I am so very grateful to so many for the support and encouragement, critique and correction, gifts and insights that made this project possible.

I begin by thanking the academic community at Regent College for creating a space where I could explore theology and begin to put pieces together. I am first a pastor, and I trained at Regent with ministry in view. But people like J. I. Packer and Don Lewis encouraged me to pursue research as well as parish ministry. And then they showed me how that research might happen. Don introduced me to Oliver Crisp, who gave me a reading list that propelled me deeper into Edwards, and J. I. Packer gave me both a model for what churchly academics can look like and also coached me, encouraged me, and gave recommendations that charted my course. Bruce Hindmarsh similarly refined my vision for the role studying early evangelicals can play in bearing fruit for the church today. And while Kyle Strobel is not part of the Regent community, he welcomed me to the world of Edwards and gave me a map for charting my way through a sometimes bewildering landscape.

And then of course I must thank my dissertation supervisors and my universities that fostered the first version of this book. Alister McGrath launched my PhD work and his encyclopedic knowledge of the great Christian tradition taught me to put Edwards in a larger context of the

Christian movement. When he left Kings College London, Steve Holmes graciously opened the door for me to complete my research with him at the University of St. Andrews. Dr. Holmes's critical eye and deep knowledge of Edwards brought my work into focus. I am deeply grateful to both.

All the work of this book has been done while I have pastored in congregations. And I give my deep thanks for all the parishioners at St. John's Vancouver, St. James Muswell Hill, and Emmanuel New York City. God disciples pastors through their congregations, and these congregations allowed me to unite the ministry of preaching and pastoring with research, giving both a deeper richness. Much of the work for this book happened while I served at St. James Muswell Hill in London, and so I give special thanks to Kim Swithinbank, Chris Green, and the whole church for the support and encouragement and time I was given there.

Words fail to express the gift God has given me in my family. I want to thank my father, who knew I should study theology before anyone else did, along with my mother and brothers who have been a constant source of encouragement. I thank my sons for their affection and their way of filling me with delight, and, in many ways, for teaching me to pray.

There is no one to whom I owe more than to my wife, Amber. Where would I be without your wisdom, your encouragement, your rebuke, and your teaching? The words *thank you* cannot bear the weight of gratitude I owe you.

Above all I thank God, Father, Son, and Holy Spirit, in prayer that all that is true in this book may contribute to his people being filled with his fullness, and all that is not may be quickly forgotten, and its author forgiven. Amen.

Abbreviations

HTR *Harvard Theological Review*
IJST *International Journal of Systematic Theology*
SJT *Scottish Journal of Theology*
ThTo *Theology Today*
WJE Works of Jonathan Edwards. New Haven, CT: Yale University Press, 1957–2009

Introduction

G od's best gift is himself. That is a small sentence that will take the saints all eternity to fully grasp. But big as this small statement is, it is the bold claim Christianity makes. Consider the prayers of Christ and of Paul. Jesus, shortly before his arrest in John's Gospel, prays to the Father: "I have made known to them your name, and I will continue to make it known, that the love with which you have loved me may be in them, and I in them" (Jn 17:26). Jesus' great aim, his great desire, is that the Father will give himself in love to the saints just as the Father has always given himself in love to the Son. This is Jesus' aim in revelation, and considering he prays this just moments before his crucifixion, it is the aim of his redeeming acts. And do not miss Jesus' desire to indwell the saints. Jesus' prayer shows that the Trinity's great gift is the Trinity. Paul's prayer makes the same point, except that the Holy Spirit joins the stage.

> For this reason I bow my knees before the Father, from whom every family in heaven and on earth is named, that according to the riches of his glory he may grant you to be strengthened with power through his Spirit in your inner being, so that Christ may dwell in your hearts through faith—that you, being rooted and grounded in love, may have strength to comprehend with all the saints what is the breadth and length and height and depth, and to know the love of Christ that surpasses knowledge, that you may be filled with all the fullness of God. (Eph 3:14-19)

This is the language of a bold son who knows his Father will withhold nothing of value. Paul peers into the Father's treasury as if to ask, "Father, give the church what you value most." The content of these "riches of his glory" turns out to be the Spirit and the Son. Again, the Trinity's great gift is the Trinity. The Father gives the Spirit, who binds the saints to Christ in his truth and his love. The result is that the saints are "filled with all the *fullness* of God." It is the purpose of Christ's redemption to procure this fullness, the purpose of the Spirit to impart it, the aim of Scripture to reveal it, and the role of the church to enjoy its reality forever in constant adoration. The purpose of this book is to follow one theologian's attempt to describe this great gift.

Jonathan Edwards (1703–1758) believed that true grace in the heart of a saint is a communication and participation in divine fullness. This book is a sustained response to the basic question, What does he mean? In particular, how did Edwards navigate the Creator-creature distinction? Further still, how does Edwards's view of grace as participation in divine fullness relate to his Reformed heritage?

In brief, when Edwards spoke of divine grace, he understood that the fullness that characterizes the Trinity and the incarnate Christ is given, with measure, to the saints. This divine fullness is not vested in created nature. Rather, it is above and discontinuous with created nature. It is "something of God."[1] However, at the same time this communication of divine fullness does not impart the divine essence. Thus, when God gives special grace, God gives *himself* to the creature, establishing a profound and even infinite union between Creator and creature. Yet, this communication never fuses the creature with the Creator. Rather, for all eternity God and the saints will enjoy a christologically mediated bond in the Spirit, which will increase perpetually but still never violate the Creator-creature distinction. This communication and participation in divine fullness is the end purpose of creation and redemption. Edwards believed that God's great gift is himself, and that God designed creation to receive this grace and redeemed humanity in order to give this grace.

Edwards's doctrine of true grace amounts to a species of what the Christian tradition has often called deification or theosis or divinization.[2] Deification is a difficult category to define, but in broad terms it refers to a

---

[1] Jonathan Edwards, "True Grace Is Divine (1738)," in *Jonathan Edwards: Spiritual Writings*, ed. Adriaan C. Neele, Kyle C. Strobel, and Kenneth P. Minkema, Classics of Western Spirituality (New York: Paulist Press, 2019).
[2] I will use these terms interchangeably.

"comprehensive vision for the Christian life that centers on the saint's participation in the divine nature, through the economic activity of the Son and the Spirit." Theosis does this in a way that maintains the Creator-creature distinction, so that the human nature is not abrogated but brought to its ultimate goal.[3] Many Edwards scholars have presented Edwards's thought as a form of deification, and this study will validate that claim. However, calling Edwards's doctrine a form of deification creates possible tension with his Reformed heritage. Deification language has never been common in Reformed circles. The absolute importance of maintaining the Creator-creature distinction led the mainstream Reformed tradition to shy away or repudiate words such as *deification* and *theosis* and *divinization*. Edwards himself abstained from deploying these words, despite the fact that he read and learned from theologians who did use them.

Nevertheless, if Edwards did not deploy the word *deification*, he did espouse a concept of grace that delivers its substance. Or perhaps better: Edwards's doctrine of grace achieves the same broad aims as classical accounts of deification, but the result is a particularly Reformed subspecies of deification thought. I say it this way because, as I will argue, Edwards presents his vision of participation in divine fullness in defense of his Reformed heritage and as a development of Reformed categories and insight. It is not a foreign import. Edwards's allegiance to his tradition did not mean he followed received patterns slavishly. Rather, his allegiance to his tradition moved him to look for ways to articulate its insights more fully. This led him to articulate special grace in a way that emphasized both the Creator-creature distinction and a real participation in fullness between them. For this reason I argue that Edwards's doctrine of special grace represents a resource for contemporary Reformed theology's engagement with participation soteriology and deification.

Deification, Participation, and Ontology in Contemporary Theology

In order to grasp more fully the significance and context for this project, it is helpful to have some deeper background on the state of current

---

[3]James Salladin, "Theosis," in *The Jonathan Edwards Encyclopedia*, ed. Kenneth P. Minkema, Harry S. Stout, and Adriaan C. Neele (Grand Rapids, MI: Eerdmans, 2017), 563-564.

participation scholarship and how Edwards's doctrine of grace relates to this conversation.

Over the course of the last thirty years, deification—or the functionally synonymous ideas of divinization and theosis—has become something of a "theological desideratum" for contemporary theology.[4] In the early twentieth century, it was viewed as primarily an Eastern Orthodox doctrine, and many Westerners viewed it as a Hellenistic aberration.[5] That has now changed. Luther scholars are claiming deification for Luther, Calvin scholars are claiming it for Calvin, Wesley scholars for Wesley, and as part of the larger trend, Edwards scholars are claiming it for Edwards.[6] This widespread embrace of deification grew, in part, out of the twentieth century's Russian diaspora. As Russian scholars such as Vladimir Lossky and John Meyendorf and others presented their understandings of deification to the West, Western theologians responded by asking whether this idea is present in

---

[4] See Paul Gavrilyuk, "The Retrieval of Deification: How a Once-Despised Archaism Became an Ecumenical Desideratum," *Modern Theology* 25, no. 4 (2009): 647-59.

[5] Norman Russell, *The Doctrine of Deification in the Greek Patristic Tradition*, Oxford Early Christian Studies (Oxford: Oxford University Press, 2006), 3-7.

[6] Luther scholars: Carl E. Braaten, "The Finnish Breakthrough in Luther Research," *Pro Ecclesia* 5, no. 2 (1996): 141-43; Carl E. Braaten and Robert W. Jenson, *Union with Christ: The New Finnish Interpretation of Luther* (Grand Rapids, MI: Eerdmans, 1998); Jonathan Linman, "Little Christs for the World: Faith and Sacraments as Means to *Theosis*," in *Partakers of the Divine Nature: The History and Development of Deification in the Christian Traditions*, ed. Michael J. Christensen and Jeffery A. Wittung (Grand Rapids, MI: Baker Academic, 2008), 189-99.

Calvin scholars: J. Todd Billings, "John Calvin: United to God Through Christ," in Christensen and Wittung, *Partakers of the Divine Nature*, 200-218; Carl Mosser, "The Greatest Possible Blessing: Calvin and Deification," *SJT* 55, no. 1 (2002): 36-57. For a debate regarding whether Eastern Orthodox essence-energies distinction should be received in the Reformed tradition, see Gannon Murphy, "Reformed Theosis?," *ThTo* 65, no. 2 (2008): 191-212; Myk Habets, "'Reformed Theosis?' A Response to Gannon Murphy," *ThTo* 65, no. 4 (2009): 489-98.

Wesley scholars: Michael J. Christensen, "Theosis and Sanctification : John Wesley's Reformulation of a Patristic Doctrine," *Wesleyan Theological Journal* 31, no. 1 (1996): 71-94; Christensen, "John Wesley: Christian Perfection as Faith Filled with the Energy of Love," in Christensen and Wittung, *Partakers of the Divine Nature*, 219-29.

Edwards scholars: see, e.g., Kyle Strobel, "Jonathan Edwards and the Polemics of Theosis," *HTR* 105, no. 3 (2012): 260; Strobel, "Jonathan Edwards's Reformed Doctrine of *Theosis*," *HTR* 109, no. 3 (2016): 371-99; Michael J. McClymond, "Salvation as Divinization: Jonathan Edwards, Gregory Palamas and the Theological Uses of Platonism," in *Jonathan Edwards: Philosophical Theologian*, ed. Oliver D. Crisp and Paul Helm (Burlington, VT: Ashgate, 2003), 139-60; Michael J. McClymond and Gerald R. McDermott, "The Theme of Divinization," in *The Theology of Jonathan Edwards* (Oxford: Oxford University Press, 2012), 410-23; Brandon G. Withrow, *Becoming Divine: Jonathan Edwards's Incarnational Spirituality Within the Christian Tradition* (Eugene, OR: Cascade Books, 2011); Oliver D. Crisp, *Jonathan Edwards on God and Creation* (Oxford: Oxford University Press, 2012), 172-73.

their own traditions.⁷ This has led many Western scholars to use the category of deification to describe their own tradition's views on salvation.

However the Russian diaspora is not the only twentieth-century source for interest in deification theology. Theologians from both the Roman Catholic tradition and the Reformed tradition began redeploying the concept in their work. Adam Cooper argues that Reginald Garrigou-Lagrange, Karl Rahner, and Henri de Lubac, despite great differences, all espoused versions of deification soteriology.⁸ Similarly, Thomas Torrance called for a recovery of deification thought long before it was common among Protestants.⁹ These thinkers differed significantly in their approaches, but they demonstrate that deification was a growing concern for a wider portion of the church than just the Eastern Orthodox tradition. The West was already (re)discovering deification in its own traditions by the middle of the twentieth century.

Contemporary theology also shows a growing interest in ontological participation in God. That is, increasing numbers of theologians are taking up old questions of metaphysics and arguing that Christian tradition must recover a strong view of direct dependence on God for its very being. Radical Orthodoxy insists that a strong view of participatory metaphysics is key to resisting modern secularity and constructing a coherent Christian view of the world.¹⁰ Hans Boersma argues for a sacramental ontology that seeks to ground all reality in a teleological framework. This world exists to point beyond itself, and this world is fulfilled in Christ.¹¹ Creation, these thinkers

---

⁷For fuller rehearsal of twentieth-century scholarship of the theme of theosis, see Russell, *Doctrine of Deification*, 3-7. Maarten Wisse gives several helpful reasons for the West's strong interest in theosis. See Wisse, *Trinitarian Theology Beyond Participation*, ed. Ian A. McFarland, John Webster, and Ivor Davidson, T&T Clark Studies in Systematic Theology (London: T&T Clark, 2011), 303-4.

⁸Adam C. Cooper, *Naturally Human, Supernaturally God: Deification in Pre-conciliar Catholicism* (Minneapolis: Fortress, 2014).

⁹T. F. Torrance, *Theology in Reconstruction* (London: SCM Press, 1965).

¹⁰See John Milbank, Catherine Pickstock, and Graham Ward, eds., *Radical Orthodoxy* (New York: Routledge, 1999); Simon Oliver, "What Is Radical Orthodoxy?," in *The Radical Orthodoxy Reader*, ed. John Milbank and Simon Oliver (New York: Routledge, 2009), 3-27; James K. A. Smith, *Introducing Radical Orthodoxy: Mapping a Post-secular Theology* (Grand Rapids, MI: Baker Academic, 2004).

¹¹See Hans Boersma, *Heavenly Participation: The Weaving of a Sacramental Tapestry* (Grand Rapids, MI: Eerdmans, 2011); Boersma, *Seeing God: The Beatific Vision in Christian Tradition* (Grand Rapids, MI: Eerdmans, 2018); Boersma, "Sacramental Ontology: Nature and the Supernatural in the Ecclesiology of Henri de Lubac," *New Blackfriars* 88 (2007): 242-73.

insist, is not disconnected from God. Resisting any hint of pantheistic or process theology, they all aim to demonstrate how it is that this creation relates to, depends on, and finds its ultimate fulfillment in God. The relationship between Creator and creature is a pressing concern.

The Significance of This Study

What is the significance of these concerns? It may be in vogue to speak of deification and participatory metaphysics, but what does it matter? The answer helps locate the relevance of this book. I take it that all of these interests are ways of reconnecting God and God's gift. The Christian tradition is a theology of grace. The church has always been concerned with God's gift. Christianity has always understood that God is generous; he gives many gifts. God gives creation its being. God gives sustenance and preserves creation. God orchestrates his creation in his providence and care. Beyond all these common graces are special graces. God gives justification and reconciliation. God gives sanctification and glorification. God elects, redeems, calls, and preserves his saints. All this is grace. Yet, strange as it may seem, these categories can sometimes sound distant from God himself. Put differently, Christian theology can sometimes speak of ontology or soteriology without speaking about theology proper. The doctrine of God and the doctrines of creation and salvation seem sometimes so distinct as to be disconnected. Theology at its best never allows this, and I take it that underneath the present interest in participatory metaphysics and deification in particular is an instinct to draw together the doctrines of God and salvation. T. F. Torrance makes just this point in his appeal for a rediscovery of theosis (his preferred term):

> At this point let me plead for a reconsideration by the Reformed Church of what the Greek fathers called *theosis*. This is usually unfortunately translated *deification*, but it has nothing to do with the divinization of man any more than the Incarnation has to do with the humanization of God. *Theosis* was the term the Fathers used to emphasize the fact that through the Spirit we have to do with God in his utter sublimity, his sheer Godness or holiness; creatures through we are, men on earth, in the Spirit we are made to participate in saving acts that are abruptly and absolutely divine, election, adoption, regeneration or sanctification and we participate in them by grace alone. *Theosis*

describes man's involvement in such a mighty act of God upon him that he is raised up to find the true centre of his existence not in himself but in Holy God, where he lives and moves and has his being in the uncreated but creative energy of the Holy Spirit. By *theosis* the Greek fathers wished to express the fact that in the new coming of the Holy Spirit we are up against *God* in the most absolute sense, God in his ultimate holiness or Godness.[12]

"We are up against *God*": Christian theology is wrestling with what that means for both creation in general, and salvation in particular.

This book is a partial response to Torrance's plea. Edwards operated within the Reformed tradition, and precisely from that starting point sought to show how all of creation is right up against God. All things participate in God for being, argues Edwards. But this participation is for purpose. All things participate in God for being *so that* God can communicate his divine fullness to his elect. This divine fullness is God giving himself, but it is a gift mediated by Christ and appropriate to a created receiver. Throughout his vision, Edwards maintains the Creator-creature distinction and does so precisely so as to show how God in Christ and by the Spirit bridges that chasm. All of this presents Edwards as a resource for Reformed reflection on both creational and soteriological participation.

The project, then, is oriented by the following question and thesis. Given the ecumenical conversation regarding theologies of deification and soteriological participation in general, and given the wide acceptance among Edwards scholars that he taught a strong version of soteriological participation, what is Jonathan Edwards's particular contribution to this wider conversation? More specifically, how does Jonathan Edwards's approach to the Creator-creature distinction contribute to a Reformed engagement with participation soteriology?

The argument I will develop in response is that Jonathan Edwards's particular contribution to ecumenical interest in deification is his doctrine of special grace. This doctrine of special grace is a communication and participation in divine fullness, such that the fullness is simultaneously infinitely above created nature, and yet also not the divine essence. This manner of navigating the Creator-creature distinction achieves much that

---

[12]Torrance, *Theology in Reconstruction*.

is associated with theosis, but does so (1) pursuant of Reformed polemical interests and (2) as a sympathetic development of the Reformed tradition of special grace. It therefore represents a resource for contemporary Reformed theology's engagement with participation soteriology.

Is It Appropriate to Call Edwards's Doctrine of Grace "Deification"?

It is important to address the question of whether it is accurate or helpful to characterize Edwards's doctrine of grace with the term *deification* or *theosis*. Indeed, some scholars argue that nearly all Western appropriations of deification are problematic. Both Andrew Louth and Gosta Hallonsten have critiqued Western appropriations of deification from an Eastern Orthodox perspective. Bruce McCormack has critiqued the category of deification from a Reformed perspective.[13] The debates center, in large part, on the question of definition. Some scholars have presented a minimal definition for deification. This approach allows many Western theologies to qualify as forms of deification.[14] Others adopt a maximalist approach. This tends to restrict deification to the East alone.[15] More recently, there is a growing

---

[13] Andrew Louth, "The Place of Theosis in Orthodox Theology," in Christensen and Wittung, *Partakers of the Divine Nature*, 32-44; Gosta Hallonsten, "Theosis in Recent Research," in Christensen and Wittung, *Partakers of the Divine Nature*, 281-93; Bruce L. McCormack, "Participation in God, Yes, Deification, No: Two Modern Protestant Responses to an Ancient Question," in *Denkwürdiges Geheimnis: Beiträge zur Gotteslehre. Festschrift für Eberhard Jüngel zum 70. Geburtstag*, ed. Johannes Fischer, Hans-Peter Großhans, and Ingolf U. Dalferth (Tübingen: Mohr Siebeck, 2004), 347-74. Oliver Crisp has critiqued McCormack's argument in *Jonathan Edwards on God*, 167-72.

[14] A. N. Williams's work represents a prime example of the minimalist approach. She sought to demonstrate that both Thomas Aquinas and Gregory Palamas taught notions of theosis, and that their differences were not as overwhelming as often thought. In order to make her case, she identifies three criteria for a doctrine of theosis. In order for a concept to be named theosis, it must first include the idea of human participation in divine life, rather than merely the divine dwelling within the human. The second requirement is a concept of union, where that union is understood to entail humanity's incorporation into God, with this signifying the destiny of humanity generally. The third is adoption, although Williams does not seem to think that this third criterion carries the same weight as the first two. See Williams, *The Ground of Union: Deification in Aquinas and Palamas* (New York: Oxford University Press, 1999), 32. McClymond is one of the leading proponents of viewing Edwards in terms of theosis, and he explicitly bases his argument on Williams's criteria. See McClymond, "Salvation as Divinization"; McClymond and McDermott, "Theme of Divinization."

[15] These scholars include Andrew Louth, Gosta Hallonsten, and Paul Gavrilyuk, among others. See Louth, "Place of Theosis"; Hallonsten, "Theosis in Recent Research"; Gavrilyuk, "Retrieval of Deification"; Roger Olsen, "Deification in Contemporary Theology," *ThTo* 64 (2007): 186-200;

consensus that even if the terms associated with deification are missing, the concept itself is often present in many iterations.¹⁶ In other words, there is room for a theologian who is not drawing on Eastern sources, and who does not use the term *deification*, to nevertheless contribute to the ecumenical conversation around the concept.

But should Edwards's view of special grace bear the label *theosis* or *deification*? I have some hesitancy with the term. Edwards does not use the term, even though he read people who did. Further, the terms *deification*, *theosis*, and *divinization* are often associated with Eastern Orthodox theology. This is still true despite the Western appropriations of the concept. Given this association, there is a risk that in applying the terms to Edwards's view of grace, one will imply that his thought borrows from the East or at least is eccentric to his Reformed heritage. Edwards was not reading Gregory Palamas, and I argue that his doctrine of grace was deeply rooted in his Reformed heritage. Given all of this I have been slow to label Edwards's doctrine as deification.¹⁷

Yet despite this hesitancy, I believe it helpful to view Edwards's doctrine of grace as a species of deification for the following reasons. First, deification scholarship, as I mentioned above, has begun to settle on the idea that a concept of deification may be present even if the word is absent and that the concept exists in more than just the Eastern Orthodox tradition. Second, this study is not simply a description of Edwards's thinking. It is also a contribution toward Reformed engagement with deification and soteriological participation theology. That is, I present Edwards's thought not just as a historical curiosity but as a resource for constructive theology in the Reformed tradition. If Reformed thought is going to take Torrance's advice and engage with soteriological participation and deification (or his preferred

---

Norman Russell, "Why Does *Theosis* Fascinate Western Christians?," *Sobornost* 34, no. 1 (2012): 14-15. Within Edwards studies, Kyle Strobel has argued that Edwards meets Hallonsten's criteria for theosis, though he does recognize the differences between Edwards and the East (Strobel, "Jonathan Edwards and the Polemics").

¹⁶Daniel A. Keating, "Typologies of Deification," *IJST* 17, no. 3 (2015): 267-83. See also Jared Ortiz, ed., *Deification in the Latin Patristic Tradition* (Washington, DC: Catholic University of America Press, 2019).

¹⁷See James Salladin, "Nature and Grace: Two Participations in the Thought of Jonathan Edwards," *IJST* 18, no. 3 (2016): 290-303; Salladin, "Essence and Fullness: Evaluating the Creator-Creature Distinction in Jonathan Edwards," *SJT* 70, no. 4 (2017): 427-44.

term, *theosis*), then Edwards is one thinker to consult. Finally, *deification* and *theosis* are simply the words presently used in ecumenical conversation about soteriological participation. Every word has strengths and weaknesses, but in order to communicate one has to use the words available. In the eighteenth century, the term *grace* meant things that it does not often mean now. Similarly, today *deification* and *theosis* mean things that they did not mean then. Given the theological conversation around soteriological participation, the term *deification*, or *theosis*, seems the best fit for Edwards's doctrine of grace.

This study takes the current deification conversations as a challenge to *resource* Jonathan Edwards's doctrine of grace.[18] It will show a particularly Reformed attempt to achieve many aspects that are often associated with deification, while at the same time maintaining core Reformed commitments. Some of these Reformed commitments will disqualify Edwards's doctrine of grace from being termed deification by some theologians.[19] Many other scholars will view Edwards's doctrine of grace as a prime example of a Western, Protestant account of deification. The real benefit will be for that portion of the church called Reformed to investigate Edwards's doctrine of grace and evaluate whether it opens opportunities for contemporary reflections on the nature of God's gift in salvation.

In 1961 an ecumenical study of the doctrine of grace argued that central to the divide between Roman Catholic and Orthodox theology on the one hand, and the Reformation on the other, was the Reformation's suspicion of the idea of participation in the life of God. The study appreciated much that is in the Reformation tradition and sought to present the three major branches of Christianity in the best possible light. But in the course of this, it challenged the Reformed churches to consider whether they might embrace the notion of participation as central to the doctrine of grace, just as Torrance did from within the tradition. Today, Reformed traditions are still cool to the notion, but there is reason to think the water is warming. Scholars such as Julie Canlis, Todd Billings,

---

[18]See Gavrilyuk's characterization of deification theology as a *ressourcement* movement ("Retrieval of Deification," 656).

[19]Gavrilyuk suggests that a synergistic understanding of anthropology is implied in a more advanced theology of deification. This alone would call into question any recognizably Reformed account of the category ("Retrieval of Deification," 652-55, 657).

and Carl Mosser have argued that participation, in a particular iteration, is central to John Calvin.[20]

This study contributes to this move and presents Edwards as embracing the notions of participation while not surrendering the values that have been central to the Reformed project. This is a key element of its value. The current surge of interest in deification and accompanying themes grew, in large part, out of Eastern Palamism's entrance into Western theological conversations. While this has been helpful in many respects, it has meant that deification-related conversations often proceed in a Palamite-centered universe. That is, the conversations can tend to take their cues from a Palamite gold standard.[21] When Western theologians do this, two main problems can arise. First, there is a danger of misunderstanding or diminishing the East's vision. Few Western scholars will take on the entire Palamite theological vision, so there can be a picking and choosing, which may not do justice to the East's theology.[22] Second, this approach carries dangers for the West's own theological systems, because it can lead Western theologians to take on categories and concepts that are ill suited to their own tradition and dogmatic systems.[23]

This study attempts to avoid both dangers by (1) interpreting the current interest in deification and related concepts as a call for each tradition to a

---

[20]Julie Canlis, "Calvin, Osiander, and Participation in God," *IJST* 6, no. 2 (2004): 169-84; Canlis, *Calvin's Ladder: A Spiritual Theology of Ascent and Ascension* (Grand Rapids, MI: Eerdmans, 2010); J. Todd Billings, "United to God Through Christ: Assessing Calvin on the Question of Deification," *HTR* 98, no. 3 (2005): 315-34; Billings, *Calvin, Participation, and Gift: The Activity of Believers in Union with Christ* (Oxford: Oxford University Press, 2007). See also Carl Mosser, "The Earliest Patristic Interpretations of Psalm 82, Jewish Antecedents, and the Origin of Christian Deification," *Journal of Theological Studies* 56, no. 1 (2005): 30-74; Mosser, "Greatest Possible Blessing"; Mosser, "An Exotic Flower? Calvin and the Patristic Doctrine of Deification," in *Reformation Faith: Exegesis and Theology in the Protestant Reformations*, ed. Michael Parsons (Milton Keynes, UK: Paternoster, 2014); Yang-ho Lee, "Calvin on Deification: A Reply to Carl Mosser and Jonathan Slater," *SJT* 63, no. 3 (2010): 272-84; Jonathan Slater, "Salvation as Participation in the Humanity of the Mediator in Calvin's *Institutes of the Christian Religion*: A Reply to Carl Mosser," *SJT* 58, no. 1 (2005): 39-58.

[21]For instance, Olsen would have the term reserved for theologies that explicitly employ the Eastern Orthodox distinction between essence and energies ("Deification in Contemporary Theology," 193, 199).

[22]This is part of Louth's concern ("Place of *Theosis*").

[23]Gavrilyuk recognizes this but considers it a good thing. He writes, "Deification . . . works like a time-bomb in due course producing a 'creative destruction' of the soteriological visions developed by the Churches of the Reformation" ("Retrieval of Deification," 657). He argues that the creative part of this would be the incorporation of more Eastern Orthodox dogmatic apparatuses into Western thought. This is a polemical move against the West's theologies.

renewed investigation of its own theory of grace, and (2) relating Edwards's theology of grace to these conversations not because his view is so similar to Palamism but because he represents a native Western and Reformed engagement with the themes of interest. Put differently, Western theology needs to explore its own heritage of divine participation without cutting and pasting from the East. There are many Western theologians who might provide rich insights for this pursuit, and this work presents Jonathan Edwards as one example, operating from a Reformed perspective.[24]

Terminology

Terminology requires care. The ecumenical deification conversation, and the related scholarly conversations regarding various approaches to participation thought, use a sometimes confusing array of terms. With respect to this study, I will use *deification* and *theosis* synonymously. When I speak of Edwards's own doctrine of deification, I will often use his own formula: grace (true or special) is a communication and participation in divine fullness. I will unpack this formula in the first chapter. For short, I will sometimes speak of "Edwards's doctrine of grace."

This study will also deal with the broader concept of participation theology. Participation theology comes in several forms, and I will delineate those differing forms of participation with distinct terms. I will sometimes describe deification with the term *soteriological participation*. In distinction from this, I will also speak of *ontological participation*. In some theologies these two types of participation—the participation that saves and the participation that undergirds being—are continuous. In those theologies there is little need to distinguish them. Edwards, however, made significant distinction between them, and I will show that this allowed him to parse out created nature and divine grace as truly distinct and yet related things. In the same vein, I will sometimes refer to two Greek words: *methexis* and *koinōnia*. Although these are sometimes near-synonyms in ancient Greek sources, contemporary participation scholarship uses these two Greek words as labels for two varieties of participation thought. *Methexis* is sometimes used to describe ontological participation in which the thing shared

---

[24]Thomas Torrance would be another candidate for the Reformed tradition. See Myk Habets, *Theosis in the Theology of Thomas Torrance* (Burlington, VT: Ashgate, 2009).

is being, substance or essence. *Koinōnia* is sometimes used to describe participation in which the thing shared is relationality, often between persons. I will use the terms in this way in part because they have become something of a convention in participation theology and therefore help map my argument to wider conversations outside Edwards studies. I will explain the *methexis-koinōnia* distinction in greater detail in chapter one.

Position Within Edwards Studies

This study builds on the work of a great many scholars who have read Edwards deeply. While Edwards scholarship is too big a field to rehearse here, contemporary Edwards scholars can be divided into two broad camps that are relevant to the present work. First, there are scholars who tend to be influenced by the work of Sang Hyun Lee.[25] These scholars tend to read Edwards as somehow operating on the edges of the Reformed tradition. Sometimes this means that Edwards valued his Reformed heritage, but that it was not at the center of his project, and other times it means that in certain areas of his philosophy he left his Reformed heritage behind him. These scholars will often view this move as the expression of Edwards's theological or philosophical genius: his thought was more creative than his tradition could hold. On the other hand, more recently there are a group of scholars who read Edwards as operating within his Reformed heritage, and in such a manner that his thought cannot be understood without close reference to his Reformed theology.[26] That is, this group thinks Edwards was a *Reformed*

---

[25]See Sang Hyun Lee, "Jonathan Edwards's Dispositional Conception of the Trinity: A Resource for Contemporary Reformed Theology," in *Toward the Future of Reformed Theology: Tasks, Topics, Traditions*, ed. E. David Willis, Michael Welker, and Matthias Gockel (Grand Rapids, MI: Eerdmans, 1999), 444-55; Lee, *The Philosophical Theology of Jonathan Edwards* (Princeton, NJ: Princeton University Press, 1988); Michael J. McClymond, "Hearing the Symphony: A Critique of Some Critics of Sang Lee's and Amy Pauw's Accounts of Jonathan Edwards' View of God," in *Jonathan Edwards as Contemporary: Essays in Honor of Sang Hyun Lee*, ed. Don Schweitzer (New York: Peter Lang, 2010), 67-92; McClymond and McDermott, *Theology of Jonathan Edwards*; Amy Plantinga Pauw, *The Supreme Harmony of All: The Trinitarian Theology of Jonathan Edwards* (Grand Rapids, MI: Eerdmans, 2002); W. J. Danaher Jr., *The Trinitarian Ethics of Jonathan Edwards* (Louisville, KY: Westminster John Knox, 2004); Anri Morimoto, *Jonathan Edwards and the Catholic Vision of Salvation* (University Park: Pennsylvania State University Press, 1995).

[26]See, e.g., Stephen R. Holmes, *God of Grace and God of Glory: An Account of the Theology of Jonathan Edwards* (Edinburgh: T&T Clark, 2000); Holmes, "Does Jonathan Edwards Use a Dispositional Ontology? A Response to Sang Hyun Lee," in Crisp and Helm, *Jonathan Edwards: Philosophical Theologian*, 99-114; Oliver D. Crisp, "Jonathan Edwards's Ontology: A Critique of Sang Hyun Lee's Dispositional Account of Edwardsian Metaphysics," *Religious Studies* 46, no. 1

theologian first, before he was anything else. This group would readily highlight Edwards's creative development and critique of his Reformed heritage, but they would tend to read him in light his fundamental loyalty to his theological heritage.[27]

This present work falls in line with the second group. In particular, I am very indebted to the work of Stephen Holmes, Oliver Crisp, John Bombaro, and Kyle Strobel. Within this group, I tend to follow Crisp and Bombaro on Edwards's approach to creation and created nature, and I tend to follow Strobel on questions pertaining to Edwards's doctrine of the Trinity and Edwards's doctrine of salvation. Crisp and Bombaro have shown how Edwards viewed all creation to be immediately dependent on God for its being. This will undergird my account of created nature. On the other hand, Strobel has shown the congruity between Edwards's doctrine of God as Trinity and his doctrine of grace. This congruity between theology proper and soteriology is the foundation of the doctrine of grace as participation in divine fullness that I will unpack. My work synthesizes the work of these scholars, presenting it in a new way, in order to leverage Edwards's thought for contemporary Reformed reflection on soteriological participation.

Overview of the Argument and Approach

I will therefore aim to present Edwards's theology of grace, with particular attention to how Edwards navigated the Creator-creature distinction, with a view to showing its relevance to Reformed development of participation soteriology. Edwards argues that special grace is a communication and

---

(2010): 1-20; Crisp, "Jonathan Edwards on the Divine Nature," *Journal of Reformed Theology* 3, no. 2 (2009): 175-201; Crisp, *Jonathan Edwards on God*; Crisp, *Revisioning Christology* (Surrey, UK: Ashgate, 2011); Crisp, *Jonathan Edwards Among the Theologians* (Grand Rapids, MI: Eerdmans, 2015); John J. Bombaro, "Jonathan Edwards's Vision of Salvation," *Westminster Theological Journal* 65 (2003): 45-67; Bombaro, *Jonathan Edwards's Vision of Reality: The Relationship of God to the World, Redemption History, and the Reprobate* (Eugene, OR: Pickwick, 2012); Kyle Strobel, *Jonathan Edwards's Theology: A Reinterpretation*, T&T Clark Studies in Systematic Theology (London: T&T Clark, 2013); Strobel, "Jonathan Edwards and the Polemics"; Strobel, "Jonathan Edwards's Reformed Doctrine."

[27]For example, Crisp says, "[Edwards] wants to hold onto the doctrine of his Reformed heritage, but he refines and reshapes it in important respects. . . . His proposal is not without its difficulties, however" (*Jonathan Edwards Among the Theologians*, 58). Crisp's comment is in specific reference to Edwards's doctrine of the Trinity, but it could also stand as a typical comment on his overarching relationship to the Reformed tradition: sympathetic and loyal, willing to modify, with some new difficulties created in the process.

participation in divine fullness. This divine fullness, the central gift of divine grace, is not embedded within created nature, and neither is it the divine essence. This Creator-creature distinction is key to Edwards's overall vision of soteriological participation, and it is key to how this vision contributed to Reformed interests. By placing divine fullness infinitely above created nature, Edwards aimed to close the door on an Arminian or synergistic account of grace. Divine fullness differs in kind from created nature, not only in degree. On the other hand, Edwards could not risk fusing Creator and creature by affirming a union of essence between the two. This had been argued by various enthusiast groups before him. Therefore, Edwards developed a theory of divine fullness that distinguished both from created nature and the divine essence. Yet, while maintaining a strong distinction between Creator and creature, Edwards always made this distinction with a view to bridging it in a relational union of profound intimacy. It is this navigation of the Creator-creature distinction and relation that is so interesting and useful for developing a Reformed account of soteriological participation.

I will demonstrate these themes through a close reading of Edwards's primary sources and also a critical engagement with contemporary theosis and participation theology. Chapters one and four are primarily explorations of key texts for Edwards's doctrine of special grace. These chapters serve to demonstrate that Edwards is operating in a Reformed framework, while making creative modifications to that framework. Chapter one shows Edwards's Reformed polemical uses for special grace, and chapter four shows how Edwards synchronized key Reformed doctrines in his development of special grace. These two chapters form a sort of *inclusio* for chapters two and three. These middle chapters focus more on contemporary challenges or problems or objections to soteriological participation, and show how Edwards's thought provides resources for dealing with these difficulties. All the chapters are united as an exploration of the Creator-creature distinction in Edwards's doctrine of grace. This overall approach allows the study to be simultaneously grounded in exegesis in Edwards's corpus and constructively engaged with contemporary theosis and participation scholarship, and to support the overall aim of presenting Edwards's thought as a resource for Reformed reflection.

Chapter one will provide a broad overview of Edwards's doctrine of special grace, with particular focus on clarifying the category of divine fullness, as well as the meaning of the notions of *communication, participation,* and *communion*. Edwards states that divine fullness is both infinitely above created nature and also not the divine essence. I will argue that the divine fullness is the Holy Spirit, poured out in uncreated love to the saint, in a way that provides relational *koinōnia* without impinging on created quiddity. This participation is a relational *koinōnia*-participation, as distinct from a *methexis*-participation focused on establishing ontology. I will then show how Edwards deployed this doctrine of special grace in polemical resistance against both Arminianism on the one hand and enthusiasm on the other. I will develop this argument by an exegetical approach to several key texts in Edwards's corpus. I begin with an exposition of a sermon in which he develops the category of "divine fullness" and relates it to the Creator-creature distinction. This sermon is a helpful starting point because it is a public presentation rather than a private reflection, plus it is a single work that addresses the key aspects of his doctrine of grace and relates it to the Creator-creature distinction. One would have to synthesize a great many of Edwards's works in order to piece together the thought that Edwards presents in one place in this sermon. Therefore, I begin with this sermon and then validate and expand it in light of other material in Edwards's corpus.

Chapter two will then take up the question, In what way can divine fullness be infinitely above created nature? I will explore this question in context of contemporary challenges from theosis and participation scholarship. This will require delving into Edwards's theology of created ontology. I will argue that Edwards does employ a notion of what I will call "common participation." This is a participation that grounds all created ontology in God for being. It is therefore a form of *methexis*-participation. However, while this participation theology undergirds all created nature, it does not account for special grace or divine fullness. There is another form of participation at work in Edwards that accounts for special grace and divine fullness. It is a relational *koinōnia*-participation that unites the creature and the Creator in intimacy, without touching their respective quiddities. This distinguishes Edwards from participation theologies that ground soteriology in ontological participation.

Chapter three then explores the other side of the same Creator-creature distinction. If Edwards distinguished between created nature and divine fullness (chap. two), then how did he distinguish divine fullness from the divine essence? Again I will situate this question in light of contemporary theosis and participation scholarship. I will argue that throughout Edwards's thought, beginning in his doctrine of the Trinity, right through his Christology and pneumatology, and finally in his soteriology, Edwards consistently distinguishes a relational union in divine fullness from an ontological union in the divine essence. I will then submit this fullness-essence distinction to the critique leveled by Reformed theologians toward the Palamite distinction between energies and essence. If Edwards is going to be useful as a resource for Reformed exploration of soteriological participation, then his categories must withstand challenges from within the Reformed tradition. His fullness-essence distinction is at least verbally similar to the Palamite energies-essence distinction, and thus I will explore whether his distinction succumbs to the Reformed critiques leveled against Palamism.

Chapter four then turns from the question of distinction, to the question of relation. I will have shown how divine fullness and grace is distinct from created nature (chap. two), but now in chapter four I will need to explore how they *relate* to each other. Edwards's theology of divine grace is always aimed at showing the relation of intimacy between Creator and creature; it does not stop at distinction. I will argue that Edwards posited a teleological relationship between created nature and divine grace. That is, God created the universe in order for it to participate in the divine fullness, through the reception and return of that divine fullness in intelligent creatures. I will show this through an exposition of Edwards's *The End for Which God Created the World*. My exposition and interpretation will differ from one of the most influential interpreters of Edwards's thought.

This will demonstrate that I follow (broadly) in the line of Holmes, Crisp, Strobel, and Bombaro, all of whom emphasize Edwards as a *Reformed* theologian. This is over against the school of thought begun by Sang Hyun Lee and continued by Anri Morimoto, Gerald McDermott, Michael McClymond, and others. The Lee school emphasizes an alleged dispositional account of ontology within Edwards, which would place him on the fringes of Reformed orthodoxy. In presenting Edwards as operating within the Reformed tradition, I do not intend to imply that Edwards slavishly followed a precisely traditional line of thought. Rather, I will show in chapter four that Edwards creatively developed and modified his inherited doctrine of special grace, but did so primarily by synchronizing the Reformed doctrines of the Trinity, special grace, and creational teleology. This was a creative development of Reformed thought, but a fundamentally sympathetic one.

All of this will combine to present Edwards's doctrine of grace as participation in divine fullness as a robust account of soteriological participation. In this it deserves a seat at the table of ecumenical reflection on these matters, but not simply because his thought vaguely echoes Eastern Orthodox thought. Rather, Edwards developed his thinking in creative and sympathetic modification of his own Reformed heritage, with a view to reinforcing traditional polemical frontiers, while at the same time achieving a vision for intimacy between Creator and creature that encapsulates the whole of the Christian life and reaches out into eternity future. This is a bold vision for the Christian life, and one that pressed the Creator-creature distinction and relation. We turn now to explore it in greater detail.

1

Grace and Fullness

On the evening of July 12, 1739, a young man walked alone and wrestled with God. He was a religious man; he knew his Puritan theology, and his soul writhed within him, at least in part, because he hated its core doctrine. God's sovereignty was central to the system that formed his tradition, and it precluded any easy means of escape. He had sought to make himself sincere in religious devotion. He had strived to pray and fast well. He had rehearsed the doctrines of grace and tried to persuade himself, perhaps even God, that he renounced any hint of merit in his efforts. Yet, in the early weeks of July he came to see that all his religion was nothing more than "self-worship."[1] This carried a terminal diagnosis. If his best efforts could not turn his heart to God, then there could be no cure, and he stood on the brink of eternal damnation. He was learning a lesson he had not known previously, "that there could be no way prescribed whereby a natural man could, of his own strength, obtain that which is supernatural and utterly above the utmost stretch of nature to obtain by its own strength or out of the reach of the highest angel to give."[2] The natural could not touch the supernatural. The path from below was blocked. But what of the path from above?

> Then, as I was walking in a dark thick grove, "unspeakable glory" seemed to open to the view and apprehension of my soul. . . . It was a new inward apprehension or view that I had of God, such as I never had before. . . . I stood still and wondered and admired! I knew that I had never had seen before

---

[1] WJE 7:138.
[2] WJE 7:124.

anything comparable to it for excellency and beauty: it was widely different from all the conceptions that ever I had had of God, or things divine.... And my soul "rejoiced with joy unspeakable" to see such a God, such a glorious divine being; and I was inwardly pleased and satisfied, that he should be God over all forever and ever.... Thus God, I trust, brought me to a hearty disposition to exalt him and set him on the throne, and ... to aim at his honor and glory as King of the universe.[3]

David Brainerd's conversion was dramatic, but it was not unique. Puritans and those under their influence had long experienced something like it, and the years just before and just after Brainerd's conversion were particularly filled with episodes that followed the familiar pattern. What was needed, however, was a theological explanation of it.

By the time Brainerd experienced his new "apprehension ... of God," Jonathan Edwards was already deeply engaged in providing just such a theological explanation. He knew the experience firsthand, and he followed his Puritan forbearers in venturing a theologized theory of how the Spirit of God affects this work.[4] Edwards's approach was creative and innovative, and particularly so in how he framed the Creator-creature distinction.

The question of how God, as Creator, and humanity, as creature, related to each other was always just underneath the surface of eighteenth-century theological debate. Edwards's Reformed heritage meant that he needed to avoid the Scylla of Arminianism, on the one hand, and the Charybdis of radical enthusiasm on the other.[5] Both of these views were popular, and both represented a theory of the Creator-creature distinction that threatened Edwards's orthodoxy.

Arminianism addressed the Creator-creature distinction and relation by allowing greater autonomy to the creature. The creature's natural endowments allow, at least in principle, for a reaching out and an embrace of its end. Arminianism was always diverse, but even considered in its broad

---

[3]WJE 7:138-39.
[4]WJE 16:792-93.
[5]WJE 4:56. See WJE 4:4-18 for an overview of New England theology's gradual shift from federal theology and the halfway covenant to Arminian ideas that God is obliged to save those who fulfill the demands of the covenant. Edwards's polemical opponent Charles Chauncy accused the Great Awakening of "enthusiasm." Edwards sought to defend it and also guard it against its own extremes. See George M. Marsden, *Jonathan Edwards: A Life* (New Haven, CT: Yale University Press, 2003), 272-73, 275.

range it tended toward optimism about the creature's natural capacity to embrace what God asked. Though Brainerd would not have owned the term *Arminian* during his spiritual struggle, the natural effort to grasp one's supernatural end was his intuitive approach to religion.[6] Ostensibly this established a degree of distance between God and the creature, because there was scope for the creature to act on its own. Yet on the other hand, by giving the creature autonomy, in whatever degree, Arminianism attributed to creatures (at least) one attribute that the Reformed tradition reserved for the Creator, for only God could be truly autonomous. Thus the Reformed tradition could view the Arminian effort to validate the creature's natural autonomy as a thinly veiled attempt at a false self-deification, inevitably resulting in what Brainerd called self-worship.

At the same time the various radical enthusiast groups envisioned the creature's direct union with God. These groups had waxed and waned for the previous century, and they often grew out of the Puritan mainstream. In their most radical forms they spoke of being "Godded with God," so that the creature came to partake of the divine essence.[7] If Arminianism ostensibly respected the distinction between creature and Creator, then the radical enthusiasts ostensibly achieved an intimacy between them. Yet, once again, and with a certain irony, the assertion of essential union with God served to undermine the notion of monotheism and collapsed the supernatural into the natural. Thus the Reformed tradition could view the enthusiast effort to achieve intimacy between Creator and creature as a profound failure that resulted in the naturalization of God.

Edwards's doctrine of special grace aimed to reject both alternatives and provide a Reformed, if innovative, approach to the Creator-creature distinction. Just months before Brainerd's conversion, Edwards presented his doctrine of special grace as "a communication or a participation of God's fullness or of his own good."[8] The central gift of grace is the divine fullness, and Edwards uses this category to navigate his polemical Scylla and Cha-

---

[6] WJE 7:124.
[7] See Paul C. H. Lim, *Mystery Unveiled: The Crisis of the Trinity in Early Modern England* (Oxford: Oxford University Press, 2012), 13.
[8] Jonathan Edwards, "True Grace Is Divine (1738)," in *Jonathan Edwards: Spiritual Writings*, ed. Adriaan C. Neele, Kyle C. Strobel, and Kenneth P. Minkema, Classics of Western Spirituality (New York: Paulist Press, 2019), 354.

rybdis. The one who has this grace has "something above created nature. . . . [It is] something of God. . . . The creature that has true grace and holiness in his heart has something infinitely above himself in him."⁹ Divine grace is profoundly (infinitely!) discontinuous with created nature. This is aimed to undermine Arminian optimism about nature. It is intended to persuade people like David Brainerd that their natural efforts will never bring about supernatural ends.¹⁰ Yet does this avoid Scylla only to fall into Charybdis? What of the danger of radical enthusiasm? Once again, Edwards's category of divine fullness charts his course. Divine grace "is not a communication of God's essence, but it is a communication of that which the Scripture calls God's fullness."¹¹ Here Edwards steers clear of essential union. When Brainerd or anyone else receives true grace, they gain something that is entirely foreign to their nature, something of God, and yet at the same time not the divine essence.

The present study is an exploration of this doctrine of grace. More specifically, it is an exploration of Edwards's doctrine of grace as a communication and participation in the divine fullness, with particular focus on the Creator-creature distinction and relation, and in contribution to contemporary scholarly discussions around soteriological participation theology. Edwards scholars regularly note the strong themes of divine participation within his thought, and it is increasingly common for Edwards scholars to use the term *theosis* to describe these ideas. These themes of divine participation, or theosis or deification or divinization, are sometimes presented as creating a tension with Edwards's Reformed heritage. Michael McClymond and Gerald McDermott begin their chapter exploring these themes in Edwards by stating, "Scholars have long recognized that certain elements in Edwards's theology were in tension with traditional Calvinism." McClymond and McDermott then note at least apparent affinities between Edwards's participation thought and that of Eastern Orthodoxy.¹² The

---

⁹Edwards, "True Grace Is Divine (1738)," 354.
¹⁰WJE 7:124.
¹¹Edwards, "True Grace Is Divine (1738)," 354.
¹²Michael J. McClymond and Gerald R. McDermott, *The Theology of Jonathan Edwards* (Oxford: Oxford University Press, 2012), 410. See also McClymond, "Salvation as Divinization: Jonathan Edwards, Gregory Palamas and the Theological Uses of Platonism," in *Jonathan Edwards: Philosophical Theologian*, ed. Oliver D. Crisp and Paul Helm (Burlington, VT: Ashgate, 2003), 139-60. They note Jaroslav Pelikan's comparison between Edwards's thought and Eastern Or-

implication is that Edwards's participation thought is eccentric to his Reformed heritage.

This may reflect a larger hesitancy among some in the Reformed tradition to the whole notion of soteriological participation, and especially the category of theosis or deification.[13] Other voices have critiqued the Reformation tradition for not embracing a form of soteriological participation, and some within the Reformed tradition have argued that it finds a more comfortable home within a Reformed, monergistic framework than it does elsewhere.[14] All of this creates a context for this present study and this particular chapter. Within the wider debates concerning the Reformed tradition and soteriological participation, there are the underlying questions: To what extent may the Reformed tradition embrace soteriological participation? One may target the question more pointedly at Jonathan Edwards: To what extent is Edwards's doctrine of grace as a participation in divine fullness a departure or a development of his Reformed heritage? If his doctrine of grace is a sympathetic development of the Reformed heritage, then what resources may it provide contemporary constructive efforts toward a Reformed doctrine of soteriological participation? I will take up this last question in chapters two and three. But before I suggest ways that Edwards's doctrine of grace may provide resources for Reformed constructive work in

---

thodox notions of theosis. See Jaroslav Pelikan, *The Christian Tradition: A History of the Development of Doctrine*, vol. 5, *Christian Doctrine and Modern Culture (Since 1700)* (Chicago: University of Chicago University Press, 1989), 161, cited in McClymond and McDermott, *Theology of Jonathan Edwards*, 410n1.

[13]See, e.g., McCormack's critique of theosis and deification as categories, and his own alternative notion of participation. Bruce L. McCormack, "Union with Christ in Calvin's Theology: Grounds for a Divinization Theory?," in *Tributes to John Calvin: A Celebration of His Quincentenary*, ed. David W. Hall (Philipsburg, NJ: P&R, 2010), 504-29; Bruce L. McCormack, "Participation in God, Yes, Deification, No: Two Modern Protestant Responses to an Ancient Question," in *Denkwürdiges Geheimnis: Beiträge zur Gotteslehre. Festschrift für Eberhard Jüngel zum 70. Geburtstag*, ed. Johannes Fischer, Hans-Peter Großhans, and Ingolf U. Dalferth (Tübingen: Mohr Siebeck, 2004), 347-74.

[14]See Habets and Murphy's debate concerning a Reformed appropriation of theosis. They agree that it fits well within a Reformed framework, though they disagree about the use of the essence-energies distinction from Eastern Orthodox Palamism. See Gannon Murphy, "Reformed Theosis?," *ThTo* 65, no. 2 (2008): 191-212; Myk Habets, "'Reformed Theosis?' A Response to Gannon Murphy," *ThTo* 65, no. 4 (2009): 489-98. For those who have critiqued the Reformation tradition for not embracing a form of soteriological participation, see Charles Moeller and G. Philips, *The Theology of Grace and the Oecumenical Movement*, trans. A. Wilson (London: Mowbray, 1961), 44. The critique is aimed not just at the Reformed tradition but at the entire Reformational and Protestant project.

soteriological participation, I must answer the prior questions.

This present chapter has two primary aims. First, this chapter will provide an overview of Edwards's doctrine of grace as participation in divine fullness, with particular focus on how Edwards navigated the Creator-creature distinction. Second, this chapter will argue that this is a sympathetic development of his Reformed heritage. I will argue this on the basis that his doctrine of grace was aimed to protect Reformed orthodoxy against Arminianism on the one hand and radical enthusiasm on the other. It was not aimed at denying or repudiating Reformed interests.

I now turn to the primary focus of this first chapter: an overview of Edwards's doctrine of grace as participation in divine fullness and its polemical use in a defense against Arminianism and radical enthusiasm. I will explore the doctrine and its polemical use by expositing a sermon titled "True Grace Is Divine." This will provide the basic vocabulary and grammar of Edwards's doctrine of special grace. I will then clarify its central categories by reference to his wider corpus. With this in place I will show the polemical purpose this doctrine served, which will suggest that Edwards's doctrine of grace and participation was a servant of Reformed interests, not an opponent.

Exposition of "True Grace Is Divine"

Why begin with this sermon? Edwards published and wrote about his view of grace in many works and many sermons, and often at greater length and detail than this one sermon provides. There are four reasons for investigating this sermon at the outset. First, "True Grace Is Divine" provides a concise statement of Edwards's doctrine of grace as participation in divinity, and more specifically *divine fullness*. Edwards speaks of participation in divine fullness in many contexts, but that voluminous body of work makes distilling a systematic and concise statement difficult. In this one sermon Edwards provides a summary of his view, which can then provide a systematic lens for grasping how the doctrine of grace functions throughout the rest of his writings. Second, in this sermon Edwards outlines a view of the category of divine fullness that contrasts it from both created nature and the divine essence. That is, he addresses the Creator-creature distinction in a targeted manner, and in a way that relates divine fullness to both created nature and the divine essence within the same argument. Edwards makes a similar contrast in other works, but here it is his particular focus. Given that it is also a particular interest of the present study, it seems a legitimate starting point. Third, the sermon shows the polemical edge of his approach to grace and participation. Last, Edwards's sermons and notes toward the end of his life indicate that his view expressed in this sermon remained constant through the rest of his life.[15]

Jonathan Edwards preached "True Grace Is Divine" in December 1738: a year of great preaching and growing notoriety. It had been four years since God's "surprising work" broke into the town of Northampton, and Edwards's account of the revival had been published in London one year before. Yet in spite of his growing fame, his congregation's spiritual life languished. The revival had ended abruptly and spectacularly with the suicide of Joseph Hawley Sr. in June 1735, and Edwards had become embroiled in a bitter ecclesiastical dispute regarding the alleged Arminianism of a local pastor named Robert Breck. The years following the revival were a time of disappointment and struggle for the pastor Jonathan Edwards.

Yet it was also a time of profound preaching. Was he motivated by the spiritual decline after revival, or had he matured in his theological reflections such that he was ready to display some of his most profound thinking? In any regard, he set about preaching two sermon series that would come to be remembered as some of his best. The first is now known as "Charity and Its Fruits," preached between April and October 1738.[16] It is an exposition of 1 Corinthians 13, and it argues that charity, or love, is the essence of all saving virtue, and that without it there can be no salvation. The second sermon series occurred in early 1739, titled "The History of the Work of Redemption."[17] This was Edwards's attempt to situate his Northampton parish within the macro movements and purposes of God in history. Both series aimed at a pastoral provocation: Edwards wanted to rouse his sleeping congregation to their earlier zeal. But he also had a theological agenda, one that touches a

---

[15]For similar discussions of divine fullness later in Edwards's life see "Approaching the End of God's Grand Design" (WJE 25:113-26), preached in 1744, especially 116. See also "True Grace, Distinguished from Devils" (WJE 25:608-40), last preached in 1752, especially 639. See also the later *Miscellanies*, such as *Miscellanies* 1266(a) (WJE 23:213), *Miscellanies* 1352 (WJE 23:498), *Miscellanies* 1218 (WJE 23:152). See also Edwards's *Blank Bible* discussion of Eph 3:19 in WJE 24:1101.
[16]WJE 8:129-397.
[17]WJE 9.

central concern throughout his career. His theological concern in both series is to answer the question, What is the distinguishing center of God's work? There are many ways of framing saving virtue, but what is its center? The answer: charity. There are many ways of telling the story of history, but what is the true center? The answer: God's work of redemption.

It is this theological aim that seems to drive "True Grace Is Divine." Edwards preached this sermon in between the two great series, and like in them both, Edwards is exploring the question, What is the distinguishing center of, in this case, saving grace? His answer, strikingly, is, grace is participation in divine fullness.

Edwards followed standard Puritan preaching tradition, and therefore his sermons follow a threefold division: exposition, doctrine, and application. His text is 1 John 4:12—"No man hath seen God at any time. If we love one another, God dwelleth in us, and his love is perfected in us" (KJV). Edwards begins by pointing out a key concern of 1 John: distinguishing the true center of God's work. "The special design of this chapter, seems to be to give some distinguishing marks, whereby the true Spirit may be distinguished from false spirits." Edwards exegetes the verse and points out that love (the sum of Christian grace) is a principle in the heart that allows (1) a saint to see God, (2) mutual indwelling between God and the saint, and (3) love to reach the effect God intends. Edwards then settles down to his doctrine statement: "True grace in the hearts of the saints, is something divine."[18]

The doctrine is provocative. It is provocative in part because it is abrupt. The biblical text says nothing about either grace or divinity and entirely focuses on love, yet Edwards's doctrine introduces both grace and divinity and leaves love aside.[19] But it is mainly provocative because of the claim itself. What does it mean that grace is divine? Edwards anticipates this question and launches into a discussion of four different possible references for the adjective *divine*.

First, *divine* may describe any work of God. Creation, humanity, and so on can all be called divine in the sense that they are works of God. Here the idea is that the adjective *divine* describes the origin, or perhaps better, the

---

[18] Edwards, "True Grace Is Divine (1738)," 350–52.

[19] The reason Edwards can move so easily between love and grace is that he views them as fundamentally one and the same (see WJE 21:166).

originator of the thing under discussion. In this way common grace may be termed divine, but this is not the way in which special grace is divine.[20]

Second, Edwards continues, the term *divine* can refer to something that reflects or typifies God in some manner. Here Edwards refers to creation and humanity again, to the sun and the stars, and to the human mind. Edwards is showing his interest in typology: all these things are designed to display some aspect of God and his glory. Where the first reference of the word *divine* pointed to the origin, this use of the term *divine* refers to the deeper typological meaning of a thing. An item may not be divine *in itself*, ontologically considered (see the next reference for *divine*), but it may point to God. But again, this is not the way in which special grace is divine.[21]

Third, the term *divine* can designate the divine essence. Thus, when one says, "God is divine," one means to refer to the fact that God's essence is divine. Importantly, Edward denies that grace is divine in this way. Grace is not divine in the way in which God himself is divine. This is important because it represents one of the ways that Edwards protects the Creator-creature distinction. This is always a concern when discussing divine participation—whether the Eastern theosis version or similar themes in Western iteration. Christianity's monotheism means that creatures must remain creatures, and one of the hallmarks of orthodox treatments of divine participation is to establish this critical boundary. This is Edwards's concern here: "Nor is it in this sense, that grace in the hearts of the saints is a divine thing. To be divine, then, is to be divine in an infinitely higher sense than any creature can be. For the creature can't partake of the divine essence, or any part of the divine essence: for the essence of God is not divisible nor communicable."[22]

I come now to the last possible meaning for divinity, and this is the meaning that applies to grace. Edwards writes, "Things are said to be divine, as they are a supernatural communication of something of that good which God himself possesses, and 'tis in this sense that grace is something divine. It is not a communication of God's essence, but it is a communication of

---

[20]Edwards, "True Grace Is Divine (1738)," 353.
[21]Edwards, "True Grace Is Divine (1738)," 353.
[22]Edwards, "True Grace Is Divine (1738)," 354.

that which the Scripture calls God's fullness."[23] Edwards is charting a narrow course and using very technical language to do it. He wants to say several things at the same time. He clearly wants to say that grace is divine in a way that is not true of all God's other gifts (creation, life, food, etc.).[24] But he also wants to guard the creature-Creator distinction. The divine essence is divine in a way that grace is not. He accomplishes both aims by employing the terms *supernatural* and *fullness*. The category "supernatural" allows him to affirm that grace is divine above "natural" gifts. The category "fullness" allows him to speak of something other than the divine essence, but nevertheless still of God in a very real way. Edwards defines *fullness* as the good that characterizes a particular thing. He derives this definition from a study of the term *fullness* in Scripture and concludes that fullness is "the good anyone possesses, either good of excellency, or beauty, or wealth, or happiness."[25]

With these distinctions in place, he can move to bold and positive statement regarding grace: "Grace is a communication or a participation of God's own fullness or of his good, a partaking of his riches, his own treasure, a partaking in some sort of his own bounty and happiness."[26] Edwards avoids ambiguity here: grace is divine participation. Yet again the subtleties are important. Clearly the words *communication* and *participation* are central, but I will leave analysis of these categories aside for the moment. At this point, it is the less obviously technical words that need comment and in particular, the term *own* and Edwards's use of the possessive *his*. Notice how the small word *own* comes up three times in one sentence. Grace, Edwards labors to say, is not merely a participation in *some* good but in *someone's* good. It is not merely a participation in *some* sort of fullness but in a fullness that properly belongs to a person, namely, God. It is God's *own* fullness that is the object of communication and participation. I will explore Edwards's notion of fullness in short order, but for now it is important to see how closely Edwards joins this category to God himself. To share in the divine fullness is to share in direct proximity to God.

---

[23]Edwards, "True Grace Is Divine (1738)," 354.
[24]He will state this explicitly in short order.
[25]Edwards, "True Grace Is Divine (1738)," 354.
[26]Edwards, "True Grace Is Divine (1738)," 355.

Grace and Fullness

At this point Edwards has asserted the main aspects of his argument and now turns to two further sections that clarify what he means. He clarifies first by considering creatureliness and then by considering divinity. I continue to follow Edwards's argument very closely here because he introduces distinctions that are important throughout the rest of this book.

Edwards argues three ways a creature may have an attribute. There are some attributes that are part of the creature's nature or essence. These are those things without which the creature ceases to be what it is. There are other things that are not part of the creature's essence but may be added to an individual creature by some sort of natural development. A person's rationality is of the essence of being human, but discretion is a development from essential rationality. Rationality illustrates the first way a creature may have an attribute (part of its essence), and discretion illustrates the second. The key thought in this second way of gaining an attribute is that it is a natural development of something latent in the essence. Discretion is a development of rationality, which is essential to being human. Edwards characterizes both as natural and not supernatural.[27]

The third way a creature may gain an attribute, however, fits into neither of these two options. "There is another kind of things in some creatures, that do neither belong to their nature and essence, nor the result of those things that are: and these things are called supernatural or divine." These are two important assertions for Edwards's doctrine of grace and divine participation. The first assertion is that a creature may gain an attribute (let us designate it "attribute X") without it being already resident in principle in the creature's essence. This opens the door to the implied idea that a creature may gain attribute X, which is foreign to its nature or essence, without attribute X undermining the creature's fundamental ontology. That is, the creature remains the same *sort of creature*, but with the addition of something entirely new. Edwards has not stated this as such, but it is the strong implication of this thinking. However, if this first assertion opens a door, the second assertion closes a door. The second assertion is that attribute X, which is not resident in principle within the nature or essence of the creature, is also not something that the creature may acquire by exercising the

---

[27]Edwards, "True Grace Is Divine (1738)," 355-56.

resources latent in it. That is, while attribute X is compatible with creaturely ontology, so that it is possible for the creature to have attribute X, it remains outside the reach of the creature to acquire it, at least on its own. What then is an example of attribute X? The answer is "true grace or holiness."[28]

What is Edwards's aim in this line of argument? His aim is twofold. First, he wants to lay the groundwork for a notion of immediacy and differentiation between Creator and creature. Is it possible to bridge the Creator-creature ontological chasm? Can a creature receive an attribute that is discontinuous with its own essential ontology? If so, does the creature cease to be a creature? Edwards is preparing the reader (or listener) to accept the possibility of immediate closeness between God and creature, without undermining their differentiation. His second aim is to ensure that this immediacy between God and creature runs from God and toward the creature. This is important because it protects gratuity. Grace cannot be taken or achieved. This is not merely because the creature cannot earn it—that is not Edwards's point—it is because the creature lacks the ontological capability to achieve it in any manner. Instead, the direction of travel must run the other way: God must *give* it, and the creature must *receive* it. "[True grace or holiness is] something entirely of a different kind from any thing that is human or angelical and something entirely above both. For 'tis something immediately from God and of God, a participation of that fullness that is in God and so is something supernatural and divine."[29] Note both the immediate communication from God and the fact that the creature remains creature. Humans or angels who receive grace are still humans and angels, yet they receive something that is essentially different from their own ontology. The Creator-creature distinction is protected, but the chasm is also bridged in a particular grammar of gratuity.

Now Edwards focuses in on this gratuitous bridge. If Edwards's concern in the previous paragraphs has been to distinguish grace from anything in creaturely ontology, he now turns to show how grace is intimately related to God himself. Grace is divine and supernatural, argues Edwards, in at least two ways.

---

[28] Edwards, "True Grace Is Divine (1738)," 356. Note that Edwards regularly equates true and grace and holiness.
[29] Edwards, "True Grace Is Divine (1738)," 356.

The first way grace is divine and supernatural is that it is immediately *from* God. The key concept here is immediacy. Immediacy is an important concept in Edwards's thought, and here he explains what he means: "not by the intervention of natural causes." God gives many lesser gifts by enhancing natural causes and natural processes. This is how he acts in common grace, but it is not the case with special grace. True grace is his immediate action on the creature. Just in case there was doubt whether grace may rely on any other processes besides God, Edwards adds that grace is "according to his arbitrary pleasure."[30]

But grace is divine by virtue of an even more close relationship to God. Not only is grace immediately *from* God, it is a participation *of* God. Here Edwards struggles for the right words. He speaks of grace being *produced* immediately by God, but then abandons production words and prefers communication language: "'Tis not only divine because of the way it is produced, but also from the nature of the thing produced, in that *it is rather a communication than a production*. 'Tis a participation of God, for where grace dwells, there God dwells."[31]

The shift in language from production to communication is significant, because it personalizes Edwards's view of grace. If grace is divine simply because it is produced immediately by God, then grace may well be a some*thing*—an impersonal product. The doctrine of creation traditionally speaks of God creating *ex nihilo*, which means that God created some*thing* that was not God, and did so immediately, because there was nothing else to use beside himself. Thus, had the sermon ended with the idea that grace is divine by its immediate production, one might conclude that this is nothing other than a sort of created grace.[32] Yet Edwards has already committed himself to say more than this alone. He has already said that some things are called divine simply because they are created by God—for example, creation itself—and that this is not the way grace is divine. So when Edwards

---

[30] Edwards, "True Grace Is Divine (1738)," 356-57.
[31] Edwards, "True Grace Is Divine (1738)," 357, emphasis added.
[32] Anri Morimoto argues, I believe wrongly, that Edwards's theology of grace includes both created- and uncreated-grace perspectives. See Morimoto, *Jonathan Edwards and the Catholic Vision of Salvation* (University Park: Pennsylvania State University Press, 1995), 7-8, 42-44. John J. Bombaro has refuted Morimoto on this point. See Bombaro, *Jonathan Edwards's Vision of Reality: The Relationship of God to the World, Redemption History, and the Reprobate* (Eugene, OR: Pickwick, 2012), 240-44.

turns from the origin of grace to the nature of grace itself, production language does not sit well. The gift given is not simply a *product* but rather a new sort of relatedness, and Edwards chooses words that can support personal relation between ontologically diverse beings: *communication* and *participation*. Both words can mean different things in different contexts and philosophical systems, but they have the capacity to indicate a relational union in which difference is maintained but intimacy achieved.[33] Note how Edwards's thought ends. Grace is a participation of God, because grace indicates God's dwelling in the saint and the saint's dwelling in God. Gracious participation, then, is a union between persons.[34] This explains why Edwards's rhetoric at this point in the sermon begins to soar in the way his theology of grace stretches the Creator-creature boundary without breaking it:

> [Grace or holiness] is super human or super angelical. It is something above all created nature. 'Tis natural to none but God. 'Tis something higher than the whole universe, yea higher than heaven itself. It is both super[-terrestr]ial and supercelestial, being something divine, something of God who is infinitely above both heaven and earth.
>
> The creature that has true grace and holiness in his heart has something infinitely above himself in him. He is gloriously honored and dignified by it, for he dwells in God, and God in him.[35]

There is nothing timid about this doctrine. It is a bold statement of intimacy between God and creature. The two are united in a bond of union in which the creature gains what is not its own. The reason Edwards can state this so strongly is that he has set careful boundaries to protect the Creator-creature distinction, and yet he has also established categories that facilitate the bridging of that distinction.

---

[33] For a similar idea in Calvin, see Julie Canlis, *Calvin's Ladder: A Spiritual Theology of Ascent and Ascension* (Grand Rapids, MI: Eerdmans, 2010), 13.

[34] As we will see, this union between persons (God and the saint) is a finite repetition of the union found within the Trinity. For studies that go into detail on this, see Robert W. Caldwell III, *Communion in the Spirit: The Holy Spirit as the Bond of Union in the Theology of Jonathan Edwards*, Studies in Evangelical History and Thought (Milton Keynes, UK: Paternoster, 2006). See also Kyle Strobel, *Jonathan Edwards's Theology: A Reinterpretation*, T&T Clark Studies in Systematic Theology (London: T&T Clark, 2013); Strobel, "Jonathan Edwards and the Polemics of Theosis," *HTR* 105, no. 3 (2012): 2 259-79; Strobel, "Jonathan Edwards's Reformed Doctrine of *Theosis*," *HTR* 109, no. 3 (2016): 371-99.

[35] Edwards, "True Grace Is Divine (1738)," 359.

It is helpful to summarize the contours of Edwards's thought in several assertions before focusing more narrowly on two decisive categories: fullness and participation. Edwards's doctrine of grace follows these contours:

1. Special or true grace is a communication and participation in divine fullness.
2. Divine fullness is not latent within created nature's ontology.
3. Created nature has no native capacity to acquire divine fullness.
4. Divine fullness is something of God's own good and something of God himself.
5. Divine fullness is not the divine essence.
6. Divine fullness is given immediately to the creature by God.
7. Special or true grace, or the communication and participation in divine fullness, achieves mutual indwelling between God and creature.

These assertions will provide a succinct point of reference as I continue exploring Edwards's doctrine. However, I now must turn to Edwards's wider corpus to answer two critical questions. First, Edwards's concept of the divine fullness remains murky: What, more specifically, does he mean by it? Second, Edwards relies on the notions of communication and participation a great deal: What, more specifically, does he mean by them?

Divine Fullness in Wider Frame

Edwards's concept of divine fullness functions like a great road junction, or perhaps better as a great roundabout where multiple roads conjoin with one another. The roundabout provides entrance to each road and in that sense *is* each road, or at least is an extension of each road. Yet the roundabout also functions to unite each road with all the other roads. That is a bit of how Edwards uses the category of divine fullness. It may be equated with several other categories, yet it also unites each of these categories to the others. In this way divine fullness fulfills the job of a technical category within a theory. Theories are designed to provide a simple explanation for the complex data under consideration. That is what divine fullness does in Edwards's thought. Edwards does not provide a systematic exploration of the notion of divine fullness. That is, it is rarely the object of study or analysis. When it is the object of study, it is generally a rehearsal of the biblical uses of the term as a way of justifying Edwards's use in a particular context. But even here he explores divine fullness only on the way to something else.

However, one can explore the richness of this roundabout category by following the argument of Edwards's *Treatise on Grace*.[36] As the title suggests, *Treatise* unpacks the doctrine of grace, and does so in ways that corroborate the line of thinking discussed above in "True Grace Is Divine." In the course of the argument Edwards arrives at the notion of divine fullness and, in so doing, fills out the picture of the concept in far greater detail. I will provide a brief sketch of the argument in order to demonstrate the richness of this roundabout category.

Treatise on Grace is divided into three chapters, and each chapter penetrates more deeply into the nature of divine grace. Chapter one is primarily concerned to show that special grace is not resident within created nature. It is a larger elaboration of the point that has already been made from the exposition of "True Grace Is Divine" above. Chapter two turns to a deeper consideration of what grace is in itself. Edwards recognizes that there are many virtues and characteristics that are often called graces. However, Edwards argues that this can be misleading. It is not so much that there are many graces or many sorts of grace that differ from each other in a fundamental way. Rather, argues Edwards, all grace resolves to one single virtue: love. The remainder of the chapter is a compelling argument that underscores and confirms this thesis.

For our purposes I note that Edwards's argument in the *Treatise* brings a question and also suggests a solution to it. "True Grace Is Divine" resolves grace to a participation in divine fullness. Is Edwards contradicting himself when he reduces grace to love in the *Treatise*? Recall that "True Grace Is Divine" is based off 1 John 4:12, which itself is entirely about love. I noted with interest how Edwards's exposition section of the sermon deals with the category of love, but then that category fades to the background in the doctrine section. There the category of divine fullness takes over. This suggests a strong relation between divine love and divine fullness, and we will discover that divine love is one of the roads that leads in and out of the roundabout of divine fullness.

---

[36]WJE 21:153-97.

With grace firmly grounded on divine love, chapter three then asks the question, "How does saving grace partake of the nature of that Spirit?"[37] Edwards keeps the conclusion of chapter two in clear view—grace is summarily love. The question in chapter three is, How does grace relate to the Holy Spirit, given that both can be identified with love? This is where the argument becomes precise and very important for every aspect of Edwards's notion of special grace. Edwards begins by uniting the Holy Spirit and divine love. That is, he argues that the Bible sees a particular connection between the Spirit and love. Just as the eternal Son may be called the Logos, so the Spirit may be designated as Agapē.[38] Then Edwards gets more specific and places the entire discussion in the context of his trinitarianism. The Holy Spirit is not only divine love, but more specifically the love, delight, happiness that binds together the Father and the Son *ad intra*.

> God's love is primarily to himself, and his infinite delight is in himself, in the Father and the Son loving and delighting in each other. We often read of the Father loving the Son, and being well-pleased in the Son, and of the Son loving the Father. In the infinite love and delight that is between these two persons consists the infinite happiness of God. . . . The Holy Spirit proceeds from, or is breathed forth from, the Father and the Son in some way or other infinitely above all our conceptions, as the divine essence entirely flows out and is breathed forth in infinitely pure love and sweet delight from the Father and the Son.[39]

At this point Edwards's discussion has moved from grace, a soteriological category, to the heights of trinitarian theology proper, for his assertion that the Spirit is divine love shared between the Father and the Son refers to their relations *ad intra*. Yet from this height, he turns back toward soteriology and argues that this divine love between the Father and the Son, which issues forth as a third person, coessential with the Father and the Son, is also the gift given to the creature in grace. Speaking of the Spirit as the bond of love between the Father and the Son, Edwards writes, "[It is this] person that is poured forth into the hearts of angels and saints."[40] This is the crucial piece

---

[37]WJE 21:180.
[38]WJE 21:183.
[39]WJE 21:184.
[40]WJE 21:186.

of the puzzle, and although Edwards has not introduced the category of divine fullness, it is this notion that the Holy Spirit, as bond of love between the Father and the Son, is the love given in divine grace that allows us to see the various roads approaching each other in the roundabout. As we draw nearer to the metaphorical junction, Edwards points out that the Spirit, who is love, is also both the holiness of God and the happiness of God. These are not separate realities but the same reality viewed from differing angles.[41]

With that in place, I arrive at the roundabout itself. Note the introduction of the term *fullness*:

> From what has been said, it follows that the Holy Spirit is the sum of all good. 'Tis the *fullness of God*. The holiness and happiness of the Godhead consists in it; and in the communion or partaking of it consists all the true loveliness and happiness of the creature. All the grace and comfort that persons have here, and all their holiness and happiness hereafter, consists in the love of the Spirit.[42]

This passage in itself falls short of the category of divine fullness as a roundabout where various categories join together. Taken on its own, this one reference to divine fullness could just be a description of the Holy Spirit rather than a technical category that it clearly is in "True Grace Is Divine." However, Edwards does employ *fullness* in a technical way in the *Treatise*, and in a way that functions to unite various other categories together. Consider the following. First, Edwards dubs the Spirit as God's fullness, and then he defines fullness in reference to the Scriptures, before uniting trinitarian processions, grace to the saints, and christological mediation all around the category of fullness.

> Hence we learn that God's fullness does consist in the Holy Spirit. By "fullness," as the term is used in Scripture, as may easily be seen by looking over the texts that mention it, is intended the good that anyone possesses. Now the good that God possesses does most immediately consist in his joy and complacence that he has in himself. It does objectively, indeed, consist in the Father and the Son; but it doth most immediately consist in the complacence in these elements. Nevertheless the fullness of God consists in the holiness and happiness of the Deity. Hence persons, by being made partakers of the Holy Spirit,

---

[41] WJE 21:186-87.
[42] WJE 21:188, emphasis added.

> or having it dwelling in them, are said to be "partakers of the fullness of God," or Christ. Christ's fullness as mediator consists in his having the Spirit given him "not by measure" (John 3:34); and so it is that he is said to have "the fullness of the Godhead," is said "to dwell in him bodily" (Colossians 2:9); and so we, by receiving the Holy Spirit from Christ and being made partakers of his Spirit, are said to receive "of his fullness, and grace for grace" [Jn 1:16]. And because this Spirit, which is the fullness of God, consists in the love of God and Christ; therefore we, by knowing the love of Christ, are said "to be filled with all the fullness of God." (Ephesians 3:19)[43]

I venture this long quotation because it (1) provides a technical definition of fullness in the abstract: "the good that anyone possesses"; (2) provides a technical definition of the fullness of God in the concrete: "his joy and complacence that he has in himself"; (3) attributes this same concrete fullness as the gift given in soteriological participation, or grace: "persons, by being made partakers of the Holy Spirit, or having it dwelling in them, are said to be 'partakers of the fullness of God'"; and finally (4) indicates that the category of divine fullness relates to other areas of Edwards's theology, especially Christology: "Christ's fullness as mediator consists in his having the Spirit given him 'not by measure.'" This passage gives us a tour around the roundabout. Divine fullness, the central gift of special grace, is the Holy Spirit, which in turn is the love between the Father and the Son *ad intra*, poured out *ad extra*, through christological mediation, to the saints. All of this content is nested in the little category, fullness.

This account of Edwards's notion of divine fullness needs to withstand an objection. Edwards appears to give a different definition in *The End for Which God Created the World*. I will address this now before proceeding further.

Edwards's *The End for Which God Created the World* is a masterpiece of material distilled from his entire intellectual career, and the category of divine fullness is central to its entire thesis.[44] Throughout the dissertation Edwards argues that the end of creation is God's glory (traditional Reformed line), but that this glory is achieved in the communication (or "emanation") of divine fullness.[45] I will explore this idea in chapter four. Yet for now the

---

[43]WJE 21:187-88.
[44]WJE 8:405-536.
[45]For instance, see WJE 8:527-28.

important thing is Edwards's definition of divine fullness. Does he equate it with the Holy Spirit as he does in *Treatise on Grace*? Not precisely. Here, God's fullness consists in three things: God's knowledge, his holiness, and his happiness. Yet these can reduce to two: holiness and happiness are both particularly grounded in the divine will because both are expressions of love. Thus, God's fullness consists in God's knowledge or understanding, and God's love or will. This fullness is communicable: the communication of God's knowledge is designated "truth," and the communication of God's love is designated "grace."[46] Does this then indicate a contradictory view of divine fullness? Did Edwards change his mind over time on this question? Taken within the context of Edwards's trinitarian theology, there is no reason to conclude this.

Edwards's trinitarian theology allows one to see Edwards's two definitions of divine fullness as being fundamentally continuous. Edwards's trinitarianism is the animating center of his thinking, and I will not venture a full exposition here.[47] Rather, I will simply point out how it provides a larger context for understanding divine fullness. When Edwards speaks of God's knowledge and God's love, or God's understanding and God's will, he is referring to trinitarian persons. Edwards understood God's knowledge to refer to God's Son, and God's will or love to refer to God's Spirit. This is clear earlier in *Treatise on Grace* when Edwards speaks of the Son as the Logos and the Spirit as Agapē.[48] *Discourse on the Trinity* details how the inner-trinitarian processions function. The Father, as the fountainhead of the Godhead, considers himself in self-reflection.[49] This mental self-idea is the Father's understanding, and because it is a perfect consideration of himself, it issues forth in a second person of the Trinity, the Logos or Son. The Father and the Son then (with no temporal implication) unite in a bond of delight and love as they contemplate each other. This delight and love is pure act, and thereby issues forth in a third person, the Holy Spirit.[50]

---

[46]WJE 8:441-43, 528-30.
[47]Chapter three will go into far greater depth on Edwards's trinitarianism.
[48]WJE 21:183.
[49]WJE 21:113-44.
[50]See Strobel's analysis of the unity and personhood of the Trinity, along with the question of "real attributes" in Strobel, *Jonathan Edwards's Theology: A Reinterpretation*, 40-64. For a view that both appreciates and critiques Strobel's work, and especially critiques Strobel's account of the real attributes, see Oliver D. Crisp, *Jonathan Edwards Among the Theologians* (Grand Rapids, MI: Eerdmans, 2015), 36-59.

With this in mind we can return to Edwards's two definitions of divine fullness and reconcile them. In *End of Creation*, Edwards describes divine fullness as, functionally, the Son and the Spirit together. In *Treatise on Grace*, he restricts divine fullness to the Spirit alone. However, the difference between these two is simply one of elaboration and abbreviation. The Spirit's procession *ad intra* between the Father and the Son, and the Spirit's communication *ad extra* to the saints, are both mediated by the Son. That is, within the Trinity *ad intra*, the Spirit only proceeds by virtue of the Father's contemplation of the Son, and therefore the Spirit is logically dependent on the Son. The Spirit "proceeds from the Father mediately by the Son, viz. by the Father's beholding himself in the Son."[51] Given this fact, there can be no divine fullness without God's knowledge, because God's will is dependent on it. A similar dynamic happens in the gracious communication of the divine fullness. The communication of the Spirit to the saint (special grace) is always mediated by Christ, who is the divine knowledge incarnate.[52] Thus, sometimes Edwards can identify the divine fullness with the Spirit alone, and other times he can identify the divine fullness with the Spirit and the Son. He is not contradicting himself. Rather, when he mentions the divine fullness as the Spirit, Christ (the divine understanding) is always implied. The gift of grace is the Spirit, mediated by Christ, such that the divine will is shared through the divine understanding. There is one gift, with two aspects.[53]

Kyle Strobel has recently provided further clarity on this question through what he calls God's "communicative natures."[54] Strobel points out that within Edwards's doctrine of the Trinity, God's understanding (the Son) and God's will or love (the Spirit) are perichoretically shared between the three persons of the Godhead, such that the Son is the Father's and the Spirit's understanding, and the Spirit is the Father's and the Son's will or love. This means that within the Godhead, God's natures of understanding and will are shared between the three persons, and Strobel argues that this sets the stage for a

---

[51] WJE 21:143.
[52] See Christ's mediation of divine fullness in WJE 21:187-88. See also Jonathan Edwards, "Sermon 180. John 1:16," in *Sermons, Series II, 1729-1731*, WJE Online vol. 45.
[53] "Knowledge of God... is always mediated *Christologically* through a *pneumatologically* achieved union" (Strobel, *Jonathan Edwards's Theology: A Reinterpretation*, 169).
[54] Strobel, "Jonathan Edwards's Reformed Doctrine." See also Strobel, *Jonathan Edwards's Theology: A Reinterpretation*, 177-207 (especially 202-5).

similar dynamic in the economy. That is, in a way that echoes perichoresis within the Trinity, God shares his natures of understanding and will (the Son and the Spirit) to the saint. Importantly, God shares the nature of his Spirit (divine love) in a manner that binds the saint to Christ (God's self-understanding), in a way that echoes the trinitarian processions and perichoretic communion.

What Strobel terms God's "communicable natures" is a helpful way of describing the internal dynamic within the divine fullness. Strobel's account of the communicable natures is strengthened if one categorizes it under the larger category of the divine fullness. This is the case, first, because it is what Edwards does (as is most obvious in *End of Creation*), and second, because the category of divine fullness points out that the gift of grace is one gift. If one speaks only in terms of God's two communicable natures, then it might sound as if there are two gifts or two graces. In fact, there is one gift, with two aspects: the Spirit uniting the saint to Christ, or, the divine love binding the saint to God's self-understanding. Grace is the divine fullness, which, if opened up, includes two aspects, which map to Strobel's communicable natures. This explains why Strobel's account and mine are mutually informative and complementary, and it also explains why Edwards can move between speaking of God's nature communicated and God's fullness communicated with such ease.

All this means that when Edwards describes divine fullness as consisting in the Holy Spirit or divine love, Christ is always implied. Because Christ is implied, divine knowledge is also in play. Thus the definition of divine fullness in *Treatise* is not materially different from the definition in *End of Creation*. In this study I will tend to use the shorthand version.[55] However, the importance of christological mediation must not be forgotten.

This section functions as a short ride around the roundabout of Edwards's notion of divine fullness. Roundabouts are important for organizing traffic patterns, and familiarity with them is important for anyone wanting to navigate effectively. The same is true in Edwards's doctrine of grace as participation in divine fullness. Divine fullness is central. It touches every other

---

[55]Recall that even in *End of Creation* Edwards uses the word *grace* to designate the communication of the Spirit (see WJE 8:529-30). It therefore follows that when divine fullness is used in the context of special grace that the Spirit will be the particular focus of attention.

category in Edwards's system of grace, and it regulates how they interact. Just as a roundabout may be considered on its own, yet still is joined to the various roads entering it and exiting it, and yet further *is* each of those roads in a very real way, so divine fullness operates. Divine fullness touches or relates directly to the doctrine of the Trinity (especially the Holy Spirit), Christology, soteriology, and many other areas of doctrine, and often functions to relate them to each other. But divine fullness not only relates to various other categories; it is also simply the extension, or even the synonym for many of them. The divine fullness, given in grace, *is* the Holy Spirit; it *is* divine love; it *is* the gift of salvation; it *is* that which unites the human and divine natures in Christ; it *is* the bond between the saint and Christ. It is the *ad extra* expression of the love between the Father and the Son *ad intra*. Changing the image, it is a theoretical category, describing a wide array of theological notions. This complexity, nested in a single category, will be important throughout the remainder of this study.

Communication, Participation, and Communion in Wider Frame

Edwards's definition of true grace falls into two basic halves: it is a communication and participation in divine fullness. We have gained some clarity on divine fullness, but we need now to explore what Edwards means by saying that grace is a *communication and participation* in divine fullness. What does he mean by the categories of communication and participation, and how do they affect his vision of saving grace? Together with the related category of communion, these concepts permeate Edwards's discussions of special grace, and given that they can mean different things in different philosophical and theological traditions, one needs to clarify their meaning within Edwards in order to understand his vision of special grace. The present discussion will be preliminary and limited in scope. My aim at the moment is merely to give an initial analysis of how these concepts are used in the context of Edwards's discussion of special grace and the Creator-creature distinction.

The definitions of these terms are not difficult. The three terms share a semantic range, so they can become almost synonyms. Their meanings converge around the idea of sharing something between parties. Yet around this convergence each term has the capacity to emphasize ideas that the other two generally do not. *Communication* can hold several meanings but has the capacity to emphasize the act of giving, so that "to communicate" is to give something that is to be shared between parties. Similarly, *participation* can hold several meanings but has the capacity to emphasize the act of receiving the thing shared. Communion, again, can mean several things but has the ability to emphasize the mutual act of sharing between parties.

Robert Caldwell confirms that these emphases reflect Edwards's typical usage. Discussing their function with Edwards's trinitarianism, he writes:

> Thus we have a triad of concepts that are used to describe the relationality of the immanent Trinity. The term "communion" (or fellowship, the terms are virtually synonymous in Edwards's writings) describes the common good that the Father and the Son partake of in their eternal love for each other.... "Communication" references the active transfer of divine riches from one member to another. "Participation" by contrast is the reception of good that is communicated from another and the common enjoyment of good with another.[56]

These definitions are helpful because they show the three concepts to be three distinct roles in the same dynamic, and I will refer to these dynamics and roles throughout the study.[57] However, they do not exhaust the question: What, more specifically, does Jonathan Edwards mean when he says that grace is a *communication and participation* in divine fullness?

---

[56]Caldwell, *Communion in the Spirit*, 55. Claghorn and Tan equate the three terms. They are correct that they all together describe the same dynamic, but in making a simple equation, they miss the action of giving (communication), receiving and returning (participation), and sharing (communion) that is important to Edwards's use of the terms (see WJE 8:631). Also see Seng-Kong Tan, *Fullness Received and Returned: Trinity and Participation in Jonathan Edwards* (Minneapolis: Fortress, 2014), 293.

[57]In this study I will follow custom and use the term *participation* when referring to the entire dynamic, without having a particular role in view. However, at other times, when I am focusing on a particular aspect of the participatory dynamic, I will use *communication* to refer to the act of giving, *participation* to refer to the act of receiving and returning the thing shared, and *communion* to refer to the mutual act of sharing. In Edwards's theology of grace—in general—God is the subject of the verb *communicate*, whereas creatures are generally the subject of the verb *participate* or *partake*, and both are often the subjects of the notion of communion. Context will make clear when I am using *participation* in the more general sense and when I am using it in the more restricted, specific sense of creaturely receiving and returning. In subsequent chapters we will see that these three concepts are rooted in trinitarian relations, and in that context, the persons of the Trinity become the subjects of all three concepts. But this will wait for chapter three.

Aid in answering this question comes from contemporary participation scholarship's work on distinguishing different types of participation thought.[58] Recent scholarship justifies distinguishing at least two broad approaches to the concept. Julie Canlis, in her recent study of John Calvin, argues that Western Christian theology produced (at least) two lineages of participation thought. The first grew out of Christian engagement with Platonism and is propounded today by movements such as Radical Orthodoxy.[59] The primary concern in this lineage is with how created reality gains quiddity, substantiality, and being.[60] That is: How does creation derive *being* from "eternal realities"?[61] However, Canlis argues that Christian theology also gave rise to a more relational tradition of participation thinking. Here, the concern is with "intimacy and differentiation, not consubstantiality"; that is, the focus in this type of participation is not on quiddity per se but rather on union between parties, such that their distinction remains.[62] In Christian context, it often refers to a relational sharing between distinct persons, based on the Trinity. Canlis locates Irenaeus and Calvin in this camp. W. Ross Hastings follows Canlis and refers to the first variety of participation with the term *methexis*, and the second, more relational iteration with the term *koinōnia*.[63] Both *methexis* and *koinōnia* may be translated into English as "participation," but they can serve the current discussion as labels for the two iterations of participation thought.[64]

---

[58] This paragraph draws from James Salladin, "Nature and Grace: Two Participations in the Thought of Jonathan Edwards," *IJST* 18, no. 3 (2016): 290-303.

[59] Canlis, *Calvin's Ladder*, 18.

[60] Andrew Davison notes rightly that any discussion of creaturely substantiality must be understood to refer to a "derived substantiality." This is the point of common participation. See Davison, *Participation in God: A Study in Christian Doctrine and Metaphysics* (Cambridge: Cambridge University Press, 2019), 296n54.

[61] T. F. Torrance, *Theology in Reconstruction* (London: SCM Press, 1965), 184.

[62] Canlis, *Calvin's Ladder*, 13. See George Hunsinger's characterization of *koinōnia* as "unity-in-distinction." Hunsinger, "Baptism and the Soteriology of Forgiveness," *IJST* 2, no. 3 (2000): 248-49.

[63] W. Ross Hastings, *Jonathan Edwards and the Life of God: Toward an Evangelical Theology of Participation* (Minneapolis: Fortress, 2015), 56-58; see also 39-40, 102, 441-42, 444.

[64] T. F. Torrance also employed the *methexis-koinōnia* in this way. See Torrance, *Theology in Reconstruction*, 184-85. Seng-Kong Tan uses the term *koinōnia* for relational participation (*Fullness Received and Returned*, 118). Similarly, James K. A. Smith uses the term *methexis* to describe Radical Orthodoxy's approach to participation. See Smith, *Introducing Radical Orthodoxy: Mapping a Post-secular Theology* (Grand Rapids, MI: Baker Academic, 2004), 74-75, 98-99. For an account of theosis based on *methexis*, see Daniel Haynes, "The Metaphysics of Christian Ethics: Radical Orthodoxy and Theosis," *Heythrop Journal* 52 (2011): 659-71.

This dissection of participation thought allows for analysis of Edwards's meaning of *communication, participation,* and *communion,* within the context of special grace, as a species of *koinōnia*. I will demonstrate it as a species of *koinōnia* by highlighting several items I observed in "True Grace Is Divine" and *Treatise on Grace,* and then relate these observations to George Hunsinger's description of *koinōnia* participation. With this in place I will note an important question that will require deeper exploration in chapters two and three.

"True Grace Is Divine" and *Treatise on Grace* provide several clues indicating that Edwards's idea of participation, within the context of special grace, is not aimed at ontological participation that undergirds quiddity, but rather a relational participation that achieves unity while protecting personal differentiation. Recall the seven contours of Edwards's doctrine of special grace identified earlier.

1. Special or true grace is a communication and participation in divine fullness.
2. Divine fullness is not latent within created nature's ontology.
3. Created nature has no native capacity to acquire divine fullness.
4. Divine fullness is something of God's own good and something of God himself.
5. Divine fullness is not the divine essence.
6. Divine fullness is given immediately to the creature by God.
7. Special or true grace, or the communication and participation in divine fullness, achieves mutual indwelling between God and creature.

The first three points above indicate that whatever Edwards means by *participation*, at least in the context of special grace, he does not mean a participation by which a thing gains its quiddity. *Participation* can often signify a sharing in an ontological fundamental such as essence or substance. This is what I called *methexis* above. Indeed, I should point out that even in "True Grace Is Divine" Edwards can describe God as partaking of the divine essence.[65] He is quick to deny that special grace is this sort of participation but illustrates that the concept of participation, within Edwards's thought as

---

[65] Edwards, "True Grace Is Divine (1738)," 353.

beyond it, can carry heavy ontological weight. However, when Edwards describes special grace and participating in divine fullness, he clearly denies that this participation is the sort that gives the creature quiddity. Point two above makes that clear: divine fullness is not latent within the created nature's ontology. That is, a creature can be a fully ontologically stable creature without any partaking in the divine fullness. Point three stresses this by saying that even if the creature developed all the endowments implied in its essence, the creature could still never acquire divine fullness. Both sides of the creature's ontology are out of bounds: participation in divine fullness does not ground the creature's quiddity, and it is out of reach of the creature's ontological capacity to achieve it on its own. Point five above puts participation in divine fullness even further from fundamental ontology by denying that it is the divine essence. Participation in divine fullness does not ground the creature's fundamental ontology, and it does not ground the deity's fundamental ontology either. Edwards is laboring to place this sort of participation in another field of discourse besides quiddity.

This denial that participation in divine fullness establishes quiddity also provides an important positive clue in uncovering what sort of participation Edwards intends. Whatever this participation means, it will necessarily preserve ontological differentiation. If participation in divine fullness does not impinge on creaturely quiddity or the essence of God, then it will follow that the creature's quiddity and God's quiddity remain intact in this participation. If the creature is an ontologically real creature before partaking in the divine fullness, and if by participating in the divine fullness the creature does not share in the divine essence, then one would expect that in participation in divine fullness the creature remains a creature of the same ontological species. If that is the case, then the creature remains creature, and God remains God. They remain distinct and differentiated.

All of this suggests a large ontological barrier between God and the creature, but that would be misleading. Point six above bridges this chasm in a bold statement of intimacy. Divine fullness is given immediately by God. Immediacy here means that grace is given "not by the intervention of natural causes."[66] That is, in this type of participation, there is no third entity. It is not the creature plus some supercreature or intermediary between God and

---

[66] Edwards, "True Grace Is Divine (1738)," 356.

the creature. The divine and the natural relate without mediation other than God himself. This brings up many questions, but it serves to heighten the closeness, the intimacy, between God and the creature without melding them or betraying differentiation. This point is confirmed and pressed further by point seven. The participation in divine fullness culminates in mutual indwelling between God and the creature. This is profound intimacy while preserving differentiation. It is the culmination of Edwards's theory of special grace.

This pattern of participation thought in Edwards fits with what Hunsinger calls the "Chalcedonian pattern" of *koinōnia* relations. Hunsinger writes:

> Formally and paradigmatically, a *koinonia*-relation is a relation of mutual indwelling between two terms (e.g. between Christ and the church). Term *a* dwells in term *b*, even as *b* dwells in *a*, with the result that they coexist in a unity-in-distinction. In such a relation neither *a* nor *b* loses its identity, but rather the distinctive identity of each is sustained, fulfilled and enhanced. The two terms are thus related without separation or division (unity) and without confusion or change (distinction).[67]

Edwards's description of participation in divine fullness follows this description closely. The culmination of special grace is mutual indwelling. God and the creature represent the two terms, and each dwells within the other. Yet this mutual indwelling is not such that God and creature stop being distinctly God and distinctly creature. In *Treatise on Grace* Edwards describes this dynamic in unmistakably relational, even social terms: "To have communion or fellowship with another, is to partake with them of their good in their fullness, in union and society with them."[68] This language follows his Reformed forebearer John Owen quite closely. Owen defined communion as "the mutual communication of such good things as wherein the persons holding that communion are delighted, bottomed upon some union between them."[69] In both Edwards and Owen, the notion of union is personal, social, and relational, which in turn emphasizes the differentiation

---

[67] Hunsinger, "Baptism and the Soteriology," 248.
[68] WJE 21:188.
[69] John Owen, *Communion with God: Of Communion with God the Father, Son, and Holy Ghost, each person distinctly, in love, grace, and consolation; or, The saints' fellowship with the Father, Son, and Holy Ghost unfolded* (Oxford: Benediction Classics, 2017), 1.1, p. 8.

that remains. When Edwards speaks of special grace as a communication and participation in divine fullness, he is describing a species of *koinōnia*, marked by "unity-in-distinction."

This fact is confirmed further when one recalls the particular direction of travel that operates in Edwards's doctrine of grace. The divine fullness is communicated, or given, immediately by God. It is not achieved by the creature but received by the creature. Once this fullness is given (communicated) and received (partaken of), God and the creature share (communion) in mutual indwelling. Hunsinger points out that this sort of dynamic, or grammar, as he calls it, is typical of *koinōnia* relations.

> Very often (though not always) in Christian soteriology a third formal element is also involved. This element may be called the principle of asymmetry. The asymmetrical ordering principle obtains in those cases where *a* is logically prior and *b* logically subsequent, so that *a* can be defined without reference to *b*, but *b* cannot be defined without reference to *a*. . . . I have described this formal or grammatical paradigm, involving an asymmetrical unity-in-distinction, as "the Chalcedonian pattern."[70]

Edwards's doctrine of special grace retains this asymmetry in the giving (communicating) and receiving (partaking) of divine fullness. The divine fullness obtains in God due to trinitarian relations. In the economy, on the basis of the incarnation and ministry of Christ, God communicates the Spirit (his divine fullness) to creatures. Their reception and return of divine fullness (mutual indwelling) is always entirely dependent on the ongoing communication of God. Edwards follows the Chalcedonian pattern of asymmetrical unity-in-distinction that is characteristic of *koinōnia* relations.

The term *koinōnia* is particularly appropriate for Edwards's participation in divine fullness because he grounds his understanding of communion in the Spirit, in an important way, on an exegesis of 2 Corinthians 13:14. This is the famous grace benediction in which Paul invokes the "fellowship of the Holy Spirit." The word translated "fellowship" or "communion" is the Greek word *koinōnia*. This is also the word used in 2 Peter 1:4, another key passage for Edwards's theology of grace. Edwards conveniently describes what he

---

[70] Hunsinger, "Baptism and the Soteriology," 248-49.

means by the term *communion* and grounds it in 2 Corinthians 13:14 when he states:

> Persons are said to have communion with each other, when they partake with each other in some common good; but anyone is said to have communion of anything, with respect to that thing they partake of, in common with others. Hence, in the apostolical benediction, he wishes the "grace of the Lord Jesus Christ, and the love of God the Father, and the communion" (or partaking) "of the Holy Ghost" [2 Cor 13:14]. The blessing wished is but one, viz. the Holy Spirit. To partake of the Holy Ghost is to have that love of the Father and the grace of the Son.[71]

This sort of communion and participation differs from ontological participation or *methexis*. Here Edwards's focus is relationality and sharing between persons in a common good. He references his understanding of communion and partaking to the *koinōnia* of the Spirit. All this validates distinguishing this approach to participation from the more Platonic lineage of thought. Yet, here a caution is in order. It is true that when Edwards describes special grace, he intends a version of participation thought that one should rightly designate as a form of *koinōnia*. However, he also engages questions of ontology and quiddity in significant detail. In these situations he carries notions that approximate *methexis*-participation. Therefore, while one can be confident that Edwards's doctrine of special grace is a participation in the sense of *koinōnia*—unity-in-distinction—one must expect him to also have a theory of *methexis*-participation. These two participations will be important aspects of this study in chapters two and three. They are not competitive with each other but fill complementary roles in his thinking. Their interaction with each other in Edwards's thought will clarify how he distinguishes Creator and creature, and so how he relates them together in special grace.

Grace as Divine Fullness Within Reformed Polemical Context

I now return to a question raised at the beginning of the chapter. In its most basic sense the question is this: To what extent may this doctrine of grace as

---

[71]WJE 21:188.

participation in divine fullness be considered Reformed? There are at least two reasons why this is an important question. The first is that Edwards scholars sometimes frame Edwards's emphasis on trinitarian participation in a way that views it as more or less eccentric from his Reformed tradition.[72] Is this the right way to think of these themes? Second, the wider Reformed theological community is increasingly interested in participation theology, and there is debate as to how well it fits within the Reformed tradition. Some scholars argue strongly that Reformed theology is well suited to soteriological participation, even framing it in terms of theosis, divinization, or deification.[73] Other Reformed theologians show significant caution.[74] This wider conversation suggests that if Edwards's doctrine of grace represents a sympathetic development of his Reformed heritage, then it may provide resources for contemporary constructive work in Reformed efforts to appropriate participation thought. It is therefore an important question both within Edwards studies as well as within the wider Reformed conversation around participation theology.

However, the question of whether Edwards's doctrine of grace is Reformed is not easy to address. This is at least because the Reformed tradition has always struggled with its own identity.[75] One of the characteristics of Reformed tradition is that it is dynamic, it is *ecclesia reformata et semper reformanda* (church reformed and ever being reformed), and therefore it has regularly returned to the Word of God in order to repent in the light of contemporary challenges.[76] This has resulted in a movement that is diverse

---

[72]See especially McClymond, "Salvation as Divinization"; Michael J. McClymond, "Hearing the Symphony: A Critique of Some Critics of Sang Lee's and Amy Pauw's Accounts of Jonathan Edwards' View of God," in *Jonathan Edwards as Contemporary: Essays in Honor of Sang Hyun Lee*, ed. Don Schweitzer (New York: Peter Lang, 2010), 67-92; Michael J. McClymond and Gerald R. McDermott, "The Theme of Divinization," in McClymond and McDermott, *Theology of Jonathan Edwards*, 410-23. These works do not argue that Edwards's emphasis on trinitarian participation betrays his Reformed heritage, but rather they strongly imply that they are themes that are distinguishable from and in some sense stand alongside his Reformed heritage. The point is that McClymond and McDermott do not appear to believe that the soteriological and trinitarian participation themes are an organic outgrowth of Edwards's Reformed tradition.

[73]Habets, "'Reformed Theosis?' A Response"; Murphy, "Reformed Theosis?"

[74]McCormack, "Union with Christ in Calvin's Theology"; McCormack, "Participation in God, Yes." See also John Webster, *Holiness* (London: SCM Press, 2003), 57, 62.

[75]Eberhard Busch, "Reformed Strength in Its Denominational Weakness," in *Reformed Theology: Identity and Ecumenicity*, ed. Wallace M. Alston Jr. and Michael Welker (Grand Rapids, MI: Eerdmans, 2003), 20.

[76]Alston and Welker, *Reformed Theology*, x-xi.

and difficult to define in absolute terms. However, it is also a movement that, while challenging to define according to precise criteria, does exhibit recognizable commonalities.[77] That is, there is a family resemblance within the Reformed tradition that can help one locate Edwards's thought.

The Reformed tradition, in its pursuit to reform unto the Word of God, developed a particular polemical, confessional, and intellectual heritage. It was birthed in polemics against both Roman Catholic and Lutheran theologies, and then later over against Anabaptist thought on the Continent and (with qualifications) over against the Church of England in Britain.[78] This English Puritan form gave rise to the established churches of the New England colonies. During its early years the tradition developed further through its traumatic internal polemics, especially against the rise of Arminianism. All of this polemical strife drove the development of dogmatic precision and the resulting symbolic confessions.[79] The Heidelberg Catechism, the Canons of Dort, and the Westminster Confession and Catechism stand out among many others.[80] No one of these confessions defines the entire movement, nor do they do so collectively. Still, the polemical arguments and the resulting dogmatic confessions serve to shape the character of the tradition. The tradition was further shaped by the creative and dynamic thought of influential theologians and their works. Huldrych Zwingli, Heinrich Bullinger, John Calvin, Theodore Beza, William Ames, William Perkins, John Owen, Richard Baxter, Peter Van Mastricht, Francis Turretin,

---

[77] On contemporary Reformed theologians' capacity to recognize and understand each other in spite of plurality, see Alston and Welker, *Reformed Theology*, xii. Muller notes both continuity and change within the Reformed Orthodox movement. See Richard A. Muller, *Post-Reformation Reformed Dogmatics: The Rise and Development of Reformed Orthodoxy, ca. 1520 to ca. 1725*, vol. 1, *Prolegomena to Theology*, 2nd ed. (Grand Rapids, MI: Baker Academic, 2003), 41, 44-46.

[78] These divisions were still porous at times. John Owen, for instance, could invoke Anglican Richard Hooker to defend his own view. See John Owen, *A Vindication of some Passages in a Discourse concerning Communion with God* (London, 1674), 13-24.

[79] Jan Rohls notes that Karl Barth resisted the idea of a pan-Reformed confession, but in the context of polemical crisis in Germany, supported the Barmen Declaration. See Jan Rohls, "Reformed Theology—Past and Present," in Alston and Welker, *Reformed Theology*, 36-37.

[80] In Edwards's case the specifically relevant confession was the Savoy Declaration, as received by the Boston Synod of 1680. "A Confession of Faith; owned, and consented to by the Elders and Messengers of the Churches, Assembled at Boston in New-England, May 12. 1680. Being the Second Session of that Synod," in *Magnalia Christi Americana: or, The Ecclesiastical History of New-England from Its First Planting in the Year 1620, Unto the Year of our Lord, 1698. In Seven Books*, ed. Cotton Mather (London: Printed for Thomas Parkhurst, at the Bible and Crown in Cheapside, 1702).

and many others all have their place in this group. Whether or not their works ever became official church doctrine, they shaped the minds and thinking of generations of pastors and congregants. These thinkers often disagreed, sometimes with each other explicitly, but still there remain recognizable themes that unite them.[81]

This polemical, confessional, and intellectual heritage can help locate where Edwards's doctrine of grace might (or might not) fit within it. I believe Edwards's doctrine of grace is a self-conscious modification of his received tradition. I will show this over the course of this work, and especially in chapter four. However, this modification alone is not sufficient cause to conclude that Edwards's view stands over against his Reformed heritage. The opposite conclusion might be as easily argued. Reformed tradition has always been self-critical, and therefore dynamic and diverse. That is, it is a *characteristic* of Reformed thought to critically engage, and at times rework, received wisdom. The polemical and confessional aspects of Reformed heritage provide helpful tools for evaluating Edwards's thought. That is, one may ask a polemical question: *How did Edwards's doctrine of grace relate to the polemical arguments that shaped the Reformed tradition?* And one may ask a confessional question: *How did Edwards's doctrine of grace comply or not comply with received Reformed confessions?* If one asks these questions and finds that Edwards's doctrine of grace is aimed at defending key Reformed polemical positions, and also that his view complies with Reformed confessions, then one will have good reason to view his doctrine as operating within the Reformed tradition. If, on the other hand, one finds either that his doctrine of grace has little to do with the polemical battles of the Reformed tradition or that his view contradicts important confessions, then one would have reason to question his Reformed credentials further. This second result would not be conclusive in itself; it would simply demand further inquiry.

I will now take up the polemical question above: How did Edwards's doctrine of grace relate to the polemical arguments that shape the Reformed

---

[81]See Letham's description of principle themes in Reformed theology in R. W. A. Letham, "Reformed Theology," in *New Dictionary of Theology: Historical and Systematic*, ed. Tim Grass Martin Davie, Stephen R. Holmes, John McDowell, and T. A. Noble (Downers Grove, IL: InterVarsity Press, 2016), 747-50.

tradition? I will show that Edwards utilized his doctrine of grace in order to combat two traditional polemical foes: Arminianism, on the one hand, and enthusiasm, on the other. More specifically, Edwards's Creator-creature distinction was aimed to disallow both an Arminian approach to nature and grace, and an enthusiast approach to union with God. This point will give good reason, if provisional, for viewing Edwards's doctrine of grace as a sympathetic development of Reformed thought. I will wait on addressing the confession question mentioned above until chapter four. There I will show that Edwards's key modification was aimed at demonstrating the harmony and synchronization of three key Reformed doctrines: the Trinity, the doctrine of grace, and creation's end. All three of these doctrines feature prominently in the Reformed confessions and catechisms, and Edwards, far from denying the teaching of these confessions, sought to demonstrate their inner coherence. However, for the moment I turn to the polemical use of Edwards's doctrine of grace.

Edwards's doctrine of grace and polemics: Arminianism. Arminianism is the Reformed tradition's old foe. It is not the only foe. Roman Catholicism, Lutheranism, and various forms of enthusiasm are all notorious opponents. But Arminianism always represented a particular threat because it grew from within the Reformed movement. In that way it seemed something of a Trojan horse. One could identify Roman Catholics and Lutherans because they were tribally distinct. Arminians were different. Jacob Arminius himself was from within the fold, and those whom the Reformed Orthodox dubbed with his name did not necessarily learn their views from the original Arminius. Rather, they often developed their views by a gradual departure from standard Reformed thought. Robert Jenson states:

> [Arminianism] was not necessarily advocacy of the particular principles of the Dutch theologian Jacob Arminius, but rather a religious and theological mood of which Arminius had been the most notorious instance in Puritan memory. Broadly, "Arminianism" was New England's name for a kind of religion that appears in all times and places of the church, and has other times been known as "semi-Pelagianism," "synergism," etc."[82]

---

[82]Robert W. Jenson, *American's Theologian: A Recommendation of Jonathan Edwards* (Oxford: Oxford University Press, 1988), 53.

The danger of Arminianism was seared on English-speaking Puritan minds because of their history with the Church of England. The rise of Arminianism in the Church of England contributed a great deal to the eventual split between the Anglicans and the nonconformists. The Church of England's Articles of Religion, though broadly Reformed in content, were unable to stem the rise of Arminian thought. If it happened once, it could happen again. This was the fear in Edwards's day. The same theological mood was growing, and it was deeply alarming to him. In 1735 Edwards joined in opposing the ordination of a minister named Robert Breck on account of his alleged Arminian tendencies.[83] Edwards considered it a real threat, and it was a threat precisely because it touched an identifiable boundary of his own Reformed tradition. Edwards employed his doctrine of grace as participation in divine fullness to combat it, including in his sermon "True Grace Is Divine."

As was common among Puritan preachers, Edwards concluded this sermon with an explicit section titled "Application." Given the doctrine that Edwards has expounded and the way his rhetoric soars at end of the doctrine section, one might expect his application to be a call to seek this grace. It is such a high gift, "something above all created nature . . . something divine . . . infinitely above [human nature]."[84] Surely this demands pursuit, but this is not where Edwards goes in his application. Alternatively, given that the biblical text is itself an exhortation for the Christian community to love each other as God loved them in Christ, one might expect some sort of exhortation to renewed affection for each other. Yet again, Edwards defies expectations at this point. Edward applies this doctrine in three points that defend Calvinism and undermine Arminianism. His first two points of application deal with his view of the creature, and his last has to do with the Creator.

Edwards begins his application by arguing that his doctrine statement ("True grace in the heart of the saint is something divine") demands the conclusion that God is the creature's only good. "The creature has nothing that is truly good but it is something of God. They have nothing—no beauty

---

[83]WJE 12:4-17. A decade later Edwards feared "the utmost danger that the younger generations will be carried away with Arminianism, as with a flood" (WJE 16:354).
[84]Edwards, "True Grace Is Divine (1738)," 359.

and no happiness—contained in their own nature simply considered, nothing of themselves but all infinitely above themselves, all in God."[85] The important point here is to observe something of Edwards's doctrine of creation. He does not want to give creation any good outside God (note his use of the word *truly*—he leaves open the possibility of apparent goods for the creature outside God). Nature has no independent or autonomous end in itself. It is not that God is a *better* option or even the *best* option for creation; it is the creature's only option for happiness and excellence. Any notion of a creaturely happiness with a coherent reality without God—whether espoused by deists or Pelagians or any of Edwards's opponents whom he liked to call "Arminians"—is ruled out. This is true regardless of the fall. Creatureliness is an inherently *empty* thing. Consider Edwards's language here, and note in particular the language of emptiness: "Every creature, every man and angel, is wholly empty in himself, or in his own nature, not only fallen man but unfallen man and unfallen angels. And their emptiness can be filled no other way but by partaking of the fullness of God that has been spoken of."[86]

Edwards believed that creation, taken in itself and without respect to the fall, is in need of special grace, in particular divine fullness. That is, *emptiness and need for divine fullness is a built-in part of God's original design.* Arminians are sometimes accused of having an underdeveloped notion of sin's corrupting effect on the human will. Here Edwards's critique is aimed elsewhere. It is not so much that Arminians have an underdeveloped view of sin's effect, but rather that they have an exaggerated understanding of creaturely capacity from the very beginning. Creatures, according to Edwards, were designed from the very beginning to be empty and to be filled with divine fullness. This need, from the very beginning, was only ever going to be given through the work of Christ. "Christ fills the capacity of the angels as well as men. He fills all things in heaven as well as on earth. For this end he descended to the earth that he might fill our emptiness here."[87] The need for divine fullness is not down to corruption, but rather it is down to creatureliness itself.

However, while creaturely need for divine fullness does not derive from fallen corruption, it does explain why corruption occurs. This is Edwards's

---

[85]Edwards, "True Grace Is Divine (1738)," 359.
[86]Edwards, "True Grace Is Divine (1738)," 360.
[87]Edwards, "True Grace Is Divine (1738)," 360.

second point in the application. Given that participation in divine fullness (grace) is the creature's only good, creatures without this grace will be thoroughly corrupt. Edwards argues that unfallen humanity (Adam and Eve) existed in grace; that is; they participated in God in the way Edwards has argued is true of the redeemed saint. When they fell, this participation in God ceased, and they were left only with natural capacities for love.[88] This meant an inward turning toward self-love, and all corruption derives from this.[89] Depravity is creatureliness without divine participation; it is not "a positive cause but only human nature left to itself."[90] Here Edwards promotes one line of Reformed hamartiology. Janice Knights writes, "For Cotton, Sibbes, Preston, Davenport, and Norton, human sin is often presented as a lack, as an absence of good rather than an active principle of evil. . . . This is not to say that they abandoned the reformed conviction of man's sinfulness, but that faith in God's diffusive goodness guaranteed their assurance of salvation."[91] This captures Edwards's thought well. His polemical aim is not to magnify the power of sinfulness, but rather to heighten the creature's natural need for God. This undermines even the theoretical possibility that a creature could own a natural goodness in itself, and it sets the stage for Edwards to emphasize "God's diffusive goodness."

Edwards's application finale comes by arguing that this view of creaturely need and emptiness reinforces "the reasonableness of the doctrine of immediate efficacious and arbitrary infusion of special grace."[92] His first two points of application deal with the creature, and this last point deals with the nature of God's gift. If the first two points sketch the negative space of

---

[88] See Crisp's more detailed analysis and reconstruction of Adam's fall in Oliver D. Crisp, *Jonathan Edwards and the Metaphysics of Sin* (Aldershot, UK: Ashgate, 2005), 32-33.

[89] While outside the scope of this book, this logic may help account for Edwards's doctrine of hell. If created nature has no good outside God, and if this good (happiness) is only gained through grace (divine participation), then when this divine participation is withheld, the result will be total nonhappiness and nongood: hell. This may go some distance toward bridging the concepts of divine participation and Edwards's notions of final judgment.

[90] Edwards, "True Grace Is Divine (1738)," 361.

[91] Janice Knight, *Orthodoxies in Massachusetts: Rereading American Puritanism* (Cambridge, MA: Harvard University Press, 1994), 86. See Knight's discussion of the trope of *emptiness* on 113. See also S. Mark Hamilton's discussion of corruption in Reformed thought as *privation* and/or *acquisition* in "Jonathan Edwards, Hypostasis, Impeccability, and Immaterialism," *Neue Zeitschrift für Systematische Theologie und Religionsphilosophie* 58, no. 1 (2016): 220-21.

[92] Edwards, "True Grace Is Divine (1738)," 361.

his portrait, his main polemical subject now comes into view. He calls his "Arminian" opponents by name and argues that his view of grace undermines their entire system and upholds God's gratuity in a way the Arminian system cannot. The words *immediate*, *efficacious*, and *arbitrary* are tribal makers of his Reformed heritage and their attempt to refute Arminianism. Edwards's doctrine of grace, with all its soteriological-participation content, is aimed at reaffirming the tradition summarized in the Savoy Declaration's statement on effectual calling. "This effectual call is of God's free and special grace alone, not from any thing at all foreseen in man, who is altogether passive therein, until being quickened and renewed by the Holy Spirit he is thereby enabled to answer this call, and to embrace the grace offered and conveyed in it."[93] Edwards's doctrine of divine participation seeks to explain and defend Savoy's assertion that grace is "not from any thing at all foreseen in man," and it seeks to do so against the traditional old Arminian opponent.

Edwards's doctrine of grace and polemics: Enthusiasm. I now turn to Edwards's defense of another boundary of Reformed thought. In addition to contrasting divine fullness with created nature, Edwards also contrasts divine fullness over against the divine essence. Grace in the saint is not the divine essence: "For the creature can't partake of the divine essence, or any part of the divine essence: for the essence of God is not divisible nor communicable. . . . It is not a communication of God's essence, but it is a communication of that which the Scripture calls God's fullness."[94] This fullness-essence distinction is one that is critical in Edwards's thought. A few years later, in *The Religious Affections*, Edwards elaborates this distinction more fully: "Not that the saints are made partakers of the essence of God, and so are 'Godded' with God, and 'Christed' with Christ, according to the abominable and blasphemous language and notions of some heretics; but, to use the Scripture phrase, they are made partakers of God's fullness."[95] This is a telling passage, because it indicates the polemical opponents Edwards had in view. Edwards's strong denial that the saints participates in the divine essence, combined with the phrase "'Godded' with God, and 'Christed' with Christ," indicates that Edwards was taking a specific side in a polemical battle

---

[93]"Confession of Faith; owned," chap. 10, p. 10.
[94]Edwards, "True Grace Is Divine (1738)," 354.
[95]WJE 2:203.

Grace and Fullness

that was already nearly a century old. Edwards was siding with the orthodox Puritan party, and distinguishing his view of participation from the radical enthusiast sect called the Familists and the thought of Henry Nicolas.[96]

By Edwards's time the Puritan movement in both Old England and New England had experienced a century of polemical struggle around the doctrine of God. The Puritan movement was never without controversy, but the middle of the seventeenth century saw a sort of double-sided attack on the classical doctrine of the Trinity.[97] On the one hand, some from within the Puritan fold broke ranks and began to deny the Trinity along Socinian lines. Some rejected the classical doctrine of the Trinity precisely because they held to a Puritan doctrine of Scripture and did not believe it could be proven from the Bible.[98] Others rejected it as a remnant of Roman Catholic or even Platonic thought.[99] Yet this was not the only attack on the classical doctrine of God. If this first side of the attack emphasized an intellectual assault, the second side of the attack was more mystical and experiential. During the 1640s and 1650s especially, groups such as the Ranters and the Familists asserted mystical and essential union with God. The Ranters employed the category of "fullness," and the Familists used the phrase "Godded with God," and while the Familists did not formally deny the Trinity, Paul Lim argues that they functionally dissolved classical monotheism by fusing the Creator-creature distinction.[100] This was a real problem for the Puritan movement. The Puritan spiritual tradition had long emphasized both a robust intellectual engagement with doctrine and a close experimental intimacy with Christ. If the Socinian or Unitarian movement attacked the first characteristic, the enthusiasts posed a threat to the second. Could Puritanism rebuff the enthusiast error without losing its own spiritual vitality?

The response was a swift and energetic rebuttal, and it followed two broad movements. The first was to reaffirm the ontological chasm between Creator and creature, and the fact that this chasm could never close. In 1648 Samuel Rutherford published a scathing account of various sects and heresies that had risen since the Reformation, and he gave focused attention to the

---

[96] Strobel, "Jonathan Edwards and the Polemics," 265-66.
[97] Lim, *Mystery Unveiled*, 73-75.
[98] For instance, John Biddle. See Lim, *Mystery Unveiled*, 50.
[99] Lim, *Mystery Unveiled*, 67-68.
[100] Lim, *Mystery Unveiled*, 86, 95, 104.

Familists and their "Godded with God" slogan.[101] He points out that these sects assert that the saints partake of not only the divine nature but also the divine *being*.[102] The idea of participating in the divine *nature* was not the cause of great concern—it is a quote from 2 Peter 1:4. It was the idea of participating in the *being* of God that was considered heresy. The words *nature* and *being* can both carry strong ontological weight, but *nature* is more ambiguous because it has many meanings.[103] *Being*, on the other hand, was understood to imply participation in the essence of God. By 1653 John Owen, with others, drafted policy documents for Parliament designed to restrain heresy and promote Puritan orthodoxy. In this document he takes aim at the enthusiasts by insisting "that this God who is the Creator, is eternally distinct from all the creature in his *being* and blessedness."[104] This statement comes at an interesting location in the document. Owen is outlining doctrine that should be enforced by the state because it is necessary to salvation. He begins with an article on the authority of Scripture, and then a second article on the existence of God. The Creator-creature distinction then comes in third place, before the doctrines of the Holy Trinity, Christology, and soteriology. Clearly, this was an important point, and it demanded a privileged location in the order of saving doctrine that required protection.

Yet the defense needed more than just a denial of essential union and an affirmation of the Creator-creature distinction. The second movement in orthodox defense against the enthusiasts came in the form of reaffirming historic Christian accounts of grace and even deification. The word *deification* was used by a number of authors in this period, and many of them took a dim view of it. It appears that it was generally associated with

---

[101] Samuel Rutherford, *A Survey of the Spiritual AntiChrist* (London: J. D. & R. for Andrew Cooke, 1648). See Lim's analysis: *Mystery Unveiled*, 97-98.

[102] Strobel, "Jonathan Edwards and the Polemics." 266.

[103] See, e.g., Edwards's famous "Unpublished Letter on Assurance and Participation in the Divine Nature," where Edwards responds to a critic who thought that he espoused essential union. Edwards points out the word *nature* need not imply *essence*, but has many possible meanings (WJE 8:638-39).

[104] John Owen et al., *Proposals for the furtherance and propagation of the Gospell in this Nation. As the same were humbly presented to the Honourable Committee of Parliament by divers Ministers of teh Gospell, and others, as also, Some Principles of Christian Religion, without the beliefe of which, the Scriptures doe plainly and clearly affirme, Salvation is not to be obtained, Which were also presented in the explanation of one of the said Proposals* (London: R. Ibbitson, 1653), article 3, p. 8, emphasis added. See also Lim, *Mystery Unveiled*, 45-46.

ontological and essential union, and therefore it was a code word for heresy. John Turner, for instance, states:

> 'Tis enough for us to that we believe the Person of Christ, and the Persons of Believers to remain distinct after all the Union that intercedes between them: Let us be thankful for the Influences of his Grace, and for the In-dwellings of his Holy Spirit; but let us detest those swelling Words of Pride and Ignorance, of being Christed and Deify'd; for whatsoever be the nature and kind of the Union between Christ and Christians, that the same shou'd be Hypostatical, cannot without Blasphemy be imagined.[105]

Notice how Turner dismisses the Familist slogan "Christed" and also the word *Deify'd*, while at the same time returning to the notion of grace as a union between the believer and Christ such that distinction remains. This is a reaffirmation of the traditional lines of Puritan and Reformed doctrine of the mystical union, the ground of Puritan spirituality and experiential tradition. The polemic is not only to deny something but to point to the real sort of union that Puritanism always supported. There were other thinkers who rebuffed the enthusiast essential-union thesis by noting the existence of an orthodox version of either deification or at least robust soteriological participation. Henry More was not a Puritan—he was famously a Cambridge Platonist—but he was known and read by Jonathan Edwards. He published a refutation of enthusiasm, and in it he affirms his own account of "deification" (his word), based on the Scriptures, the church fathers, and the *Theologia Germanica*.[106]

Even from within the Puritan world, Edward Leigh recognized that the church fathers could speak of *theopoiesis* and other theosis categories in an orthodox way. Still, he warns that it is easy to abuse these statements from the Fathers. He includes Martin Luther in a list of orthodox thinkers whose thought could be mistakenly read to include essential union. Part of the problem is that the orthodox (Fathers along with Luther) were given to hyperbole: "The Fathers hyperboles this way, followed by Luther." Like

---

[105] John Turner, *A Phisico-Theological Discourse* (London: Printed by F.C. for Timothy Childe at the White Hart at the West End of St. Paul's Church-yard, 1698), 221. See also Lim's discussion and quotation in *Mystery Unveiled*, 96.

[106] Henry More, *Enthusiasmus Triumphatus, or, a Discourse of the Nature, Causes, Kinds, and Cure of Enthusiasme* (London, 1656), 298-300.

Turner, he refutes the error by restating his understanding of the real nature of union with Christ. Interestingly, given the present discussion of Edwards's approach to participation as a form of *koinōnia*, Leigh warns against confusing essential union with communion between distinct persons. "We must not apply that to Union which is proper to Communion, Communion is the common union of all the members with Christ. It is folly to apply that to one part which is proper to the whole body."[107] In the context he argues that to posit essential union is to assert a sort of union that exceeds even the christological union, for even there the divine and human natures remain distinct. Rather, in grace the believer is united to the body of Christ, but the believer is never more than a portion of the body. That is, the believer cannot be said to become identical with the body of Christ. Distinction remains.

All of this is to show that Puritan and Reformed polemics, or in the case of Henry More even Anglican Platonic polemics, followed the pattern of maintaining the Creator-creature distinction, denying essential union, and then reaffirming an orthodox understanding of union or communion in which personal distinction remains.

Nearly one hundred years later, this controversy was still relevant to Jonathan Edwards. He gained entrance to the debates at least through Samuel Rutherford's *Display of the Spiritual Antichrist*.[108] The controversy hit closer to home when Charles Chauncey, one of Edwards's greatest opponents, suggested a connection between the enthusiasts such as the Familists and the revivalists defended by Edwards.[109] Chauncey's attacks came in the early 1740s, a few years after Edwards preached "True Grace Is Divine."[110] However, Chauncey's attacks arrived before the publication of *The Religious Affections*. This may help explain why in the sermon Edwards simply denies essential union and moves on, whereas in the *Affections* he issues a stronger statement and explicitly includes the enthusiast slogan "Godded with God and Christed with Christ" as the position he rejects. Edwards responded by creating a sharp break with the entire idea of

---

[107] Edward Leigh, *A Systeme or Body of Divinity* (London: Printed by A.M. for William Lee at the Signe of the Turks-head in Fleet Street over against Fetter-lane, 1662), 673-74.
[108] WJE 2:287. See also Strobel, "Jonathan Edwards and the Polemics," 265.
[109] Strobel, "Jonathan Edwards and the Polemics," 267-68.
[110] "True Grace Is Divine" was preached in 1738. Chauncey's attacks came in 1742. See Strobel, "Jonathan Edwards and the polemics of Theosis," 267.

participating in the divine essence or of any idea of a mingling with God's *being* per se. It is the divine fullness that is given, but this is not the divine essence. That distinction makes all the difference, but it is not where Edwards stopped. He followed the pattern of his forbears in the Reformed Puritan tradition by denying essential union, reaffirming the Creator-creature distinction, and then also presenting an approach to special grace and union marked by communion between distinct parties. This is not to say that Edwards's theology of divine grace followed convention at every turn.[111] But it does mean that Edwards deployed his doctrine of grace to defend Puritan polemical interests, and that he did so in a way that signaled his loyalty to the Reformed orthodoxy of the previous century.

Yet I must say something more. It would be wrong to suggest that Edwards incorporated enthusiast interests; but it would be right to say that he refused to surrender a robust vision of intimacy between God and believer. That is, while he maintained the Creator-creature distinction, his ultimate aim was not that the two remain separate but rather that he account for their relational union. Throughout Edwards's corpus he is captivated by the way special grace *bridges* the ontological chasm without undermining it. His first *Miscellanies* entry states that holiness is "almost too high a beauty for any creatures to be adorned with; it makes the soul a little, sweet and delightful image of the blessed Jehovah."[112] This beauty still captivated him at the end of his life. Speaking of the union that results from the communication of divine fullness, Edwards writes:

> The union will become more and more strict and perfect; nearer and more like to that between God the Father and the Son; who are so united, that their

---

[111] For instance, Edwards Leigh asserted that believers partake of the divine nature (2 Pet 1:4), but not the divine fullness. He had in view the christological fullness of Col 2:6. Edwards, as we have seen, strongly asserted Christ's communication of divine fullness and viewed the divine *nature* of 2 Pet 1:4 as a near synonym. John Cotton denied that grace in the heart of the saint was the Holy Spirit, but rather the created effect of the Holy Spirit (created grace). Edwards, on the other hand, viewed the divine fullness in grace to be the Holy Spirit poured out into the saint (uncreated grace). These are merely two examples of how Edwards's solutions could differ from others in the Puritan world. However, the larger point is that the polemical boundaries that helped form the identity of the Reformed movement were held in common. See Leigh, *Systeme or Body*, 674. See also John Cotton, *The covenant of Gods free grace, most sweetly unfolded and comfortably applied to a disquieted soul. Whereunto is added, A profession of faith, made by J. Davenport*, ed. Thomas A. Schafer (London: John Hancock, 1645), 30-31.

[112] WJE 13:163.

interest is perfectly one. If the happiness of the creature be considered as it will be, in the whole of the creature's eternal duration, with all the infinity of its progress, and infinite increase of nearness and union to God; in this view, the creature must be looked upon as united to God in an infinite strictness.[113]

This is not essential union, but it is a union of profound intimacy. It is *koinōnia*, a communion between distinct persons, united in the bond of love that unites the Father and the Son, economically poured out. Edwards held the Reformed line against the enthusiasts, but he also pressed forward a vision of participation that shows itself creative and compelling.

Conclusion

David Brainerd was a changed man when he went to sleep the night of July 12, 1739. His experience was in many ways traditional and perhaps even conventional. Many lives had been changed in a similar way before him, and his own conversion took place on the eve of one of the greatest religious awakenings in American history. Perhaps for that very reason, precisely because it was not all that unique, it was an experience that demanded explanation. What was it that had happened to him?

Jonathan Edwards published Brainerd's conversion story and the account of his life because he thought it vividly displayed the nature of true and special grace.[114] In particular, Edwards points to "what passed in his [Brainerd's] own heart, the wonderful change that he experienced in his mind and disposition, the manner in which that change was brought to pass, how it continued."[115] It was this change within Brainerd that captivated Edwards, and he sought to provide his own theological explanation for what it was that had happened in the soul of the future missionary and all those who share in the same experience. What was Edwards's explanation? Brainerd, and all other true saints, had received a communication of divine fullness, immediately, effectually, and arbitrarily communicated by God.

This divine fullness was nothing latent within Brainerd, nor in any other would-be convert. It was this fact, that supernatural grace (divine fullness)

---

[113]WJE 8:533-34.
[114]WJE 6:89-91. Edwards does not use the word *grace*, but he clearly presents Brainerd as an example of what true religion looks like.
[115]WJE 6:91.

was infinitely above created nature, that meant Brainerd could never achieve it from below; it could only be received from above. The very sovereignty that so dominated his Puritan tradition, and so provoked him to despair, was also the basis for how grace could eventually break in and change him. Grace, argued Edwards, was a communication of God himself. But in what way was it something of God himself?

It was something of God because it was a finite communication of the Holy Spirit. The Spirit, for Edwards, is the bond of love between the Father and the Son. Their mutual good is their fullness, which in turn is their mutual love and delight and joy. This is the fullness that was communicated economically to Brainerd, and in and through his faculties returned to God himself.[116] This is why Brainerd's experience was a new "view and apprehension." It was not that he saw something with his eyes; it was that his soul was suddenly captivated with a spiritual sight of God's divine beauty. "It appeared to be divine glory that I then beheld. And my soul 'rejoiced with joy unspeakable,' to see such a God, such a glorious divine being."[117] This is the same bond of union enjoyed by the Father and the Son in the Spirit, finitely communicated to the young Brainerd. Brainerd's enjoyment of it was his participation in divine fullness.

This communication and participation remained constant, not in degree but in kind, throughout the rest of Brainerd's life. In this ongoing communion, Brainerd remained Brainerd, ontologically nothing more than creature; and the Holy Trinity remained the Holy Trinity, ontology nothing less than Creator. Yet Creator and creature were eternally bound in a *koinōnia* that when viewed from eternity, "must be looked upon as . . . [a union of] . . . infinite strictness."[118]

This first chapter has aimed to provide an overview of Edwards's doctrine of grace as participation in divine fullness and to argue that it functioned polemically to defend two key Reformed boundaries. It resisted both Arminian and enthusiast errors. This polemical use of Edwards's doctrine of

---

[116]"So that true saving grace is no other than that very love of God; that is, God, in one of the persons of the Trinity, uniting himself to the soul of a creature as a vital principle, dwelling there and exerting himself by the faculties of the soul of man, in his own proper nature, after the manner of a principle of nature" (WJE 21:194).
[117]WJE 6:138-39.
[118]WJE 8:534.

grace should justify at least a provisional conclusion that it operates within the Reformed sphere of thought. On this basis, I now turn to two chapters that explore the Creator-creature distinction in greater detail, with the aim of contributing insight to contemporary conversations in soteriological participation theology. Behind these next two chapters is an underlying question: Given that Reformed theology is exploring participation thought, what insights might Edwards's approach to grace, and particularly his understanding of the Creator-creature distinction, give to this pursuit?

2

Grace and Nature

THE PREVIOUS CHAPTER PROVIDED an overview of Jonathan Edwards's doctrine of special grace as a communication or participation in divine fullness, and how it functioned to reinforce Reformed polemical interests. With this overview in place, I now must investigate more thoroughly the relationship between divine fullness and created nature in Edwards's thought. To what extent, and in what way, did Edwards distinguish nature and grace? This has always been an important question within Christian thought, and it has been particularly important for Augustinian tradition. Ever since the Pelagian controversy Western Christianity has striven to demonstrate the gratuity of divine grace, while at the same time preserving integrity and value for created nature in itself. This question is perhaps heightened further when grace is presented in terms of divine participation. If one says that grace is participation in divinity, what does that mean for created nature in itself? Do all things, by virtue of their being, partake of divinity? If so, then to what extent is divine grace gratuitous? If not, then one must ask difficult questions about the way in which created nature gains its being.[1]

This set of questions is relevant to any Christian theology of grace, but it is increasingly poignant in current scholarly discussions of participation theology. Participation theology often covers both questions of ontology and questions of soteriology, and therefore it is crucial to ask the question,

---

[1]Much of this chapter draws from James Salladin, "Nature and Grace: Two Participations in the Thought of Jonathan Edwards," *IJST* 18, no. 3 (2016): 290-303.

How do these spheres of participation thought relate to each other in any given thinker's theology? I will sharpen this question in reference to current participation and theosis scholarship.

Paul Gavrilyuk provides a helpful overview and critique of contemporary interest in participation thought, and in the soteriological notion of theosis more specifically. He notes the wide consensus that theosis or deification or divinization is grounded on a theology of participation. This consensus is correct: the concept of participation is "constitutive of the notion of deification," but he complains that some scholars reduce theosis to (merely) "participation in God." Gavrilyuk sees this as an overly minimal definition, partially because it can mean that everything is, at least a little, deified: "One corollary of this definition, on the assumption of participatory metaphysics, is that all things are deified to unspecified degree: by participating in being, all existing things participate in God. As central as the notion of participation is for understanding deification, greater precision in using the term is in order."[2]

This is an astute observation, and it highlights the relevance of this present chapter. If participation theologians tend to ground *ontology* itself in God, then what is left for *soteriology*? Is the participation that grounds created nature in God the same sort of participation that elevates created nature in salvation? Gavrilyuk suggest there is a way to be more precise. What might such greater precision look like? Is there a way to ground all being as a participation in God, while also stating that soteriology is a participation that is somehow distinct from this?

Maarten Wisse is more critical of the entire theosis project, and is cautious of participatory metaphysics generally, but shares something of Gavrilyuk's observation at this point. If, argues Wisse, theosis is rooted in participation in God, then it may well end up that theosis is less about becoming something new and more about realizing what one already is.[3] This, in Wisse's mind, is a theological failure. Salvation must be somehow distinct from created nature and ontology. There must be something new, some real transformation, rather than simply realizing what is already there in principle. All of this indicates that current participation thought requires greater

---

[2]Paul Gavrilyuk, "The Retrieval of Deification: How a Once-Despised Archaism Became an Ecumenical Desideratum," *Modern Theology* 25, no. 4 (2009): 651.
[3]Maarten Wisse, *Trinitarian Theology Beyond Participation*, ed. Ian A. McFarland, John Webster, and Ivor Davidson, T&T Clark Studies in Systematic Theology (London: T&T Clark, 2011), 305.

precision. In particular, there is need for greater precision regarding the relationship between ontological participation and soteriological participation. In other words, there is need for greater precision in distinguishing created nature and divine grace.

This present chapter will contribute to this need for greater precision by exploring how Edwards distinguished created nature from divine grace. More specifically, I will rearrange Gavrilyuk's observation into a question. He asserts that when theosis is reduced to participatory metaphysics, then all ends up deified to an unspecified degree. My question is, Is this true of Edwards's view of special grace? For the purpose of this chapter, I will state the question in more specifically Edwardsean terms: Given that Edwardsean special grace is a communication and participation in divine fullness, does this imply that all things participate in divine fullness to some degree?

The answer to this question is no: only the elect saints and angels participate in divine fullness, and God communicates his divine fullness only to these particular creatures. However, to show this, I will need to argue that Edwards has what amounts to two types of participation theology. Perhaps better: there are two ways that a creature can be said to participate in God. These two versions of participation map, in broad terms, to the two types of participation mentioned earlier. In Edwards's thought, there is one way in which all things can be said to participate in God. I dub this "common participation," and I will show that it has strong similarities to the Platonic approach, or what one may call *methexis*. However, there is a second way that creatures may participate in God, and this second way is only true of the elect saints and angels. When Edwards speaks of communication and participation in divine fullness, he means this second way. I dub this second version of participation "special participation." This special participation has strong similarities to what Canlis calls "trinitarian Participation," or what one may call *koinōnia*.[4] Edwards employs both approaches to

---

[4] Canlis argues that Calvin exhibits "trinitarian participation," based on *koinōnia*, rather than the Platonic version, based on *methexis*. In employing this typology and utilizing Canlis's helpful work, I am not intending to argue that Edwards relied on Calvin for his participation theology. In fact, I will argue that Edwards differs from Calvin, as presented by Canlis, at least in that Edwards uses both approaches to participation and not only the second. For "trinitarian participation" see Julie Canlis, *Calvin's Ladder: A Spiritual Theology of Ascent and Ascension* (Grand Rapids, MI: Eerdmans, 2010), 142.

participation.[5] He does not employ them in a competitive or incoherent way but in a complementary manner. Where Julie Canlis argues that Calvin's participation theology is a form of relational *koinōnia*, and is therefore an alternative to the Platonic approach, I will argue that Edwards unites the two approaches in a constructive whole.[6]

I will make this argument by exploring both approaches to participation within Edwards's thought, beginning with common participation and showing how it undergirds Edwards's doctrine of common grace and nature, before exploring special participation and showing how it undergirds his view of special grace. In this way I will clarify the meaning of participation in Edwards and show how participation in divine fullness is specific to the redeemed and grounded in their trinitarian communion.

COMMON PARTICIPATION

Our understanding of what I call common participation must begin with Edwards's view of common grace and the way it is rooted in God's action. Edwards followed his Reformed heritage in making a fundamental distinction between these two forms of grace. There is grace that God extends, to some extent, toward all creation. Edwards calls this "common grace." On the other hand, there is grace that is unique, or specific, to those who will be saved. This is "special" or "saving" grace. Edwards was very concerned to show that these two types of grace differ at a fundamental level. It is not that they describe two different extents of God's grace. It is not that special grace is simply greater in degree than common grace. Rather, "special or saving grace . . . is not only different from common grace in degree, but entirely diverse in nature and kind."[7] Both common grace and special grace describe the immediate action of God, but God does different things in the

---

[5] W. Ross Hastings suggests Edwards employs both *koinōnia* and *methexis*, and suggests more work is required for developing the *methexis* aspect of Edwards's thought. See Hastings, *Jonathan Edwards and the Life of God: Toward an Evangelical Theology of Participation* (Minneapolis: Fortress, 2015), 56-58; see also 39-40, 102, 441-42, 444.

[6] Canlis recognizes that the Platonic tradition of participation and the *koinōnia* approach are not necessarily in competition with each other (*Calvin's Ladder*, 18). I agree with this and present Edwards's theology as an example of the two working together in one thought system. For a helpful analysis of how the Christian tradition has leveraged both Greek philosophy and New Testament teaching in symbiosis, see Henri de Lubac, *Catholicism: Christ and the Common Destiny of Man* (San Francisco: Ignatius, 1950), 40-41.

[7] WJE 21:154.

two types of grace. Edwards distinguishes the two in numerous places, but consider the following from his sermon "A Divine and Supernatural Light":

> Common grace differs from special, in that it influences only by assisting of nature, and not by imparting grace, or bestowing anything above nature. The light that is obtained, is wholly natural, or of no superior kind to what mere nature attains to; though more of that kind be obtained, than would be obtained if men were left wholly to themselves. Or in other words, common grace only assists the faculties of the soul to do that more fully, which they do by nature.[8]

Notice the relation between common grace and nature. God acts and influences what is natural within the human person, and this is what Edwards means by common grace. What is interesting here is that there is nothing incongruous between common grace and nature. It is true that when Edwards uses the term *common grace* he usually speaks of God's action of influencing and directing what is natural in the human person, and this could imply a strong distinction between common grace and nature. However, Edwards has no view of nature that is not directed or supported or influenced by God's immediate action, and therefore he has no view of nature that is not a result of common grace. As Norman Fiering rightly says, "Any discussion of the powers of nature as conceived of by Edwards must presuppose the role of common grace."[9] One therefore cannot understand common grace without asking about Edwards's view of the natural world. More specifically, in order to understand common grace more fully, one must ask how the natural world relates to God. The answer to this question will launch one into the world of Edwards's metaphysics.[10]

---

[8] WJE 19:410.

[9] Norman Fiering, *Jonathan Edwards's Moral Thought and Its British Context* (Chapel Hill: University of North Carolina Press, 1981), 61. Fiering then goes on to cite the same passage from *A Divine and Supernatural Light*.

[10] Edwards's metaphysics has produced a large amount of literature, and I will not attempt to address all the issues raised in this conversation. My aim in this section is merely to argue that Edwards held to a view of natural participation in God for its being. Sang Hyun Lee began an important debate by arguing that Edwards departed from traditional essentialist/substantialist metaphysics and preferred a "dispositional ontology." This view has been rejected by Crisp and Bombaro, as well as Stephen Holmes and others. See Lee, *The Philosophical Theology of Jonathan Edwards* (Princeton, NJ: Princeton University Press, 1988). For the larger conversation regarding Edwards's metaphysics and critiques of Lee's perspective, see Oliver D. Crisp, *Jonathan Edwards on God and Creation* (Oxford: Oxford University Press, 2012); John J. Bombaro, *Jonathan*

Edwards believed that created being was an immediate and continuous gift from God. This was, in many respects, not a new thought, but it was unpopular at his time. He lived and wrote in a time that was busy jettisoning older ways of viewing ontology. The Enlightenment was shining brightly, and the new learning in science and new ways of thinking in philosophy were reimagining a world that nearly ran itself. Laws and mechanisms explained the phenomena humans observed, and there was less felt need for a theory that included a God who acted within history. Nature was becoming autonomous. This new natural autonomy took different forms: Thomas Hobbes's notion of materialism collapsed God into corporality, whereas the deists kept God far enough away so that nature could run its course.[11] Edwards would have none of this. It is not that he was a blind traditionalist or an intellectual dinosaur, unable to acclimate to the modern world. Edwards engaged as much of the learning of his day as he could, and sought to use the emerging scientific and intellectual insights to support his Christian convictions.[12] Among these was the conviction that the natural world depended, radically and at every moment, on God's immediate power. It was as this conviction engaged the scientific and philosophical controversies of his day that he grasped a view of natural dependence that approximates a *methexis* approach to participation.

To say that the natural world depends radically on God's immediate power could be nothing more than classical creation *ex nihilo*. Yet, Edwards meant more. Stephen Holmes recounts that one of the key intellectual

---

Edwards's Vision of Reality: The Relationship of God to the World, Redemption History, and the Reprobate (Eugene, OR: Pickwick, 2012); Stephen R. Holmes, *God of Grace and God of Glory: An Account of the Theology of Jonathan Edwards* (Edinburgh: T&T Clark, 2000); Holmes, "Does Jonathan Edwards Use a Dispositional Ontology? A Response to Sang Hyun Lee," in *Jonathan Edwards: Philosophical Theologian*, ed. Oliver D. Crisp and Paul Helm (Burlington, VT: Ashgate, 2003), 99-114.

[11] Hobbes writes, "'Incorporeal substance' is merely an 'insignificant sound,' like 'round quadrangle.'" See Thomas Hobbs, *Leviathan, or The Matter, Forme, & Power of a Common-wealth Ecclesiastical and Civill* (London: Printed for Andrew Crooke, at the Green Dragon in St. Paul's Church-yard, 1651), 1.4, cited in Holmes, *God of Grace*, 82. For discussion of Edwards's ontology as a response to materialism and other Enlightenment thought, see WJE 6:52-75. For a more comprehensive account of Edwards's thought in the context of the Enlightenment, see Michael J. McClymond, *Encounters with God: An Approach to the Theology of Jonathan Edwards*, Religion in America (New York: Oxford University Press, 1998).

[12] McClymond, *Encounters with God*, 7. For Edwards's intellectual context and engagement with other contemporary thinkers, see Fiering, *Jonathan Edwards's Moral Thought*. See also Peter J. Thuesen, "Introduction," in *Catalogues of Books*, ed. Peter J. Thuesen, WJE 26.

difficulties of Edwards's age was the question of how to reconcile Newtonian physics with the notion of a nonmaterial reality. Even if Hobbes's materialism was denied, it was not at all clear how the nonmaterial world interacted with the material. The difficulty was great enough that some imminent thinkers simply retreated from questions of metaphysics altogether. Edwards responded with the bold move of grounding all substance in God alone.[13] In an early reflection on the nature of physics Edwards writes, "The substance of bodies at last becomes either nothing, or nothing but the Deity acting in that particular manner in those parts of space where he thinks fit. So that, speaking most strictly, there is no proper substance but God himself (we speak at present with respect to bodies only). How truly, then, is he said to be *ens entium*."[14]

When Edwards investigates the deepest foundation of nature, he finds God's direct action, such that the natural world—indeed the whole of creation—has no substance other than God.[15] This does not imply pantheism—God is independent of creation, and his aseity remains intact.[16] It is, however, a very strong view of nature's direct, immediate dependence on God for its substance and even for its being.[17] God's action is nature's substance, and God is the *ens entium*, the "being of beings."

This leads to Edwards's view of continuous creation. When he grounds nature's substance in the action of God, Edwards commits himself to framing this as a *continuous action*. If deists believed that God created and then

---

[13] Holmes, *God of Grace*, 80-84.
[14] WJE 6:215.
[15] While the category "substance" is generally associated with Aristotelian philosophy, and "participation" more often with Platonic, the two can exist together. They certainly existed together in Thomas Aquinas. See Rudi A. Te Velde, "General Introduction," in *Participation and Substantiality in Thomas Aquinas* (New York: Brill, 1995), esp. xi. By the same token, whereas Aristotle used *substance* to describe immanence, to some degree over against Platonic participation, one might question whether Edwards, in grounding nature's substance in God's immediate action, reconciles the two traditions or swallows up "substance" into "participation." As Te Velde asks, "If a creature is a participation of God's being, how then can it be understood to be a substance which is endowed with a nature of its own?" ("General Introduction," xii).
[16] Oliver Crisp rehearses the debate regarding whether Edwards is a pantheist and argues instead that he holds a panentheist vision of creation. See especially chaps. 4 and 7 in *Jonathan Edwards on God and Creation*. See also Bombaro, *Jonathan Edwards's Vision of Reality*, 80-83.
[17] Edwards's aim is to ground or perhaps "suspend" creation from God, much as Radical Orthodoxy describes how the "Platonic account of participation (*methexis*) . . . suspends the immanent order from a transcendent source." See James K. A. Smith, *Introducing Radical Orthodoxy: Mapping a Post-secular Theology* (Grand Rapids, MI: Baker Academic, 2004), 98-99.

stepped away to let the machine run on its own, then Edwards turned this image around with clockwork precision. Nature's substance can only endure if God continues to substantiate it.[18] This activity of God is identical with the initial creation of the world *ex nihilo*: "'Tis certain with me that the world exists anew every moment, that the existence of things every moment ceases and is every moment renewed."[19] Oliver Crisp describes this concept of continuous creation with the image of a cinema:

> Edwards's doctrine of God's relation to the world he creates is rather like that of a projectionist and the motion picture he is responsible for projecting onto the theatrical screen: each world-stage God creates is similar to a discrete photographic still that is one of many such stills in a series, segued together in sequence on a reel that is then projected onto the silver screen of a movie theatre, giving the illusion of continuous action across time.... Creation comprises a set of world-stages that God orders into a series as he sees fit. And God is the only causal agent acting in this way. Creatures are merely the occasions of this divine act.[20]

Thus far we have seen that the natural world derives its substance from God's immediate action and that this action must be repeated every moment in order for the natural world (creation) to endure. But what is this action? What action of God explains substance and being in nature? Edwards answers by pointing to God's act of knowing. "I demand in what respect this world has a being, but only in the divine consciousness."[21] In a move reminiscent of his contemporary George Berkeley, Edwards undermines Enlightenment autonomy with a form of idealism, and this idealism hangs in the background of his thought on both creation and God himself.[22] When

---

[18] Thomas Morris discusses the concept of continuous creation as an element of creaturely dependence and frames it as, in a broad sense, a form of Platonism. In many respects his discussion is similar to Edwards's doctrine. See Thomas V. Morris, *Our Idea of God: An Introduction to Philosophical Theology* (Vancouver: Regent College Publishing, 1991), 154-58.

[19] *Miscellanies* 125.a (WJE 13:288). See also *Miscellanies* 18 (WJE 13:210), *Miscellanies* 346 (WJE 13:418).

[20] Crisp, *Jonathan Edwards on God and Creation*, 9.

[21] WJE 6:204.

[22] For similarities and differences between Berkeley and Edwards, and that Edwards was not likely relying on Berkeley as a source, see WJE 6:63, 76, 76n3, 102-3. Bezzant expects Edwards did encounter Berkeley's thought. See Rhys Bezzant, *Jonathan Edwards and the Church* (Oxford: Oxford University Press, 2014), 50. For a brief overview of Berkeley's idealism, see Lisa Downing, "George Berkeley," in *The Stanford Encyclopedia of Philosophy*, ed. N. Zalta Edward, 2013 ed., https://plato.stanford.edu/archives/spr2013/entries/berkeley.

Edwards describes the Trinity, he grounds the begetting of the Son in the perfect idea that the Father has of himself. Similarly, the Spirit is the perfect and infinite loving of the Father's idea of himself (which is the Son).[23] That which is real—as much in the Trinity's internal relations as in creation itself—is real because God thinks it.[24] If God were to cease thinking of a thing, then the thing would cease to exist. Thus Edwards can ask the question, "What then is become of the universe?" and answer with, "Certainly, it exists nowhere but in the divine mind."[25] Edwards's concern throughout his doctrine of creation is to present God as the active agent, and creation as the thoroughly dependent result. Irenaeus distinguished Creator from creature by saying, "God makes, humanity is made."[26] Edwards makes the same point, adding the idea that creation is "something [God] has done, and is doing and will do, in a particular manner."[27]

This brief rehearsal of Edwards's metaphysics and ontology is sufficient to offer two important insights regarding Edwards's theology of grace and participation: First, Edwards's thought shows a strong continuity between common grace and nature, and, second, this view of common grace amounts to a theory of participation in being.

First, common grace and nature, in Edwards's view, are fundamentally continuous with each other. As already seen, common grace is God's activity of assisting or influencing nature, but not in a way that adds anything above nature. Nature is also derived from God's immediate activity and has no being, substance, existence without this activity. This would appear to imply that the distinction between common grace and nature is one of activity and

---

[23]For a discussion of how Edwards's idealism relates to his view of the Trinity, along with the related notions of communicative disposition and excellency, see Robert W. Caldwell III, *Communion in the Spirit: The Holy Spirit as the Bond of Union in the Theology of Jonathan Edwards*, Studies in Evangelical History and Thought (Milton Keynes, UK: Paternoster, 2006), 20-24.

[24]Stephen Holmes adds that along with God's knowledge, God's love is also required in order to establish the being of the universe. He bases this, in part, on Edwards's view of excellency. See Holmes, *God of Grace*, 92.

[25]WJE 6:206.

[26]See Canlis's description of Irenaeus's dictum *Deus facit, homo fit*, in *Calvin's Ladder*, 178-88. I am not suggesting that Edwards consciously borrowed from Irenaeus, but simply that Edwards stands in continuity with him at this point but in his own idiosyncratic manner.

[27]Editor's comment in WJE 6:67. See Oliver Crisp's critique of Edwards's occasionalism and how it implies that God is cause of evil. Crisp, *Jonathan Edwards Among the Theologians* (Grand Rapids, MI: Eerdmans, 2015), 169-79.

result.²⁸ Common grace describes the action of God, and nature refers to its effect. God upholds the natural world by his continuous creation. This continuous action of God gives the natural world its being, but through it God is also directing and orchestrating the unfolding story of that natural world. This action of God, giving the natural world its being, and in so doing also directing it and influencing it moment by moment, is God's common grace.

Second, this view of the natural world depending on God's common grace for its being and its unfolding action amounts to something near to what Canlis calls the Platonic approach to participation (sometimes designated with the Greek term *methexis*). Canlis defines this approach as oriented around the question of substantiality.²⁹ We have already seen that Edwards grounds all substantiality and being in God's action. God and creature do not share substantiality, but the creature's substantiality is derived from God. It is true that Edwards seldom employs the term *participation* or *partaking* when describing this natural dependency on God.³⁰ Yet even when the term is missing, the concept is everywhere present. Total dependence of the creature on the Creator is always what Christian Platonists meant to affirm with the concept of participation. Cornelio Fabro writes, "In the Platonic tradition, the term 'participation' signifies the fundamental relationship of both structure and dependence in the dialectic of the many in relation to the One and of the different in relation to the

---

²⁸Consider the following line of thought: If (1) common grace is God's activity toward nature; (2) nature results from God's activity; (3) common grace adds nothing above nature; then it appears to follow that (4) common grace is the activity that undergirds nature.

²⁹There is more than one way to describe *methexis*. Russell describes *methexis* as occurring "when an entity is defined in relation to something else." It accounts for both "being and becoming," and exists between ontologically diverse things. This relationship is "(a) substantial, not just a matter of appearance, and (b) asymmetrical, not a relationship between equals." In Russell's account, *methexis* may not establish quiddity, but it will be the basis of some sort of attribute (for instance, holiness). Still, Edwards's common participation fits these criteria. Creation is defined in relation to God; God and creation are ontologically diverse, but creation derives its substantiality from God, and therefore it is an asymmetrical relationship. See Norman Russell, *The Doctrine of Deification in the Greek Patristic Tradition*, Oxford Early Christian Studies (Oxford: Oxford University Press, 2006), 2.

³⁰Edwards speaks of God communicating himself toward creation and creation partaking of him, in this natural way, in WJE 8:461-62. Notably, Crisp quotes this passage when he begins his chapter titled "Panentheism," in which he argues for viewing Edwards in a Neoplatonic light (*Jonathan Edwards on God and Creation*, chap. 7).

Identical, whereas in Christian philosophy it signifies the total dependence of the creature on its Creator."[31]

Fabro's description of the Christian use of Platonic participation fits Edwards well.[32] Edwards aimed to defend creaturely dependence on God against the modern momentum toward natural autonomy. He pursued this on a path that was well trod before him by the Christian Platonic thought. Crisp may be overenthusiastic when he states, "Edwards is nothing if not a Christian Neoplatonist."[33] It is, however, clear that he was influenced by the Neoplatonic tradition, and also that he modified it in very important ways.[34] By the same token, Christian theologians always modified the Hellenistic traditions they engaged.[35] Edwards followed a similar line and grounded nature such that "participation in God and participation in

---

[31] Cornelio Fabro, "The Intensive Hermeneutics of Thomistic Philosophy: The Notion of Participation," *The Review of Metaphysics* (1974): 449.

[32] As does Te Velde's definition. Speaking of Platonic participation, particularly the concept of *methexis*, Te Velde writes, "Participation signifies a relation of sharing in a common character, of having communion, in whatever way, with the absolute and self-subsistent idea" ("General Introduction," xi).

[33] Crisp, *Jonathan Edwards on God and Creation*, 9.

[34] Edwards was influenced by the Cambridge Platonists, such as Henry More (see WJE 6:73). See also Michael J. McClymond, "Salvation as Divinization: Jonathan Edwards, Gregory Palamas and the Theological Uses of Platonism," in Crisp and Helm, *Jonathan Edwards: Philosophical Theologian*, 139-60; Michael J. McClymond and Gerald R. McDermott, "The Theme of Divinization," in *The Theology of Jonathan Edwards* (Oxford: Oxford University Press, 2012), 410-23.

Stephen Holmes argues that Edwards's reliance on the Trinity for his doctrine of creation undermines the idea that his emanationism is Platonic. Bombaro agrees with Holmes. I also agree that Edwards cannot be viewed as an unmodified Platonist, and this is particularly the case in his use of *emanation* in *End of Creation*. However, it is possible to call something broadly Platonic and mean that it reflects characteristics shared by a long and varied tradition of thinkers who were loosely influenced by Plato, without thereby implying that it agrees with Plato, or any one of his followers, in every regard. For those resisting the Platonic label in Edwards, see Holmes, *God of Grace*, 59; Bombaro, *Jonathan Edwards's Vision of Reality*, 77n32. For those arguing in favor of viewing Edwards in terms of Platonism, see Crisp, *Jonathan Edwards on God and Creation*, 9; McClymond, *Encounters with God*, 13. Kyle Strobel argues, rightly, that while Neoplatonic categories and influences run through Edwards's thinking, it is not the orienting tradition. Rather, Reformed orthodoxy is the orienting tradition. See Strobel, *Jonathan Edwards's Theology: A Reinterpretation*, T&T Clark Studies in Systematic Theology (London: T&T Clark, 2013), 152n6.

[35] Pelikan points out that in the early church's engagement with the Greek tradition, it was always more subtle than simply taking on the pagan ideas. There was always Christian modification. "Taken as it stands, 'hellenization' is too simplistic and unqualified a term for the process that issued in orthodox Christian doctrine." See Jaroslav Pelikan, *The Christian Tradition: A History of the Development of Doctrine*, vol. 1, *The Emergence of the Catholic Tradition (100-600)* (Chicago: University of Chicago Press, 1971), 45.

being or existence come to the same thing."[36] This vision of natural dependence on God is what I dub "common participation," and it represents Edwards's iteration of a long tradition of Christian participatory metaphysics that grew out of engagement with Neoplatonism.

I now need to return to primary question I posed at the beginning: In light of Gavrilyuk's observation that when theosis is reduced to participatory metaphysics, all things become deified to some extent, does this apply to Edwards? Put more accurately, does Edwards's view of participation mean that all things participate in divine fullness to some degree?

Given the discussion so far, one might conclude the answer to be yes. I have argued that Edwards's view of natural dependence, what I call common participation, states that all created things derive their substance, their existence, and their being from God. God is the being of beings, or "being in general," the only proper substance, who gives substance by his continuous action of creating, which in turn is grounded in his own mind. All of this leads to the conclusion that, in at least one sense, all things participate in God.

Furthermore, it might appear that this participation in God undergirds Edwards's equivalent to the wider tradition's theosis. Edwards regularly speaks of the Spirit influencing people in a common, natural way, such that they are influenced in a positive moral direction.[37] Edwards is even willing to concede that these common, natural influences of the Spirit "are in some respects the nature of the Spirit of God." This is at least because "every effect has in some respect or another the nature of its cause," and because the influences of the Spirit include illuminations of truth, and truth shares in the Spirit's nature.[38] This means that God can influence and assist humanity *in*

---

[36]Bombaro, *Jonathan Edwards's Vision of Reality*, 77.

[37]WJE 2:265. In *Treatise on Grace*, Edwards writes, "The Spirit of God is supposed sometimes to have some influence upon the minds of men that are not true Christians; and that those dispositions, frames and exercises of their minds that are of a good tendency, but are common to them with the saints, are in some respect owing to some influence or assistance of God's Spirit" (WJE 21:153).

[38]WJE 21:180. See also *Miscellanies* 626, where Edwards asserts that convictions may come from the Spirit of God, but that these are still the Spirit assisting natural faculties, rather than communicating a supernatural principle, in what Edwards calls a "habitual" manner. It is this habitual, abiding, new principle (supernatural) that is true saving grace (WJE 18:155). See also *Miscellanies* 732, where Edwards discusses that the Spirit gives common illuminations to natural men and that this is fundamentally a created, natural principle. This amounts to the creation of the will, which is part of the natural image of God in humanity (WJE 18:357-59).

a moral manner, all the while operating within the sphere of common participation. Can this lead to salvation? Can this lead to true holiness? Put in specifically Edwardsean language, Can this lead to a participation in divine fullness? One could wonder whether participating in divine fullness is simply a matter of God influencing and assisting the saint, in a manner continuous with his relation to the rest of creation, except that he directs the saint to develop in a moral direction, to an extraordinary degree.

Yet Edwards explicitly denies this line of thinking. The first chapter in *Treatise on Grace* is entirely taken up with the thesis that common grace and special grace differ in nature and kind, not simply in degree.[39] Throughout the chapter he attempts to demonstrate that however much one may be influenced by the Spirit, so long as this influence is only an expression of common grace, or what I have called common participation, then there is no amount of special grace at all. How can Edwards claim this? To clarify, I will show how Edwards consistently distinguishes natural principles, rooted in common grace or common participation, from supernatural principle, rooted in participation in divine fullness. Once I have shown how Edwards distinguishes these principles, I will proceed to investigate his notion of participation as it functions in special grace.

Natural and Supernatural Principles

The relationship between nature and grace is a question that has troubled and intrigued the church since its earliest days. At least since the Pelagian controversies, orthodox Christianity has insisted on the priority of grace, but precisely how nature and grace relate has been a source of tension. N. P. Williams traces the tension between what he calls "once born" thinkers—those who emphasize that grace is a matter of developing and influencing and directing what is given in nature—verses "twice born" thinkers—those who see grace as breaking in on nature from outside it and imparting something new and above human ability.[40] Cassian and the semi-Pelagians (or

---

[39] See WJE 21:153-65; *Miscellanies* 683 (WJE 18:245-48).
[40] N. P. Williams, *The Grace of God* (London: Longmans, Green, 1930), 4-6. This distinction is useful, though perhaps sometimes too neat. Yarnold represents an approach to the theology of grace that at once emphasizes that grace is a "second gift" that is "infinitely above our natural powers" (xiii), and that converting grace is "extraordinary grace, as there is nothing in man to prepare for it" (198). However, Yarnold also emphasizes that exercises of actual grace, resting

perhaps semi-Augustinians) number with the first group, and Augustine and his followers number with the second. Another way to frame this debate is in terms of this question: Is that which undergirds nature continuous or discontinuous with the grace that effects salvation? To this question Jonathan Edwards gives a decisively twice-born answer; that is, Edwards holds a strong distinction between nature and grace, and this in spite of his strong view of nature's dependence and participation in God for its being. This can be seen in Edwards's notion of creaturely emptiness.

In Edwards's *Notes on Scripture*, entry 448, he explores the meaning of the expression תֹהוּ וָבֹהוּ, *tohu wabohu*, "empty and void," in Genesis 1:2. Edwards interprets this to signify something about the nature of creatureliness "in itself": "Thus God was pleased in the first state of the creation to show what the creature is in itself; that in itself it is wholly empty and vain." With this somewhat pessimistic assertion in place, he moves on to state where the goodness of creation comes from:

> that its fullness or goodness is not in itself, but in him and in the communications of his Spirit, animating, quickening, adorning, replenishing, and blessing all things. . . . Thus the fullness of the creature is from God's Spirit. If God withdraws from the creature, it immediately becomes empty and void of all good. The creature, as it is in itself, is a vessel, and has a capacity, but is empty; but that which fills that emptiness is the Spirit of God.[41]

There are several points in this quote that are important to understanding Edwards's relation of nature and grace.[42]

---

on habitual grace, are "expressions of myself" (199). Yarnold's commitment to created grace allows him to emphasize both a "twice born" approach and an emphasis that grace makes a genuine transformation of the human being. Edwards, while rejecting the idea that grace is created, does espouse a version of compatibilism that bears similarity. On Edwards and created grace, Anri Morimoto argues, I believe wrongly, that Edwards espoused what amounts to both a view of uncreated and created grace. See Morimoto, *Jonathan Edwards and the Catholic Vision of Salvation* (University Park: Pennsylvania State University Press, 1995), 7-8, 42-44. Bombaro has sought to refute Morimoto on this point. See John J. Bombaro, "Jonathan Edwards's Vision of Salvation," *Westminster Theological Journal* 65, no. 1 (2003): 45-67; Bombaro, *Jonathan Edwards's Vision of Reality*, 240-44. Finally, see Seng-Kong Tan's discussion of uncreated/created grace, and grace as habit in Jonathan Edwards. See Tan, *Fullness Received and Returned: Trinity and Participation in Jonathan Edwards* (Minneapolis: Fortress, 2014), 281-302.

[41] WJE 15:530.

[42] Compare to Edwards's comments on Eph 3:19 in the *Blank Bible*, where he connects this passage in Genesis to God's fulfillment in grace (WJE 24:1101).

The first thing to observe is that the creature "in itself" must still imply common participation. That is, Edwards's overarching participatory metaphysics, his entire doctrine of creation, means that there cannot be a creature that does not exist through God's immediate action. If God withdrew common participation, then, in Edwards's understanding, the creature would immediately cease to exist. But here, he describes a creature that exists, but without any of God's fullness. Stated more directly, this implies that Edwards's notion of nature's dependence and participation in God still does not mean that God communicates any proper good when he communicates being. Nature exists by a common participation in God, but in spite of this, it is still "empty."

Second, this emptiness implies a teleology.[43] The creature in itself may have no good, but it does have capacity for it. Edwards envisions nature like an empty cup. Cups exist for a purpose: to be filled and to be used. Similarly, Edwards's notion of nature implies a teleology, a purpose, that is fulfilled when nature is filled with fullness.

Third, this natural emptiness is the basis for Edwards's notion of total depravity. The previous chapter explored Edwards's sermon "True Grace Is Divine," and Edwards addresses just this point in that sermon. In the application section, Edwards rehearses the notion of creaturely emptiness and then argues that it is the basis for corruption.

> Hence we may learn how the nature of man came to be so corrupt.... All the goodness the creature has is something above its own nature, being something of God, and that created nature in itself is wholly ruined without a participation of God, who is all its goodness and all its blessedness.
>
> Man, in his first estate, had this supernatural divine principle, even a principle of holiness and divine love, by the indwelling of God in him by his Spirit.

---

[43]Cherry argues that Edwards does not speak of a Thomistic inclination toward virtue. See Conrad Cherry, *The Theology of Jonathan Edwards: A Reappraisal* (Garden City, NY: Anchor Books, 1966), 59, 227. However, Anri Morimoto argues that Thomas Aquinas and Edwards converge on many points (*Jonathan Edwards and the Catholic Vision*, 8-10). Similarly, if Thomas's notion of the natural desire for the vision of God is viewed not as the seed of grace, but as the seedbed, that is, that nature is designed for the supernatural, and that the supernatural is its fulfillment, then there are important points of contact between Thomas's notion and Edwards's. However, Edwards's emphasis on *emptiness*, as the image of what is fulfilled, does contrast with Thomas's notion of *desire*. For Thomas's notion of natural desire for the beatific vision as the seedbed, see Edward Yarnold, SJ, *The Second Gift: A Study of Grace* (Slough, UK: Society of St. Paul, 1974), 38.

> But when man rebelled against God, the Spirit of God justly left him, for it was not meet that the Spirit of God should continue to dwell in the heart of one that was not at peace with God. And God, being gone out of his heart, it follows from what has been said, that all that was good left his heart. Divine love was extinct, and man was left wholly under the dominion of mere nature and natural principles, or those principles that are essential to his nature, such as self-love or love to his own pleasure [or] his own honor and without any divine principle to regulate this love. . . . Love of God ceased, the love of the world ensued.

Then Edwards states his view of nature and grace with clarity and brevity: "Created nature of itself will necessarily be corrupt without something divine added to it."[44]

It is remarkable here that, for Edwards, fallenness and depravity do not derive from an active change of something in nature. Rather they result from nature being left by itself.[45] It is not so much that the cup is broken or shattered by the fall, but rather that the cup remains empty. The natural capacity is left unfilled, and the result is inevitable corruption. Another way to frame this, in light of the earlier argument in this chapter, is to say that common participation, by itself, can never lead to salvation, but rather leads to enmity between the creature and the God from whom the creature derives its being. More starkly still: common participation, by itself, results in deformity, not deiformity; emptiness, not theosis. Thus, what Edwards has achieved is a view of nature that is grounded in participatory metaphysics, with God as the immediate source of all nature, and yet still retaining a strong distinction between nature and grace.

The fourth item to notice from these passages is Edwards's distinction between two principles in created existence: there are natural principles, and then there is a supernatural or divine principle. These principles are implied in the passages from *Notes on Scripture*, mentioned explicitly in "True Grace Is Divine," and stated most clearly in *Original Sin*:

---

[44] Jonathan Edwards, "True Grace Is Divine (1738)," in *Jonathan Edwards: Spiritual Writings*, ed. Adriaan C. Neele, Kyle C. Strobel, and Kenneth P. Minkema, Classics of Western Spirituality (New York: Paulist Press, 2019), 360-61.

[45] Edwards specifically rejects the notion that original sin results from a "positive influence" or an "infusion" of evil into the human nature (WJE 3:381-82). Oliver Crisp notes that Edwards sometimes speaks as though God gave Adam "sufficient" grace, but not "confirming" grace, so that with merely sufficient grace, Adam could have not sinned (*Jonathan Edwards and the Metaphysics*, 32-33).

> The case with man was plainly this: when God made man at first, he implanted in him two kinds of principles. There was an *inferior* kind, which may be called *natural*, being the principles of mere human nature. . . . Besides these, there were *superior* principles, that were spiritual, holy and divine, summarily comprehended in divine love . . . which are called in Scripture the *divine nature*. These principles may, in some sense, be called *supernatural*.[46]

This distinction between the two principles—one set natural and one set supernatural—is fundamental to Edwards's concept of nature and grace and to the question of this chapter: Given Edwards's participatory metaphysics, and given his assertion that grace is a participation in divine fullness, do all things, to some extent, share in this grace? These two principles—natural and supernatural—help clarify the answer.[47] In one sense all things participate in God for being. This is common participation, and it is characteristic of all created reality—both fallen and redeemed. It is this common participation that allows existence, and it undergirds Edwards's natural principles—it must, otherwise the natural principles themselves would immediately cease to exist. Left by itself, this common participation, with the natural principles that it supports, leads not to salvation or holiness or virtue but to corruption. What is needed is the supernatural principle. As I pointed out in the last chapter, and as the passages already cited in this chapter reflect, Edwards often connects this supernatural principle with the category of divine fullness. God must fill nature with divine fullness, the supernatural principle, in order for holiness, goodness, virtue, salvation, and so on to obtain. Following his Augustinian tradition: "Grace does not destroy nature, it perfects it."[48] Edwards might phrase it, the supernatural does not destroy nature; it fills its emptiness. The two principles are complementary but distinct.[49]

---

[46]Emphasis original. Edwards identifies two types of the *imago Dei*—one natural and one spiritual—with these two sets of principles. He also clarifies that by *supernatural*, he means something that does not belong to the essence of a natural creature but is above it (see WJE 3:381).

[47]See Kyle Strobel's discussion of the two principles, and how they relate to the grace and the Holy Spirit (*Jonathan Edwards's Theology: A Reinterpretation*, 198-205).

[48]See James A. Carpenter, *Nature and Grace: Toward an Integral Perspective* (New York: Crossroad, 1988), 8.

[49]Consider St. Athanasius's argument that at creation God granted two gifts: one was creation itself, but then the second gift was the grace of God's own image. This second gift was ruined in the fall. This two-gift typology is very similar to Edwards's two principles. See Athanasius, *St. Athanasius on the Incarnation: The Treatise De Incarnatione Verbi Dei*, trans. A Religious of

The significance of this two-principle approach to nature and grace becomes clearer by way of contrast. John Smith was a Cambridge Platonist, a preacher and teacher, and a source for Edwards.⁵⁰ There are many ways in which Smith and Edwards sound similar. Smith can say "True *Religion* is a . . . *participation of the divine Nature.* . . . *True Religion* is such a Communication of the Divinity, as none but the Highest of created Beings are capable of."⁵¹ Like Edwards, Smith grounds all created being by way of participation in God.⁵² However, when Smith discusses the creation of humanity, the fall, and the gift of grace, a subtle and significant difference emerges. Smith argues that God gave human beings "*Truths of Natural inscription*," which are "*Fundamental principles* of Truth which Reason by a naked intuition may behold in God, or those necessary *Corollaries* and *Deductions* that may be drawn from thence." God, Smith argues, gave humanity a natural reason that had the native ability to perceive God "by reflecting into himself." This reasoned reflection "into himself" allowed prefallen humanity to "behold there the glory of God . . . [and] see within his Soul all those Ideas of Truth which concern the Nature and Essence of God, by reason of its own resemblance of God; and so beget within himself the most free and generous motions of love to God."⁵³ Smith sees God's gift of reason to be sufficient to guide the human toward knowledge of God, and that this gift is part of nature. Nature and grace are, at least at this point, embedded—one within the other. This changes when Smith deals with the fall, but it is also here that the great difference between Smith and Edwards comes out clearly. Smith

---

C.S.M.V. (London: Mowbray, 1953), 1.3. Note also Yarnold's analysis of this argument and its relevance to the doctrine of grace. He uses this passage to orientate his entire study of grace (Yarnold, *Second Gift*, 2-3).

⁵⁰Smith and the other Cambridge Platonists, particularly Henry More and Ralph Cudworth, are often cited as sources for Edwards's thought on a variety of subjects. For the Cambridge Platonists as background for Edwards's theory of divinization, see McClymond, "Salvation as Divinization"; McClymond, "Theme of Divinization," esp. 413-14. See also Bombaro, *Jonathan Edwards's Vision of Reality*, 13n47; Stephen A. Wilson, *Virtue Reformed: Rereading Jonathan Edwards's Ethics* (Leiden: Brill, 2005), 98n2. For Edwards's intellectual sources and background, see WJE 10:6-9; 26:2-14.

⁵¹C. A. Patrides, ed., *The Cambridge Platonists* (Cambridge: Cambridge University Press, 1969), 148. One page before this quote, Smith states, "[True religion] comes from Heaven, and constantly moves toward Heaven again." This sounds very similar to Edwards's language of emanation and remanation in *End of Creation* (see WJE 8:531).

⁵²"Indeed God hath copyed out himself in all created Being" (Patrides, *Cambridge Platonists*, 148).

⁵³Patrides, *Cambridge Platonists*, 149.

writes: "Since Mans fall from God, the inward virtue and vigour of Reason is much abated. . . . Those Principles of Divine truth which were first engraven upon mans Heart with the finger of God are now, as the Characters of some ancient Monuments, less clear and legible then at first."[54]

Edwards's and Smith's descriptions of nature and grace before and after the fall differ at important points. For Edwards, nature after the fall has not changed. The only difference is that the supernatural principle is gone, but this was never part of nature in the first place. Smith is nearly the opposite. Nature, before the fall, had a reason that was sufficient to lead to the knowledge of God, and after the fall, that nature is damaged. This leads the two thinkers to very different understandings of the result of the fall. For Edwards, nature without supernatural principles is corrupt. For Smith, nature has greater difficulty in perceiving God than before. Smith goes on to describe the necessity of grace in order for people to return and grasp God rightly, and his descriptions of grace share many similarities to Edwards's own view. However, in spite of these similarities, their differences regarding nature lead to a fundamental difference in their conception of grace. For Smith, divine grace rehabilitates a damaged nature. Nature is grounded in participation in God's being, and from this participation there proceeds the exalted reason that is sufficient to guide the unfallen human to God.[55] This reason is damaged but not destroyed in the fall, and grace reveals God and gives the soul an impression of God, rehabilitating it to its prefallen state. In this framework, grace is God's special revelation and internal movement, but not the impartation of something entirely new.[56] Smith's view is characteristic of Christian Platonism: "Platonist anthropology, even as corrected by the Greek Fathers, in order to deal with the dynamic aspect of Christianity, sees in man a being capable from the very

---

[54]Patrides, *Cambridge Platonists*, 150.

[55]On the Cambridge Platonists' assertion that human reason was free to develop their participation in divine reason, and how they still affirmed the need for grace, see Wilson, *Virtue Reformed*, 120-25. George Turnbull was more radical than the Cambridge Platonists in asserting that humans could become like God on the basis of their native resources alone (see Wilson, *Virtue Reformed*, esp. 123-25).

[56]The Cambridge Platonists spoke of the "candle of the Lord as a God-directing gift of God" (Patrides, *Cambridge Platonists*, 18; see also 38). This remains after the fall. Edwards, when he speaks of fallenness, also uses the image of the candle, but for him "the candle is withdrawn: and thus man was left in a state of darkness" (WJE 3:382). One wonders whether Edwards employs the candle imagery in conscious rejection of the Cambridge Platonist view.

beginning of reaching the highest degree of spiritual life, union with God, although unable to reach it by his own efforts."[57]

This is the sort of relation between nature and grace that concerns Maarten Wisse. According to Wisse, when theosis is grounded in participatory metaphysics, the result may be that salvation is less about a transformation and more about a realization of what was already the case to some extent.[58] In fairness to Smith, he does speak of transformation through grace, but this transformation is a recovery of something that is already partially present in nature. It is partially present in nature because nature participates in God. In the final analysis, Smith is illustrative of Wisse's concern and of Gavrilyuk's observation: when soteriological participation reduces to participatory metaphysics, then nature is always, at least a little, deified.

Edwards takes a different path. By radically distinguishing nature and grace, rather than embedding one in the other, Edwards is able to avoid Wisse's concern and give Gavrilyuk a clear no. At least at this point, Edwards is deeply divergent from standard Platonic accounts of human capability for union with God. For Edwards, grace is a radical transformation, and insofar as it is a participation in divine fullness, it is a sort of participation that is above nature *in itself*. Furthermore, Edwards's two-principle approach allows him to affirm a strong view of total depravity, as well as God's sovereignty in communicating grace—two themes that are central to his Reformed heritage. Edwards's polemic against Arminianism and his defense of Reformed tradition are always present when he discusses nature and grace. "True Grace Is Divine," his *Treatise on Grace*, and *Original Sin* all deal with similar themes of nature and grace, and all are aimed at attacking theologies that fused the two together. Edwards almost certainly learned positively from John Smith, but he also developed a view of grace that critiqued theologies such as Smith's at a fundamental level.

---

[57]Charles Moeller and G. Philips, *The Theology of Grace and the Oecumenical Movement*, trans. A. Wilson (London: Mowbray, 1961), 39.

[58]Canlis describes Aquinas's theology of created grace as approximating something very similar to this. "Aquinas clearly locates God's grace toward the creature within its natural capacity, turning grace into an anthropological asset" (*Calvin's Ladder*, 38). This appears to be part of Canlis's concern with the Platonic-*methexis* approach to participation, especially when it undergirds grace. Later, Canlis contrasts Calvin's emphasis on communion with Thomistic medieval emphasis on naturalization (*Calvin's Ladder*, 44).

This also means that Edwards differs from some influential accounts of participation theology on offer today. Over the past decades, Radical Orthodoxy has represented a vigorous reappropriation of the concept of participation for Christian theology. Indeed, participation is right at the heart of the entire movement.[59] Radical Orthodoxy uses the notion of participation in a polemical move against the entire notion of secularity. The movement reads secularity as a result of a theological failure to ground all being uniquely in God. Beginning with Duns Scotus, the West began to view the created sphere as possessing *being* in the same way that God possesses being. This led to the idea that the created sphere (nature) can be viewed and engaged as if God were not there. It is, in this view, a closed coherent system of being. Radical Orthodoxy sees this as a great failure and reasserts the idea that only God truly, finally, *is*, and all created being is a participation in God for being. This means that the secular, the sphere of reality that might be engaged without reference to God, is incoherent.[60] To this point Radical Orthodoxy shares interests and solutions with Edwards's thought. What I have called common participation in Edwards is very similar, both in aims and in solution, to Radical Orthodoxy's view of participation. Both are varieties of *methexis* aimed at grounding all being in God, in such a way that there is no room for autonomy in created existence.

However, there is also a critical point of departure. Radical Orthodoxy also employs the concept of deification. And when it employs the notion of deification, it tends to be grounded in ontological participation. That is, whereas Edwards draws strong distinction between created nature and divine grace, Radical Orthodoxy tends to emphasize the continuity between nature and grace. The gift of deifying grace is somehow anticipated in created nature's ontology. I point out two examples.

First, Daniel Haynes, in his discussion of deification in Radical Orthodoxy, suggests that the grace of deification is "not extrinsic to the human being. Instead, there is a paradoxical supernatural empowering of an already graced 'created' nature."[61] This statement suggests a distinction between

---

[59]John Milbank, Catherine Pickstock, and Graham Ward, eds., *Radical Orthodoxy* (New York: Routledge, 1999), 3.

[60]Simon Oliver, "What Is Radical Orthodoxy?," in *The Radical Orthodoxy Reader*, ed. John Milbank and Simon Oliver (New York: Routledge, 2009), 3-27.

[61]Daniel Haynes, "The Metaphysics of Christian Ethics: Radical Orthodoxy and Theosis," *Heythrop Journal* 52 (2011): 668.

supernatural grace and created nature. The question, however, is what Haynes means by "graced 'created' nature." This appears to refer to the ontological participation that undergirds all creation. Haynes cites Acts 17:28, in which the apostle Paul implies that all being is grounded in God, as a text that describes deification.[62] The application of Acts 17:28 to soteriological deification suggests that Haynes's view moves from ontological participation that explains nature to soteriological participation that explains deification, as if the difference were one of degree, rather than one of kind.[63] Radical Orthodoxy aims to continue the tradition of the Cambridge Platonists, and so it is not surprising to see a strong grounding of grace in nature, perhaps even embedding grace in nature *to some degree*.[64]

Simon Oliver links grace to nature, not by way of degree but by way of obligation. Oliver leverages the thought of Henri de Lubac as the basis for Radical Orthodoxy's vision for how nature and grace are both distinguished and blended.[65] De Lubac followed a long tradition in asserting that there is a natural desire for a supernatural end (Oliver speaks in terms of the beatific vision). That is, built into nature per se is an appetite and desire that is only fulfilled in the supernatural gift of grace. Oliver then argues that this natural desire obligates God to give the satiating gift of grace. If God has planted the hunger or desire in nature, then this desire must be fulfilled, because unfulfilled desire causes distortion of the nature and thus suffering. This presupposition, that a nature that does not achieve its end is frustrated and consigned to suffering, implies for Oliver that God has placed himself under obligation to give supernatural grace and the beatific vision. Gratuity remains, because the obligation is grounded in God's creative act of designing

---

[62]Haynes, "Metaphysics of Christian Ethics," 560.

[63]Milbank views deification as directly related to created ontological dependence on God. See John Milbank, "Postmodern Critical Augustinianism: A Short Summa in Forty-Two Responses to Unasked Questions," in Milbank and Oliver, *Radical Orthodoxy Reader*, 54.

[64]Specifically, Radical Orthodoxy aims to continue the tradition of Ralph Cudworth. See Fergus Kerr, "A Catholic Response to the Programme of Radical Orthodoxy," in *Radical Orthodoxy? A Catholic Enquiry*, ed. Laurence Paul Hemming (Aldershot, UK: Ashgate, 2000), 49; Milbank, Pickstock, and Ward, *Radical Orthodoxy*, xi. Norman Russell views Radical Orthodoxy's approach to theosis as more Neoplatonic than Greek or patristic. See Norman Russell, "Why Does Theosis Fascinate Western Christians?," *Sobornost* 34, no. 1 (2012): 9-10.

[65]Simon Oliver, "Henri De Lubac and Radical Orthodoxy," in *T&T Clark Companion to Henri de Lubac*, ed. Jordon Hillebert (New York: Bloomsbury, 2017), 393-417.

humanity with the desire for the supernatural.[66] The creature cannot demand or hoist obligation on God, for this would destroy gratuity. Rather, God places himself under obligation in the manner with which he chose to create.

This is a subtle and elegant argument. Important for present purpose is its difference from Edwards. Oliver's vision of created nature bears in itself the seed, so to speak, for divine grace. If Haynes seemed to suggest the seed within created nature was grace itself, in small degree, then Oliver argues the seed is not so much grace in small degree, but grace (universally?) anticipated by principle. God committed himself to give supernatural grace in the design of creation. Oliver distinguishes nature and grace in clearer form than does Haynes, but still there is an in-principle embedding of grace within nature. Edwards explicitly rejected both accounts. I have already emphasized Edwards's account of creaturely emptiness—there is no trace of divine grace in created nature per se. Acts 17:28 refers (in Edwards's vision) to natural dependence on God for being, but it is not the basis for the gift of divine grace. However, Edwards also railed against the idea that God can be obligated to give true grace. In strenuous opposition to Arminian theology, Edwards preached, "If we obtain the saving grace of God by virtue of an obligation that God has laid himself under, to us in common with the rest of mankind, [then] his grace ceases to be of the nature of a present."[67] Edwards believed that gratuity and obligation are mutually exclusive. To ground divine grace in some sort of gift already embedded (or implied) in created nature will undermine the uniqueness of grace and the gratitude the saints owe to the Lord.

For both Haynes and Oliver, grace and nature, while distinguished, grow from the same sort of participation. Gavrilyuk's words, "All things are deified to unspecified degree," might apply to Haynes's account, while Wisse's concern that soteriological participation ends up being about realizing something that is already there, at least in principle, might apply to Oliver's.[68] As I have shown to this point, Edwards's concern to ground all existence in common participation shares much in common with Radical Orthodoxy's concern. Yet, Edwards's concern that special grace differs in

---

[66]Oliver, "Henri De Lubac and Radical Orthodoxy."
[67]Edwards, "True Grace Is Divine (1738)," 361.
[68]Gavrilyuk, "Retrieval of Deification," 651; Wisse, *Trinitarian Theology Beyond Participation*, 305.

kind and not just in degree from nature, and without any claim to obligation, indicates that his vision represents an important alternative vision for soteriological participation.[69]

Yet this raises a serious question: Does Edwards's distinction between created nature and divine fullness (true grace) amount to a "separated theology"? During the mid-twentieth century de Lubac sharply critiqued a neo-Thomist account of nature and grace that separated them rather too sharply. Hans Boersma summarizes the position de Lubac critiqued:

> This conservative Thomist tradition speculatively posited the notion of *pura natura*, completely unaffected by the realm of grace and as a result without any natural desire (desiderium naturale) for the eternal vision of God. While the purpose was no doubt to safeguard the gratuitous character of the beatific vision, de Lubac observes in this neo-scholastic approach an extrinsicism or "separated theology," which regarded grace as something that came strictly from the outside and had no intrinsic connection with created human nature.[70]

De Lubac's critique of this extrinsicism, or separated theology, influenced Radical Orthodoxy and the sacramental ontology of Boersma deeply. So the question arises: Given that I have just pitted Edwards's distinction between created nature and divine fullness against two versions of Radical Orthodoxy's approach, does Edwards's view fall into a form of extrinsicism? I respond with three reasons for a qualified no.

First, recall that Edwards understood all created nature to depend on God for its being. This is what I have dubbed "common participation," and it means that there is no natural autonomous sphere. Indeed, there is no natural sphere that is without grace, so long as it is common grace one is considering. This presses back on one of the philosophical foundations of extrinsicism. During the late Middle Ages Duns Scotus rejected the previous Christian Platonic ontology and asserted that creaturely being and divine being have being in the same manner. That is, when one speaks of God's being on the one hand and creaturely being on the other hand, one means

---

[69]Boersma notes that Radical Orthodoxy's emphasis on ontological participation may arguably leave little need for an emphasis on Christology and can end up blurring the "boundaries between the divine and the human." See Hans Boersma, *Heavenly Participation: The Weaving of a Sacramental Tapestry* (Grand Rapids, MI: Eerdmans, 2011).

[70]Hans Boersma, "Sacramental Ontology: Nature and the Supernatural in the Ecclesiology of Henri de Lubac," *New Blackfriars* 88 (2007): 249.

the same thing by the word *being*. This univocity of being was a massive shift from previous Christian Platonic accounts of ontology. Previously Christians tended to view the created world as profoundly dependent on God for its being, and thus not at all autonomous. Duns Scotus and his univocity of being changed this.[71] The effect was that now philosophers and theologians could investigate created nature on the one hand and God on the other as separated spheres of inquiry. The separation of God and created nature had begun.

Edwards lived in an early modern era that was taking full advantage of this separation and pressing it forward by asserting autonomy to the natural sphere. Edwards, as already seen, pressed against this move vigorously, and he did so by his notion of common participation. All things partake of God for being, and therefore there is no autonomy for the created sphere, and also no space to consider created nature without respect to God. In fact, chapter four will reveal God and created nature as so closely linked that God's love for the creature is not inconsistent with God's own self-love. God and created nature are distinct for Edwards, but they are never separate. Still, this common participation, undergirding created nature and common grace, is not the special participation that explains divine fullness (true or saving grace). Thus, while all created nature is rooted in real participation in God for being, this does not mean that divine fullness is fused to natural being per se. Is this then where Edwards falls into a "separated theology"?

Again, we can say no for a second reason: created nature was designed for union with divine fullness. I have argued vigorously that created nature does not depend on divine fullness for its being, but it is also true that created nature is fulfilled in divine fullness. This will be the burden of chapter four, but for right now note the difference between Edwards's vision and the concept of *pura natura* (pure nature). Pure nature was posited by conservated Thomists as a vision of created nature, before the fall, that was untouched by grace.[72] This does not fit Edwards's view. Earlier I quoted *Original Sin*, where Edwards distinguishes natural principles from supernatural principles. There I emphasized their distinction. But the same quote also

---

[71] On univocity of being, see Smith, *Introducing Radical Orthodoxy*; Boersma, *Heavenly Participation*, 68-83.
[72] Boersma, *Heavenly Participation*.

demonstrates that, while distinct, the natural and the supernatural were united before the fall:

> The case with man was plainly this: when God made man at first, he implanted in him two kinds of principles. There was an *inferior* kind, which may be called *natural*, being the principles of mere human nature.... Besides these, there were *superior* principles, that were spiritual, holy and divine, summarily comprehended in divine love ... which are called in Scripture the *divine nature*. These principles may, in some sense, be called *supernatural*.[73]

The natural and the supernatural were designed from the beginning for union. Chapter four will unpack this teleology in detail and there we will discover that the natural and the supernatural were in union before the fall and will continue in union for eternity. Pure nature does not fit in Edwards's vision. Indeed, this is why the natural without the supernatural, without divine fullness, is *empty* in Edwards. Does this emptiness imply extrinsicism?

It is certainly the case that when Edwards speaks of fallen created nature as *empty*, one feels the separateness of nature and divine fullness. Edwards was, after all, a Reformed theologian who held to the doctrines of grace with their associated views on depravity. Where other theologies speak of a natural desire for the supernatural, Edwards speaks of emptiness and candles snuffed out.[74] Fallen humanity is indeed separated from divine fullness. On the other hand, this image of natural emptiness is also a sort of link to the supernatural. It is not a positive link but a negative link. It is a link that emphasizes need, but teleological need nonetheless. A cup's emptiness points to its purpose. Nature's emptiness in itself points to its teleology in divine fullness. Put differently, the separation of nature and the supernatural in fallen humanity preserves the tragedy of sin and the urgency of redemption. Common participation needs special participation. I turn now to consider special participation in greater detail.

Special Participation

So far I have argued that Edwards based his view of nature on what I have called common participation, and that this is not to be confused with

---

[73]Emphasis original. Edwards identifies two types of the *imago Dei*—one natural and one spiritual—with these two sets of principles. He also clarifies that by *supernatural*, he means something that does not belong to the essence of a natural creature but is above it (see WJE 3:381).
[74]See WJE 3:382.

Edwards's doctrine of special grace—the supernatural principle. Common participation is a sharing in being, by which nature gains its substance and existence, and therefore undergirds the entirety of creation. However, Edwards views nature, and the common participation that undergirds it, as empty and corrupt without the supernatural principle of divine grace. The last chapter revealed how divine grace is a communication and participation in divine fullness. I have termed this "special participation." The question now remains, How do these two types of participation differ? In the remainder of the chapter I will show that, whereas common participation is an Edwardsean variation on *methexis*—ontological participation—and similar to what one often finds in Neoplatonic tradition, special participation is more oriented around the sharing in trinitarian relations. I will first point out an important way the two versions of participation are similar and then show that they differ in content, quality, and aim.[75]

As I explore the way common participation and special participation differ, it is important to keep in mind the clear ways they are similar. The most obvious thing to say, but nevertheless important, is that they are both forms of participation. That is, both common participation and special participation describe a sharing between God and creature. Not only do they both describe a sharing between Creator and creature, but they also share a structure of activity. In both kinds of participation, it is God who gives and the creature who receives. God communicates being by his immediate action—this is common participation. Similarly, God communicates divine fullness by his immediate action—this is special participation.[76] In both

---

[75] The notion of two complementary but distinct ways of participating in God is not unknown in the English tradition. Richard Hooker argues that all participate in God by creation, but only saints participate in God as Savior, and this through union with Christ. This section of Hooker was quoted at length by John Owen to defend his own view of participation in Christ. Owen quotes Hooker favorably for nine pages, although his quote does not include Hooker's reference to participating in God as Creator, only to participating in God as Savior. Still, it is interesting to note that in defending his own view of saving participation, Owen points to Hooker as an authority, and Hooker explicitly distinguishes two ways of participating in God. Owen quoted Hooker as part of a defense against Anglican opponents. See Hooker, *The Lawes of Ecclesiastical Polity*, vol. 2, ed. John Keble (Oxford: Clarendon, 1888), 5.56, 247-49; Owen, *A Vindication of some Passages in a Discourse concerning Communion with God* (London, 1674), 13-24. Also see Paul C. H. Lim, *Mystery Unveiled: The Crisis of the Trinity in Early Modern England* (Oxford: Oxford University Press, 2012), 209-10.

[76] See sermons: Edwards, "True Grace Is Divine (1738)"; "A Divine and Supernatural Light" (WJE 17:408-26).

cases, God continues this act of giving. I have already noted Edwards's doctrine of continuous creation, and he has an answerable iteration in his discussions of divine grace. God does not only communicate grace (or the supernatural principle, or divine fullness) once but must continue that communication constantly in order for the saint's participation to endure.[77] In both sorts of participation, Edwards keeps the priority on God, with the creature receiving the gift.[78]

But here the first important difference appears: special participation differs from common participation in its content. The gift is different. Common participation is a sharing in being, substance, and existence, whereas special participation is a sharing in divine fullness.[79] As noted in chapter one, *divine fullness* becomes a technical term for Edwards that signifies the good enjoyed within the Trinity. This good is the knowledge and love, or happiness, or delight within God. But in *Treatise on Grace*, it especially refers to the Holy Spirit as the love between the Father and the Son, poured out in economic gift. This, then, is the gift shared in special participation. It is a participation *of* the Holy Spirit, and *with* the Father and the Son. The prepositions are important to Edwards. He defines *communion* or *partaking* in something as a sharing between parties in a common good. In divine grace, the saint partakes *with* the Father and the Son—they are the parties with which the gift is shared. But the saint partakes *of* the Holy Spirit—the Spirit is the gift itself.[80] "What Christ purchased for us, was that we might have communion with God in his good, which consists in partaking of or having communion of the Holy Ghost . . . in partaking of the fullness of Christ, their head and Redeemer, which, I have observed, consists in partaking of the Spirit that is given him not by measure."[81] This is the fundamental difference between common participation and special

---

[77]WJE 21:196-97.
[78]Just as in creation "God makes, and humanity is made" (Irenaeus), so in redemption, Edwards keeps the same framework of action: God saves, humanity is saved—and this in continuous action.
[79]See chapter one for a discussion of Edwards's doctrine of special grace as a communication and participation in divine fullness.
[80]See WJE 21:187-88. See also Edwards's argument that the *koinōnia* with the Father and the Son in 1 Jn 1:3 is the Holy Spirit in *Miscellanies* 376 (WJE 13:448). For a definition of *communion* see *Miscellanies* 482 (WJE 13:524).
[81]WJE 21:190.

participation. Common participation allows for the Spirit to influence natural faculties, but this is not special participation. The Spirit may direct or influence, but in special participation, the Spirit communicates his own nature "in a peculiar manner."[82] The content of special participation is creaturely communion in trinitarian love.

This fact implies the second significant difference between common participation and special participation. The two differ in the quality of participation or communion. Special participation is more relational and personal in quality than is common participation. This naturally results from special participation's content. If special participation is a sharing with persons (the Father and the Son) in love (which itself is a person, the Holy Spirit), inevitably the participation itself will have a relational-personal quality. Further, not only does the content color the participation, but the subjects of special participation are only persons. Special participation is restricted to humans and angels. "This communication is really only to intelligent beings."[83] Common participation is a sharing in being, which is not a personal category, and is shared by inanimate and well as personal entities. Special participation is relational in content and personal in subject. This relational-personal quality in special participation also derives from the New Testament texts that shaped Edwards's thought. The New Testament's primary term for participation between God and humanity is *koinōnia*. Of the several Greek words that can signify "participation," *koinōnia* carries a more personal quality than the more typically Platonic term, *methexis*.[84] Edwards maintained this relational and personal quality in his view of special participation.

---

[82]WJE 21:180. See also how Edwards contrasts the Spirit's work toward inanimate objects versus his communicating holiness to the saint (WJE 21:192).

[83]"The great and universal end of God's creating the world was to communicate himself. God is a communicative being. This communication is really only to intelligent beings: the communication of himself to their understandings is his glory, and the communication of himself with respect to their wills, the enjoying faculty, is their happiness" (*Miscellanies* 332, in WJE 13:410). See also "man, the consciousness or perception of the creation, is the immediate subject of this [the communication and happiness of the Son of God]" (*Miscellanies* 104, in WJE 13:272). Kyle Strobel emphasizes the relational aspect of gracious participation when he states, "This participation is not mediated in a metaphysical register, as if humanity were somehow to merge into the essence of God, but is fundamentally a relational notion (upholding persons as such)." See Strobel, "By Word and Spirit: Jonathan Edwards on Redemption, Justification, and Regeneration," in *Jonathan Edwards and Justification*, ed. Josh Moody (Wheaton, IL: Crossway, 2012), 48.

[84]See Canlis's discussion in *Calvin's Ladder*, 8-12.

The third way common participation and special participation differ is in aim. Edwards achieves complementary but distinct things in exploring the two ways creatures participate in God. The aim of common participation is, at least in part, to establish a clear distinction between Creator and creature. Edwards is responding to the Enlightenment pursuit of natural autonomy by asserting natural dependence. At least part of the problem with natural autonomy is that, by allowing a space in nature where God is not needed, nature takes on characteristics of divinity—self-sufficiency. Against this, Edwards grounds all substance in God alone. While some have read this as a fusing of Creator and creature, Robert Jenson suggests Edwards's move functioned in an inverse direction: "The category of substance is part of a notion of deity, so that its application elsewhere is either polytheism or mere confusion."[85] By grounding substance in God, Edwards was denying nature any hint of deity *in itself*. God makes, creatures are made—continually.[86] The aim of special participation, in contrast, is to unite Creator and creature in "one society, one family; that the church should be as it were admitted into the society of the blessed Trinity." Christ "descends from the infinite distance and height above us," so that the church, through union with him, may "ascend up to God, through the infinite distance." This ascending is special participation: "We being members of the Son, are partakers in our measure, of the Father's love to the Son."[87] The Creator-creature distinction is still maintained, but the ontological chasm is bridged by relational communion.[88]

Conclusion

This chapter has clarified how Edwards distinguishes created nature from divine fullness or grace. I pursued this by asking whether participation in divine fullness is implicit in all of creation, or whether it is unique to a portion of it. This relates to Gavrilyuk's observation that when deification is reduced to (merely) participation in God, the result is that all creation is

---

[85] Robert W. Jenson, *American's Theologian: A Recommendation of Jonathan Edwards* (Oxford: Oxford University Press, 1988), 25.
[86] A modification of Irenaus: *Deus facit, homo fit*.
[87] WJE 19:593-94.
[88] Athanasius achieved something similar. He posited an ontological gulf between Creator and creature that critiqued aspects of Hellenism and at the same time bridged it by the incarnation. See Cheslyn Jones, Geoffrey Wainwright, and Edward Yarnold, SJ, eds., *The Study of Spirituality* (London: SPCK, 1986), 161-62.

somewhat deified. Similarly, Wisse cautions against participatory metaphysics because it can end up turning Christian soteriology into a form of self-realization, rather than transformation. With these observations and concerns in mind, I argued that there is one way in which all things participate in God. This is what I have called Edwards's doctrine of common participation, and its aim is to ground all nature in God's immediate action. This maps, in broad strokes, to what one may call Platonic *methexis*. However, this is not the participation Edwards intends when he discusses divine grace. He means another concept entirely. Nature has being without any measure of participation in divine fullness. God created the world with its natural principles, which are grounded in common participation, and supernatural principles. The supernatural principles vacated nature entirely at the fall, and divine grace represents their restoration. There is therefore no direct line between common participation in God for being and participation in divine fullness. This undermines an Arminian or synergistic approach to divine participation and is central to Edwards's polemical concerns. Yet, the supernatural principles are also based on a variety of participation theology, what I have called special participation. This is rooted in Edwards's doctrine of the Trinity and seeks to achieve a profound level of relational-personal intimacy between Creator and creature, all the while maintaining their differentiation.

The task now is to understand this participation in divine fullness more deeply. In order to do that, I will explore Edwards's doctrine of the Trinity and how the communion within the Trinity is extended toward finite creatures through the gifts of incarnation and the Spirit. I turn now to these topics.

3

Grace and God

THE PREVIOUS CHAPTER asked the question, Does Edwards's doctrine of grace as divine participation imply that all of nature participates in God's fullness to some extent? In other words, is there a real distinction between nature and grace? I answered first no and then yes: no, Edwards's doctrine of grace does not imply that all of nature participates in God's fullness; and therefore, yes, there is a real distinction between nature and grace. Both nature and grace may be said to participate in God, but they do not participate in the same way; or, perhaps better, they are founded on different types of participation. Nature, and common grace that undergirds it, participates in God for its being. That is, God continually creates, sustains, and directs (influences) the natural world, giving it being and providential leading. The gift of special grace, however, is a different gift altogether. It is not a gift of being but a gift of relational *koinōnia* with the Trinity, "that the church should be as it were admitted into the society of the blessed Trinity."[1]

Yet to say that special grace is a *koinōnia* in the "society of the blessed Trinity" brings up another question. Having asked how grace is related to nature, this chapter looks at the other end of the ontological spectrum and asks a similar question: How is grace related to God? Does Edwards's doctrine of grace achieve sufficient intimacy between God and the saints to be called divine participation while maintaining sufficient differentiation between God

---

[1] WJE 19:594. Much of this chapter draws on James Salladin, "Essence and Fullness: Evaluating the Creator-Creature Distinction in Jonathan Edwards," *SJT* 70, no. 4 (2017): 427-44.

and the saints to maintain the Creator-creature distinction? This chapter will argue that Edwards achieved both through a distinction between God's *essence* and God's *fullness*. This distinction allowed Edwards to posit an ontological chasm between God and humanity, while at the same time relating them together such that saints enjoy a real participation (*koinōnia*) in the life of God. However, I must sharpen the question before I proceed.

One of the most pressing difficulties in any approach to divine participation is grasped by the question, How can a saint participate in God without becoming identical with God?[2] Eastern Orthodox Palamism famously addresses this by distinguishing between God's essence, which is incommunicable and inaccessible, and God's energies, which may be shared with the saint.[3] Gregory Palamas inherited this distinction from Maximus the Confessor and earlier church fathers but also developed it in response to his own polemical situation.[4] His aim was to posit real participation in God without sacrificing the Creator-creature distinction. This distinction became a standard of Eastern Orthodox theology and has been central to the West's renewed engagement with theosis ideas in the recent past.[5]

This, however, is a controversial distinction. Bruce McCormack and Myk Habets have both argued against this distinction from a Reformed perspective. Both believe the distinction drives a wedge between the immanent and economic Trinity, such that, ironically, the distinction serves to make God too distant, unreachable, and, according to McCormack, at

---

[2]As Lossky describes it: "The question of the possibility of any real union with God ... thus poses for Christian theology the antimony of the accessibility of the inaccessible nature. How is it possible that the Holy Trinity should be the object of union ... ?" See Vladimir Lossky, *The Mystical Theology of the Eastern Church* (Plymouth, UK: Latimer, Trend, 1957), 69.

[3]For a discussion of the Eastern Orthodox distinction between essence and energies, see John Meyendorff, *A Study of Gregory Palamas* (London: Faith Press, 1964), 202-27; Meyendorff, "Doctrine of Grace in St Gregory Palamas," *St Vladimir's Seminary Quarterly* 2, no. 2 (1954): 17-26; Lossky, *Mystical Theology*, 67-90; Norman Russell, "Theosis and Gregory Palamas: Continuity or Doctrinal Change?," *St Vladimir's Theological Quarterly* 50, no. 4 (2006): 357-79.

[4]Russell, "Theosis and Gregory Palamas."

[5]Gavrilyuk mentions Protestant theologian Roger Olsen as following Lossky and Mantzanaridis in viewing the essence-energies distinction as basic to any view of theosis. See Paul Gavrilyuk, "The Retrieval of Deification: How a Once-Despised Archaism Became an Ecumenical Desideratum," *Modern Theology* 25, no. 4 (2009): 652. Gavrilyuk cites Roger Olsen, "Deification in Contemporary Theology," *ThTo* 64 (2007): 199; George Mantzaridis, *The Deification of Man* (Crestwood, NY: St. Vladimir's Seminary Press, 1984); Lossky, *Mystical Theology*.

risk of seeming "unreal."⁶ McCormack elsewhere argues that the concept of God's energies can only make sense if it refers to some sort of created grace.⁷ Habets argues that the essence-energies distinction divides God's being from God's act and therefore serves to demote the Son and the Spirit to "intermediaries of God, not God himself."⁸ McCormack and Habets differ in terms of their solutions to these problems. McCormack leaves behind the category of deification entirely, while Habets strongly supports it.⁹ Both McCormack and Habets aim their critiques at the Eastern Orthodox distinction of essence and energies, or to Western appropriations of this distinction.

How are these critiques of the essence-energies distinction relevant for this study? Jonathan Edwards, after all, did not incorporate the Eastern distinction between essence and energies, and almost certainly never came in contact with the developed Palamism that defined it. However, he did strongly espouse a distinction that sounds very similar.¹⁰ Edwards

---

⁶Bruce L. McCormack, "Participation in God, Yes, Deification, No: Two Modern Protestant Responses to an Ancient Question," in *Denkwürdiges Geheimnis: Beiträge zur Gotteslehre. Festschrift für Eberhard Jüngel zum 70. Geburtstag*, ed. Johannes Fischer, Hans-Peter Großhans, and Ingolf U. Dalferth (Tübingen: Mohr Siebeck, 2004), 373-74.

⁷Bruce L. McCormack, "Union with Christ in Calvin's Theology: Grounds for a Divinization Theory?," in *Tributes to John Calvin: A Celebration of His Quincentenary*, ed. David W. Hall (Philipsburg, NJ: P&R, 2010), 505-6.

⁸Myk Habets, "'Reformed Theosis?' A Response to Gannon Murphy," *ThTo* 65, no. 4 (2009): 494.

⁹McCormack prefers "relational and historical ontologies of Barth and Jungel" as the basis of his account for how participation in the life of God relates to Christian salvation (McCormack, "Participation in God, Yes," 373-74). Habets strongly supports the category of deification explicitly as a Reformed theologian. He agrees with Gannon Murphy that theosis finds its best home in the Reformed tradition. See Habets, "'Reformed Theosis?' A Response"; Murphy, "Reformed Theosis?"

¹⁰Michael McClymond, in an important chapter observing similarities between Edwards and Palamas, notes they both were concerned to "define the relationship between spiritual experience and the divine essence." See McClymond, "Salvation as Divinization: Jonathan Edwards, Gregory Palamas and the Theological Uses of Platonism," in *Jonathan Edwards: Philosophical Theologian*, ed. Oliver D. Crisp and Paul Helm (Burlington, VT: Ashgate, 2003), 145. Kyle Strobel also, while noting important differences, argues that Edwards's essence-nature distinction functions similarly to Vladimir Lossky's account of the essence-energies distinction. See Strobel, "Jonathan Edwards and the Polemics of Theosis," *HTR* 105, no. 3 (2012): 278. See also Strobel, *Jonathan Edwards's Theology: A Reinterpretation*, T&T Clark Studies in Systematic Theology (London: T&T Clark, 2013), 203; Strobel, "Jonathan Edwards's Reformed Doctrine of *Theosis*," *HTR* 109, no. 3 (2016): 371-99. Strobel is particularly helpful in pointing out that the divine understanding and the divine will are "communicable natures" given in grace. While Strobel is right that Edwards speaks in the essence-*nature* categories, I believe that when he is focused on the Creator-creature distinction, his preferred distinction is essence-*fullness*. The essence-*nature*

distinguished the divine essence, which is not communicated in grace, from the divine fullness, which is communicated in grace.[11] In *Religious Affections*, the most influential of Edwards's works on grace, he describes grace in terms of divine participation and qualifies himself by saying:

> Not that the saints are made partakers of the *essence* of God, and so are "Godded" with God, and "Christed" with Christ, according to the abominable and blasphemous language and notions of some heretics; but, to use the Scripture phrase, they are made partakers of God's *fullness* (Ephesians 3:17-19, John 1:16), that is, of God's spiritual beauty and happiness, according to the measure and capacity of a creature; for so it is evident the word "fullness" signifies in Scripture language. Grace in the hearts of the saints, being

---

distinction stems from two primary sources: First, he does speak of the Holy Spirit's communication of himself in his own "proper nature." This language occurs prominently in Edwards's sermon "A Divine and Supernatural Light," and, more importantly for this present purpose, in *Religious Affections*. However, it is in *Religions Affections* that Edwards denies a communication in *essence*, and therefore it is the more important for establishing which category is placed in opposition to essence in Edwards's thought. In the relevant passage in *Religious Affections*, Edwards denies that grace is a communication of divine essence and affirms that it is, rather, a communication of fullness, and then explains divine fullness in terms of nature. Similarly, in the sermon "True Grace Is Divine," Edwards juxtaposes essence over against *fullness*, rather than nature. He seems to prefer to use fullness as the category when contrasting with essence, and it is for this reason that I focus on the essence-fullness distinction. Part of the reason the essence-nature distinction has some prominence among scholars is a letter fragment from Edwards. In this letter fragment, he responds to a critic of *Religious Affections* who misconstrued Edwards's language about the Spirit communicating his own nature as signifying the communication of essence. Edwards responds that he explicitly denies this in *Religious Affections* and points out that the term *nature* does not need to mean "essence." This is an important letter for understanding divine grace in Edwards, but it should not be used to supplant Edwards's preference for the category of *fullness*, as the letter focuses on *nature* because of the critic's misunderstanding and not because it was Edwards's primary category over against essence. Based on the key passage in *Religious Affections*, it appears that divine *fullness* is the larger category that can then be explained in terms of *nature*. Thus, Edwards writes, "Not that the saints are made partakers of the *essence* of God . . . but . . . to use the Scripture phrase, they are made partakers of God's *fullness*. . . . Grace in the hearts of the saints, being therefore the most glorious work of God, wherein he communicates of the goodness of his *nature*" (emphasis added). Notice here that essence is denied, fullness is affirmed, and fullness is explained as the "goodness of his nature." The *nature* that the Spirit communicates (or per Strobel, the "communicable natures" of the divine understanding and will) is the content of the *fullness* communicated. *Fullness* and *nature* are, therefore, near synonyms, with *nature* being one way of referring to the content of divine fullness, and divine fullness being the larger category that is properly juxtaposed against essence (see WJE 2:202-3; 17:408-25). See also Jonathan Edwards, "True Grace Is Divine (1738)," in *Jonathan Edwards: Spiritual Writings*, ed. Adriaan C. Neele, Kyle C. Strobel, and Kenneth P. Minkema, Classics of Western Spirituality (New York: Paulist Press, 2019). For the letter from Edwards on divine participation, see WJE 8:636-40.

[11] See, e.g., "It is not a communication of God's essence, but it is a communication of that which the Scripture calls God's fullness" (Edwards, "True Grace Is Divine (1738)," 354).

therefore the most glorious work of God, wherein he communicates of the goodness of his nature, it is . . . above the power of all creatures.[12]

The saints do not partake of the *essence* but instead the *fullness* of God. What did Edwards mean by this distinction? While neither McCormack's or Habets's critiques are aimed at Edwards's distinction, it is reasonable to ask whether their critiques apply to it. Their arguments are all the more relevant given that they are both writing from a Reformed perspective. If Reformed theology resists the essence-energies distinction of the East, should it also resist Edwards's essence-fullness distinction?[13] This chapter will leverage McCormack and Habets to interrogate Edwards's distinction in the following two key questions:

1. Is there a coherent difference between the divine essence and the divine fullness in Edwards's thought? If so, what is it?[14]

2. Does this distinction drive a wedge between God's immanent and economic life, or between God's being and act?[15]

This chapter will argue that there is a coherent distinction between divine essence and divine fullness, and one that does not drive a wedge between the immanent and the economic Trinity. I will show this by tracing the concepts of the divine essence and the divine fullness through Edwards's doctrines of the Trinity, Christology, and grace. In each case I will show how Edwards utilizes two complementary approaches to participation. Here I will use the same typology employed in the previous chapter. The Christian tradition has employed two distinct but not necessarily contradictory approaches to participation. The first may be termed *methexis* and is oriented around sharing of substance. This is most often associated with the Platonic tradition. The second may be termed *koinōnia* and is oriented around shared relationship, marked by intimacy and differentiation. In the previous chapter

---

[12] WJE 2:203, emphasis added.
[13] Although some Reformed theologians embrace the essence-energies distinction; see, e.g., Murphy, "Reformed Theosis?"
[14] McCormack believes the theosis conversation often lacks sufficient clarity, especially when theologians posit a participation in uncreated energies and not in uncreated essence. He sees the distinction as incoherent, at least so long as both are regarded as *uncreated* (McCormack, "Union with Christ," 505-6).
[15] As Habets argues occurs in Palamite essence-energies distinction. See Habets, "'Reformed Theosis?' A Response," 493-94.

this typology helped clarify the relationship between nature and grace in Edwards. In this chapter the same typology clarifies the distinction between the divine essence and the divine fullness. The divine essence is grounded on the first type of participation—*methexis*—whereas the divine fullness is grounded on the second type of participation—*koinōnia*. I will show how both are operative in the immanent Trinity, both are operative in a different way in Edwards's Christology, and both are operative in a modified manner in the graced saint. Once I have traced these two participations through the Trinity, Christology, and the graced saint, I will return in the conclusion to the two questions above, in an effort to determine whether Edwards's distinction between essence and fullness is vulnerable to Reformed critiques of the Palamite distinctions.

Overview of Edwards's Doctrine of the Trinity

Edwards's doctrine of the Trinity represents the animating core of his thought.[16] Sang Hyun Lee writes, "Everything Edwards wrote about the Trinity expresses the intertwining connectedness of the Trinity and the Christian's experience of God as the Creator, Savior, and Sanctifier, and thus between the immanent and the economic Trinity."[17] This is the case even though Edwards never published a treatise on the Trinity. Nevertheless, throughout Edwards's published writings, and particularly when he writes on the nature of grace, or salvation, or God's end in creation, his doctrine of the Trinity looms in the background, even if it is not explicit. With this in mind it will not be surprising to find that, in order to understand how Edwards achieved both intimacy and differentiation between Creator and creature in his theology of grace, one must begin in his doctrine of God. What follows is not intended to be a full account of Edwards's theology proper—entire monographs are dedicated to that task.[18] Rather, I will

---

[16] This is the increasing consensus among Edwards scholars. See in particular Danaher's rehearsal of differing and changing views toward the centrality of Edwards's doctrine of the Trinity to Edwards's thinking, and especially his moral thought. See W. J. Danaher Jr., *The Trinitarian Ethics of Jonathan Edwards* (Louisville, KY: Westminster John Knox, 2004), 1-5.

[17] WJE 21:3.

[18] Amy Plantinga Pauw's monograph on Edwards's doctrine of the Trinity was the watershed study on the subject and has provoked vigorous debate. She argues that Edwards developed what amounts to two models for the Trinity: a psychological model derived from his Augustinian heritage, and a social model that in some respects anticipates modern moves in trinitarianism. Studebaker and Caldwell reject this thesis, and argue that Edwards's Trinity is thoroughly

provide an overview of Edwards's trinitarian thought as background for a closer inspection of how his ideas of participation lead to his distinction between essence and fullness in his theology of grace.

Trinitarian happiness and goodness. Edwards's God is a God who is happy and good. On the face of it, this appears to be a simple, perhaps simplistic, place to begin thinking through the great doctrine of the Christian church. Yet, there is a way in which his entire doctrine grows from this fundamental insight. Happiness and goodness are, for Edwards, inextricably linked: one implies the other.

To be perfectly good is to incline to and delight in making another happy in the same proportion as it is happy itself, that is, to delight as much in

---

Augustinian and of the mutual-love model. Kyle Strobel has sought to refute both views by arguing that Edwards's Trinity is best described using an idiosyncratic model of "personal beatific delight" or "religious affection in pure act." By this he means to point out that Edwards arranged his doctrine of the Trinity in continuity with the goal of salvation: the beatific vision. Each perspective has its strengths and weaknesses. Pauw is strongest in relating Edwards's trinitarianism to contemporary trends in the social Trinity movement but likely overplays the extent to which the two models really are distinct. Studebaker and Caldwell helpfully show Edwards's continuity with his own tradition but perhaps underestimate his unique contributions. Strobel is helpful in pointing out Edwards's unique moves and how this relates to his polemical context and his soteriology, and provides the most coherent account of Edwards's unique theological vision. Oliver Crisp has also engaged critically with a range of issues in Edwards's view of God in *Jonathan Edwards on God and Creation* (Oxford: Oxford University Press, 2012), 37-137. See Amy Plantinga Pauw, *The Supreme Harmony of All: The Trinitarian Theology of Jonathan Edwards* (Grand Rapids, MI: Eerdmans, 2002); Steven Studebaker, "Jonathan Edwards's Social Augustinian Trinitarianism: An Alternative to a Recent Trend," *SJT* 56, no. 3 (2003): 268-85; Steven Studebaker and Robert W. Caldwell, *The Trinitarian Theology of Jonathan Edwards: Text, Context, and Application* (Surrey, UK: Ashgate, 2012); Steven M. Studebaker, "Supreme Harmony or Supreme Disharmony? An Analysis of Amy Plantinga Pauw's *The Supreme Harmony of All: The Trinitarian Theology of Jonathan Edwards*," *SJT* 57, no. 4 (2004): 479-85; Studebaker, "The Supreme Harmony of All: The Trinitarian Theology of Jonathan Edwards," *Fides et historia* 36, no. 1 (2004): 156-57; Robert W. Caldwell III, *Communion in the Spirit: The Holy Spirit as the Bond of Union in the Theology of Jonathan Edwards*, Studies in Evangelical History and Thought (Milton Keynes, UK: Paternoster, 2006); Caldwell, "The Holy Spirit as the Bond of Union in the Theology of Jonathan Edwards," *Reformation & Revival* 12, no. 3 (2003): 43-58; Strobel, *Jonathan Edwards's Theology: A Reinterpretation*. For a defense of Plantinga Pauw, see Michael J. McClymond, "Hearing the Symphony: A Critique of Some Critics of Sang Lee's and Amy Pauw's Accounts of Jonathan Edwards' View of God," in *Jonathan Edwards as Contemporary: Essays in Honor of Sang Hyun Lee*, ed. Don Schweitzer (New York: Peter Lang, 2010), 67-92. For a critique of Strobel, see Gerald McDermott, "Jonathan Edwards and God's Inner Life: A Response to Kyle Strobel," *Themelios* 39, no. 2 (2014): 241-50. For an appreciative account and also critique of Strobel, see Oliver D. Crisp, *Jonathan Edwards Among the Theologians* (Grand Rapids, MI: Eerdmans, 2015), 36-59. For an account of Edwards's theology than relates it to the previous Western Catholic tradition, see Seng-Kong Tan, *Fullness Received and Returned: Trinity and Participation in Jonathan Edwards* (Minneapolis: Fortress, 2014), 5-49.

communicating happiness to another as in enjoying of it himself, and an inclination to communicate all his happiness; it appears that this is perfect goodness, because goodness is delight in communicating happiness.[19]

To be good is to communicate happiness, and to do so in proportion to one's own happiness. This is a deep moral insight, and one that could significantly affect a theory of ethics. However, Edwards articulates this in the context of his doctrine of the Trinity. If, as tradition taught, God is both happy and good, then God must communicate that happiness to another.[20] Two crucial insights derive from this. First is that "God is a communicative being."[21] That is, God has a fundamental disposition to communicate himself to other intelligent beings.[22] Second to this is that God must not be a monad. Edwards believed that "one alone ... cannot be excellent," and this is as true of God as any other being.[23] If God is to be good, then he must have another to whom he may communicate happiness. This receiver of his communications cannot simply be a creature, because creatures are, by definition, finite, and therefore they will never be capable of receiving the infinite communications of happiness that God's goodness demands.[24] It follows that God must be, in some sense, plural. However, in what way is God to be plural?

---

[19] *Miscellanies* 96 (WJE 13:265).
[20] WJE 13:265.
[21] *Miscellanies* 332 (WJE 13:410). Edwards makes this statement in relation to creation, but the insight is fundamental to his notion of the Trinity as well. See William M. Schweitzer, *God Is a Communicative Being: Divine Communicativeness and Harmony in the Theology of Jonathan Edwards* (London: Bloomsbury T&T Clark, 2012), 11-16.
[22] Studebaker and Caldwell assert, "The disposition of the divine nature for self communication is perhaps Edwards's most fundamental theological conviction" (*Trinitarian Theology of Jonathan Edwards*, 62-63). Within Edwards studies, this question of the role of Edwards's notion of disposition is a point of debate. Sang Hyun Lee argued that it is the basis of an entirely new ontology. His view is widely followed by Edwards scholars. Stephen Holmes sought to refute his assertion, and has gathered a following as well. See Lee, "Jonathan Edwards's Dispositional Conception of the Trinity: A Resource for Contemporary Reformed Theology," in *Toward the Future of Reformed Theology: Tasks, Topics, Traditions*, ed. E. David Willis, Michael Welker, and Matthias Gockel (Grand Rapids, MI: Eerdmans, 1999), 444-55; Lee, "Editor's Introduction," in *Writings on the Trinity, Grace, and Faith*, ed. Sang Hyun Lee, WJE 21; Lee, *The Philosophical Theology of Jonathan Edwards* (Princeton, NJ: Princeton University Press, 1988). See also Holmes, "Does Jonathan Edwards Use a Dispositional Ontology? A Response to Sang Hyun Lee," in Crisp and Helm, *Jonathan Edwards: Philosophical Theologian*, 99-114; WJE 21:1-10. In defense of Lee and Plantinga Pauw, who follows Lee in a limited way, see McClymond, "Hearing the Symphony."
[23] This is because one alone will not be able to consent to another being. Edwards's notions of consent, communication, love, harmony are all closely related concepts (WJE 6:337).
[24] *Miscellanies* 96 (WJE 13:264).

Trinitarian idealism: The generation of the Son. Edwards's answer to this question comes in the packaging of his idealism.[25] In his *Discourse on the Trinity*, he rehearses an axiom that God must have a perfect idea of himself.[26] This would follow from the traditional notion of omniscience. However, for Edwards, a perfect idea is a substantial thing. That is true in Edwards's doctrine of creation, as explored in the previous chapter, but it is far more potent when God turns God's thoughts toward himself. When God thinks of himself, his idea is perfect in every way, and "this idea of God is a substantial idea and has the very essence of God, is truly God, to all intents and purposes, and that by this means the Godhead is really generated and repeated." The reason God's idea generates the very essence of God is explained in Edwards's notion of spiritual ideas. A spiritual idea is always a sort of repetition of the thing itself. The idea of love or fear is a repetition, however imperfect, of love or fear itself. Edwards argues that, in a similar sort of way but to an infinitely greater extent, when God views himself mentally, God repeats himself. "Therefore as God with perfect clearness, fullness and strength understands himself, views his own essence (in which there is no distinction of substance and act, but it is wholly substance and wholly act), that idea which God hath of himself is absolutely himself." This perfect idea of God is a distinct, but identical, consubstantial, coeternal, subsistence of the Godhead. This is Edwards's understanding of the Son's generation. The Son is the Father's perfect idea of himself, and Edwards reinforces this assertion by pointing out the many biblical references to Christ's role as revealer of God. Why is Christ the Logos? Why is it that Christ points to himself when the disciples ask to see the Father? Why does Hebrews point to Jesus as the exact representation of God? It is because the eternal Son is the Father's idea of himself.[27]

Trinitarian love: The procession of the Spirit. Edwards's idealism has, at least to his mind, explained how there can be two coessential subsistences or persons in the Godhead. However he has not yet explained God's goodness and happiness. Recall that a being is perfectly good when there is

---

[25]Tan provides a helpful historical context for Edwards's thought on the generation of the Son in *Fullness Received and Returned*, 7-13.
[26]WJE 21:113-44.
[27]WJE 21:114, 116-21.

a disposition to communicate happiness to the same extent that one is happy in oneself. How does this obtain within Edwards's doctrine of God? The answer to this question ushers in the Holy Spirit. At the same time that the Father views himself in his idea—which is to say, at the same time as the Father views himself in the person of the Son—the Father loves his own image of himself, and the Father's image returns this love simultaneously. The Father and the Son are united in a mutual bond of perfect love, delight, happiness, and joy. This communicated happiness, delight, love, and joy is a third subsistence of God: the Holy Spirit. Why does it follow that the Father's love to the Son, and the Son's return of that love, issues forth a third person of the Trinity? Edwards's answers this by leveraging pure act tradition.

> The Godhead being thus begotten by God's having an idea of himself and standing forth in a distinct subsistence or person in that idea, there proceeds a most pure act, and an infinitely holy and sweet energy arises between the Father and Son: for their love and joy is mutual, in mutually loving and delighting in each other. . . . This is the eternal and most perfect and essential act of the divine nature, wherein the Godhead acts to an infinite degree and in the most perfect manner possible. The Deity becomes all act; the divine essence itself flows out and is as it were breathed forth in love and joy. So that the Godhead therein stands forth in yet another manner of subsistence, and there proceeds the third person in the Trinity, the Holy Spirit, viz. the Deity in act: for there is no other act but the act of the will.[28]

Edwards's argument is not nearly as full as his idealist argument for the deity of the Son. However, in the text just before this quote he asserts that there can be no distinction between substance and act in God. This presupposition helps explain his thinking here. God's substance and act are one, and God's perfect, infinite, and pure act is his act of the will. His will is inclined in love toward himself, in his perfect image of himself, his Son. This perfect act of love cannot be other than God's substance and essence flowing forth between the Father and the Son. This, then, leads Edwards to view the Holy Spirit as the communicated happiness, love, delight, and joy between the Father and the Son.

Trinitarian attributes, perichoresis, and personhood. At this point Edwards has shown how God can be happy and good: God is good because

---

[28]WJE 21:121.

God communicates happiness (which is an aspect of love) within the deity.[29] This self-communication is infinite and perfect, resulting in (and requiring) God, God's idea or understanding, and God's will or love. Edwards believes that these three constitute the only real distinctions that are to be found in God. Further, these three (God, God's idea, God's will) explain all of God's attributes.[30] Or perhaps better, all of God's attributes reduce to these three "real attributes."[31] Here Edwards creatively engages the divine simplicity tradition.[32] Christian theology regularly denies that there are distinguishable "parts" of God. All that God is, is God. When one describe God's attributes, they are ways of describing all that God is and not merely a part of God. Yet here Edwards critiques the traditional language. All that one can say about God reduces to God, God's understanding (or his idea), and his will (or his love). One might speak of God's omniscience, but that is merely

---

[29] See Tan's discussion of the procession of the Spirit in *Fullness Received and Returned*, 13-17.
[30] WJE 21:131-32.
[31] There is a debate between Kyle Strobel and Oliver Crisp on Edwards's view of "real attributes." Strobel argues that Edwards's real attributes (God, God's understanding, and God's will) are attributes that are intrinsic to God, or "God without reference to anything else," whereas all God's other traditional attributes are "relative attributes" (infinity, eternity, omnipresence, etc.), extrinsic to God, that is, they describe God in reference to something else (Strobel, *Jonathan Edwards's Theology: A Reinterpretation*, 234-42). Crisp, on the other hand, argues that God has intrinsic attributes that predicate to the shared divine essence other than the three real attributes. Crisp wants to retain essentialism in Edwards, as does Strobel. However, Crisp critiques Strobel as failing to realize that what Strobel calls the "relative attributes" describe God himself and therefore must be intrinsic. If they are intrinsic, then they cannot be accidental; if they are not accidental, then they must be essential (Crisp, *Jonathan Edwards Among the Theologians*, 52-59). I take Crisp's view to be a possible critique of Edwards's assertions in the *Discourse on the Trinity* (see WJE 21:132), but I take Strobel's account to be the more accurate account of what Edwards actually says. However, in this debate Crisp is not intending to critique Edwards but describe his thought and critique Strobel's reading. I have not been persuaded by Crisp on this point, and I follow Strobel's account.
[32] There is vigorous debate among Edwards scholars as to whether Edwards creatively engaged the divine simplicity tradition, or modified it radically, or else perhaps did not understand it. For scholars questioning Edwards's adherence to the divine simplicity tradition, see WJE 6:84; Pauw, *Supreme Harmony of All*, 59-80, 69-72; McClymond, "Hearing the Symphony." Stephen Holmes argues that by situating attributes in the persons of the Trinity, instead of in the divine essence, Edwards was innovating in the tradition. See Holmes, *God of Grace and God of Glory: An Account of the Theology of Jonathan Edwards* (Edinburgh: T&T Clark, 2000), 69-71. For scholars arguing that Edwards, while creative, still operated within the divine simplicity tradition, see Studebaker and Caldwell, *Trinitarian Theology of Jonathan Edwards*, 129-31; 144-51. Oliver Crisp notes the difficulties of Edwards's unique account but also argues that he is seeking to accomplish what the divine simplicity tradition aims to do. See Crisp, "Jonathan Edwards on Divine Simplicity," *Religious Studies* 39, no. 1 (2003): 23-41; Crisp, *Jonathan Edwards on God and Creation*, 96-107; Crisp, *Jonathan Edwards Among the Theologians*, 36-59.

a description of God's understanding, relative to all that might be known. One might speak of God's grace or mercy, but this is merely God's will (his love) relative to needy creatures or sinners. Even God's holiness reduces to a form of excellency, which in turn is composed of consent between two beings, which again resolves in God's will or love.[33] Therefore, argues Edwards, whatever attributes we may use to describe God, they will always end up being descriptions of God, his understanding, and his will.

Yet this idea brings up a problem. If the deity is God, his understanding, and his will, then this sounds more like a modern definition of one person than it does a Christian Trinity.[34] Edwards defines a *person* as something with both an understanding and a will.[35] This modern definition of personhood was one shared by his theological opponents, and therefore it was important to his polemical strategy.[36] Yet, by identifying the Son with God's understanding and the Spirit with God's will, he would appear to be succeeding in giving a Unitarian doctrine of God. The question then arises, How are there *three* persons?

Edwards answers this question in yet another creative use of the tradition. Beginning with Maximus the Confessor, Christian trinitarian theology has often described the distinction-in-unity of the persons in terms of perichoresis (circumincession). Each person of the Trinity is present in the other persons, without mingling or absorbing each other, such that when one person is said to do something, all persons are implicated. It was designed

---

[33] WJE 6:337.
[34] Studebaker and Caldwell point out that Edwards's definition of a person as one who has understanding and will is a modern definition. This is distinct from the traditional understanding of a person as an instance of a rational nature (Studebaker and Caldwell, *Trinitarian Theology of Jonathan Edwards*, 77-78).
[35] WJE 21:133. There is debate regarding Edwards's preferred understanding of personhood. The more traditional definition of personhood, as it relates to the trinitarian persons, is that of subsistence: a given instance of a rational nature. Edwards does seem to employ this approach—both in the discourse and in the *Miscellanies*—yet he also, as here, employs the modern definition of persons as that which has understanding and will. Studebaker and Caldwell argue that Edwards oscillates between the two, but that the traditional subsistence language is more foundational. Strobel argues that Edwards changes his mind on the nature of the essence and persons, and conceives of essence in more personal terms. See Studebaker and Caldwell, *Trinitarian Theology of Jonathan Edwards*, 77-83; Strobel, *Jonathan Edwards's Theology: A Reinterpretation*, 31-71.
[36] See Strobel's argument regarding the polemical background of Edwards's *Discourse on the Trinity* in *Jonathan Edwards's Theology: A Reinterpretation*, 31-71.

to avoid both tritheism and modalism.[37] Edwards employs the concept toward a similar but modified end: he uses it to establish personhood for each member of the Trinity. The Father, Son, and Holy Spirit are all three persons because they each have understanding and will. Yet they do not each have a separate understanding and will but share the understanding through perichoresis. That is, the Son wills because the Spirit is perichoretically "in" him as the will of the Son and the Father. The Son understands because he is the Father's understanding. The Spirit understands because the Son is perichoretically "in" him, and the Spirit wills because he is the will of the Father and the Son. The Father understands and wills because he begets and spirates the Son and Spirit respectively, and they are "in" him perichoretically.

This argument appears to be a new way of employing the perichoretic tradition.[38] Edwards employs it to establish a Trinity of persons, where persons are defined as that which has understanding and will. However he does this without conceding three centers of consciousness or falling into something similar to a contemporary social model of the Trinity.[39] In this way, his use of perichoresis allows him to describe the divine essence in

---

[37]Jacques Fantino, "Circumincession," in *Encyclopedia of Christian Theology*, ed. Jean-Yves Lacoste (New York: Routledge, 2005), 315.

[38]For a critique of Edwards's employment of perichoresis, see Ralph Cunnington, "A Critical Examination of Jonathan Edwards's Doctrine of the Trinity," *Themelios* 39, no. 2 (2014): 238-39.

[39]Studebaker and Caldwell, *Trinitarian Theology of Jonathan Edwards*, 77-78. In this Edwards narrowly avoids what Stephen Holmes considers the error of modern theologies of the Trinity. Holmes points out a change in the way the notion of personhood is understood, such that the persons of the Trinity can be viewed as three centers of consciousness. He argues that this social model is a departure from earlier consensus. See Stephen R. Holmes, *The Holy Trinity: Understanding God's Life* (Milton Keynes, UK: Paternoster, 2012), 13-16, 195, 200. Of course, Amy Plantinga Pauw argues precisely that Edwards does achieve a social model, though one that is built on a more traditional Augustinian mutual-love model. It is this achievement of the social model that Pauw argues can be resourced in contemporary trinitarian theology (Pauw, *Supreme Harmony of All*, 10-11). However, Strobel's reading of Edwards's trinitarian doctrine points out how his use of perichoresis to establish personhood serves to distinguish his thought from aspects of Augustinian tradition (contra Studebaker and Caldwell) without embracing a social model (contra Pauw). Edwards retains essence language but explains it in personal terms, while at the same time personalizing the divine attributes. See Strobel, *Jonathan Edwards's Theology: A Reinterpretation*, 40-64; see also 65-71 for how Edwards fits neither the Augustinian model (as conceived by Studebaker and Caldwell) nor the social model (as conceived by Pauw and Danaher). Oliver Crisp, while critical of Strobel's account of real and relative attributes, affirms Strobel's analysis of the use of perichoresis in Edwards's trinitarian doctrine (*Jonathan Edwards Among the Theologians*, 57).

personal categories, achieving both threeness and oneness.[40] As Strobel says, "[Edwards] utilizes both perichoresis and the divine essence to talk about plurality and unity, unity grounded by one essence and personhood existing through perichoresis."[41]

Trinitarian aim: "Illustrative of gospel doctrine." Edwards developed his doctrine of God in order to defend the classical trinitarianism that he inherited and that he believed the Bible taught; but he also sought to develop it further than it had been previously understood. He was not aiming at explaining the Trinity in its entirety, as if the mystery could be set aside.[42] Rather, he believed that his theological creativity and development was pressing further what Scripture and reason encouraged the church to believe.[43] More specifically, he believed that this account of the Trinity opened up the doctrines of redemption in greater clarity. In the middle of his *Discourse on the Trinity*, Edwards readily admits that his account leaves many questions and perhaps even opens up new problems and questions that will need resolution. Yet, Edwards states that his aim is "to say something further of [the Trinity] than has been wont to be said." That is, Edwards wants to contribute to the tradition and press it forward. In his next sentence he gives a clue of what sort of contribution that might be. "It seems to me that what I have here supposed concerning the Trinity is exceeding analogous to the gospel scheme, and agreeable to the tenor of the whole New Testament, and abundantly illustrative of gospel doctrines; as might be particularly shown,

---

[40] By synchronizing trinitarian persons with divine attributes (real attributes), Edwards unites the two primary spheres of a traditional doctrine of God. As Beeke and Jones comment, "The doctrine of God may be understood in a twofold sense, either essentially or personally. Understood essentially, the doctrine refers to the essence of God and His attributes; a personal understanding refers to the doctrine of the tri-personality of the Godhead, or the doctrine of the Trinity." See Joel R. Beeke and Mark Jones, *A Puritan Theology* (Grand Rapids, MI: Reformation Heritage Books, 2012), 85. When this is applied to grace and participation in the economy, Strobel points out that it also unites two strains of theosis theology (Strobel, "Jonathan Edwards and the Polemics," 279).

[41] Strobel, *Jonathan Edwards's Theology: A Reinterpretation*, 47. Strobel has shown very helpfully how Edwards's view of essence is fundamentally personal. Crisp has confirmed this view in *Jonathan Edwards Among the Theologians*, 36-59.

[42] "I am far from pretending to explaining the Trinity so as to render it no longer a mystery" (WJE 21:134).

[43] "I think the Word of God teaches us more things concerning it to be believed by us than have been generally taken [notice of]" (WJE 21:139). On the role of reason for trinitarian reflection, see Edwards's famous acclamation: "I am not afraid to say twenty things about the Trinity which the Scripture never said" (*Miscellanies* 94 in WJE 13:257).

would it not exceedingly lengthen out this discourse."[44] Edwards believed that his contribution was not that he had resolved the difficult questions of the Trinity but that he had explained New Testament gospel doctrines—soteriology—more clearly.[45] This suggests that Edwards's pursued the doctrine of God in order to clarify the doctrines of soteriology, with grace holding a central place.[46] I will now turn to consider one way in which Edwards's articulation of the Trinity clarifies his doctrine of grace.

Essence and Fullness *Ad Intra*: The Trinity

Jonathan Edwards's distinction between the divine essence and fullness is grounded in his doctrine of the Trinity. The processions of the persons and the relations of the persons set a pattern that then follows through, with important modifications, into the doctrine of grace. More specifically, Edwards's doctrine of the Trinity allows for two types of participation—one that is a sharing in essence (*methexis*) and another that is fundamentally relational (*koinōnia*). Edwards can speak of a type of participation that explains quiddity and another type of participation that explains how distinct persons share in love.[47] Edwards does not explicitly distinguish the two forms of participations in his discussion of the Trinity *ad intra*. However, the distinction is present implicitly, and it becomes explicit as Edwards moves from the doctrine of the Trinity *ad intra* to the doctrine of grace. In order to show this distinction, I will focus on the person of the Son within Edwards's Trinity *ad intra*, with particular attention to how the Son partakes of the divine essence and how the Son partakes of the divine love.

The Son ad intra *as pattern for graced saint*. What is the reason for focusing in on the Son generation and relation within the Trinity? The Son's reception and return of divine love becomes the model for the dynamic of

---

[44]WJE 21:134.

[45]Could this be why Edwards never published on the Trinity? On the other hand, he published early and often on soteriological concerns that leveraged his trinitarian reflections. Consider, for instance, "God Glorified in Man's Dependence," and how this early published sermon grows so naturally from his trinitarian reflections (see WJE 17:200-214).

[46]When Strobel describes Edwards's Trinity as "religious affection in pure act," he captures the union between theology proper and soteriology in Edwards's thought (*Jonathan Edwards's Theology: A Reinterpretation*, 70).

[47]"I believe Edwards maintains divine-essence language in talking about God's 'stuff,' his *quiddity*" (Strobel, *Jonathan Edwards's Theology: A Reinterpretation*, 238).

grace. This is an early insight for Edwards. In *Miscellanies* 104 Edwards argues that there is an analogy between the Father's communicative disposition that undergirds the Trinity and the Son's communicative disposition that undergirds the creation and redemption of the church. That is, just as the Father inclines to self-communication, and this is communication of happiness is entirely fulfilled in his self-communication to the Son, so the Son also inclines toward self-communication. The Son's self-communication obtains in the communication of love and delight to the church. This is the end of creation, and in a remarkable statement, Edwards says it results in "an image of the eternal Trinity; wherein Christ is the everlasting father, and believers are his seed, and the Holy Spirit, or Comforter, is the third person in Christ, being his delight and love flowing out towards the church. In believers the Spirit and delight of God, being communicated unto them, flows out toward the Lord Jesus Christ."[48] For the moment, notice that within the image of the Trinity, Christ takes the place, as it were, of the Father, and the church takes the place, as it were, of the Son, while the Spirit replicates its same role in both the Trinity proper and in this trinity of grace. This means that the church's reception and return of the Holy Spirit in the economy of grace is patterned on the Son's reception and return of the Holy Spirit within the Trinity *ad intra*. For this reason I turn to investigate the Son's generation and relation *ad intra* in search of insight into the dynamic of grace.

The Son's participation in the divine essence and divine fullness. I begin by asking the question, How does the Son come to partake in the divine essence? The answer will show that the Son's participation in the divine essence is a species of *methexis*. Recall the discussion above regarding the Father's act of begetting the Son. The Father reflects on himself. This is a nonvolitional movement that is fundamental to his personhood and essence.[49] As the Father thinks on himself, God's self-understanding generates. This self-understanding is perfect and infinite, such that it must issue forth in a coessential, consubstantial, subsistence that is nevertheless

---

[48] WJE 13:273-74.
[49] "The divine essence is independent and underived in another respect, i.e. it is not dependent on any arbitrament or voluntary communication" (WJE 21:148). Edwards elsewhere states, "[The Son's] proceeding from the Father in his eternal generation, or filiation, argues no proper dependence on the will of the Father; for that proceeding was natural and necessary and not arbitrary" (WJE 19:571-72).

relationally distinct from the Father.[50] The Son is therefore a "partaker of the divine essence."[51] It is important to note that the Son's participation in essence is sufficiently established by the ideation of the Father. One should view this participation in divine essence as an example of *methexis*-participation. As I have used the term, *methexis* is a variety of participation thought that is oriented around shared substance or essence. It can be contrasted with the notion of *koinōnia*, which does not imply a shared essence but rather relational intimacy in differentiation.[52] It will become clear that the Son relates to the Father in a *koinōnia* in the Spirit as well. But it remains that the Son partakes of the divine essence by way of a *methexis*, on the basis of the Father's ideation.

If the Son partakes of the divine essence by virtue of the Father's ideation, then how does the Son partake of the divine happiness or love? This is a key question for Edwards, because as noted earlier, Edwards's doctrine of God is not yet a Trinity without the communication of happiness. This communication occurs through the mutual love between the Father and the Son. The Father views himself in the Son, and the Son views himself in himself, and this spirates delight, happiness, and love (all synonymous) in the person of the Spirit.[53] Importantly, however, the procession of the Spirit is a sharing in love between the Father and the Son, *and not the basis of their sharing in the divine essence*. The Father's and Son's participation in the divine essence is established prior (logically, not temporally) to their

---

[50]It is instructive to note that when the Father reflects on the divine essence, his mental image is a *person*, not a set of abstract attributes. This would appear to confirm Strobel's more personal account of the divine essence. "It is more immediately relevant to talk of God as 'whom' rather than 'what'" (*Jonathan Edwards's Theology: A Reinterpretation*, 46).

[51]Jonathan Edwards, "Sermon 321. Hebrews 1:3," in *Sermon Series II, 1729–1731*, WJE Online vol. 45. Edwards also speaks of the divine persons partaking in the divine essence in "True Grace Is Divine (1738)," 353.

[52]I draw this typology, as from the previous chapter, from Julie Canlis's helpful analysis in *Calvin's Ladder: A Spiritual Theology of Ascent and Ascension* (Grand Rapids, MI: Eerdmans, 2010), 13. See also T. F. Torrance's distinction between *methexis* and *koinōnia*. Torrance describes *methexis* as a sharing in "eternal realities," whereas *koinōnia* is the type of participation that Chalcedon relied on to relate the divine and human natures of Christ without any mixing of essence. I follow both Torrance and Canlis (who herself cites Torrance) in designating participation oriented around shared substance or essence as *methexis*, and participation oriented around shared intimacy in differentiation as *koinōnia*. See T. F. Torrance, *Theology in Reconstruction* (London: SCM Press, 1965), 184–85.

[53]"[The Spirit] proceeds from the Son immediately by himself by beholding the Father in himself" (WJE 21:143).

participation in mutual love. In other words, the Father and the Son can share in divine love—the Holy Spirit—without that act of sharing impinging on their quiddity.

At this point I must make some careful observations. The Spirit itself partakes of the divine essence by virtue of the Father's and Son's pure act. If act and substance cannot be distinguished in God, then the Father's and Son's pure act of love must be substantial and essential. Thus, just as the Son partakes of the divine essence by virtue of a *methexis*, on the basis of the Father's ideation, so the Spirit partakes of the divine essence by virtue of a *methexis*, on the basis of the Father's and Son's pure act of love. Once again, Edwards utilizes *methexis*-participation when he is describing the consubstantiality of the persons of the Trinity.

However, while it is true that the Father's and Son's act of mutual love establishes the Spirit's participation in divine essence (*methexis*), *it does not work the other way around*. The Father-Son mutual love does not establish *the Father's and the Son's* participation in the divine essence. That is, the Father's and the Son's participation in divine essence (*methexis*) is not dependent on their communion in the Spirit.[54] "The Son derived the divine essence from the Father, and the Holy Spirit derives the divine essence from the Father and the Son."[55] It is true that their mutual love is logically inevitable and necessary because of their divine essence, but it does not follow that their sharing in the essence *is based* on their act of mutual love. Classical trinitarian doctrine affirms that each divine person shares the essence of God, but that the persons may be distinguished as to their relations of origin: the Father unoriginate, the Son begotten, and the Spirit proceeding.[56] Edwards is doing something similar here. The Father, the Son, and the Holy Spirit all share one essence, yet they partake of the essence in distinct ways. While the Spirit's participation in essence is dependent on the pure act of

---

[54] I use the word *dependent* because Edwards could speak of mutual dependence between the persons in the Trinity. For example, "That there is a dependence in the Godhead of one person on another—if we don't understand it of an arbitrary [dependence] or a depending on another's will—is not at all inconsistent with a perfect equality in glory. There is a dependence every one has on another, though necessary and of different kinds" (WJE 21:147; see also 146). See also *Miscellanies* 1062 (WJE 20:430).

[55] WJE 21:147. Edwards clarifies immediately that the divine essence is undivided as to its being but that this does not exclude the idea of personal relations.

[56] See Holmes's fifth point in his summary of classical trinitarian doctrine (*Holy Trinity*, 200).

the Father and the Son, the Father's and Son's participation in the divine essence is logically prior to that act.

The Son's two participations:* Methexis *in essence and* koinōnia *in fullness. We can begin to discern two complementary yet distinguishable types of participation: one that is a sharing in essence, undergirding being (*methexis*), and another that is a sharing in love between distinct persons (*koinōnia*). In order to make the *koinōnia* participation more clear, focus again on the Son's relation to the Father. On the one hand, the Son derives essence on the basis of the Father's ideation. This participation explains *being* or quiddity, but Edwards presses further. The Father and the Son relate to each other not merely through the Father's ideation but on the basis of shared love (the Holy Spirit). Edwards designates this shared love as the fullness of the deity.[57] The entrance of this third party (the Holy Spirit, or divine fullness), shared between the Father and the Son, which is not itself the basis of their shared essence, but rather their shared love, propels Edwards into the realm of *koinōnia* participation. That is, with the entrance of the Holy Spirit as the bond of love between the Father and the Son, Edwards is no longer talking about shared substance or essence (*methexis*), but rather about relational intimacy in differentiation (*koinōnia*).

Edwards explicitly invokes the New Testament *koinōnia* tradition in developing this idea. He describes the shared fullness between the Father and the Son in terms of *partaking, fellowship*, and *communion*, and he does so all while reflecting on 2 Corinthians 13:14. This is the famous grace blessing, in which Paul employs the term *koinōnia*. Edwards defines this communion/partaking/fellowship as a sharing between persons in a common good. Notice the emphasis is on differentiated persons sharing in a third thing—a common good. He defines the common good between the Father and the Son as their shared holiness and happiness (which for Edwards are equivalents for love, the Holy Spirit, and divine fullness). The result is that the divine fullness shared between the Father and the Son is their *koinōnia* in the Spirit.[58] Put differently, the Son shares a *methexis* with the deity by

---

[57] "The fullness of God consists in the holiness and happiness of the Deity. . . . The fullness of God consists in the Holy Spirit" (WJE 21:187-88).

[58] It is important to point out that the passage in the *Treatise on Grace* where Edwards discusses this is in particular relation to the doctrine of grace. Edwards's point is that grace is a partaking of the divine fullness shared between the Father and the Son. This passage is aiming at the

virtue of the Father's ideation, but the Son shares a *koinōnia* with the Father by virtue of his reception and return of the Holy Spirit (divine fullness). Seng-Kong Tan puts it this way:

> The Son's reception of the Spirit is not a reception of being or essence (as that happens in the Son's generation), but a reception of love or *koinonia*. As the Son's generation and the Spirit's procession from the Father are simultaneous, the Son receives the divine essence, *koinonia* (the Father's love), and identity (individuality and a unique filial disposition). Yet this eternal, identity-constituting "movement" of the Spirit does not terminate in the Son: the Holy Spirit proceeds from the Father through the Son, who returns the Spirit to the Father.[59]

The Spirit's dignity as koinōnia. Edwards reserved a particular dignity for this *koinōnia* between the Father and the Son. Recall that from an early stage Edwards asked the question, How is it that God can be infinitely happy and good?[60] Goodness is the disposition to communicate happiness, and Edwards develops his doctrine of the Trinity with this question and this assumption in mind. It is perhaps for this reason that Edwards's development of the Trinity is not satisfied merely to prove that each of the three persons share in one essence. This is important for orthodoxy, and it was important for his polemical situation, but Edwards wanted to show more. He wanted to show not only that each person shares one divine essence, but also that God is happy and good. He achieves this only when he shows the Father and the Son in a communion of divine love. The relational communion (*koinōnia*) between the Father and the Son therefore carries a particular dignity, along with the essential

---

doctrine of grace, but Edwards bases it on his doctrine of the Trinity *ad intra*, which is why I justify drawing it into the discussion here. See the following: "By *fullness*, as the term is used in Scripture, as may easily be seen by looking over the texts that mention it, is intended the good that anyone possesses. Now the good that God possesses does most immediately consist in his joy and complacence that he has in himself. It does objectively, indeed, consist in the Father and the Son; but it doth most immediately consist in the complacence in these elements. Nevertheless the fullness of God consists in the holiness and happiness of the Deity.... Hence our communion with God the Father and God the Son consists in our partaking of the Holy Ghost, which is their Spirit: for to have communion or fellowship with another, is to partake with them of their good in their fullness, in union and society with them. Hence it is that we read of the saints having fellowship or communion with the Father and with the Son, but never of their having fellowship with the Holy Ghost, because the Holy Ghost is that common good or fullness which they partake of, in which their fellowship consists" (WJE 21:187-88).

[59]Tan, *Fullness Received and Returned*, 118.

[60]*Miscellanies* 96 (WJE 13:264-65).

participation (*methexis*), precisely because it is the relational communion that establishes God's goodness. When Edwards discusses the equality of the divine persons, he notes that they each have complementary dignities that mark them out as unique and honorable. The Father and the Son each have their particular honor and dignity, but the Spirit "has this particular dignity.... He is as it were the end of the other two, the good that they enjoy, the end of all procession."[61]

Koinōnia *in fullness as gift of grace.* Now I am ready to pivot toward the doctrine of grace. The "end of all procession," the relational communion between the Father and the Son (the Holy Spirit) is the *ad intra* antecedent to the divine fullness shared in grace.[62] "The Holy Spirit is the sum of all good. 'Tis the *fullness of God*. The holiness and happiness of the Godhead consists in it; and in the communion or partaking of it consists all the true loveliness and happiness of the creature."[63] Edwards's move from theology proper to a theology of grace is easy to miss but crucially important. The happiness of the Trinity consists in the communion or partaking of the Holy Spirit. The same is true of the creature. The term *divine fullness* grasps both. The relational *koinōnia* in the Holy Spirit between the Father and the Son is the gift given in grace.

This idea provides insight into the distinction between the divine essence and the divine fullness in Edwards's thought. Within the context of the Trinity *ad intra*, divine essence is, predictably, a question of quiddity and unity. It is based on the processions, and it refers to that which is God. The Father, the Son, and the Holy Spirit all partake of the divine essence, and this participation is a form of *methexis*. But alongside this question of what God is, there is the question of how God is good. Here Edwards moves from impersonal categories of ontology to personal categories of relationship. Goodness requires a communication of happiness, which is achieved through a relational communion or partaking or fellowship between the Father and the Son.[64] The thing that is shared between the Father and the Son is personal love, the Holy Spirit. It is this *koinōnia* in fullness, and not

---

[61]WJE 21:146.
[62]See Tan, *Fullness Received and Returned*, 15–17.
[63]WJE 21:188, emphasis added.
[64]*Communion, partaking,* and *fellowship* can all describe the same dynamic in Edwards.

a *methexis* in essence, that is given in grace. Just as the Son's sharing in divine love with the Father does not impinge directly on his being or quiddity or participation in essence, so the saints' sharing in divine love with Christ in grace does not impinge directly on their being *as creature*.

But I am getting ahead of myself. One must tread carefully when moving from theology proper (the Trinity *ad intra*) to the doctrine of grace. Christian theology moves from theology proper to soteriology by way of Christology. This is true in Edwards, as in the wider tradition.[65] Divine fullness is always mediated to the creature *through* Christ incarnate, and therefore one will not see how the creature may partake of the divine fullness *as creature* until one sees how the human Jesus partakes of it *as creature*.

I will not attempt a full rehearsal of Edwards's Christology, but I will point out how Edwards's Christology continues patterns already begun to be seen. Just as the Son *ad intra* can receive and return the Spirit (divine fullness) without this establishing his participation in divine essence, so the human Jesus can receive the Spirit "without measure" without thereby implying any change in his human essence. This will form the basis for how the divine fullness can be communicated to the saints in grace.

Essence and Fullness *Ad Extra*: Christology

The incarnation of the Son of God is the Christian church's explanation for how the infinite ontological chasm between the Creator and the creature may be bridged. This was so from the earliest days of the church: to be united to Christ, who is the fullness of deity, is to be filled with the fullness of God (Col 1:19; Eph 3:19). The battle for this soteriological import drove the early church to defend the full deity of the eternal Son against the Arian heresies in the fourth century. Yet even after the debates of Nicaea and Constantinople and their respective creeds, there still remained a major challenge. If Christ is *homoousion* with the Father, then in what way is he really human? The definition of Chalcedon established the framework of

---

[65]Traditional Puritan theology saw a close relationship between the communion between the persons of the Trinity *ad intra* and the saints' communion with God but still strongly affirmed that, properly speaking, the communion *ad intra* between the trinitarian persons was incommunicable (see Beeke and Jones, *Puritan Theology*, 90-91).

orthodoxy for the person of Christ.[66] According to the Chalcedonian fathers, Christ is:

> perfect Godhood and also perfect manhood ... consubstantial with the Father according to the Godhead, and consubstantial with us according to the manhood ... to be acknowledged one and the same, Christ, Son, Lord, Only-begotten, of two natures, inconfusedly, unchangeably, indivisibly, inseparably, the distinction of natures being by no means taken away by the union, but rather the propriety of nature being preserved, and concurring in one Person and one subsistence, not parted or divided into two persons, but one and the same Son.[67]

Yet this definition of orthodox boundaries was not simply about Christology or theology proper, as if either could be explored or explained apart from the saving purposes of God. Chalcedon was a statement of soteriology: How can the Creator and the creature unite without confusion? The answer to this—that in Christ the divine Son united to the human Jesus such that their natures did not fuse, but also such that Christ is one person, truly God and truly human—became a model for how the saint may *participate* in divine life. T. F. Torrance writes:

> Reformed theology interprets participation in the divine nature as the union and communion we are given to have with Christ in his human nature, as participation in his Incarnate Sonship, and therefore as sharing in him in the divine Life and Love. That is to say, it interprets "deification" precisely in the same way as Athanasius in the *Contra Arianos*. ... Yet the difficulty ... concerns the concept of *participation*. Is it *koinonia* or *methexis* that is meant: a participation governed by the Chalcedonian doctrine of the union of divine and human natures in Christ or by the Greek notion of participation in the eternal realities?[68]

---

[66]"The formulae of Chalcedon are regarded ... as the Spirit-given framework of all orthodox Christology. ... They are precisely framework and nothing more; indeed perhaps we might better think of them as scaffolding." Robert W. Jenson, "Christ in the Trinity: Communicatio Idiomatum," in *The Person of Christ*, ed. Stephen R. Holmes and Murray A. Rae (London: T&T Clark, 2005), 63. As framework and scaffolding, the formulae of Chalcedon do not close the christological conversation but rather facilitate its pursuit within a church-unifying set of boundaries.

[67]William Andrew Hammond, ed., *The Definitions of Faith and Canons of Discipline of the Six Oecumenical Councils with the Remaining Canons of the Code of the Universal Church, Translated with Notes Together with the Apostolical Canons* (New York: Sparks, 1844), 97.

[68]Torrance continues, "Even before Chalcedon Athanasius pointed out that if we interpret the union in Christ in terms of *methexis* we destroy the *homoousion*, and make impossible the faith

Torrance argues that Chalcedonian *koinōnia*, and not *methexis*, is the basis of divine participation in the Reformed tradition. Edwards exemplifies this approach. Like the Reformed tradition that shaped him, Edwards looked to the hypostatic union in Christ as the basis for how the sinner may become saint. Yet Edwards pressed further than most in his tradition by making the hypostatic union not only the basis but also the grammar for how Creator and creature may enter a *koinōnia* in divine fullness.[69] He developed his own explanation of Chalcedonian Christology, wherein the Holy Spirit binds together the divine Son and the human Jesus such that they become one person without mixing the two natures. Edwards frames this Christology as a *koinōnia* between the natures and in the Spirit. In this way he continues the themes introduced in the immanent Trinity, but now it is deployed between God and creature, and therefore between two different essences. Here the *koinōnia* of the immanent Trinity becomes exportable to the creature, and precisely for that reason it becomes the basis *and grammar* for grace. That is, the hypostatic union of Christ incarnate not only makes it possible for saints to partake of the divine fullness (basis), but it also sets the pattern for how that participation takes place (grammar).[70] There is a very real way in which, for Edwards, "the mystery of grace is the mystery of Christ."[71]

I will now explore this mystery further in order to discover how the human and divine natures may be joined in a *koinōnia* of divine fullness, without undermining the integrity of either nature and without fusing the essence of Creator and creature. With this in place, I will relate these findings

---

of the Church that in the communication of himself to us Christ communicates to us the very Life of God" (*Theology in Reconstruction*, 184).

[69] Caldwell points out that, in contrast with Turretin and most of the Reformed tradition, Edwards emphasized the commonalities between the hypostatic union and all other unions of Christianity (Caldwell, *Communion in the Spirit*, 86-87).

[70] That is, Christ is an effective mediator because of his union with the divine Logos, which is by the Spirit. See *Miscellanies* 487 (WJE 13:530-31). Bruce McCormack argues that Reformed Christology disallows theosis theories by rejecting the Lutheran approach to the communication of divine attributes to Christ's human nature. Kyle Strobel has shown how Edwards's approach to Christology and grace achieves theosis via a different path. Rather than basing it on a communication-of-attributes theory, Edwards achieves it through a *relational* sharing in divine attributes. See Strobel, "Jonathan Edwards's Reformed Doctrine," 392-98. See especially Strobel's comment on 396 that "on Edwards's understanding of *theosis*, the question is not: How is the human 'nature' divinized? but is instead, how is the human person ushered into the life of God?"

[71] Torrance, *Theology in Reconstruction*, 186.

to unpack how Edwards can distinguish essence and fullness in his doctrine of grace.

Edwards's Christology: Koinōnia *in divine fullness.* Any doctrine of Christ that seeks continuity with the Chalcedonian tradition must address at least two sets of questions. First, it must be able to account for how the divine Son is truly consubstantial, *homoousion*, with the Godhead, as well as how the human Jesus is truly consubstantial with humanity. That is, the first step is to give an account for how the incarnate Christ can truly have two natures. The second movement will be to show how these two relate to each other. Given the integrity of the two natures, how do they join together, establishing one person, without mixture or separation? These two sets of questions are convenient for consideration of Edwards's Christology, because he employs idealist conceptions of the *methexis* tradition in addressing the first, and a Spirit-focused account of *koinōnia* for the second. I will address them in turn.

Distinction of Christ's natures. Jonathan Edwards establishes essence—both divine and created—through this idealist conception of being. I have already rehearsed how this is true in the generation of the divine Son (or Logos). God's perfection in happiness, goodness, and omniscience implies that God will have a perfect mental image of himself. The act of God's self-reflection generates a perfect replication, or repetition of himself, which is nevertheless legitimately distinct. The distinction is not in essence, but in personhood and relatedness. That the divine Logos (Son) shares the same essence follows from the object of God's reflection. God is thinking about himself, and therefore the image is identical in essence with God. This explains why it is a type or species of *methexis*. If one takes *methexis* to be characterized by a sharing in substance, or perhaps as a sharing in eternal realities, then it certainly applies to this view of the Son's generation.[72] It hardly needs mentioning that this divine Son, the Logos, is the same person who, in the economy, assumes humanity in the incarnation.

But when one turns to consider the humanity of Jesus, one sees that Edwards establishes the natural, created humanity in a way that also follows his idealist conception of being. Similarly, this idealist conception of being

---

[72]Canlis, *Calvin's Ladder*, 13; Torrance, *Theology in Reconstruction*, 184-85.

can be categorized as an iteration of *methexis*-participation, albeit with important differences to the *methexis* that characterizes the Trinity *ad intra*. As noted in the previous chapter, Edwards grounds all created being in God. God is the "being of beings," and all created substance finally finds its reality in God alone.[73] This is by God's continuous action of creating the world. This world, in Edwards's view, does not have an autonomous ability to persist in time. Every moment of created reality is the result of God's immediate action of creating the world. And this activity of creating is the act of thinking: God's ideas are the basis of created reality, created substance, created essence.[74] In the previous chapter I dubbed this idealist approach to continuous creation, and the way it explains natural substance, "common participation." In this way, Edwards viewed all natural reality to be grounded as a participation in God.[75] The creation of Jesus' human nature follows this pattern.[76] The Trinity resolved to create and redeem humanity, and designated the Son as the one who would assume created reality. The created, human nature of Jesus shares the same ontological grounding as the rest of creation, depending on God's immediate action for its essence as human and created, and therefore grounded on common participation (*methexis*).[77]

---

[73] WJE 6:215, emphasis original.

[74] WJE 6:204. At this point I am using *substance* and *essence* as equivalent general terms referring to that which a thing is in itself.

[75] John J. Bombaro, *Jonathan Edwards's Vision of Reality: The Relationship of God to the World, Redemption History, and the Reprobate* (Eugene, OR: Pickwick, 2012), 77.

[76] Although there appears to be subtle differences. Commenting on *Miscellanies* 958, Tan writes, "All creation is *per filium* as 'God created the world by his Son,' with the exception of Christ's human nature, which was more a work of the Father. By this distinction, Edwards could say that all creation is 'more immediately' a manifestation of 'the glory of the Son of God,' while Christ's humanity is 'from the glory of the Father'" (*Fullness Received and Returned*, 57); see also WJE 20:234-39.

[77] One of the potentially troubling aspects of Edwards's doctrine of creation, as it relates to his Christology, is that his view of continuous creation implies that there are infinite incarnations because God is continually creating Jesus' human nature and body. See Oliver D. Crisp, "Jonathan Edwards, Idealism, and Christology," in *Idealism and Christian Theology*, ed. Joshua R. Farris and S. Mark Hamilton (New York: Bloomsbury, 2016), 161.

Oliver Crisp points out that Edwards's metaphysics, especially his commitments to immaterialism, metaphysical antirealism, occasionalism, and what Crisp calls "pure act panentheism," combine to create tensions in Edwards's Christology. Crisp argues that some of them provide resources to resolving problems in classical Christology, and some of them (especially pure act panentheism) create new and unresolved problems (Crisp, "Jonathan Edwards, Idealism, and Christology," 145-67).

The creation of Jesus' human nature has similarities to the Father's generation of the Son in eternity, but they are also very different. Both are explanations of being and how being, essence, substance obtains—or, to use Torrance's expressions, both are explanations of how being partakes of eternal realities.[78] However, one must also note the colossal differences between the creation of the human Jesus and the eternal generation of the Son. The most obvious difference is that in the latter, God is reflecting on himself, issuing forth in an identical subsistence of the divine essence. In the former, God thinks not of himself but of the creation, and therefore creation issues forth with an entirely distinct essence. Further, the essential *methexis* within the Trinity is nonvolitional, whereas God decides to create.[79] God is the actor, who continually gives creation its being, whereas creation is the recipient of being, contributing nothing back to God.[80] Edwards is not a pantheist, and it is important that one avoids reading Edwards's natural ontology in a pantheistic manner, especially when considering the humanity of Jesus. The reason is that pantheism would evacuate all significance from the incarnation. If natural substance is already indistinguishable from God, then either the incarnation is already implied in creation, or the entire Chalcedonian distinction between the divine and

---

[78] Torrance, *Theology in Reconstruction*, 184-85. S. Mark Hamilton shows that Edwards's immaterialism provides some resources for resolving the problem of interaction between the spiritual and material substances in Christology and elsewhere. In short, there is a problem regarding how immaterial spiritual realities can interact with material substances. Edwards, by grounding all substances in God's ideas, denies the reality of material, and therefore even Jesus' human body is immaterial, in that it is an idea in the mind of God, communicated to created minds. Whatever other possible difficulties this might suggest, it helps explain one way to avoid the interaction problem in Christology. See Hamilton, "Jonathan Edwards, Hypostasis, Impeccability, and Immaterialism," *Neue Zeitschrift für Systematische Theologie und Religionsphilosophie* 58, no. 1 (2016): 206-28; see also Crisp, "Jonathan Edwards, Idealism, and Christology."

[79] That is, God decides to create in a compatibilist sense. Oliver Crisp argues that Edwards's God must create, and must create this world, but does so without sacrificing freedom and aseity, due to Edwards's compatibilist framework (Crisp, *Jonathan Edwards on God and Creation*, 8).

Edwards writes concerning the nonvolitional essential *methexis* within the Trinity, "The divine essence is independent and underived in another respect, i.e. it is not dependent on any arbitrament or voluntary communication" (WJE 21:148). See also Tan, *Fullness Received and Returned*, 59-60.

[80] It is true that God is praised and glorified by creation, but that is not a true contribution to God. As Edwards says, "It don't make God the happier to be praised, but it is a becoming and condecent and worthy thing for infinite and supreme excellency to shine forth: 'tis not his happiness but his excellency so to do" (WJE 13:410). See Stephen Holmes's discussion of God's aseity, and how Edwards developed the relation between God and creation without surrendering God's aseity in *God of Grace*, 33-44, esp. 40.

human natures is simply incoherent.[81] For the present purposes, one must see that Edwards employs an idealist approach to *methexis*-participation to undergird and distinguish the divine and human natures of Christ. The divine essence and a created human essence are drawn together, without mixing them or separating them.

Union of Christ's natures. Yet how does this union occur? How is it that the Logos (divine Son) and the human Jesus are united without essential mingling—as required by Chalcedon? Here the questions turn from questions of being, and how an essence or substance may obtain, to questions of relation: How is it that distinct beings may be in union with each other? Edwards addresses this question by deploying his Spirit Christology. The divine and human natures in Christ are bound together in a communion—a *koinōnia*—in the Holy Spirit. Edwards rolls out this view in *Miscellanies* 487—his charter entry on the incarnation.[82] He writes, "All divine communion, or communion of the creatures with God or with one another in God, seems to be by the Holy Ghost. 'Tis by this that believers have communion with Christ, and I suppose 'tis by this that the man Christ Jesus has communion with the eternal Logos."[83] This is a provocative assertion: Edwards is assuming a high degree of continuity between the hypostatic union and the mystical union of believers with Christ, and he is employing communion categories and pneumatology to flesh out the continuity. But what is the nature of this communion between the Logos and the human Jesus? What does it mean that the communion between the human Jesus and the Logos is "by the Holy Spirit"? Edwards argues that there are two aspects to this communion. The first is a communion of love, and the second is a communion of personal faculties.

Christ: A communion of love. The Logos is bound to the human Jesus, in the first instance, through a communion of love. God the Father, argues

---

[81] Edwards clearly distinguishes divine essence from created essence, but it is instructive to remember that the difference between them is not that one is immaterial and one is, at least sometimes, material. Rather, Edwards is an immaterialist, and so even Jesus' human body is immaterial, strictly speaking. Crisp argues that this does not imply docetism, because Jesus' immaterial body is no different (in this regard) from all other human bodies, and that Edwards's view can uphold the Chalcedonian definition (Crisp, "Jonathan Edwards, Idealism, and Christology," 157-60).

[82] Caldwell, *Communion in the Spirit*, 85n35.

[83] *Miscellanies* 487 (WJE 13:529).

Edwards, loves the human Jesus with the same love he pours out on the eternal Logos. Indeed, the Father loves the human Jesus in precisely the same way and with the identical love that he pours out eternally toward the Son. This means that the human Jesus and the divine Logos *share* the same love of the Father. This love of the Father is nothing other than the Holy Spirit, proceeding as the Father's Spirit. This sharing in the Father's love, between the eternal Logos and the human Jesus, establishes a communion between them. Recall Edwards's definition of communion: "a common partaking of goods, either of excellency or happiness."[84] He states this definition in the context of commenting on the *koinōnia* of 2 Corinthians 13:14, and it clearly reflects his thinking in *Miscellanies* 487. The Logos and the human Jesus share in a common good, namely, the Father's love, which Edwards explicitly identifies as the Holy Spirit.[85] Significantly, Edwards has taken the communion between the Father and the Son *ad intra* and made it the basis for the communion between the Logos and the human Jesus *ad extra*. This continuity of thought will be crucial as I proceed.

Christ: A communion of personal faculties. But Edwards must press further: the union is not only a communion of love; it is also a communion of personal faculties. If Edwards stopped at stating that the Logos and the human Jesus commune by virtue of their shared reception of the Father's love, then we might imagine them to be two persons—one divine and one creaturely—who merely share relation to the Father. This might imply a deification of the human Jesus, but it would not necessitate a true incarnation. Edwards guards against this by stating that there is also a communion of personal faculties. As previously seen in the discussion of Edwards's trinitarianism, Edwards often described a person as a being with understanding and will. Edwards argues that the Logos and the human Jesus are one person precisely because the Spirit unites the Logos's understanding and will to the answerable faculties in the human Jesus.[86] This is "such that there is the same consciousness."[87] The Gospels describe Jesus as having

---

[84] WJE 21:129-30.
[85] WJE 13:529.
[86] For how the hypostatic union and Edwards's immaterialism can help preserve impeccability, see Hamilton, "Jonathan Edwards, Hypostasis, Impeccability."
[87] WJE 13:529. There is discussion among scholars as to how to class Edwards's Christology. Most see an Alexandrian line as primary, but with Antiochene themes present as well. For scholars

access to memory and information that would only be possible for the divine Logos (Edwards cites Jn 17:5), and this is because the Spirit unites the understanding of the Logos to the human understanding of Jesus. Something similar happens with the will. The Logos's will, as seen in the discussion of the Trinity, is the Spirit, poured out in filial love to the Father. This will of the Logos, or the Spirit of the Son, is given to the human Jesus "not by measure," such that the human Jesus loves the Father just as the eternal Son loves the Father.[88] This union of faculties—understanding and will—causes the divine Logos and the human Jesus to be one person.[89] The consciousness or personality of the human Jesus is indistinguishable from the consciousness of the Logos, except for the creaturely limitations implied in Jesus' humanity.[90]

Christ: A communion of the Father's and Son's mutual love. It is instructive to notice how these two aspects of the incarnational communion map to the procession of the Spirit in Edwards's Trinity *ad intra*. The incarnational communion is first the Father's love toward the human Jesus. This is an economic echo of the immanent procession of the Spirit from the Father to the Son. Second, the incarnational communion is the Spirit uniting the human Jesus' faculties to the eternal Logos. This means that the human Jesus knows and loves as the eternal Logos, and therefore this love is an economic echo of the immanent procession of the Spirit from the Son to the Father. Just as the Son receives and returns the Spirit *ad intra*, so the incarnate Christ receives and returns the Spirit *ad extra*. Edwards is applying the Spirit's procession *ad intra* between the Father and

---

arguing in an Alexandrian direction, see Pauw, *Supreme Harmony of All*, 143. Seng-Kong Tan argues that Cyrillian Alexandrian is primary, while Antiochene is the minor key (*Fullness Received and Returned*, 143, 158). Alternatively, Caldwell argues that Edwards shows Alexandrian flavor without undermining his basic Reformed orientation (*Communion in the Spirit*, 96-97).

[88] WJE 13:529.

[89] Oliver Crisp points out that there is a difficulty in Edwards's Christology with respect to the agency of the human Jesus. If God is the only causal agent in creation, then in what way does the human Jesus truly obtain as an agent? However, this is less a problem for Christology than for the rest of creation, because catholic orthodoxy requires a union of wills between the Logos and the human Jesus (Crisp, "Jonathan Edwards, Idealism, and Christology," 162-65).

[90] Following his Reformed heritage, Edwards believed that Christ, as to his human nature, is finite (*finitum non capax infiniti*), whereas the eternal Logos retains the divine infinity (*extra calvinisticum*). See John Calvin, *Institutes of the Christian Religion*, vol. 2, ed. John T. McNeill, Library of Christian Classics (Louisville, KY: Westminster John Knox, 1960), 1393, 1403. See also Caldwell, *Communion in the Spirit*, 94-95; Tan, *Fullness Received and Returned*, 196.

the Son to the Spirit's work of bonding the human Jesus to the Godhead. The *koinōnia* between the Father and the Son *ad intra* is repeated economically in the *koinōnia* between the Son and the human Jesus. Or, to put it differently, the fullness of the Trinity *ad intra* is the fullness of the incarnate Christ *ad extra*.[91]

This helps explain why there can be a personal union between the Logos and the human Jesus without implying a union of essence. Chalcedonian orthodoxy requires this, but it is instructive to see how Edwards's Spirit Christology achieves it. I observed earlier that the *koinōnia* in the Spirit between the Father and the Son (*ad intra*) was not the basis of their participation in the essence of the Godhead. Their communion in the Spirit does not impinge on their essential participation, because their essential participation in the Godhead is established prior (logically). In other words, when Edwards speaks of *koinōnia* or communion in the Spirit, it does not touch questions of quiddity or essence or substance of the two participating parties (the Father and the Son *ad intra*). This is also true in Edwards's Christology. The *koinōnia* or communion in the Spirit between the Logos and the human Jesus does not imply any change or impact to the two natures. The divine essence of the Logos and the human essence of Jesus are both intact, viable, and coherent, without any mixture or comingling. The incarnate Christ can share in the divine fullness, without measure, without in any way undermining the coherence of his human nature. Thus Edwards is consistent between his doctrine of the Trinity and his doctrine of Christ—in both cases the communion in the divine fullness does not impinge on quiddity, being, or essence. Rather, it effects relatedness and goodness. The divine fullness implies intimacy of relatedness, and distinction between the related parties. This is what makes the Trinity good—that is, happy. This is what makes Christ one person, and a partaker of the Trinity's good—that is, the Trinity's happiness.

Objection considered: *Are* methexis *and* koinōnia *overly distinct?* Here I must pause to consider an objection. In this rehearsal of Edwards's Christology, I have sought to emphasize the distinction between the creation of the humanity of Jesus and the *koinōnia* given between the divine and human

---

[91]"The Holy Ghost is the fullness and riches of the Godhead" (*Miscellanies* 487, in WJE 13:529).

natures of Christ. Jesus' humanity was given being in a manner continuous with how God gives being to all creation: through his continuous creative act. I have labeled this continuous creative activity of God as common participation and argued that it can be analyzed as a type of *methexis*, because it is a participation in God for (derived) being. But I have also argued that God granted the human Jesus a *koinōnia* with the divine Logos, in the Spirit. This participation differs from common participation, or creational *methexis*, because it does not bear directly on quiddity, or how the two natures obtain being. Rather, it is a communion between two distinct essences (divine and human). But does this account overplay the distinction? This is an important objection because if the distinction fails, then the *koinōnia* in the Spirit, which effects the union between the Logos and the human Jesus, could have implications for quiddity. If, for instance, the communion in the Spirit that unites the human Jesus and the divine Logos is found to contribute somehow to the establishment of Jesus' human nature or essence, then the distinction between the *methexis* that undergirds Jesus' quiddity and the *koinōnia* that undergirds relational union with the Logos would fall apart. Does the distinction hold?

In *Miscellanies* 709 Edwards is very clear that the Logos's assumption of humanity was achieved in *one act*. Therefore, it was not as though God first created the humanity of Jesus, and then subsequently or secondarily united the humanity to the Logos in the Spirit. If the union to the Logos were subsequent (especially if this subsequence were temporal), then it would suggest something like a Nestorian or adoptionist heresy: the person Jesus was, at least at some point, merely a man, who was later united to the Logos. Edwards avoids this: the creation of Jesus' humanity and the union to the Logos was achieved as *one act*. Did this *one act* function to fuse the creation of the humanity of Jesus with the union with the Logos? Edwards skillfully avoids this alternative as well. "This assuming [of the humanity of Jesus by the Logos] may be considered as one act," writes Edwards, "but having two effects, viz. the being of the manhood, and his union with the person of the Son."[92] Edwards proceeds carefully. He wants to affirm that the assumption of Jesus' humanity was one act so that he can affirm the Chalcedonian

---

[92] WJE 18:335.

doctrine that, from the very conception, Christ was the Logos incarnate.[93] Mary was not merely *Christotokos* but *Theotokos*.[94]

Yet at the same time, this one act carried two distinguishable effects. One was the establishment of Jesus' humanity. This was a creational gift of being. Given Edwards's idealist conception of creation, and that all being is a participation in the "being of beings," one may call this effect a *methexis* in being. But then there is the other effect. The other effect, parallel with the first, is the union between the human Jesus and the divine Logos. This is a communion or a joint participation in the Spirit. The two essences are distinct and unmixed, yet joined in personal union through the communication of the Spirit. This is properly a *koinōnia*: a relational union in differentiation. The distinction then, remains, and the objection serves to clarify that in the incarnation these two effects were achieved in one act, thereby conserving the unity of the person of Christ and Edwards's commitment to christological orthodoxy.

Summary Observations

It will be helpful to pause and summarize the key observations so far before proceeding further with the argument. The overall aim of this chapter is to clarify Edwards's distinction between participation in the essence of God and participation in the fullness of God. This is an important question for understanding Edwards, because the distinction comes at a crucial point in his overall account of saving grace. It is also important for contemporary conversations around theosis. The distinction sounds similar to the Eastern Palamite categories of essence and energies, and therefore one must ask whether critiques of the Palamite categories apply to Edwards's distinction. In answer to these questions, I have argued that Edwards's distinction between

---

[93]One might ask how Edwards can speak of the incarnation occurring in *one act* when his doctrine of continuous creation means that Jesus' human nature is being created every moment. However, Edwards's point is that *at the beginning of and throughout the series of acts* that constitute God's continuous creation of Jesus' human nature, God is uniting the Logos to the continuously created human Jesus. For a discussion of the tension around continuous creation and the incarnation, see Crisp, "Jonathan Edwards, Idealism, and Christology," 161.

[94]Not that Edwards uses the title *Theotokos* but that he affirms what Chalcedon intended by it. His tradition, however, did affirm it explicitly, though with cautions. See, e.g., Francis Turretin, *Institutes of Elenctic Theology*, trans. George Musgrave Giger, ed. James T. Dennison Jr. (Phillipsburg, NJ: P&R, 1994), 2:310; John Owen, *The Works of John Owen* (Edinburgh: Banner of Truth Trust, 1981), 3:166.

essence and fullness is clarified in view of two approaches to participation thinking. On the one hand, there is a participation tradition that focuses on a sharing or continuity of substance and can be termed *methexis*. Alongside this and complementary to it, there is a participation tradition that focuses on a sharing of relatedness, while maintaining differentiation. This can be termed *koinōnia*.

I have argued that both *koinōnia* and *methexis* are present in Jonathan Edwards's theology. He uses *methexis* notions, through this idealist conception of being, to explain the Son's participation in the divine essence and also the creation's participation in being. At the same time, and in complement to it, Edwards employs notions of *koinōnia* to describe how the Father and the Son are bound together in love, and how the Logos and the human Jesus are joined in personal union. The *koinōnia* between the Father and the Son does not impinge on their participation in the essence—that is established in another way. Similarly, the *koinōnia* between the Logos and the human Jesus does not compromise the integrity of either nature. Rather, the *koinōnia* in the Spirit is precisely how Edwards unites disparate essences in Christ into a personal union *while maintaining* their distinction. This is crucial background for grasping how Edwards can assert that the saint may partake of the divine fullness without implying any compromise of the Creator-creature distinction. The divine fullness is not the basis of essence in the Godhead, nor does it change the essence of the human Jesus. I will now turn to the doctrine of saving grace to show that, in a similar way, divine fullness does not compromise the integrity of the saints' created nature.

Essence and Fullness: Special Grace

I have surveyed Jonathan Edwards's doctrines of the Trinity and Christology as background for discovering how he can make the distinction between the divine essence and the divine fullness in his discussion of saving grace. I will now show how the *koinōnia* between the Logos and the human Jesus functions as a model for the *koinōnia* between the incarnate Christ and believers, and how this draws the saints to partake in the fullness, but not essence, of God.

Christology and grace: "A likeness of union." Edwards emphasized the continuity between the hypostatic union in Christ and the mystical union of believers with Christ.[95] In doing so, he synchronized his doctrines of grace and Christology, without making them identical. This is explicit in his *Miscellanies* 487. Edwards never produced a full treatise on Christology, but *Miscellanies* 487 functions as a sort of charter entry for his thinking.[96] The entry begins with an explicit assertion of the continuity between the union of the believers with Christ and the union between the Logos and the man Jesus Christ. "There is a likeness between the union of the Logos with the man Christ Jesus and the union of Christ with the church, though there be in the former great peculiarities." Edwards is clear on the nature of the likeness: the union between the Logos and the human Jesus is by the Spirit, and the same is true for the union between the church and Christ. In fact, the connection between Christology and grace is so strong for Edwards that he seems to nearly reverse-engineer his account of the hypostatic union *from* his knowledge of grace. "As the union of believers with Christ be by the indwelling of the Spirit of Christ in them, so it may be worthy to be considered, whether or no the union of the divine with the human nature of Christ ben't by the Spirit of the Logos dwelling in him after a peculiar manner and without measure."[97]

Notice that Edwards begins the quote above (which heads the entry as a whole) with the premise that the union of Christ with the believer is by the Spirit, and then proceeds to consider whether something of the same might be true of the hypostatic union. This is important because it suggests that Edwards's account of the hypostatic union is built, so to speak, on the foundation of his theology of grace: grace and Christology are not disparate spheres of theological inquiry, but rather logically and analogically related. They are logically related in that Edwards seemed to sharpen his christological reflections on logical deductions from his doctrine of grace. They are analogically related in that Christology serves as the model for grace, without there being an identity between them. That is, there is not a one-to-one correlation between the Logos's union with the human Jesus and the believer's union with Christ; important differences remain. Yet, there is sufficient continuity that they can mutually inform each other.

---

[95]This is in contrast to many in the Reformed tradition. See Caldwell, *Communion in the Spirit*, 86-87.
[96]Caldwell, *Communion in the Spirit*, 85.
[97]*Miscellanies* 487 (WJE 13:528).

The continuity between the two unions is, as in the quote above, that each is a union in the Spirit. Edwards fleshes this out in what is by now the familiar language of divine fullness. The fullness of Christ is the fullness given in grace.

> In Christ dwells all the fullness of the Godhead bodily, Colossians 2:9 (the Holy Ghost is the fullness and riches of the Godhead); where I suppose the apostle Paul means the same thing as the apostle John. . . . "For God giveth not the Spirit by measure unto him" [Jn 3:34]. And that fullness of the Godhead which the apostle Paul speaks of, I suppose to be the same with that fullness which John speaks of (John 1:16), as being that of which we receive; for God also dwells in us, as we are often told by the same apostle, and we are partakers of the divine nature (2 Peter 1:4); and believers also are filled with the fullness of God (Ephesians 3:19), though it don't dwell in them bodily. And the way that we partake is no otherwise than by partaking of the Spirit of God; God dwells in us by his Spirit.[98]

Edwards's exegesis leads him to conclude that the fullness of deity in Colossians is the fullness given by Jesus in the Gospel of John; and it is also the fullness that results from the indwelling of the Spirit in Ephesians. This, in turn, explains for Edwards the significance of partaking of the divine nature in 2 Peter 1:4. It is a sweeping exegetical reflection, and it collects Edwards's thought on how fullness relates to both Christology and grace. It is important for this study because it justifies relating what I have observed about christological fullness to Edwards's discussions of divine fullness in grace. Christological fullness and the fullness given in divine grace are closely analogous: both represent the Holy Spirit as a bond of love.[99] This explains why Edwards can so closely relate the intimacy between the Logos and the human Jesus with the intimacy between God and the saint in grace:

> We have all reason to conclude that no degree of intimacy will be too much for the manhood of Christ, seeing that the divine Logos has been pleased to

---

[98] *Miscellanies* 487 (WJE 13:529).
[99] This continuity between christological fullness and the fullness given in grace is apparent in Edwards's sermons. "Christ has all manner of grace. . . . There is not one grace in Christ, but that there is one to answer it in the saints. This seems to be what is meant by our receiving of his fullness and grace" ("Sermon 180. John 1:16"). This also explains why Edwards can echo (whether consciously or not) the classical "exchange formula" so often associated with theosis tradition: "[Christ] became in all things like unto us that his disciples should in many things become like unto him" (WJE 17:290).

assume him into his very person; and therefore, we may conclude that no degree of intimacy will be too great for others to be admitted to, of whom Christ is the head or chief, according to their capacity.... He hath done this to the head of manhood to show forth what honor and happiness God designs for manhood, for the end of God's assuming this particular manhood, was the honor and happiness of the rest; surely therefore, we may well argue the greatness of the happiness of the rest from it.[100]

Christology and grace: Yet "*after a peculiar manner and without measure.*" However, as mentioned above, the hypostatic union in Christ and the union between Christ and believers are not one-to-one equivalents. The divine fullness in Christ—the Holy Spirit as the bond between the Logos and the human Jesus—is "after a peculiar manner and without measure."[101] Thus, while Edwards emphasizes the continuity between the two unions, he does not equate them. A difference remains, and he frames the difference in at least three different manners.

First, he uses the image of the body. Christ is the head of the body, and just as the body depends on the head for life, and in this way the head might be viewed as the source of life, so the church depends directly on Christ as the source of its divine fullness.[102] Believers in the church share in the divine fullness "by derivation from and participation with the head.... And the way that [they] partake is no otherwise than by partaking of the Spirit of God; God dwells in [them] by his Spirit."[103] This head-and-body analogy and the idea of derivation undermine any notion that a human can participate in the divine fullness apart from Christ. Edwards is allergic to notions of human autonomy, and this image, apart from its obvious biblical grounding, serves to underscore the Christocentric nature of grace and therefore of divine participation.[104]

A second key way Edwards distinguishes Christ's participation in the divine fullness and the believers' participation in the divine fullness is by the

---

[100] *Miscellanies* 741 (WJE 18:368).
[101] WJE 13:528.
[102] Questions of biology notwithstanding.
[103] WJE 13:529.
[104] One laments, in passing, that some Edwards scholars have forgotten the Christocentric focus of Edwards's account of grace and divine participation. For instance, Oliver Crisp can provide an account of theosis in Edwards without needing to reference Christ at all (*Jonathan Edwards on God and Creation*, 172-73). Seng-Kong Tan has gone a long way to redressing this in *Fullness Received and Returned*, 97-280.

notion of measure. John 3:34, in the Authorized Version, speaks of God giving the Spirit to Christ "without measure."[105] If Christ receives the Spirit (the divine fullness) without measure, then he gives the same to the saints "according to our capacities . . . [and] . . . in their measure."[106] This measure language is important for at least three reasons. First, it follows on from the derivation theme above and emphasizes creaturely dependence. Christ, as the head, receives the divine fullness without measure, and gives it to the members according to their measure. Thus there is no space for creaturely autonomy. Second, the notion of measure serves to reinforce that grace as divine fullness is received *as a creature*.[107] The Reformed tradition's principle of *finitum non capax infiniti*—the finite cannot contain the infinite—was a way of protecting authentic creatureliness. Edwards here maintains this tradition. Interestingly, Jesus himself has the divine fullness "without measure," but not "infinitely."[108] This is a subtle difference but significant. Jesus, as a creature, still has a particular capacity, albeit greatly enlarged by virtue of his union with the Logos.[109] The believers' capacity is immeasurably less than Jesus' capacity, and they receive the divine fullness according to their creaturely capacity. Thus, the finitude of the creature is key to Edwards's aim of maintaining the Creator-creature distinction.[110] Finally, and perhaps ironically, the measure and capacity language allows Edwards to posit not

---

[105] There is ambiguity as to whether *didōsin* takes "he whom God has sent" or "God" as its subject. Some modern translations therefore phrase it as Christ who gives the Spirit without measure, rather than Christ receiving the Spirit without measure. However, Edwards clearly follows the Authorized Version. See Max Zerwick and Mary Grosvenor, *A Grammatical Analysis of the Greek New Testament*, 5th ed. (Rome: Editrice Pontificio Istituto Biblico, 1996), 294.

[106] Edwards is referring to the believers' capacity and measure—the change in pronouns notwithstanding (WJE 19:593).

[107] Strobel emphasizes the finitude of creaturely participation in the divine life and christological mediation as key elements of how Edwards protects the Creator-creature distinction ("Jonathan Edwards's Reformed Doctrine," 395).

[108] Edwards follows Reformed tradition at this point, and in particular, he follows Turretin. Turretin uses the same passage (Jn 3:32) as the basis for presenting Jesus as the greatest creature, recipient of the greatest possible gifting, but nevertheless a creature still. See Stephen R. Holmes, "Reformed Varieties of the Communicatio Idiomatum," in *Person of Christ* (New York: T&T Clark, 2005), 77.

[109] See Tan, *Fullness Received and Returned*, 196. See also *Miscellanies* 81: "[The] capacity of the man Jesus is so large, by reason of the personal union with the divine nature" (WJE 13:248).

[110] Although Tan argues that Edwards stretched the Reformed *finitum non capax infiniti* toward the Lutheran *finitum capax infiniti non per se sed per infinitum*. True as this may be, it does not undermine that in speaking of believers receiving the divine fullness "according to our capacity," Edwards is maintaining the Reformed principle. See Tan, *Fullness Received and Returned*, 196.

only the infinite distance between the Creator and the creature, but also the perpetual progress of the creature toward the Creator. That is, by stating that Christ has the divine fullness "without measure" and that the believers receive it "according to their capacity," Edwards can imagine the believers ever increasing in their capacity to receive the divine fullness, and therefore perpetually grow closer in intimacy with God in an asymptotic union.[111]

A third difference between Christ's personal union with the Logos and believers' union with Christ is implied in *Miscellanies* 487. A large part of the entry is taken up with arguing that there is a union of faculties between the Logos and the human Jesus. It is therefore implied in the entry that this is unique to the hypostatic union. Jesus is united to the Logos such that the Logos is the personal consciousness of the human Jesus. This, clearly, is not the case between believers and Christ. It is true that Edwards is able to speak of a communication of faculties of understanding and will to believers.[112] Yet even there, it is more a synchronization of faculties, not a union of consciousness.

Christology and grace: "Admitted into the society of the blessed Trinity." Here I arrive at a critical juncture. As I have made clear, the divine fullness that characterizes Christ's hypostatic union is given, in measure and according to creaturely capacities, to believers in grace. However, not only is the divine fullness of grace *christological fullness*; it is also *trinitarian fullness*. That is, the divine fullness communicated in grace is a participation in the trinitarian union between the Father and the Son.

> So we being members of the Son, are partakers in our measure, of the Father's love to the Son, and complacence in him. . . . So we shall, according to our capacities, be partakers of the Son's enjoyment of God, and have his joy fulfilled in ourselves (John 17:13). And by this means, we shall come to an immensely higher, more intimate, and full enjoyment of God, than otherwise could have been. For there is doubtless an infinite intimacy between the Father and the Son; which is expressed by his being in the bosom of the Father. And saints being in him, shall, in their measure and manner, partake with him in it, and of the blessedness of it.[113]

---

[111] See WJE 8:534.
[112] See WJE 13:495; 8:441.
[113] WJE 19:593.

What is striking in this passage is the way believers' participation so closely follows the inner-trinitarian dynamic. The graced saint partakes of the *mutuality* of love between the Father and the Son. First, the believer is a partaker "in our measure, of the *Father's love to the Son*" (emphasis added). Just as the Son *ad intra* receives the Father's love, so believers partake of this *ad extra*, in their union with Christ. Second, Edwards asserts the return of this love: the believer becomes a partaker "of the Son's enjoyment of God." Just as the Son returns the love to the Father, *ad intra*, so believers return the same love through their union with Christ, *ad extra*. To be a member of the Son is to join in the trinitarian act of love, the *koinōnia* in the Spirit. Edwards concludes the sermon "The Excellency of Christ" with these momentous words: "This was the design of Christ, to bring it to pass, that he, and his Father, and his people, might all be united in one . . . that the church should be as it were admitted into the society of the blessed Trinity."[114]

Edwards could hardly be more specific. The gift of grace is a gift of admission to the society of the Trinity. The believer is caught up in Christ and allowed to partake of the *koinōnia* of the Trinity: the mutual love between the Father and the Son, in the Spirit. This chapter has followed the theme of divine fullness from its roots in the Trinity *ad intra*, through its economic expression in the doctrine of Christ, and now to the soteriological doctrine of grace. A key aim throughout has been to show that Edwards views divine fullness to be fundamentally the same in each case: it is the *koinōnia* of the Spirit, partaken in different ways in each situation. The Father and the Son *ad intra* partake infinitely. In the economy, Christ incarnate partakes "without measure." The believers, in turn, partake "according to their capacity." However, the *koinōnia* in the divine fullness remains constant in both content and in character throughout. The content is the same because it is the same Spirit who acts as love between two parties. The character is constant because it is, in each case, a *koinōnia*, a sharing in intimacy between two parties *who remain distinct*. Thomas Torrance captures a vision that fits very nicely with Edwards's when he states:

> The participation of the Church . . . in Christ must be construed in terms of *koinonia* governed by the Chalcedonian doctrine of the union of two natures

---

[114]WJE 19:594.

in Christ. This is a participation in which the human nature of the participant is not deified but reaffirmed and recreated in its essence as human nature, yet one in which the participant is really united to the Incarnate Son of God partaking in him in his own appropriate mode of the oneness of the Son and the Father . . . , through the Holy Spirit. . . . The mystery of grace is the mystery of Christ.[115]

With this in place, I return to the questions raised in the introduction before drawing the chapter to a conclusion.

Essence and Fullness: Evaluating the Distinction

I am now in a position to return to the central questions that launched the chapter. Soteriologies that place participation in the divine nature as a central component will necessarily have to deal with the question of how to distinguish between Creator and creature. Contemporary theosis scholarship has been dominated by the Palamite distinction between essence and energies. This distinction, and this approach to maintaining the Creator-creature distinction, has come under fire from Reformed circles. In particular, Bruce McCormack and Myk Habets have explicitly rejected this distinction and set forward their own preferred path for Reformed theology in this matter. This chapter is not an evaluation of their respective critiques of the Palamite distinction, nor is it an evaluation of their recommendations. Rather, their critiques of the East's distinction create pressure on Jonathan Edwards's distinction between essence and fullness. This is partly because there is such a strong verbal similarity between essence and energies (Palamite distinction) and essence and fullness (Edwards's distinction). It is also because the two distinctions pursue a similar aim: to facilitate real intimacy and participation between God and creature, without surrendering the fundamental Creator-creature distinction. Given these similarities, it is natural to raise the question: Is Edwards's essence-fullness distinction vulnerable to the critiques leveled by McCormack and Habets toward the Palamite distinction?

In order to address this question, I articulated two more specific questions, inspired by McCormack's and Habets's critiques but arranged to fit

---

[115]Torrance, *Theology in Reconstruction*, 185-86.

more specifically to Edwards's distinction. The first question is inspired by McCormack's critique that the essence-energies distinction in Palamism lacks clarity.[116] Therefore I ask, Is there a coherent difference between the divine essence and the divine fullness in Edwards's thought? If so, what is it? The second question is inspired by Habets's critique that the essence-energies distinction in Palamism divides God's being from God's act, such that the Son and the Spirit become intermediaries rather than God himself.[117] Therefore I ask, Does Edwards's distinction drive a wedge between God's immanent and economic life, or between God's being and act? I will look at these questions in turn and relate the findings of the chapter as a whole to each.

Is there a coherent difference between the divine essence and the divine fullness in Edwards's thought? If so, what is it? It is fair to say that Edwards's distinction between God's essence and God's fullness can provoke the reader to ask whether this is a distinction without a difference. Is Edwards denying essential union with God, while in the next moment affirming it, but with different terms? In other words, does this distinction resolve to a verbal trick?

This chapter finds that Edwards's distinction is not a verbal trick, that there is a real difference between the divine essence and divine fullness. Further, the difference between the divine essence and divine fullness obtains with a striking consistency throughout his theology. The distinction is rooted in his doctrine of the Trinity, maintained in his doctrine of Christ, and applied to the saint in his theology of special grace.

In his doctrine of the Trinity, Edwards follows his tradition in describing the three persons who all share in one divine essence, by virtue of their relations. The Father partakes of the divine essence as the fountain of deity, the Son as the deity's understanding, and the Spirit as the will of the deity. However, when Edwards speaks of the goodness and happiness of the Trinity, he introduces a distinguishable dynamic of divine fullness. The Father and the Son partake of this divine fullness (the Holy Spirit, divine love, happiness, and holiness), without this participation establishing or impinging

---

[116]See McCormack, "Union with Christ," 505-6.
[117]Habets, "'Reformed Theosis?' A Response," 493-94. See also McCormack's concern that the essence-energies distinction makes the immanent and economic trinities differ in content ("Participation in God, Yes," 373-74).

on their participation in essence. Essence and fullness are distinguishable in God *ad intra*.

This theme carries on and becomes clearer in Edwards's Christology. Following the Chalcedonian tradition, Edwards distinguishes the uncreated and created natures in Christ, while uniting them in a personal union. The Son's divine essence and Jesus' human essence are never mixed or made consubstantial; their integrity remains. Yet, at the same time, the two essences are united in a personal union. This union is a communion in divine fullness: the Spirit. The Logos and the human Jesus are able to share the divine fullness without the divine fullness establishing or impinging on either essence. This echoes the communion in divine fullness between the Father and the Son. However, in the incarnation, there is something new and vitally important for the Creator-creature relation: the divine fullness may be shared between two parties whose essences differ. Essence and fullness differ in Christ incarnate.

This theme carries on, once again, in the doctrine of special grace. God unites the saint to Christ by granting the divine fullness (the Spirit) to the saint according to the saint's creaturely capacity to receive it and return it. This is a relational union of love, but not one in which the essence of the saint is compromised, nor one in which the divine essence is communicated. Just as the Father and the Son are united by the Spirit without this establishing or impinging on their participation in the divine essence, and just as the Logos and the human Jesus share the divine fullness without this establishing or impinging on their differentiated essences, so Christ and the saint share the divine fullness without this establishing or impinging on their essences. Essence and fullness differ in special grace.

All of this argues that the divine essence and the divine fullness differ in both content and character. They differ in content in that, whereas essence is a category of being, fullness is a category of relationality. Essence designates what a thing is, and fullness designates a particular way a person shares in love with another person. Thus, when Edwards speaks of the saints partaking of the divine fullness, but not of the divine essence, he means that the saint is united in love to Christ, in the Spirit, thus sharing in the society of the Trinity, but without any abrogation to the saint's created being.

Not only do they differ in content, but Edwards's account of essence and fullness differ in their respective character of participation. To partake of an essence is a sort of participation distinguishable from partaking of the divine fullness. To partake of an essence (whether divine or created) is a *methexis* in God for being, when *methexis* is governed by shared substantiality. To partake of the divine fullness requires two distinct parties, joined in a relational *koinōnia* of love. Here, *koinōnia* is taken to refer to shared relational intimacy with differentiation. Essence and fullness differ, then, in that one rests on *methexis*-participation, and therefore is always primarily concerned with quiddity, whereas the other rests on *koinōnia*-participation, and therefore is always primarily concerned with relationality.

I therefore answer the question above by stating, yes, there is a coherent difference between essence and fullness in Edwards's thought: they differ both in content and in character of participation, and this difference is consistent through Edwards's doctrines of the Trinity, Christology, and special grace. What then of the second question?

Does this distinction drive a wedge between God's immanent and economic life, or between God's being and act? One of Myk Habets's critiques of the Palamite essence-energies distinction is that it implies a wedge between God's being and God's act. If God's essence is entirely transcendent and inaccessible for the creature, and God is accessible only through God's energies, then it would appear that God's energies (his acts toward creation) and God's essence differ in some way.[118] Habets argues that the *homoousion* of the Nicaean Creed shatters such a strong differentiation. *Homoousion* implies that God revealed his being—his *ousia*—in his economic action in Christ. Thus, to rend asunder essence and energies—being and act—is to undermine the reality of Christ's full divinity, remaking him into an intermediary between God and creation, rather than God himself. The same line of thought goes for the Spirit as well. This is a formidable critique, and one that would significantly undermine any classical Christian theology.[119]

Based on all that has gone before in this chapter, I argue that Edwards's distinction does not fall victim to Habets's critique for two reasons: First,

---

[118]Or at least God's immanent and economic modalities differ in some respect. See Habets, "'Reformed Theosis?' A Response," 494; McCormack, "Participation in God, Yes," 373-74.

[119]I am setting aside the question of whether Habets has adequately represented the Eastern view.

Edwards maintains a strong continuity between the divine fullness *ad intra* and the divine fullness *ad extra*. That is, the economic activity of God in grace is patterned on the immanent activity of God in the Trinity. Second, Edwards maintains the union of God's being and act, precisely because the divine fullness is a divine person (the Holy Spirit), who is mediated by a divine person (the incarnate Christ). I will take these in turn.

One of the striking elements of the Northampton pastor's theology is the way he replicates theology proper in his soteriology. The relational dynamic that describes the inner-trinitarian relations is, in a modified way, the same dynamic that describes the work of grace in the heart of the saint. This is so much so that Kyle Strobel calls Edwards's doctrine of the Trinity "religious affection in pure act."[120] The fullness of grace is the economic answer to the fullness of the Trinity *ad intra*: it is a partaking with the Father and the Son in their good, which is the Holy Spirit.[121] Similarly, the fullness of grace is the fullness of Christ, which is also the Holy Spirit.[122] It is true that there is a modification at each point, but fundamentally the point remains that Edwards means the same thing when speaking of divine fullness *ad intra* and *ad extra*. Speaking of grace in terms of the twofold work of illumination and regeneration, he states:

> This twofold way of the Deity's flowing forth *ad extra* answers to the twofold way of the Deity's proceeding *ad intra*, in the proceeding and generation of the Son and the proceeding and breathing forth of the Holy Spirit; and indeed is only a kind of second proceeding of the same persons, their going forth *ad extra*, as before they proceeded *ad intra*.[123]

Similarly, Edwards writes:

> God is glorified within himself these two ways: (1) by appearing or being manifested to himself in his own perfect idea, or, in his Son, who is the brightness of his glory; (2) by enjoying and delighting in himself, by flowing forth in infinite love and delight towards himself, or, in his Holy Spirit. So

---

[120] Strobel, *Jonathan Edwards's Theology: A Reinterpretation*, 70.
[121] "Hence our communion with God the Father and God the Son consists in our partaking of the Holy Ghost, which is their Spirit: for to have communion or fellowship with another, is to partake with them of their good in their fullness, in union and society with them" (WJE 21:188).
[122] WJE 21:190.
[123] *Miscellanies* 1082 (WJE 20:466).

> God glorifies himself towards the creatures also two ways: (1) by appearing to them, being manifested to their understandings; (2) in communicating himself to their hearts, and in their rejoicing and delighting in, and enjoying the manifestations which he makes of himself.[124]

Edwards unites God's immanent and economic life in a very close relation, without precisely equating the two. The theological distinction remains between the two, but they are so closely related that they can mutually inform each other.[125] Thus, Edwards's employment of divine fullness does not imply any disjoining of God's immanent and economic life.

Further, Edwards's theology of grace maintains union between God's act and being. It is crucial to see that in Edwards's doctrine of grace, God's act of communicating divine fullness is God's gift of himself. As seen throughout this chapter, divine fullness is the Holy Spirit. The fullness between the Father and the Son is the Holy Spirit, the fullness uniting Christ's two natures is the Holy Spirit, and the fullness communicated in grace to the saint is the Holy Spirit. This same Holy Spirit partakes of the divine *essence*, just as do the Father and the Son. The basis for Edwards's argument for the full deity of the Spirit is his presupposition that God's act and God's being are one. Speaking of the procession of the Spirit, Edwards states:

> This is the eternal and most perfect and essential act of the divine nature, wherein the Godhead acts to an infinite degree and in the most perfect manner possible. The Deity becomes all act; the divine essence itself flows out and is as it were breathed forth in love and joy. So that the Godhead therein stands forth in yet another manner of subsistence, and there proceeds the third person in the Trinity, the Holy Spirit, viz. the Deity in act: for there is no other act but the act of the will.[126]

---

[124]*Miscellanies* 448 (WJE 13:495).

[125]By this I mean that while Edwards's theology of grace proceeds logically from God's immanent life to God's economic life, Edwards's theology of grace grows exegetically from God's economic actions, revealed in Scripture, to a theological reconstruction of God's immanent life. A simple perusal of *Treatise on Grace* or *Discourse on the Trinity* will show that Edwards reasons from exegesis on Scripture dealing with soteriology and draws out implications for his theology of God's immanent life. These speculative implications on God's immanent life then form the basis for his further theorizing on grace. Thus, the immanent and economic doctrines of God are mutually informative in Edwards's theology.

[126]WJE 21:121.

The Spirit partakes of the essence of God on the basis of the pure act tradition, and therefore Edwards unites God's being and God's act. Yet this has significant implications for Edwards's doctrine of grace. For grace is this same act of God poured out toward the creature. Therefore, and one must say this strongly, when God gives grace, God is giving himself, *in an essential person of the Trinity*. Just as traditional theology always claimed Christ as *homoousion* with the Father, so Edwards's doctrine of the Holy Spirit requires one to say that the divine fullness, given in grace, is *homoousion* with the Father and the Son, because it is the Holy Spirit.

The critical reader will see a possible inconsistency, however. If the Holy Spirit is the divine essence, poured out in love, and if the Holy Spirit is the divine fullness given in grace, then how can Edwards still claim that the divine fullness is communicated without implying a communication of divine essence? This objection is addressed in ground already covered. Recall that in the immanent Trinity, the Father and the Son participate in the divine fullness, which itself partakes of the divine essence, but without this establishing or impinging on their own participation in the divine essence. Similarly, the Logos and the human Jesus share the divine fullness, which itself partakes of the divine essence, but without this establishing or impinging on either of the essences involved in the hypostatic union. Again, the saint and Christ share the divine fullness in grace, but once again without this establishing or impinging on the essences involved in the mystical union. That is, from the outset, two parties can share the divine fullness without that participation implying any communication of the divine essence. There is another way to describe this based on the distinction between *methexis* and *koinōnia*. The communication of the divine fullness (the Holy Spirit) is a *koinōnia*, a relational sharing between distinct parties. It is not, however, a *methexis*: the communication of the divine fullness is not a fusing, mixing, or sharing in being.[127]

---

[127] A complementary argument to the one above grows out of Kyle Strobel's work on the communicable natures in the Trinity. As we have seen, God's tri-personhood is achieved through a perichoretic sharing among the Father, Son, and Holy Spirit. That is, the Father, the Son, and the Holy Spirit all share the same understanding (the Son) and the same will (the Spirit) perichoretically. Thus, the natures of understanding and will are sharable (communicable) within the Trinity. Strobel points out that a similar sharing happens within the economy when these natures are shared with the saint. In this case, the divine essence is not communicated to the saint by virtue of the finitude and christological mediation that is involved. Finitude and

Thus, while it is true that the divine essence is incommunicable, it is not precisely true to say that the divine essence is *inaccessible*. The divine essence is given in the gift of Christ, but not communicated to the creature. The divine essence is also given in the gift of special grace (divine fullness, the Holy Spirit), but it is not communicated to the saint. What is communicated is a sharing in the divine act of love, binding distinct parties together.

All of this means that for Jonathan Edwards, grace is genuinely *uncreated*, and it is not a sort of semidivine intermediary. Rather, grace is God's gift of himself. McCormack argues that the Palamite essence-energies distinction can only make sense if the energies are taken for a sort of created grace. Similarly, Habets concludes that the energies must be an intermediary sort of reality. Regardless of whether this adequately reflects Palamism, neither conclusion fits Edwards. Divine fullness is *homoousion* with the Father and the Son, but the gift of divine fullness is a relational gift of sharing between beings who retain their essential and ontological integrity. This is the achievement of Edwards's distinction between the divine essence, not communicated in grace, and the divine fullness, which is communicated. This is the way in which Edwards is able to achieve such intimacy between God and creature that he can rightly call grace a divine participation, but without collapsing the ontological chasm between them.

Conclusion

Overall this study contends that Jonathan Edwards represents a Reformed resource for Western Protestant reflection on the topic of divine participation. Like Eastern Palamism, Edwards distinguished that which is communicable in God from that which is incommunicable; otherwise the very notion of participation in the divine nature fails. It will either collapse into a sort of pantheism, by fusing Creator or creature, or else it will fail to achieve sufficient intimacy between Creator and creature to warrant the term *divine participation*. Edwards and the East share this common goal. Not only so, but their distinctions show at least superficial similarity. Palamism distinguishes God's essence from God's energies, and Edwards

---

christological mediation serve to strain out the divine essence. Thus, God communicates his understanding and will without communicating his essence. See Strobel, "Jonathan Edwards's Reformed Doctrine."

distinguishes the participation in divine essence from the participation in divine fullness. This chapter has not aimed at showing the extent of continuity or discontinuity between Palamism and Edwards on these distinctions. More modestly, this chapter took Reformed critiques of Palamism and asked whether Edwards's distinction could stand against them. This narrowing of scope is due to the contention mentioned above: Edwards is a resource for *Reformed* appropriation of divine participation tradition. Therefore, as a Reformed resource, his thought must stand under the light of Reformed critique. One finds that, regardless of the degree of continuity between Edwards and the East, and regardless of whether the Reformed critiques of the East are entirely fair, they do not undermine Edwards's distinction. The Northampton pastor's distinction between essence and fullness is consistent throughout his doctrines of the Trinity, Christology, and grace. They correspond to different traditions of participation, and they relate to differing fields of discourse: one to questions of quiddity and the other to questions of relationality. Therefore, Edwards establishes profound intimacy between Creator and creature, without fusing them, such that God gives himself in grace without abrogating the created essence of the saint.

4

Grace and Creation

THE PREVIOUS TWO CHAPTERS have focused on drawing out how Jonathan Edwards distinguishes special grace from both created nature and the divine essence. However, it is not enough to simply *distinguish* grace from created nature and the divine essence. It is also necessary to show how grace and created nature *relate* to each other more positively.[1] Christianity is not only concerned with how God and created nature differ, but also how they relate. Indeed, one might argue that the first concern (distinction) is only a stage on the road to the second (relation). Christianity's most distinctive doctrine is not the otherness of God; other religions agree at that point.[2] Christianity's bold claim is that this transcendent God "was made man."[3] Not only does historic Christianity posit the incarnation, but it also proclaims the gift of the Holy Spirit. The whole Christian doctrine of God—the Trinity—is framed in terms of a transcendent God who nevertheless achieves a Creator-creature *relation*. This Creator-creature *relation* is the particular interest of the divine-participation tradition.

This brings up a question I anticipated in chapter two: Does Edwards's doctrine of nature and grace amount to a sort of extrinicism? Extrinicism

---

[1] Chapter three concerned both the distinction and the relation between divine fullness and the divine essence. What remains is to show the positive relation between divine fullness (grace) and created nature.

[2] E.g., Judaism and Islam.

[3] Consider how Athanasius posited both a strong ontological gulf between Creator and creature, and also the incarnation as the bridge for that gulf. See Cheslyn Jones, Geoffrey Wainwright, and Edward Yarnold, SJ, eds., *The Study of Spirituality* (London: SPCK, 1986), 161-62.

is the idea that grace is so distinct, so separate, from nature that nature can be viewed *without respect* to grace. The aim in this sort of thinking is admirable: extrinicists desire to guard the gratuity of grace. Grace is really *outside* nature, and there is no intrinsic link between the two. Henri de Lubac famously resisted this line of thought in Roman Catholic circles, and Radical Orthodoxy more recently took up the concern. Simon Oliver speaks of the "blending of grace and nature."[4] The concern to press against extrinicism is also admirable. If it is important to protect gratuity of grace, it is also important to demonstrate that created nature is *for* a supernatural end in grace. If nature gains too much autonomy, then it can devolve to support a sort of modern account of secularity. God is not necessarily relevant except in respect to salvation narrowly conceived. In chapter two I argued that Edwards shares the extrinicists' concern for gratuity but avoids any hint of natural autonomy by virtue of his vision of common participation. All things partake of God to gain being, and therefore God is everywhere relevant for all aspects of created nature. Yet there is now more to say. Not only does created nature depend on God for its being, but God has designed all being *for* participation in divine fullness. Divine fullness is not the same as being (Creator-creature *distinction*), but being finds its fulfillment in divine fullness (Creator-creature *relation*).

This Creator-creature *relation* is a crucial interest in Edwards's doctrine of grace. Throughout Edwards's reflections on grace, he distinguishes it from (especially) created nature only in order to emphasize the intimacy between them.[5] In fact Edwards makes a direct link between the intimacy between Creator and creature achieved in the incarnation, and the intimacy intended for the saints:

> We have all reason to conclude that no degree of intimacy will be too much for the manhood of Christ, seeing that the divine Logos has been pleased to

---

[4] Simon Oliver, "Henri De Lubac and Radical Orthodoxy," in *T&T Clark Companion to Henri de Lubac*, ed. Jordon Hillebert (New York: Bloomsbury, 2017), 399-400.

[5] See, e.g., Edwards's three chapters in *Treatise on Grace*. Chapter one distinguishes common grace from special grace, and this is one way of supporting a strong distinction between Creator and creature. God's activity in and through the natural world (common grace) is distinct from God's self-gift in special grace. Yet chapters two and three both argue toward a strong view of participation in divine fullness, which is itself a participation in the Holy Spirit. Creator and creature are distinguished, only in order to show their relation (WJE 21:153-97).

assume him into his very person; and therefore, we may conclude that no degree of intimacy will be too great for others to be admitted to, of whom Christ is the head or chief, according to their capacity: . . . for the end of God's assuming this particular manhood, was the honor and happiness of the rest.[6]

This concern for the positive relation between Creator and creature in grace goes right back to Edwards's earliest theological reflections. His first *Miscellanies* entry muses on the nature of true holiness (a synonym for true grace) and states, "Holiness is a most beautiful and lovely thing. . . . Tis almost too high a beauty for any creatures to be adorned with; it makes the soul a little, sweet and delightful image of the blessed Jehovah."[7] Edwards is captivated not so much with the distinction, important as that is, but with the *relation* between grace and created nature. The task of this chapter will be to explore this positive relationship and show how Edwards achieves the intimacy he envisions.

I will address this relationship by returning to the distinction between common participation and special participation used in the previous two chapters. I will argue that throughout Jonathan Edwards's thought, common participation exists or is given for the purpose of special participation. Put differently, in Jonathan Edwards's thought, being is for *koinōnia*.[8] I will begin by showing that this teleology is rooted in Edwards's trinitarianism. Edwards states that the Holy Spirit is "the end of all processions." The Trinity's own end and teleology is fulfilled in the *koinōnia* between the Father and the Son in the Holy Spirit. Put in terms from chapter three, the Son's *methexis* in the Father for being and essence finds its end in the *koinōnia*

---

[6] *Miscellanies* 741 (WJE 18:368).
[7] *Miscellanies* a. (WJE 13:163).
[8] The reader may ask how this assertion, that being is for *koinōnia*, relates to hell. That is, if all being exists for fulfillment achieved in *koinōnia* with God, then in what way do the damned realize this end? Space does not allow an extensive answer. However, recall that all being is established by *methexis* in God for being. Further, the saints and angels receive *koinōnia* in divine fullness and return love to God in exultant joy and delight. The damned participate in God for being (common participation), but they do not partake of divine fullness to any degree. How do they contribute to creation's end of *koinōnia* in God? The saints see God's glory and attributes in the punishment of the damned, and this contributes to the saints' joy in God. In this the damned fulfill a role similar to inanimate objects in creation. The saints see God's glory depicted in the world around them, in the history of redemption, and also in the punishment of the damned, and all this contributes to their glorification of God. The saints see God's glory and rejoice in it due to their participation in divine fullness. See *Miscellanies* 279 (WJE 13:379). See also *Miscellanies* 288 (WJE 13:381). For a sermon on how the damned fulfill their purpose in creation, see WJE 46, sermon 210, on Prov 16:4. For the saints' joy in God's glory through viewing inanimate creation, see WJE 17:323.

between the Father and the Son. This teleology in the doctrine of God sets the pattern for his teleology in creation. I will exposit Edwards's reflections on the end of creation to show that, once again, participation in creational being (common participation) is teleologically oriented toward participation in divine fullness (special participation). That is, whereas chapter two showed Edwards distinguish created nature from divine grace, now it is clear that this distinction is ultimately for the purpose of relation. I noted this in chapter two, but now it remains to explore it in greater detail in the present chapter. I will reveal a consistency and a symmetry between the telic orientation of the divine being with the telic orientation of created being, and this will help justify the fundamental assertion of this chapter: *being is for* koinōnia.

This argument will address a point of confusion within Edwards studies. Edwards scholars have long debated the appropriate way to understand Edwards's ontology. Is he pantheistic? Is he panentheistic? Does he invent an entirely new approach to ontology? These questions have hung in the background of Edwards scholarship for some time, and they are larger than this study can address. However, within this larger conversation there is debate as to how to read Edwards's *The End for Which God Created the World*. More specifically, Edwards asserts that God's end in creating the world was to communicate his own divine fullness. The question of interpretation is whether this communication of divine fullness was the act of creation, or whether creation was given being with a view toward this communication. I will argue the latter, and in doing so, I will need to address one of the most influential interpreters within Edwards scholarship, Sang Hyun Lee. I will first present a reading of *The End of Creation* and then turn to Lee's work in order to address his alternate interpretation.

Once this discussion is in place, I will conclude the chapter with a consideration of how Edwards modified his Reformed tradition in espousing this view of grace as participation in divine fullness. In the first chapter I argued that Edwards's doctrine of grace was aimed to reinforce Reformed commitments over against Arminianism and enthusiasm. That is, Edwards's doctrine of grace may be viewed as Reformed at least in that it allowed him to hold historic boundary lines of that tradition. In the conclusion of this chapter I will return to this question and argue that Edwards's doctrine of grace was a sympathetic development of his Puritan and Reformed heritage, rather than a departure from it.

I begin, however, with an exploration of the relation between creature and Creator in Edwards's teleology.

BEING IS FOR *KOINŌNIA*

Teleology is central to the thought of Edwards. He followed a long line of Western thought that took the notions of purpose and intended end as central to a full understanding of an object. This teleological orientation is crucial to the way Edwards related created nature to divine grace. The aim of this section is to demonstrate that, for Edwards, creational being, grounded on what I dubbed "common participation," is teleologically related to divine *koinōnia*, or what I called "special participation." Created nature is designed by God in order for God to fulfill it as it participates in the divine fullness. Or, put most simply, *being is for* koinōnia. Edwards grounded this idea in his doctrine of the Trinity, so I will begin by leveraging the argument from chapter three. The Trinity itself is for *koinōnia*, and this sets the pattern that Edwards follows through his reflections on creational nature and its fulfillment in special grace.

***Trinity: Divine being is for* koinōnia.** In the previous chapter I explored Edwards's distinction between the divine essence and divine fullness, and this led into the world of Edwards's view of the Trinity. Edwards employs the essence-fullness distinction most commonly when he is speaking about divine grace—that is, the distinction is primarily soteriological for Edwards. Yet the best way to grasp what Edwards means by this distinction is to trace its roots back into Edwards's doctrine of God. This is because Edwards's doctrine of God is the foundation of his thought—Edwards's soteriology and ethics and philosophy (and so forth) are built on his view of God. With this in mind I found that the distinction between the divine essence and divine fullness is grounded on two types of participation in Edwards's doctrine of the Trinity. More specifically, if one looks at the divine Son's *ad intra* procession, it appears that the Son partakes of the divine essence through a *methexis* in the Father's ideation, and that the Son shares in the divine love through a *koinōnia* in the Holy Spirit. If one asks the question, How does the divine Son (*ad intra*) partake of the divine essence? Edwards answers, the Son gains quiddity by sharing in the Father's ideation. This is a form of *methexis* because it is a sharing by which one gains substance or essence. However, if one asks the question, How does the divine Son (*ad intra*) partake of divine love or happiness? Edwards gives a distinct answer: the Son gains divine love or happiness by sharing in the Holy Spirit. This is a form of *koinōnia* because it is a relational sharing between persons, without direct bearing on quiddity. These two participations *ad intra* form the basis for the essence-fullness distinction *ad extra*.

However, it is not enough simply to distinguish the Son's *methexis* from the Son's *koinōnia*. One must also see how Edwards related them, and this is where Edwards's teleology comes into view. Edwards believed that the *koinōnia* between the Father and the Son was the culmination of all the trinitarian processions. That is, the sharing in the divine love—the Holy Spirit—between the Father and the Son is the purpose of the trinitarian relations. Edwards points this out in a fragmentary reflection on the equality of the persons of the Trinity. Written around the early 1740s, the fragment records Edwards's attempt to explore the relative glory of each person of the Trinity.[9] What is interesting for our purpose is the honor Edwards ascribes to the Holy Spirit. The Holy Spirit is the last of the trinitarian persons in logical order. The Father is first, being the fountain of the Godhead. The Son is the second as God's self-image, and the Spirit, as the mutual love between the Father and the Son, is the last. One might imagine that this suggests the Spirit is least in honor, but that is not Edwards's insight. Rather, Edwards argues that the Spirit's place as (logically) last implies that the Spirit is also the *end* (teleologically) of the other two. Edwards writes, "The Holy Ghost is the last that proceeds from both the other two, yet the Holy Ghost has this peculiar dignity: that he is as it were the end of the other two, the good that they enjoy, the end of all procession."[10] The shift from logical language (*last*) to teleology (*end*) is significant. It indicates that, for Edwards, the purpose of the Trinity is gathered up in the mutual sharing in the Holy Spirit between the Father and the Son. That is, the purpose of the trinitarian processions culminates in the *koinōnia* of divine fullness, or love, or the Holy Spirit (all synonymous in this context). This telic end is inevitable *ad intra*. The trinitarian processions are all necessary, and so the *methexis* of

---

[9] WJE 21:145-46.
[10] WJE 21:146.

the Son in the Father's essence, and the *koinōnia* between the Father and the Son, are eternally coincident.¹¹ Still, in the same way that there is a logical order to them, there is also an order of teleology. For Jonathan Edwards, the divine being is for *koinōnia*.

Yet as soon as Edwards states this *ad intra* teleology, he moves to show its *ad extra* counterpart. As we saw in the previous chapter, Edwards held a strong continuity between God's being and God's act, and therefore there is a strong continuity between the Trinity *ad intra* and the Trinity's activity *ad extra*. The same is true for Edwards's teleology. The *koinōnia* that is the end, or the telic fulfillment of the *methexis* between the Father and the Son, is also the end or telic fulfillment of the Father's and the Son's activity in redemption. Edwards writes:

> He is the end of the other two in their acting *ad intra*, and also in his acting *ad extra*, in all they do in redemption and their distinct economical concerns. The end of the Father in electing is the Spirit. He elects to a possession of this benefit. His end in giving the Son [is] to purchase this. The end of the Son in all his suffering is to obtain this, to purchase this. This was the great precious thing to which all that the other two do is subordinated.¹²

Edwards's point is that just as the *koinōnia* in the Spirit between the Father and the Son is the telic end of the trinitarian relations *ad intra*, so the *koinōnia* of the Spirit, as divine grace, is the end of the Trinity's action in redemption. The Father's telic end in electing is to give of his own infinite good, namely, *koinōnia* in the Spirit. The Son's telic end in giving himself is to purchase the same thing, *koinōnia* in the Spirit.¹³ This is important

---

¹¹The trinitarian relations may be termed dependent, but not in the sense that they are arbitrary, or based on a willed action (WJE 21:147).

¹²WJE 21:146-47. There is an exegetical question regarding the referent to the first pronoun, *he*, in this quote. The previous sentence ends with "Son," which would normally indicate that the following pronoun, *he*, refers to the second person of the Trinity. However, I take it to refer to the Holy Spirit. The reason is that the previous sentence discusses how the Holy Spirit is the infinite good shared between the Father and the Son, and the sentence following continues this idea. In this context it makes most sense to take the *he* pronoun to refer to the Holy Spirit as the "end of the other two." If *he* refers to the Son, then it is much more difficult to make sense of Edwards's thought.

¹³The Spirit as the good purchased by Christ for the saints is a regular theme in Edwards (see WJE 21:136). For this theme implied in a sermon, see "God Glorified in Man's Dependence" (WJE 17:210). Edwards's first sermon in "Charity and Its Fruits" identifies the Holy Spirit's nature with love, and the love between the Father and the Son as the thing revealed in the gospel (see WJE 8:132, 143-44).

because one can see a consistency in Edwards's understanding of teleology. The divine being (*ad intra*) is for *koinōnia*, and the divine activity (*ad extra*) is also teleologically aimed at giving this *koinōnia* in grace.

Creation: Created being is for koinōnia. All of this provides the context for addressing the question that is the focus of this section: What is the positive relationship between created nature and divine grace? Edwards has (almost) answered this question already. Just as *koinōnia* in the Spirit is the telic fulfillment of *methexis* in the divine being *ad intra*, and just as *koinōnia* in the Spirit is the telic fulfillment of God's action in redemption *ad extra*, so also *koinōnia* in the Spirit is the telic fulfillment of created nature. Phrasing it that way makes it sound as if there are three different modes to this teleology. In fact, there are only really two in Edwards's thinking. God's purpose *ad intra* and God's purpose *ad extra* are distinguishable, but God's purpose in his redemptive activity and God's purpose in creating are in fact one. That is, all God's action (*ad extra*), in both creation and redemption, is teleologically oriented toward giving *koinōnia* in the Spirit (special participation or special grace) to the saints. Created being is for *koinōnia*. The most obvious and authoritative place to demonstrate this is Edwards's *The End for Which God Created the World*. I will investigate this work to show the telic priority of special grace (*koinōnia* in the Spirit), and then I will consider a major possible objection.

Overview of End of Creation. Edwards's *The End for Which God Created the World* was the culmination of a career's worth of reflection on teleology; it is his most mature reflection on the purpose of the created order.[14] This fact brings up a helpful question. I have observed Edwards's teleology within his doctrine of God—both *ad intra* and *ad extra*. However, this is drawn from private, unpublished papers. Did this teleology affect his more mature thinking? Or, did Edwards's private thought on *God's* purpose impact his more public thought on *creation's* purpose?[15] As it turns out, Edwards was

---

[14]Edwards reflected on creation's end throughout his writing life, and much, though perhaps not all, of this reflection is gathered up in his great dissertation. I will focus on the dissertation and use *Miscellanies* entries as needed. For key *Miscellanies* entries on creation's end, see 3, 92, 104, 109, 115, 271, 327(a), 332, 351, 445, 448, 461, 553, 581, 586, 662, 669, 853, 918, 993, 1063, 1066, 1080, 1081, 1082, 1084, 1094, 1099, 1140, 1151, 1182, 1208, 1218, 1225, 1266, 1275.

[15]*The End for Which God Created the World* was not published during Edwards's lifetime, but he was likely preparing it for publication, along with *True Virtue*. This justifies my description of it as his "more public thought" (see WJE 8:5).

Grace and Creation 153

very consistent. He believed that God's purpose for created nature, creational being, is fulfilled in the saints' participation in divine fullness. This maps directly to Edwards's statements about God's purpose *ad extra* in redemption mentioned above. There is no need to attempt a full analysis of *The End of Creation*.[16] Rather, I will show that created being is for *koinōnia* in the Spirit by observing Edwards's question, method, and conclusion within the work. The central question will show that Edwards's primary focus is creation's *end* rather than its *being* as such.[17] This will help distinguish created nature and divine grace in the work. Edwards's methodology will show that he is describing the same teleology in this work as he does in his trinitarian reflections examined earlier. That is, God's purpose in redemption and his purpose in creation are identical: the gift of *koinōnia* in the Spirit. Edwards's conclusion in *End of Creation* clarifies that true grace, the communication and participation in divine fullness, is the fulfillment of created nature.

All good dissertations begin with a good research question, and Edwards's *The End for Which God Created the World* is no exception. And like well-written dissertations, Edwards's work keeps the central question close at hand throughout his argument. This means that one will not read his work well without clearly understanding the question he is trying to answer, and importantly, what questions he is *not* addressing in the work. His research question comes embedded in his first sentence, and it reoccurs throughout the work. Edwards begins with these words: "To avoid all confusion in our inquiries and reasonings *concerning the end for which God created the world*."[18] The question at the heart of Edwards's work is simply this: Why

---

[16] Most major studies of Edwards's theology include a section on this dissertation. For key works, see Stephen R. Holmes, *God of Grace and God of Glory: An Account of the Theology of Jonathan Edwards* (Edinburgh: T&T Clark, 2000), 44-76; W. J. Danaher Jr., *The Trinitarian Ethics of Jonathan Edwards* (Louisville, KY: Westminster John Knox, 2004), 204-11; Kyle Strobel, *Jonathan Edwards's Theology: A Reinterpretation*, T&T Clark Studies in Systematic Theology (London: T&T Clark, 2013); Oliver D. Crisp, *Jonathan Edwards on God and Creation* (Oxford: Oxford University Press, 2012), 138-89; Michael J. McClymond and Gerald R. McDermott, *The Theology of Jonathan Edwards* (Oxford: Oxford University Press, 2012), 209-23; Seng-Kong Tan, *Fullness Received and Returned: Trinity and Participation in Jonathan Edwards* (Minneapolis: Fortress, 2014). Tan uses *The End of Creation* throughout his book.

[17] The qualification "primarily" is important—clearly Edwards does deal with ontology, and the work as a whole has ontological implications. However, that is not the primary aim. Teleology is primary.

[18] WJE 8:405, emphasis added.

did God create the world? More specifically, what was it that motivated God to create, and, in what will reduce to the same for Edwards, what was it that God sought to accomplish in embarking on the work of creation? This is, in one sense, obvious. It is all captured in the dissertation's title. Yet, I emphasize this ostensibly obvious point in order to make an easily overlooked one: Edwards's dissertation is primarily about teleology and not primarily about ontology. Put differently, Edwards's concern is with the *end* of creation, and not in the first instance with created nature per se.

Why is this important? Clearly both teleology and ontology are, at least to some extent, in Edwards's view. Why is it important to prioritize teleology as the primary focus, over against ontology? The answer is this: if we read *End of Creation* as primarily about ontology, then the distinction between created nature and divine grace in Edwards's thought will weaken or even collapse. On the other hand, if we read *End of Creation* as primarily about teleology, then there is a clear way to retain a strong distinction and relation between created nature and divine grace. This requires further clarification. The climax of *End of Creation* is the assertion that God's purpose is the "the emanation or communication of the divine fullness."[19] If the work is *primarily* about ontology, then it will be tempting to understand this as describing something God achieved in the *act of creation*. In categories developed in previous chapters, it will sound as if the communication of the divine fullness is given as an aspect of common participation, or the form of participation that undergirds creation per se (*methexis*). However, elsewhere Edwards regularly says that the communication of divine fullness is *not given* as the act of creation or preservation but only in special grace.[20] Therefore, if Edwards is now saying that divine fullness is given in the act of creation, then he appears to be changing his view, and the distinction between created nature and divine grace collapses.

However, there is no need to conclude that Edwards changed his view. In fact, there is good reason to argue that Edwards's statements about emanation and communication of divine fullness *do not* relate to creation per se,

---

[19] WJE 8:531.
[20] See argument in chapter two. See also Edwards's first chapter in *Treatise on Grace*, where he states that there is a difference in kind and not merely degree between common and special grace (WJE 21:153-65.).

nor is this communication given in the act of creation (or ongoing preservation), but rather is the unique gift of special grace. The most obvious reason to read it this way is his orienting research question. The question is not *What is the nature of creation*, or *How did God create*, but rather *Why did God create*? When this question is kept in clear view, then Edwards's consistent teleology comes into greater clarity. The Trinity's telic end *ad intra* is *koinōnia* in the Spirit. The Trinity's telic end *ad extra* is giving *koinōnia* in the Spirit (or divine fullness). Now it is clear that the telic end of creation is this same *koinōnia* in divine fullness. In this light *End of Creation* becomes one of Edwards's clearest statements on how created nature relates to grace as participation in divine fullness.

This last sentence may raise a question: The term *grace* is rarely used in *End of Creation*, so how can the work be about grace?[21] The answer to this becomes clear when one moves from considering the research question to considering Edwards's methodology. Just as all good dissertations have an orienting research question, so good dissertations have a guiding methodology. Edwards's method is to reverse-engineer creation's purpose from God's accomplishment in special grace. This is an important point. Edwards could have reflected on God's accomplishment *in the act of creating itself* and then attempted to discern God's purpose. He could have reasoned from ontology to teleology. After all, one could easily presuppose that whatever God intended to accomplish in creation was in fact accomplished with the act of creating. This, however, is not his approach. Rather, he chose to reflect on God's accomplishment in *the work of redemption* and then generalized God's purpose from that perspective. In other words, Edwards's method was to reason from soteriology to teleology. This means that Edwards's teleology is always framed in the context of God's work of grace, or at the very least, his work of redemption. It also confirms Edwards's consistent teleology. God's *telos* in his *ad extra* work of creation and redemption is the same: *koinōnia* in the Spirit.

This is clear from the second section of chapter two.[22] Edwards puts forth twelve positions, or theses, that are meant to show a reasonable method for

---

[21] Although Edwards does explicitly state that the communication of divine fullness to the will is called grace (see WJE 8:529-30).
[22] WJE 8:469-74.

how one may answer the primary question from the Scriptures. He has already addressed the question from the standpoint of reason, but even there he asserts that the question of God's end in creation will have to be answered from Scripture.[23] The second section of chapter two picks this up and considers how one should interrogate Scripture appropriately. His twelve positions, or theses, amount to principles that guide logical extrapolation from what the Bible says. For instance, position one reads, "That which appears to be spoken of as God's ultimate end in his works of providence in general, we may justly suppose to be his last end in the work of creation."[24] This is a principle that guides theological reflection, rather than an exegetical insight itself. The rest of the positions are similar.

What is important, however, is that the twelve positions become increasingly narrow in their frame of reference. The first position, as just seen, is broad in its frame of reference. It includes all of God's providential acts. Without rehearsing each position, the twelve together functions like a funnel, moving from general to specific. Edwards moves from all God's acts in providence to God's acts in the moral world.[25] If one can find God's last and chief end in the moral world, then that will be God's end in creation. Yet, Edwards narrows the field further. Not only should one investigate God's acts of providence within the scope of the moral world, but also one should specifically look at the "good portion" of the moral world.[26] But even this is not narrow enough. Edwards narrows the field yet further in positions eight through twelve: look at what God wants the saints to pursue and seek, and that will be God's end in creation.[27] But then further, one should look at the approved saints in Scripture and seek out what their aim was. Yet again, Edwards narrows the field even further, until he focuses exclusively on Christ. Christ's aim must be the decisive clue in determining God's end in the whole of creation.

> *Position* 12. Since the Holy Scriptures teach us that Jesus Christ is the head of the moral world, and especially of all the good part of it; the chief of God's

---

[23] WJE 8:419.
[24] WJE 8:469.
[25] Position 4, WJE 8:470.
[26] Position 7, WJE 8:471-72.
[27] WJE 8:472-74.

> servants, appointed to be the head of his saints and angels, and set forth as the chief and most perfect pattern and example of goodness; we may well suppose by the foregoing positions, that what he sought as his last end was God's last end in the creation of the world.[28]

The key point at the moment is simply that Edwards's methodology was to move from soteriology to teleology. He reverse-engineered creation's end from the doctrine of Christology and soteriology. This explains why much of what Edwards says in *End of Creation* only relates directly to the redeemed. In fact, Edwards explicitly mentions that nonintelligent creatures, inanimate objects, and the like can only participate in God's final end for creation in an indirect manner.[29] This is because they are not the immediate recipients of divine fullness. Only the saints are immediate recipients of divine fullness. This also means that the statements in *End of Creation* about God's purpose of communicating his divine fullness should not be taken to be a generalized communication to all of creation per se, but rather a specific communication to the saints *in particular*. This is why Edwards has so much to say about perpetual growth for the saints. The communication of divine fullness to the saints will require eternal and perpetual growth in intimacy between God and the saints because they are by definition finite. This is the way in which creation achieves its true end—in the eternal communication of grace from God to the saints, and their participatory return of that fullness to him.

But this does not occur simply in the act of creation itself. As suggested above, Edwards could have reflected from God's act of creation to God's purpose or motive for that act. Apparently, Edwards's problem with this method is that it would fail to yield God's chief end. God's act of creating undoubtedly accomplished many ends, and perhaps ultimate ends, but that is not Edwards's question. Edwards's question regards God's *chief end* or *last end*—which, in Edwards's understanding, must be both an ultimate end and a highest end.[30] For this question, he must look not only at God's act of creating; he must look beyond it to how God glorifies himself in the soteriological communication of fullness to the saints, as exhibited in Christ

---

[28]WJE 8:474. See there Ramsey's intriguing footnote (n1) that argues Edwards's position must be viewed in terms of a high Christology with a communication of properties.
[29]WJE 8:470-71.
[30]See Edwards's introductory essay on various types of ends (WJE 8:405-15).

himself. Thus he reverse-engineers God's chief and last end in creating from soteriology (which should include Christology) to teleology.

This is not to say that ontology is wholly absent. Edwards does address, briefly, common participation in God for being that applies to all creation in itself. However, this is not the primary focus of Edwards's inquiry. I will address this more fully in short order.

The purpose at present is to show that Edwards's dissertation, *End of Creation*, is a work that concerns how created nature is fulfilled in special grace, as opposed to a work that is primarily concerned to show the ontology of creation in itself. The first reason to read it this way comes from Edwards's fundamental question: it is a question of teleology and not in the first instance one of ontology. Second, Edwards reverse-engineers teleology from soteriology (with at least a nod toward Christology). Finally, Edwards concludes his work by describing God's end in creation in terms of special grace. I will explain this more clearly now.

Edwards concludes his work by answering his research question. Why did God create the world? Edwards's answer is traditional: for his own glory. This is little more than the Westminster Catechism's first question and answer. However, he gets more specific. The Bible describes this glory of God in a variety of ways, but they all fundamentally reduce to the same thing. Edwards describes it as "the emanation and true external expression of God's internal glory and fullness."[31] This, Edwards admits, is an obscure way to speak, but he makes himself clear as his conclusion unfolds.

The word *emanation* is a philosophically charged word; however, Edwards uses it synonymously with the more standard word *communication*.[32] The philosophical history of the word *emanation* might lead a reader to draw pantheistic conclusions.[33] As seen elsewhere, Edwards does speak of creation's

---

[31] WJE 8:527.
[32] Ramsey believed Edwards's use of *emanation* was synonymous with *communication* and should not be read in terms of Neoplatonic emanationism (see WJE 8:96n2). See WJE 8:531, where *emanation* and *communication* are clearly interchangeable. See also John J. Bombaro, *Jonathan Edwards's Vision of Reality: The Relationship of God to the World, Redemption History, and the Reprobate* (Eugene, OR: Pickwick, 2012), 77n32.
[33] Speaking about emanationism within pantheistic philosophies, Mander writes, "Although it would be tempting to contrast creation *ex nihilo* as theistic and emanation as pantheistic, such thoughts are probably too simple." See William Mander, "Pantheism," *Stanford Encyclopedia of Philosophy*, 2013 ed., http://plato.stanford.edu/archives/sum2013/entries/pantheism/. See also McClymond and McDermott, *Theology of Jonathan Edwards*, 206.

common participation in God for its being. However, that is not how the word *emanation* is being used here. Edwards's Reformed tradition used the term *emanation* to describe "the emanation of grace from God."[34] Its meaning is determined by its context, and the context of Edwards's argument clearly indicates that *this* emanation is to be understood as identical with the communication and participation in divine fullness given in special grace.

This becomes more clear when one asks the question, What is it that God emanates or communicates? Edwards's answer is "God's internal glory and fullness."[35] If one asks further what he means by this, one finds that his answer points decisively to the inner-trinitarian relations, which are shared with the saints in grace. Consider the following excerpt:

> The emanation or communication is of the internal glory or fullness of God, as it is. Now God's internal glory, as it is in God, is either in his understanding or will. The glory or fullness of his understanding is his knowledge. The internal glory and fullness of God, which we must conceive of as having its special seat in his will, is his holiness and happiness. The whole of God's internal good or glory, is in these three things, viz. his infinite knowledge; his infinite virtue or holiness, and his infinite joy and happiness. Indeed there are a great many attributes in God, according to our way of conceiving or talking of them: but all may be reduced to these; or to the degree, circumstances and relations of these.[36]

The word *Trinity* is missing, as are the names of the persons (Father, Son, and Holy Spirit). However, if one reads this with Edwards's *Discourse on the Trinity* in mind, it is clear that this is thinly veiled trinitarianism. Fullness or internal glory is God's personal knowledge (which, according to the *Discourse on the Trinity*, maps to the divine Son), along with God's personal will (which, according to the *Discourse on the Trinity*, maps to the divine Spirit, and includes both holiness and happiness). Edwards even leverages his idiosyncratic notion of real attributes that he developed in his *Discourse on the Trinity*.[37] Recall from chapter one that Edwards can sometimes speak of

---

[34]John Owen, *Communion with God: Of Communion with God the Father, Son, and Holy Ghost, each person distinctly, in love, grace, and consolation; or, The saints' fellowship with the Father, Son, and Holy Ghost unfolded* (Oxford: Benediction Classics, 2017), 1.2, p. 10.
[35]WJE 8:527.
[36]WJE 8:528.
[37]WJE 21:131-32. See also Sang Hyun Lee, "Editor's Introduction," in WJE 21:10-20.

the divine fullness as the Spirit, and sometimes as the divine will and the divine knowledge. I argued in chapter one that these are not contradictory. The divine fullness is one gift that includes two aspects: the infusion of the Spirit (the divine love or will) that binds the saint to Christ (who is the divine understanding). Kyle Strobel describes this dynamic in terms of God's two communicable natures (his understanding and will), and I argued that Strobel's communicable natures are the two aspects within the one gift of the divine fullness.[38] The important point here is that the internal glory or fullness of God is the divine *koinōnia* that characterizes the Trinity *ad intra*. Edwards's argument in the conclusion of *End of Creation* is that this same fullness is given to the saints in eternally increasing measure and that this is the fulfillment of creation.

> The emanation or communication of the divine fullness, consisting in the knowledge of God, love to God, and joy in God, has relation indeed both to God and the creature: but it has relation to God as its fountain, as it is an emanation from God; and as the communication itself, or thing communicated, is something divine, something of God, something of his internal fullness. . . . In the creature's knowing, esteeming, loving, rejoicing in, and praising God, the glory of God is both exhibited and acknowledged; his fullness is received and returned. Here is both an *emanation* and *remanation*. The refulgence shines upon and into the creature, and is reflected back to the luminary. The beams of glory come from God, and are something of God, and are refunded back again to their original. So that the whole is *of God*, and *in* God, and *to* God; and God is the beginning, middle and end in this affair.[39]

I quote this section at length to illustrate that all of this language is nearly identical to what one finds in Edwards's various works on divine and special grace. I say "nearly" because the word *emanation* is unusual elsewhere. Still, as seen throughout this book, Edwards's language of communication or participation in divine fullness is consistent in his corpus. It appears in his sermons, his *Religious Affections*, his *Treatise on Grace*, and now here in a work he was preparing at his death. In each case it does not refer to a gift given to creation generally, but the gift of *koinōnia* given to the saints specifically. This means that, in a very real sense, the purpose of creation is the

---

[38] Kyle Strobel, "Jonathan Edwards's Reformed Doctrine of *Theosis*," *HTR* 109, no. 3 (2016): 371-99.
[39] WJE 8:531.

same (with qualifications) as the Trinity's own purpose. The "end of all processions" in the Trinity *ad intra* is the *koinōnia* of the Spirit. The end of the Trinity *ad extra* is sharing this *koinōnia* with creation, in the saints. Being is for *koinōnia*.

Two participations in End of Creation? Edwards's teleology is strikingly consistent. For Edwards, being is for *koinōnia*. That is true of the Trinity *ad intra* and in the Trinity's *ad extra* work of creation and redemption. This *koinōnia* is special participation—the type of relational participation that defines special grace. However, this brings up a question. I argued in chapters two and three that there are two forms of participation in Edwards's thought: common participation, which is a *methexis* in being, and special participation, which is a *koinōnia* in love, fullness, or the Spirit. Hence the question: Does Edwards address common participation in *End of Creation*? The answer is yes. It is not the primary focus of *End of Creation*, but Edwards does employ it as a kind of background concept for the main argument.

The concept I dub "common participation" arises as Edwards addresses whether God's self-love, as a motive for creating, resolves to selfishness.[40] Edwards reasons that when self-love is opposed to general benevolence, then it is selfish. For instance, if Joe loves himself in such a way as to exclude love for Sally, then Joe is selfish. Joe's self-love will not necessarily lead to love of Sally. However, this is not the case with God. God's self-love implies general benevolence precisely because God is *being in general*. Edwards's thought is this: everything exists in God for its being. Therefore, God's self-love does not compete with love for all because all things participate in God for being. This is what I have called common participation.[41] It is a *methexis* because it shares in being to establish quiddity, essence, or substance.

At this point, however, it is helpful to ask, Given that Edwards employs his notion of common participation in *End of Creation*, what is its function in the argument? The answer is this: common participation allows Edwards to show how creatures can be the proper objects of God's self-love. Consider

---

[40]WJE 8:461-62.
[41]On Edwards's identification of God as *being in general*, and the ideas of love, consent, and excellency that are embedded in it, see Bombaro, *Jonathan Edwards's Vision of Reality*, 76-78. Bombaro states that "participation in God and participation in being or existence come to the same thing" (77). I would agree as long as this participation in being is not confused with the participation in divine fullness that constitutes special grace.

what this means within Edwards's larger thought. God's self-love inevitably draws one back to Edwards's trinitarianism. This is true even if it is not explicit in *End of Creation*. God's self-love is the *koinōnia*, communion, relational participation between the Father and the Son *ad intra*. It is this same *koinōnia* that God seeks to share *ad extra* in creation and redemption. How can this self-love *koinōnia* extend to creatures? At least part of the answer is common participation. If creatures share in God for being, then God's self-love *koinōnia* can, at least in principle, extend to them. When God communicates divine fullness the saints, he is loving himself in them. This is plausible, at least partially, because they were never ontologically independent from him. Once again, track the telic order implied in this line of reasoning. Common participation (created being, grounded in *being in general*) is given with a view to special participation (*koinōnia* in the Spirit, given in special grace).

However, this reading needs to stand up to challenge. Consider a key passage:

> God in his benevolence to his creatures, can't have his heart enlarged in such a manner as to take in beings that he finds, who are originally out of himself, distinct and independent. This can't be in an infinite being, who exists alone from eternity. But he, from his goodness, as it were enlarges himself in a more excellent and divine manner. This is by communicating and diffusing himself; and so instead of finding, making objects of his benevolence: not by taking into himself what he finds distinct from himself, and so partaking of their good, and being happy in them; but by flowing forth, and expressing himself in them, and making them to partake of him, and rejoicing in himself expressed in them, and communicated to them.[42]

Paul Ramsey says, "This paragraph . . . compresses a number of concepts that are elaborated more fully [elsewhere]."[43] His comment refers to the paragraph before this one, and he points to *True Virtue* as the place of greater elaboration, but the comment fits this paragraph as well. This passage could be read to contradict my argument to this point. The difficulty here is that if this quote is taken on its own, without being informed by the rest of the work and by the rest of Edwards's corpus, then it is ambiguous as to whether God's self-communication is in the act of creating or subsequent to that act.

---

[42]WJE 8:461-62.
[43]WJE 8:461n5.

Does Edwards fuse common participation and special participation? This passage does not fuse the two, but rather illustrates how common participation is given with a telic view toward fulfillment in special participation. I argue this for the following reasons.

First, the aim of this paragraph is to assert the *plausibility* that God's self-love could conceivably extend to those who are not God. Therefore Edwards emphasizes the ontological dependence of creature on Creator, as a reason for how this self-love can extend. Ontological dependence is necessary for the communication of God's self-love, but it is not Edwards's intention to argue that they are the same thing.

Second, one must read this within the larger argument of *End of Creation*. Just after the quoted paragraph above, Edwards admits, "There is a degree of indistinctness and obscurity in the close consideration of such subjects."[44] He knows he has not adequately clarified his argument. Greater clarity will come from the Scriptures, and that is where he turns next in the second chapter of *End of Creation*.[45] As seen, Edwards argues in chapter two that God is glorified in his communication of divine fullness *to the saints*, with Christ being the climatic example. This particularism, so characteristic of Edwards and his Reformed tradition, argues for viewing a distinction between God's act of creating and his self-communication in grace. If the two are fused, then Edwards's particularism is incoherent.

Third, one must read this within the larger context of Edwards's corpus. Just as particularism is a key theme in Edwards, so is the distinction between common grace and special grace. If participation in being is fused with participation in God's self-love (or Spirit, or divine fullness), then it is difficult to see how Edwards can maintain such a strong distinction between common and special grace. Yet Edwards asserts very strongly that "special or saving grace in this sense is not only different from common grace in degree, but entirely diverse in nature and kind; and that natural men not only have not a sufficient degree of virtue to be saints, but that they have no degree of that grace that is in godly men."[46] Later in the same work, Edwards defines special grace as "[consisting] in partaking of the fullness of

---

[44] WJE 8:462-63.
[45] WJE 8:463.
[46] WJE 21:154.

Christ... which... consists in partaking of the Spirit that is given him not by measure." So, partaking in the fullness of Christ, or partaking of the Spirit, belongs only to the saints. I have shown Edwards's consistency that partaking of the divine fullness maps to sharing in the *koinōnia* between the Father and the Son, given economically in the Spirit. This *koinōnia* can also be described as God's self-love. It follows, then, that God's self-love is not given to all, but rather to the saints. If this is the case, and if Edwards is consistent, then he must have distinguished between the way in which all things partake of God for being and the communication of his self-love to the saints.

How then should one read the passage above about God as *being in general*? It appears the best way to read it is to distinguish between the two types of participation: common and special. Then, one can say that common participation, or participation in being, is given with a view to special participation. That is, God gives being (creation and ongoing preservation), in order to communicate himself to the saints, so that he loves himself in them. On this reading, common participation is given with telic orientation toward fulfillment in special participation. Special participation is therefore dependent on common participation. Once again, being is for *koinōnia*, and on the other hand, of course, *koinōnia* requires being.

Alternate reading considered: Sang Hyun Lee. This reading of Edwards's *End of Creation*, and particularly the notion that Edwards implies two types of participation, must answer a serious objection. Sang Hyun Lee published *The Philosophical Theology of Jonathan Edwards* in 1988, and ever since it has held priority of place in Edwards scholarship. Lee's aim was to present a reading of Edwards's philosophy that would provide a unity for his overall thought.[47] Edwards scholarship found Lee's thesis compelling, and there developed something of a school of thought that took Lee's thesis as paradigmatic. More recently Lee's thesis has come under significant critique, but the fact remains that Lee's interpretation of Edwards is influential. The reading that I have given here, while coinciding with Lee at points, differs in some very significant ways. I will address these differences by first pointing out the most obvious divergence, then outlining key points in Lee's

---

[47]See Lee's thesis in Sang Hyun Lee, *The Philosophical Theology of Jonathan Edwards* (Princeton, NJ: Princeton University Press, 1988), 3-4.

thought that form the background for his position, before evaluating it and providing an alternative approach.

Lee asserts that God's self-communication of fullness includes the *act of creation*, rather than seeing God's communication of divine fullness as the uniquely telic goal of God's act of creation. Whereas I have argued that Edwards's *End of Creation* looks primarily at God's telos that moved him to create, and the fulfillment of creation itself, rather than God's act of creation, Lee sees these as united. For instance, Lee writes:

> The inner-Trinitarian fullness of the divine being . . . does not exhaust the divine disposition. The exercise of this disposition ad extra, according to Edwards, constitutes God's creation of the world. Created existence, then, is the spatio-temporal repetition of God's inner-Trinitarian fullness, a process which, as shall be seen, will be everlasting in duration.[48]

Lee is discussing how the Trinity *ad intra* sets the pattern for the Trinity's activity *ad extra*. That is, the same inclination or disposition (important terms for Lee) that defines the Trinity *ad intra* is now expressed *ad extra* in self-communication to creation. However, notice that, for Lee, this *ad extra* exercise of God's disposition "*constitutes* God's creation of the world."[49] For Lee "created existence" per se is the "repetition of God's inner-Trinitarian fullness." It is important to point out that Lee sees this as a process that begins at creation and continues eternally. It must continue eternally because of creaturely finitude—only Christ receives the divine fullness without measure.[50] In this way Lee is able to see God's self-communication of divine fullness as undergirding both creation's ontology per se and its ongoing telic goal at the same time. He is able to achieve this dynamic view of creation through his dispositional ontology. This dispositional ontology is the centerpiece of his systematization of Edwards's thought. I will summarize it now.

Lee's reading of Edwards turns on his argument that Edwards functionally replaced traditional essence-substance ontology with the notion of dispositions. *Miscellanies* 241 states that "all habits being only a law that God has

---

[48]Lee, *Philosophical Theology of Jonathan Edwards*, 173.
[49]Lee, *Philosophical Theology of Jonathan Edwards*, 173, emphasis added.
[50]Lee, *Philosophical Theology of Jonathan Edwards*, 173, 211-12, 227.

fixed, that such actions upon such occasions should be exerted."⁵¹ Lee takes this to be a significant development of the idea of habit and disposition, and argues that it grows to carry ontological weight. Without detailing each step, Lee argues that a "habit or an active power is . . . a law like relation between events or actions and not an accidental quality that inheres in a substance. At this point, Edwards has effectively left the old world of the substance/form metaphysics."⁵² Dispositions and habits have replaced substance and essence, establishing a reality that is fundamentally relational.⁵³

This dispositional ontology penetrates directly, argues Lee, into Edwards's doctrine of God. "God is a communicative being," writes Edwards.⁵⁴ For Lee this is more than a description; it approaches a definition. God is "inherently a tendency toward an increase or enlargement of God's own being."⁵⁵ This is the pivot point back toward Lee's doctrine of creation and its end, and the disagreement with this present study. Lee argues that this dispositional ontology in God is what undergirds the inner-trinitarian relations. Further, as seen above, "the inner-Trinitarian fullness of the divine being . . . does not exhaust the divine disposition," but rather that disposition moves God to create. Yet this disposition to create is rather more than that. The disposition is an inclination to repeat God's divine fullness, and this fullness appears to be the same thing as God's being.⁵⁶ At this point Lee's view of created ontology as dispositional joins hands with his doctrine of God as dispositional. The divine disposition motivates the act of creation, and this results in a dispositional created universe, which reaches its telic fulfillment in the eternal communications of the divine fullness.⁵⁷ This explains how

---

⁵¹WJE 13:358. I point out that this *Miscellanies* entry is about regeneration—a category of grace—and not primarily about ontology. One wonders how valid it is to put as much ontological weight on it as Lee does.

⁵²Lee, *Philosophical Theology of Jonathan Edwards*, 39.

⁵³"Relational causality implies a confluence of all entities in the system of being into a nexus of relationships in which all are involved in causing one another" (Lee, *Philosophical Theology of Jonathan Edwards*, 41).

⁵⁴*Miscellanies* 332 (WJE 13:410).

⁵⁵Lee, *Philosophical Theology of Jonathan Edwards*, 184.

⁵⁶Lee, *Philosophical Theology of Jonathan Edwards*, 8. Lee states that God's purpose for creation is to repeat God's own being. One wonders how Lee would account for Edwards's distinction between the divine essence and fullness in light of his identifying divine being with divine fullness.

⁵⁷Lee is careful to distinguish some key differences between the divine disposition and created dispositions. Still, he argues that there are key overlaps (*Philosophical Theology of Jonathan Edwards*, 183).

Lee can view created ontology as itself a repetition of the divine fullness, and still teleologically oriented toward eternal communications.

There is something important and attractive about Lee's interpretation. He argues that his approach explains why Edwards, in *End of Creation*, speaks in terms of both emanation and teleology.

> It should be noted that in discussing God's self-communication in creating the world, Edwards freely mixes emanationistic and teleological languages. In creating the world, God "aims at," and "seeks" to achieve, some ends. Edwards also asserts that the creation is a "flowing forth" or emanation of God's internal fullness. Edwards, I believe, is not being careless with his words here but speaks as he does because he sees the creation as both a purposive act and also an emanation.[58]

There is something very helpful in Lee's observation, although I disagree with the way the insight is framed, as well as its basis. Lee is right that Edwards speaks in terms of immediate ontological dependence of creation on God, or framed the other way around, God's immediate communication of being to creation. Lee is also right that Edwards speaks in terms of creation's telic goal to be an intimate, asymptotic union with the divine fullness in eternity. Lee uses the word *emanation* to describe the first reality, and *teleology* for the second. Surely Lee is right that any account of Edwards's view of God and creation must account for these two aspects of God's relatedness to creation.

Then comes Lee's explanation of these two aspects. Lee thinks the best way to explain the union of these aspects is through a dispositional ontology. This ontology is grounded in God and exported in the act of creation. This establishes creation's ontology (the first aspect above), and because that ontology is a repetition of God's disposition, creation will have an intrinsic orientation (disposition) toward God's purpose of union.

> And it is Edwards's dispositional conception of God that enables Edwards to combine the categories of emanation and teleology.... Since [disposition] is an ontological as well as an operational principle, its exertion brings about the actuality of being as well as a multiplication of that actuality. At the same time, disposition is also a teleological principle in that it is a tendency toward

---

[58]Lee, *Philosophical Theology of Jonathan Edwards*, 198-99.

the end of bringing about a certain sort of actual event or activity. That to which a disposition tends is a real possibility, and this real possibility becomes an actuality when the deposition is exercised; thus, there is a real teleological movement involved here, a movement from virtuality to full actuality. . . . God's creation of the world is both a "flowing forth" or a self-communication and also a purposive activity with a goal.[59]

Lee observes something important, and his explanation cannot be simply dismissed. At the same time, there is a better way to explain the two aspects than by reducing all to disposition. Disposition is important, and Lee is right to emphasize it. But disposition is not everything, and Lee's account struggles to explain some of Edwards's theological assertions.

Evaluation of Lee's view. This study is particularly concerned with Edwards's doctrine of grace as participation in the divine fullness. Within that overall topic, I am concerned to understand how Edwards can assert that true grace is both infinitely above created nature, and at the same time not the divine essence. I will turn the questions evaluated in chapters two and three above into questions for evaluating Lee's reading. First, does Lee's view account for the distinction between created nature and divine grace? Second, does Lee's view account for the distinction between divine fullness and divine essence?

Does Lee's view account for Edwards's distinction between created nature from divine grace? Throughout this study I have drawn attention to Edwards describing true, special grace as the communication or participation in divine fullness. This divine fullness is consistently identified with the relational communion (*koinōnia*) between the Father and the Son, in the Holy Spirit. This is an *ad intra* dynamic, which then becomes the gift of grace in the *ad extra* communications of grace in the work of redemption. The object of the communications is the saints.[60] I expect that at this point Lee would agree. However, I have also made clear that Edwards posits a strong distinction—even a *discontinuity*—between divine grace and created nature. Edwards insists strongly that, in one sense, all is grace. That is, common grace undergirds all things. This is a vehicle for Edwards's view of sovereignty

---

[59]Lee, *Philosophical Theology of Jonathan Edwards*, 199.
[60]*Miscellanies* 104 states that God created the world so that the Son could communicate himself, and the object of his communications are the saints (WJE 13:272).

and his view of ontological dependence on God. Yet, he says that this common grace is not the same thing as special grace. This is argued most pointedly in *Treatise on Grace*, but it is also woven throughout Edwards's thought about grace. In *Treatise on Grace*, Edwards clearly states that natural humans, without special grace, have no degree of the divine fullness operative within them. Further, when divine grace is given, it is precisely the divine fullness that is the gift. Or take Edwards's sermon "True Grace Is Divine."[61] Here Edwards says that there are some things that are developments or improvements of human nature. However, true grace is not one of those things. Rather, it is something different, something above human nature, something compatible with but properly distinct from the human essence.

Why is this review important? Because I do not see how Lee's view can account for such a strong discontinuity between created nature and divine grace. If the communication of the divine fullness is given *in the act of creation*, then the divine fullness is repeated, in some manner, in created nature itself. If this is the case, then the difference between created nature and divine grace *can only be by degree*, but it cannot be by kind. Yet this contradicts Edwards in *Treatise on Grace*. If the divine fullness is given in creation, then, as Paul Gavrilyuk says, "all things are deified to unspecified degree."[62]

I can imagine someone pushing back and arguing in the following way. The distinction between nature and grace could be explained in terms of potentiality and actuality. Created nature is a repetition of the divine fullness, and therefore, in Lee's language, it is an emanation. However, it is also teleologically oriented toward receiving and returning further communications of divine fullness. Therefore, the communications of God's divine grace over eternal duration secures the movement from potentiality (present in created nature) to actualized intimacy with God. Created nature, therefore, has very little of divine fullness (potentiality), and divine grace is the increasing of this to all eternity (actualization).

I would respond to this idea by saying that it sounds like a plausible way to frame the relationship between nature and grace, but it does not sound like Edwards's account. Rather, it sounds more like something the

---

[61] Edwards, "True Grace Is Divine (1738)," 356.
[62] Paul Gavrilyuk, "The Retrieval of Deification: How a Once-Despised Archaism Became an Ecumenical Desideratum," *Modern Theology* 25, no. 4 (2009): 651.

Cambridge Platonists might espouse. Edwards read the Cambridge Platonists and learned from them, but he also differed from them at this point. They famously spoke in terms of the "candle of the Lord," the light of reason that was resident in human nature. This reason was itself an emanation of God's reason.[63] Grace was God's assistance in increasing and bolstering this light through revelation and moral improvement. In their mind there was a strong continuity between nature and grace because of God's immanence in creation. Stephen Wilson writes, "In emphasizing the immanence of the divine nature, the divine reason all human beings possess, [the Cambridge Platonists] also emphasized the absolute freedom of all agents to develop and expand their participation in it."[64] Grace was in some sense embedded in nature.

This, however, was not Edwards's view. This is evident, for instance, in the way Edwards frames the doctrine of depravity in *Original Sin*. For him, created human nature, without divine grace, was not simply deficient in degree, but rather was empty. Before the fall, Adam and Eve existed with both divine grace (Edwards sometimes calls this superior or supernatural principles) and human nature. But with the fall, divine fullness or the supernatural principles were withdrawn, leaving *"mere human nature."* Without these superior principles "human nature would be human nature still."[65] But while human nature per se remained intact, it was empty of divine grace and divine love. It is not that the candle waned and flickered, but rather that the candle was extinguished.

> Therefore immediately the superior divine principles wholly ceased; so light ceases in a room, when the candle is withdrawn: and thus man was left in a state of darkness, woeful corruption and ruin; nothing but flesh, without spirit. The inferior principles of self-love and natural appetite, which were given only to serve, being alone, and left to themselves, of course became reigning principles; having no superior principles to regulate or control them, they became absolute masters of the heart.[66]

---

[63]See Wilson's discussion of the Cambridge Platonists' approach to emanationism as the basis for beauty and morality in Stephen A. Wilson, *Virtue Reformed: Rereading Jonathan Edwards's Ethics* (Leiden: Brill, 2005), 113-16.
[64]Wilson, *Virtue Reformed*, 120.
[65]WJE 3:382, emphasis original.
[66]WJE 3:382.

My point is this: any account of created nature and divine grace in Edwards must explain how the two can be thoroughly distinct and yet related to each other. By explaining both created nature and divine grace in reference to disposition and fullness, Lee's account can only differentiate them by degree. This is not strong enough for Edwards. Therefore, Lee's view requires modification to take this into account.

Does Lee's view account for Edwards's distinction between divine fullness and divine essence? I showed in the previous chapter that Edwards makes a distinction, in various contexts, between God's essence, which cannot be communicated, and God's fullness, which is the gift of grace. I argued that this distinction carries into Edwards's trinitarianism, particularly when one follows the Son's quiddity through the Father's ideation, and the Son's fullness, through *koinōnia* with the Father, in the Spirit. This carries into Christology and then soteriological grace. The saints receive the divine fullness without this impinging on their quiddity. Their essence remains human essence, and yet in receiving (and returning) the divine fullness, they partake of the relational *koinōnia* between the Father and the Son, in the Holy Spirit. In this understanding, the divine fullness can be called a disposition to love within God, which is communicated to the saints. The divine essence, however, is something that is truly incommunicable.

It is unclear, however, that Lee's view can adequately account for Edwards's distinction between the divine essence and the divine fullness. Perhaps Lee could say that, if anything, the divine essence is a disposition, and the divine fullness is the expression of that disposition. Yet even if this distinction carries, Lee can say that creation's telos is to repeat the divine being, and he can say that creation itself is the repetition of the divine fullness.[67] The divine being and the divine fullness are hardly distinguishable.[68] Even if the divine essence is a disposition and the divine fullness is its expression, then it is still difficult to map this to Edwards's assertion that the divine fullness is communicable and the divine essence is not. If the expression of a disposition is communicable, then why would the disposition

---

[67]Lee, *Philosophical Theology of Jonathan Edwards*, 173-74. "The created world is a network of divinely established habits and dispositions (or the so-called laws of nature) whose ultimate telos is to know and to love God so as to repeat in time and space God's own being" (8; see also 183).
[68]Bombaro notes that it is God's fullness rather than essence that is communicated to the saints, and he bases this on *The End of Creation* (*Jonathan Edwards's Vision of Reality*, 98).

itself not be communicable? Lee is careful to point out ways in which the divine disposition (Lee's equivalent to essence) differs from creaturely disposition, but the fact remains that the Creator-creature distinction is harder to pin down in Lee's conception than it would be with a traditional essence-substance ontology.[69]

This is where the real trouble lies. Lee dispenses with the essence-substance ontology in favor of a dispositional one. Yet such a strong thesis creates difficulty in making sense of some of Edwards's statements. If one retains a more traditional idea of essence and substance, then Edwards's distinction between the divine essence and the divine fullness becomes at least plausibly intelligible. In this study I have assumed just this. When Edwards says that creatures cannot partake of the divine essence, I have understood that to mean that creatures cannot share in being *in the same way that God is being*. On the other hand, the divine fullness is dispositional and relational, and as persons, saints can partake of relatedness in the same way that God can, though in infinitely less degree.

Am I, however, trying to have my cake and eat it too? Is there a way to retain an essence-substance ontology within Edwards and still hold onto a central role for disposition? Happily, recent scholarship suggests one can do just this.

An alternative to Lee's thesis. In 2003 Stephen Holmes published an essay calling Lee's dispositional account of God into question.[70] Holmes's concern is that Lee's account of Edwards's God, if correct, would mean that Edwards jettisoned the theological orthodoxy he claimed. Edwards was a Reformed theologian, and he owned that tradition closely. He defended it, he supported it, he promoted it, and at times he modified it. Holmes recognizes that Edwards sometimes challenged and critiqued his received tradition, but when this happens, Edwards generally acknowledges this and justifies why his adjustment is plausibly within the bounds of orthodoxy. Lee asserts that Edwards redefined God's essence in terms of disposition, so that, among other things, "God is inherently a tendency towards an increase

---

[69]Lee, *Philosophical Theology of Jonathan Edwards*, 183.
[70]Stephen R. Holmes, "Does Jonathan Edwards Use a Dispositional Ontology? A Response to Sang Hyun Lee," in *Jonathan Edwards: Philosophical Theologian*, ed. Oliver D. Crisp and Paul Helm (Burlington, VT: Ashgate, 2003), 99-114.

or enlargement of God's own being."[71] This assertion, argues Holmes, places Edwards outside the bounds of orthodoxy, and therefore there is a high burden of proof required to make the case. Holmes concludes that Lee's argument, while internally coherent, does not prove sufficiently persuasive. Rather, there are simpler explanations that can explain the data.[72]

Other scholars have followed Holmes in critiquing Lee's dispositional ontology. Oliver Crisp is notable for his argument that Edwards does retain a role for substance ontology. Where Holmes critiqued Lee as overextending disposition in Edwards's doctrine of God, Crisp critiques Lee for making created nature dispositional, to the exclusion of essentialism. According to Crisp, Edwards's ontology retains the ideas of essence, substance, and properties, and that they cannot be entirely dislodged by disposition. It is not that dispositions are absent from Edwards's thought, but rather Crisp critiques Lee's assertions that *all* an entity's properties are dispositional. Edwards's corpus simply does not require such a thesis. Like Holmes, Crisp asserts that there are simpler explanations that can explain all the data, and that the simpler explanations include the notions of nondispositional essence, substance, and properties. Crisp explores Edwards's approach to idealism, occasionalism, and continuous creation and argues that especially the last two—occasionalism and continuous creation—call Lee's dispositional ontology into real question. This is because Lee's account of ontology envisages dispositions enduring through time. Crisp argues that Edwards's occasionalism and continuous-creation doctrine deny this. God recreates reality in every moment, and these moments are linked together to form a sense of continuity.[73]

If this is correct, then it is difficult for Crisp to see how disposition—a tendency to certain action in relation to other things—can form the basis of reality. A dispostion's "tendency to action" will be nothing more than a sort of illusion based on the more fundamental reality of God's immediate and continuous creation. Therefore, there must be something more basic to reality than dispositions alone. With this in place Crisp is able to point

---

[71]Lee, *Philosophical Theology of Jonathan Edwards*, 184; Holmes, "Does Jonathan Edwards Use," 104.

[72]"I believe that most if not all of the evidence Lee offers for his reconstruction can be explained as, or more, adequately by a less implausible account of what Edwards thought" (Holmes, "Does Jonathan Edwards Use," 100).

[73]Crisp, *Jonathan Edwards on God and Creation*, 15-18, 22-23, 32.

out how Edwards does not deny created substances, but rather defends and argues for the existence of created substances. More specifically, Edwards grounds created substance in God's immediate action.[74] God himself is the deeper reality in the created world. God is the only real substance, but by his immediate action there is "ontological room ... for created substances."[75] Edwards denies any autonomous substance, but allows created substance to exist through the immediate action of God's ideation.[76] All of this leads Crisp to conclude that Edwards's unique contribution to ontology was not so much dispositionalism—taken in exclusion to essentialism—but rather "the way in which he sought to synthesize essentialism, idealism, occasionalism, and continuous creation along with orthodox theological commitments."[77]

Given Crisp's and Holmes's critiques of the Lee view, it is not surprising that scholars have come to Lee's defense. The most important for my purposes comes from the pen of Michael McClymond.[78] McClymond is a firm supporter of Lee's dispositional account of Edwards's theology. His reasons for this are several, but they are captured in an intriguing metaphor. He compares Edwards's thought to a symphony that carries several different musical lines, which all harmonize in relation to each other. Lee's interpretation, along with scholars who have followed and furthered his thought, is the best explanation for how the music fits together.[79] That is, Lee's interpretation allows Edwards readers to truly hear the whole symphony in harmony together. In particular, and importantly for my purposes, McClymond argues that Lee's interpretation "more adequately acknowledges Edwards's *soteriology*. Lee's and Pauw's writings have captured Edwards's expansive

---

[74] WJE 6:215.
[75] Crisp, *Jonathan Edwards on God and Creation*, 33.
[76] Crisp, *Jonathan Edwards on God and Creation*, 33. See WJE 6:238. Here Edwards links an entity's reality and substantiality to its proximity to God. He denies a thing's reality in itself. Crisp takes this to be a way of affirming created reality (and substantiality) in dependence on God.
[77] Crisp, *Jonathan Edwards on God and Creation*, 36.
[78] Michael J. McClymond, "Hearing the Symphony: A Critique of Some Critics of Sang Lee's and Amy Pauw's Accounts of Jonathan Edwards' View of God," in *Jonathan Edwards as Contemporary: Essays in Honor of Sang Hyun Lee*, ed. Don Schweitzer (New York: Peter Lang, 2010), 67-92.
[79] McClymond particularly seeks to defend Amy Plantinga Pauw, who follows and furthers Lee's thought. See Amy Plantinga Pauw, *The Supreme Harmony of All: The Trinitarian Theology of Jonathan Edwards* (Grand Rapids, MI: Eerdmans, 2002); Pauw, "A Response from Amy Plantinga Pauw," *SJT* 57, no. 4 (2004): 486-89.

vision of God's outflowing and overflowing love in creation and redemption, and the elect creatures' genuine participation in the life, love, happiness, blessedness, and glory of the Holy Trinity."[80] McClymond argues that this soteriological focus is central and that it is underappreciated in the accounts given by Holmes and Crisp.

McClymond's thought becomes clearer as he develops his metaphor of the symphony. He imagines Edwards's theology as an orchestra with five sections: the violins, the stringed instruments, the woodwinds, the brass, and the harmonious constitutionalism. The violins represent the theme of trinitarian communication—within the Trinity and exported in the creation. The stringed instruments map to its corollary in human participation in the Trinity's life. These together, asserts McClymond, carry the melody of the symphony in Edwards's thought and cannot be overestimated in importance. The woodwinds represent Edwards's Augustinian-Calvinistic emphasis on the will and affections, human depravity, and divine sovereignty. The brass section represents Edwards's focus on the dispositions as the decisive aspect of the human that makes them pleasing or not to God. Finally, McClymond asserts harmonious constitutionalism, in which, rather as in Thomism, "salvation is less like a chain of beads than like a net in which each part of the net holds the rest in place." All five elements of the symphony must be heard together. Yet, once again, the violins and the strings hold a certain priority. "Trinitarian communication and creaturely participation carry the tune throughout most of the symphony." And this is part of his critique of Holmes, Crisp, and others who resist Lee's dispositional ontology. Holmes, Crisp, and others are "sitting too near to the woodwind section to hear the violins and other strings."[81] That is, they overemphasize Edwards's Augustinian and Reformed heritage in such a way that what is distinct in Edwards is lost. More specifically, the distinct element McClymond thinks is lost is trinitarian communication and creaturely participation. For McClymond, this is the centerpiece of Edwards's soteriology, and Lee's school of thought preserves it best.

McClymond is a skilled apologist for Lee and Lee's school. He is right to emphasize trinitarian communication and creaturely participation and to give them a leading role in the Edwardsean symphony. Edwards's theology

---

[80]McClymond, "Hearing the Symphony," 70.
[81]McClymond, "Hearing the Symphony," 81-82.

carries this melody throughout his thought, and this melody is profoundly dispositional. Trinitarian fullness is dispositional because it is God's love—the Holy Spirit—shared between the Father and the Son. Therefore, one must say that this divine fullness penetrates to the very heart of Edwards's God. The Father begets the Son through his own self-reflection, and the two mutually adore one another, spirating the third person of the Trinity. This represents the Father's love (a disposition) and also the Son's love (the same disposition). Further, the Son also inclines to replicate this communication beyond the Godhead. This results in the intention to create the world. The aim of creation is the Son's communication to the church, and the church's participation in him.[82] Dispositions are key throughout this melody.

That said, and using McClymond's helpful image of the symphony, while one must attend to this violin and string melody, one must not lose the woodwinds. Holmes and Crisp, along with others such as John Bombaro, Kyle Strobel, and Steve Studebaker, have provided reminders that Edwards valued his Reformed Augustinian heritage. Holmes is right that Edwards was loyal to Reformed orthodoxy, and the scholars such as Crisp and others who taken this line seriously are right to do so as well. True, Edwards was not loyal in a slavish way to the Reformed tradition. Famously, he felt the Reformed tradition shortchanged the Holy Spirit's glory, and he made corrections.[83] Similarly, he felt free to modify traditional approaches to ontology in order to reemphasize creation's immediate dependence on God and address the questions of modernity. But these modifications and creative developments are always taken with a close eye to the tradition Edwards inherited. Indeed, just as McClymond notes, Reformed orthodoxy was not monolithic.[84] The fact that the Reformed tradition was composed of differing viewpoints on many matters reinforces the idea that Edwards had room to maneuver within the bounds of orthodoxy. Surely one can agree that Edwards aimed to defend, reinforce, and extend the Reformed project in his day.[85] If so, then these scholars lend a helpful voice.

---

[82] *Miscellanies* 104, 115 (WJE 13:272-74, 282). Both *Miscellanies* entries are explicit that only the saints receive this communication. Thus, this cannot be referring to the *act of creation*.
[83] WJE 21:191.
[84] McClymond, "Hearing the Symphony," 74.
[85] See, e.g., Kyle Strobel's work to place Edwards's trinitarian thought into the polemical context of his day. Edwards's creativity was spurred on, in part, by his efforts to defend key Reformed doctrine (Strobel, *Jonathan Edwards's Theology: A Reinterpretation*, 31-72).

What then should one make of this debate? Is there a way to honor the good insights on both sides and put forward a coherent way of hearing the symphony? Bombaro provides a helpful attempt to take Lee's dispositional insights seriously, while at the same time listening intently to what McClymond calls the woodwinds of Edwards's Reformed heritage.[86] In particular he argues that while Lee is right that dispositions are very important in Edwards, Lee is wrong that dispositions supplant essence-substance ontology. In this Bombaro echoes Holmes and Crisp. Yet he provides a further insight that helps relate Edwards's essence-substance ontology to his dispositionalism. Bombaro argues that Edwards uses essence-substance ontology to undergird being, and he uses dispositionalism to undergird causality. Created being is established through God's immediate communication, and Bombaro describes this in much the same way that this study does. All things exist in direct, immediate dependence on God as the being of beings. However, this created, natural being (creation in its widest frame) also includes law-like dispositions. These dispositions are not the same as being. Rather, they are a constitutive part of how God orchestrates causality.[87] Things happen in creation because God has built dispositions into the world.

All of this accords well with this study's findings, and Bombaro's approach allows something of a mediating line between Lee, on the one hand, and Holmes's and Crisp's rejection of Lee, on the other. Essence-substance ontology and dispositions do not require a binary choice in Edwards. They are both present, and they operate in a complementary fashion. Here I argue that they are both aspects of created nature, and they are undergirded by common grace, or what I have called common participation. God communicates being, continually, and this establishes created essence and substance. Bombaro is right to say that within this created matrix, Edwards conceived of dispositions as God's way of effecting providential orchestration. As Bombaro states, "God is not interventionist, but an orchestrationist."[88] This dispositionalism also falls under common participation and common grace.

---

[86]Bombaro, *Jonathan Edwards's Vision of Reality*, 73. Bombaro asserts that Edwards's "innovations" were "restrained by this Calvinistic confessional convictions" (100-101).
[87]Bombaro, *Jonathan Edwards's Vision of Reality*, 13, 22, 71-72, 75-77, 97-100.
[88]Bombaro, *Jonathan Edwards's Vision of Reality*, 72.

This means that my account of common participation follows, at least in broad strokes, the ontology put forward by Bombaro and those of the essentialist camp. Part of the reason for this is that this ontology holds explanatory power for Edwards's strong and repeated distinction between created nature and divine grace. As discussed earlier, a key concern in Lee's approach is that it becomes unclear how divine grace differs from created nature. If all is disposition, and if the created world is a communication of divine fullness, then what is distinct about divine grace, especially when Edwards uses precisely those words to describe its uniqueness? This is not to say that I take disposition to be *absent* from created nature in itself. Dispositions to self-love and habits of various forms are implied in created natures and particularly *human* essence.[89] As Bombaro argues, dispositions operate within created nature and govern causality. But two things must be said about these dispositions. First, these dispositions resident in created nature and essence are not the same as the trinitarian divine fullness. To say that they are the same is to collapse Edwards's distinction between created nature and divine grace, or between common and special grace. The second thing is this: it is one thing to say that created nature and created essences exhibit disposition; it is another thing to say that they *are* those dispositions, and nothing else. I am prepared to say the first; Lee would have one say the second.[90] With respect, I decline to take that step.

Yet even as I decline Lee's dispositionalism, my account of special participation reaffirms, strongly, McClymond's point about the melodic nature of trinitarian communication and participation in Edwards. Special grace, special participation, is robustly dispositional in Edwards—it is just that it is not the same dispositions that are given in the act of creation itself. Rather, special grace is the immediate communication of the Trinity's own disposition to mutual love between the Father and the Son. This communication, and the creaturely participation it effects, is the end or telos of God's creative act—not the act of creating itself. If it is the end of God's purpose in creating,

---

[89]For instance, "[The human soul's] essence consists in powers and habits" (*Miscellanies* 241, in WJE 13:358). I should point out, however, that this is an offhand comment. The burden of the entry is to explain the habitual nature of special grace in regeneration. Another example: "A principle of self-love, or love of his own happiness: 'tis natural to man to love happiness; it belongs to his essence" (Edwards, "True Grace Is Divine (1738)," 355).

[90]Lee, *Philosophical Theology of Jonathan Edwards*, 39.

then this reaffirms McClymond's point that trinitarian communication and creaturely participation occupy a privileged position in the Edwardsean symphony. Further, McClymond is right to emphasize the importance of this communication and participation to Edwards's *soteriology*. I agree that it is the linchpin in Edwards's soteriology. I underline this point by saying that when Edwards speaks of the communication of trinitarian *fullness* as the end of creation, he speaks specifically to *soteriology*, rather than to *ontology* more generally.

This approach also allows one to point out the ways in which Edwards's doctrine of special grace as participation in divine fullness is at the same time traditional and a development of his tradition. McClymond urges caution in viewing Edwards as following Reformed convention in a slavish way. He is correct. However, when it comes to Edwards's approach to special grace, it is not the dispositionalism that is novel, as one might imagine from reading Lee, but rather the way Edwards grounds special grace in trinitarian communication and participation. Lee makes much of Edwards's dispositional comments in *Miscellanies* 241. The burden of this entry is not ontology, though it is mentioned as an aside.[91] The burden of Edwards's discussion of habit and disposition is to describe *regeneration*, an aspect of special grace. For Edwards, special grace is a habit and a disposition.

This is no innovation. John Cotton, prominent minister of the First Church of Boston, describes grace this way: "By *gifts of Grace*, I mean holy qualities, the same the Philosophers call *vertuous habites*, or *good dispositions*, whereby the faculties and affections of the soule . . . are hereby sanctified, and lifted up to God."[92] It is true that the early Reformers were cautious about describing grace in terms of habit and disposition because they wanted to avoid associations with semi-Pelagiansim.[93] However, there was development in the tradition, so that Cotton could describe grace in habitual terms without a great deal of fanfare. Nearly one hundred years later,

---

[91]Crisp makes this point (*Jonathan Edwards on God and Creation*), 23.

[92]John Cotton, *The covenant of Gods free grace, most sweetly unfolded and comfortably applied to a disquieted soul. Whereunto is added, A profession of faith, made by J. Davenport*, ed. Thomas A. Schafer (London: John Hancock, 1645), 27, emphasis original. I modified the *s* to modern rendering.

[93]Richard A. Muller, *Post-Reformation Reformed Dogmatics: The Rise and Development of Reformed Orthodoxy, ca. 1520 to ca. 1725*, vol. 1, *Prolegomena to Theology*, 2nd ed. (Grand Rapids, MI: Baker Academic, 2003), 356-59.

Edwards was not innovative in employing dispositions in describing divine grace. He *does modify* his tradition, however, by grounding these habits and dispositions in a participation in uncreated grace. I will explore these modifications more fully in the next section. For the moment it is important to note that in this move Edwards unites a reasonably traditionally dispositional view of special grace with a strong view of trinitarian communication and creaturely participation, to achieve the melody McClymond rightly wants us to hear.

All of this allows for a return the central question of this chapter. How do created nature and divine grace positively relate to each other? Edwards distinguishes created nature from special grace. I nest the ontology of Bombaro and others in the first category, and the trinitarian communication and participation, along with much dispositional content so important to McClymond, in the second category. Yet, Edwards distinguishes these only in order to relate them. Created nature is *for* special grace. God creates the universe and gives it created essence and nature—being—which itself is a participation in God's own being. God is *ens entium* and "being in general."[94] But this created nature is not an end in itself. It exists for a larger purpose. The end for which created nature exists is the communication and participation in divine fullness—special grace. "God is a communicative being. This communication is really only to intelligent beings," that is, to the saints.[95] If this was God's great purpose in creating, then it explains why it is that this trinitarian communication and participation is always so prominent in Edwards's writings. Ontology is background for soteriology. *Being is for* koinōnia.

Edwards's Doctrine of Grace: A Modification of Reformed Tradition?

One of the questions in the background throughout this study is that of how Edwards's doctrine of grace as participation in divine fullness relates to his Reformed heritage. Is Edwards's emphasis on trinitarian participation a jettisoning of his Reformed heritage? If it is not a jettisoning, is it a foreign

---

[94] WJE 6:215; 8:461.
[95] *Miscellanies* 332 (WJE 13:410). See *Miscellanies* 104: "This was the end of the creation, even the communication of the happiness of the Son of God.... And man, the consciousness or perception of the creation, is the immediate subject of this. Therefore the church is said to be the completeness of Christ" (WJE 13:272).

appendage, something that Edwards has joined onto his theological tradition, but not something that developed from within it? Or, alternatively, is it a development of his Reformed commitments? This question is particularly relevant in the current scholarly context because of how soteriological participation has come into view. Recent interest in soteriological participation grew out of engagement with Eastern Orthodox theories of theosis. One result of this is that, when similar ideas are found in Western thinkers, it raises the question as to whether these ideas are somehow imported from elsewhere, or otherwise out of sync with native Western thought. Within Reformed thought in particular there is debate as to the propriety of emphasizing soteriological participation at all.[96] It is therefore inevitable, and important, that the question is asked: How does Jonathan Edwards's doctrine of grace as a communication and participation in divine fullness relate to this Reformed heritage? May one, in some sense, call it a *Reformed* doctrine of grace? More boldly: a *Reformed* doctrine of theosis?

One must recognize that this is not an easy question, and ultimately it is a question beyond the scope of this study. This in part due to the fact that Reformed tradition is always diverse. McClymond, quoted above, is right that the Reformed heritage is not monochrome. Reformed thinkers often put forward ideas that are at odds with other Reformed thinkers, and yet they are still viewed as loyal to the Reformed household. The most decisive way a thinker's thought may be vindicated or rejected is through a synodical or conciliar decision. However, no such synod or council has considered Edwards's doctrine of grace. Failing this, there is the longer and less decisive process in which scholars evaluate the thinker's ideas and then debate whether the idiosyncrasies serve to uphold or tear down the wider Reformed project. In this process, it is key to consider whether the thinker's ideas contribute or undermine key interests of the Reformed movement.

This study will not attempt to settle the question; however, we can add an element that helps address the question of how Edwards's doctrine of grace relates to his Reformed heritage. I will analyze three key modifications that Edwards made to his Reformed heritage and argue that these are sympathetic developments of doctrine in pursuit of Reformed interests.

---

[96]Julie Canlis, *Calvin's Ladder: A Spiritual Theology of Ascent and Ascension* (Grand Rapids, MI: Eerdmans, 2010), 13-17.

Jonathan Edwards's doctrine of special grace includes several modifications of his Reformed tradition. However, the key modifications that he made were never intended as denials of Reformed orthodoxy. Rather, they were made with a view toward showing the coherence of at least three crucial Reformed doctrines: (1) the doctrine of the Trinity, (2) the doctrine of grace, and (3) the doctrine of creation's end. The modifications Edwards made to these doctrines were intended to show how they relate to each other. That is, the modifications Edwards made in developing his approach to soteriological participation were made to synchronize these inherited doctrines, not to deny that heritage. Put differently yet again: Edwards modified the doctrine of the Trinity, *in order to show its soteriological import*; Edwards modified the doctrine of grace, *in order to show its trinitarian foundation*; Edwards modified the doctrine of creation's end, *in order to show the centrality of the first two doctrines*. All three of these doctrines unite to each other around the idea of soteriological participation, or grace as communication and participation in divine fullness. These modifications were aimed at a sympathetic development of Reformed tradition and not as a denial or departure from it.

Modifying the Trinity. Edwards's doctrine of the Trinity is striking, not least because he framed it as a foundation for his theory of soteriology. This, in itself, was nothing new in Christian theology and tradition. The Christian doctrine of God, both framed in terms of the Trinity as a whole and in terms of Christology more specifically, had framed soteriology from the patristic era. Indeed, it is fair to say that the Christian dogma of the Trinity, developed via the doctrine of Christ, grew as an address to the question of how humanity may be saved.[97] This soteriological orientation in the doctrine of the Trinity was never lost entirely in Christian tradition, but it was perhaps eclipsed by subsequent debates. The arguments between Rome and the Protestant Reformation did not center on the dogma of the Trinity. They agreed on that. What they disagreed on were questions of justification, the church, authority, the ministry, and the sacraments. These questions therefore became the particular focus of attention, with the Trinity providing the

---

[97]See Donald Fairbairn's argument that the christological controversies of the early church were in fact arguments over the doctrine of grace in *Grace and Christology in the Early Church*, Oxford Early Christian Studies (Oxford: Oxford University Press, 2006).

background and context for these debates, but it was not always clear how the doctrine of the Trinity related directly to these questions.

By Edwards's day, English Dissenters could view the Trinity as an optional interpretation of Scripture rather than a fundamental dogma. The Salter's Hall Synod of 1719 allowed ministers to be ordained without subscribing to the traditional trinitarian formula. This was because the historic dogma of the Trinity rested not only on the Scriptures but on the historic creeds as well. The synod chose not to require ministers to adhere to extrascriptural definitions.[98] Yet it was more than just a question of the Bible over against historic creeds. Amy Plantinga Pauw suggests that it was the importance of the doctrine that was set aside, rather than its truth as such.[99] In hindsight, this was harbinger of the approaching Unitarianism that grew so important in the rest of the eighteenth century. That Edwards spent so much time on and gave so much soteriological emphasis to the doctrine of the Trinity at precisely this era is part of what makes his thought so remarkable.

However, it would be wrong to imagine that Edwards was a lone pioneer in this. Rather, Edwards's own Puritan heritage carried within it a strong tradition of emphasizing the soteriological import of the Trinity. Nearly one hundred years before Edwards's *Discourse on the Trinity*, his theological forbearers were arguing that the Trinity was the basis of true Christian spirituality. Francis Cheynell states that the Trinity is "a Practicall mysterie, the very foundation and ground-worke of the mysterie of godlinesse."[100] John Owen is among the most obvious examples of a Reformed thinker who viewed the Trinity as central to every aspect of Christian theology. His magisterial work *Of Communion with God the Father, Son and Holy Ghost* is the most obvious instance. Owen writes in a way that could easily be a quotation from Edwards's discussion of special grace: "Our communion, then, with God consisteth in his *communication of himself unto us, with our returnal*

---

[98]Thomas Lewis, *The Scourge: In Vindication of the Church of England; to Which Is Added, I. The Danger of the Church-Establishment of England, from the Insolence of Protestant Dissenters; Occasion'd by a Presentment of the Forty Second Paper of the Scourge at the King's Bench Bar, by the Grand Jury of the Hundred of Ossulston; II. The Anatomy of the Heretical Synod of Dissenters at Salters-Hall* (London, 1720), 369.
[99]Pauw, *Supreme Harmony of All*, 24.
[100]As quoted in Paul C. H. Lim, *Mystery Unveiled: The Crisis of the Trinity in Early Modern England* (Oxford: Oxford University Press, 2012), 176. See n19, cited as Francis Cheynell, *A Copy of Some Papers* (1647), 11-12.

unto him of that which he requireth and accepteth, flowing from that *union* which in Jesus Christ we have with him."[101] This communion is entirely based on the doctrine of the Trinity. Indeed, Owen believed that the doctrine of the Trinity would be most strongly upheld and defended when it was properly the subject of experience.[102]

Richard Muller considers Owen's trinitarian orientation to be typical of the Reformed Orthodox.[103] Owen and Cheynell are not alone but represent a strain of the Puritan tradition that was directly in Edwards's heritage. One can see this play out further by comparing two classic Puritan confessions of faith: the Westminster Confession and the Savoy Declaration. The Savoy Declaration is, in large part, simply a Congregationalist version of Westminster. There is near verbal identity between them. It is therefore particularly interesting to find where Savoy differs from Westminster. One of those differences occurs at the very end of the chapter on the doctrine of the Trinity. Savoy follows Westminster word for word until the last line in the article. There Savoy adds a specifically soteriological application for the doctrine: "Which doctrine of the Trinity is the foundation of all our communion with God, and comfortable dependence upon him."[104] This same document, with this addition, was received by the Boston Synod in 1680.[105] All this is to say that the Puritan tradition, or at least part of it, emphasized the Trinity as a soteriological doctrine. By the time of Edwards this interest may have atrophied, but it still stands that emphasizing the Trinity as the basis for the saints' communion with God was a traditional element in Puritan and Reformed doctrine.

As seen in chapter three, Edwards's aim in his doctrine of the Trinity was to show how it was "illustrative of gospel doctrines."[106] This was a traditional

---

[101] John Owen, *The Works of John Owen*, ed. William H. Goold (Edinburgh: Banner of Truth Trust, 1976), 2:8.
[102] Joel R. Beeke and Mark Jones, *A Puritan Theology* (Grand Rapids, MI: Reformation Heritage Books, 2012), 114-15.
[103] Richard A. Muller, *Post-Reformation Reformed Dogmatics*, vol. 4, *The Trinuity of God* (Grand Rapids, MI: Baker, 2003), 145, 148; cited in Beeke and Jones, *Puritan Theology*, 101n2.
[104] "A Declaration of the Faith and Order Owned and Practiced in the Congregational Churches in England; Agreed upon and consented unto By their Elders and Messengers in Their Meeting at the SAVOY, Octob. 12, 1658" (Printed for D.L. and are to be sold in Paul's Church-yard, Fleet-Street, and Westminster-Hall, 1659), http://www.creeds.net/congregational/savoy/, 2.3.
[105] "Confession of Faith; owned," 6.
[106] WJE 21:134.

impetus. One may therefore read Edwards's development and modification of the doctrine of the Trinity as continuing the theological trajectory of his Puritan forbearers, and not least of Owen. Multiple monographs are written on Edwards's doctrine of the Trinity and address the question of whether Edwards is more or less traditional in his views.[107] However, Edwards makes two modifications that stand out as relevant for his doctrine of grace: his view of real attributes, and his assertion that the Holy Spirit is the gift purchased in salvation. Both of these were discussed in chapter three, so I will not go into great detail here. Rather, I want to point out that both of these modifications are aimed at demonstrating the soteriological import of the Trinity. That is, both modifications are aimed at pursuing the traditional Puritan theological aim of experiencing doctrine.[108]

Edwards asserts that all God's attributes can be summed up in God, God's understanding, and God's will. Alternatively, Edwards means the same thing by saying that there is God, God's Logos, and God's Agapē. These three correspond to the Father, the Son, and the Holy Spirit respectively.[109] All other traditional attributes of God resolve to these three in relation to other things. This view is controversial—some believe it undermines the traditional notion of simplicity.[110] On the other hand, it functions to unite two traditional spheres of discourse in the doctrine of God. Joel Beeke and Mark Jones write, "The doctrine of God may be understood in a twofold sense, either essentially or personally. Understood essentially, the doctrine refers to the essence of God and His attributes; a personal understanding refers to the doctrine of the tri-personality of the Godhead, or the doctrine of the Trinity."[111]

Edwards's approach clearly unites these two.[112] But this first modification was a step on the road to a second modification: presenting the Holy Spirit

---

[107]See, e.g., Pauw, *Supreme Harmony of All*; Steven Studebaker, "Jonathan Edwards's Social Augustinian Trinitarianism: An Alternative to a Recent Trend," *SJT* 56, no. 3 (2003): 268-85; Steven Studebaker and Robert W. Caldwell, *The Trinitarian Theology of Jonathan Edwards: Text, Context, and Application* (Surrey, UK: Ashgate, 2012).
[108]Beeke and Jones, *Puritan Theology*, 114-15.
[109]WJE 21:131-32.
[110]On the debate regarding Edwards and the simplicity tradition, see n32.
[111]Beeke and Jones, *Puritan Theology*, 85.
[112]For similar points, see Strobel, "Jonathan Edwards's Reformed Doctrine"; Kyle Strobel, "Jonathan Edwards and the Polemics of Theosis," *HTR* 105, no. 3 (2012): 259-79.

as not only the applier of saving gift but the gift itself.[113] Edwards argues that the Holy Spirit not only *loves* but *is God's love*, and this allows him to argue that in the gift of salvation, the Holy Spirit not only *gives God's love*, or *applies God's love*, but rather *is the love given*. Traditionally, Edwards's own tradition presented the Father as the one who purchases salvation, the Son as the price of salvation, and the Spirit as the one who applies the salvation.[114] Edwards believed this undermined the honor and glory of the Spirit, and self-consciously modified the tradition so that the Holy Spirit not only applied the gift of salvation but rather in fact was the gift itself. This was a crucial modification for Edwards. He knew he was modifying his tradition, and he defends himself as pursuing equal honor and glory for each member of the Trinity, certainly a traditional Reformed pursuit.[115] One must not miss the soteriological significance of this move. Whereas many in his Puritan heritage viewed the Trinity as the "foundation of... communion with God," Edwards has now made the Trinity into the communion itself.[116] Or more accurately, the Holy Spirit becomes the communion the saints enjoy with the Father and the Son.[117] God is no longer the giver of salvation alone; God is now the gift itself.

This is a formidable modification. Yet it is a modification that presses forward a trajectory already set by Puritan canon. Owen and others set the trajectory by drawing together the Trinity and soteriology. Edwards's modification was not a departure from this trajectory, but rather he pressed forward on the same path. This leads to the second major doctrine that Edwards modified: grace itself.

Modifying grace. When Edwards made the Spirit not only the applier of salvation but the gift of salvation itself, he committed himself to a strong view of uncreated grace. Augustinian tradition had always affirmed uncreated grace, but beginning in the Middle Ages, Western theology also posited a view of created grace. Where uncreated grace referred to the Holy

---

[113]Strobel moves from Edwards's real attributes of God *ad intra* to communicable natures in the economy. As I have mentioned previously, these communicable natures are implied within the divine fullness (see Strobel, "Jonathan Edwards's Reformed Doctrine").
[114]See, e.g., Owen, *Communion with God*, 1.2, 16-17.
[115]WJE 21:136-37.
[116]"Declaration of the Faith," 2.3.
[117]WJE 13:448.

Spirit's direct work in the lives of saints, created grace referred to the effects of that operation. Created-grace theories are particularly attractive when the Spirit is viewed as the one who applies the saving gift. In this case, the Spirit *does something* in the saint that carries created results, and these created results may be termed grace. The Spirit's work is uncreated, the Spirit's effects are created, thus the distinction. However, Edwards's conception of the Spirit as the gift of salvation places great emphasis on the uncreated nature of grace. For Edwards, grace is the Holy Spirit.[118] Edwards states this as clearly as possible: "So that true saving grace is no other than that very love of God; that is, God, in one of the persons of the Trinity, uniting himself to the soul of a creature as a vital principle, dwelling there and exerting himself by the faculties of the soul of man, in his own proper nature, after the manner of a principle of nature."[119] Notice here that the Spirit (divine love, also the divine fullness) exerts himself through the human soul, repeating his own activity in the Trinity, so that the human loves with God's own love. The last clause, "after the manner of a principle of nature," does not mean that God's Spirit gives a new principle of *created* nature, but rather that the uncreated Spirit works *after the manner of a principle of nature*. The point is that the Spirit's work in the human soul fills the same dispositional function as a principle of nature. This is uncreated activity working through created beings. In positing this, Edwards modified his own tradition.

However, before we discuss the way in which this represents a modification of Edwards's tradition, it is important to note that there is debate about whether Edwards held to uncreated grace alone or also to a view of created grace. Edwards is clear that when grace is infused or communicated to the human, that the love given is the uncreated Spirit. However, he is also clear that the human is truly the agent of the love expressed and returned back toward God. In the quote above, the Spirit "exerts himself by the faculties of the soul of man," and therefore the faculties of man are activated to love. The human saint really is loving with the Spirit's love. Elsewhere Edwards states that the saint not only reflects divine light but "becomes

---

[118]Divine grace is the gift of the divine fullness, and the divine fullness is the Holy Spirit (see WJE 21:187-88).
[119]WJE 21:194.

properly a luminous thing."[120] This leads Anri Morimoto to conclude that Edwards implies a doctrine of created grace.

Morimoto's view is based in part on his strong affirmation of Lee's dispositional ontology. As noted above, Lee understands dispositions to be the fundamental ontology underneath all things. Edwards often describes grace as a disposition. The question is whether this is a created or uncreated disposition. While Morimoto agrees that Edwards does hold a view of uncreated grace, he also argues that God creates a new disposition to love in the saint. This is how Morimoto can explain the saints' agency. If saints are luminous and not just reflectors of divine light, then they must become a secondary source (Morimoto's word, not Edwards's) for that light. This implies, for Morimoto, a view of created grace.[121] Michael McClenahan put forward a distinct but similar argument. He states, "It is of singular importance to distinguish the indwelling of the Holy Spirit from the new foundation laid in the soul by the Holy Spirit. That is, to distinguish the new indwelling vital principle from the holy principles and gracious dispositions which exist as a consequence of the renewal of the soul."[122] While he does not employ the created-grace term, he argues for something similar, and does so in part to retain an aspect of Puritan tradition that sought to protect human agency.

There is good reason to doubt both these conclusions, and scholars have critiqued both Morimoto and McClenahan on these points.[123] Indeed, there appears to be a growing consensus that Edwards taught uncreated grace without a created-grace view. Bombaro notes that Morimoto bases his argument on an apparent silence in Edwards. Morimoto does not think Edwards was likely to be aware of the created-/uncreated-grace controversy.[124] Bombaro counters this by showing that Edwards explicitly uses the categories

---

[120] WJE 2:343.
[121] Anri Morimoto, *Jonathan Edwards and the Catholic Vision of Salvation* (University Park: Pennsylvania State University Press, 1995), 7-8, 42-46.
[122] Michael McClenahan, *Jonathan Edwards and Justification by Faith* (Burlington, VT: Ashgate, 2012), 187.
[123] John Bombaro and Robert Caldwell have refuted Morimoto on this point. See Bombaro, *Jonathan Edwards's Vision of Reality*, 240-44; Robert W. Caldwell III, *Communion in the Spirit: The Holy Spirit as the Bond of Union in the Theology of Jonathan Edwards*, Studies in Evangelical History and Thought (Milton Keynes, UK: Paternoster, 2006), 109-11. See also Tan, *Fullness Received and Returned*, 281-301.
[124] Morimoto, *Jonathan Edwards and the Catholic Vision*, 43.

of created and uncreated grace, and explicitly names grace as uncreated. Bombaro quotes Edwards to say, "Yet the grace of God in men's hearts can hardly be called created. 'Tis God's own beauty and excellency that is uncreated and eternal, which is not properly made but communicated. It is as we said before the Spirit of Christ itself; it is God himself."[125] This is a very clear endorsement by Edwards of uncreated grace over against created grace, and a clear engagement with the debate. Bombaro proceeds to show that the gracious dispositions in the saint are similarly the ongoing operation of the Spirit and never become created nature in the saint.[126]

Kyle Strobel has critiqued McClenahan as failing to fully account for the way Edwards views the Spirit acting "as a habit of grace upholding the soul by *being the very love of God itself dwelling there.*"[127] Strobel goes on to argue that the work of the Spirit acting as habit within the soul does not undermine the integrity of the human person. Rather, Edwards views the dynamic in a compatibilist manner. God the Spirit does all, and at the same time the saint is truly loving, not because something new is created, but because the Spirit loves through the faculties of the saint.[128] Strobel notes that McClenahan reads Edwards in light of John Owen, but in this way fails to fully grasp the modification Edwards made to his tradition.[129]

Bombaro's and Strobel's arguments are persuasive. Morimoto reads Edwards in light of Thomism, and McClenahan reads Edwards as following Puritan convention, but neither grasps the modification Edwards made to his tradition's doctrine of grace. Edwards's approach is to posit uncreated grace, working in and through the created faculties, in an ongoing manner, such that the saint loves with God's own love.

Edwards was indeed modifying at least a portion of his tradition. Created grace was a mainstream way of distinguishing the Creator-creature distinction and relation. John Owen, Amandus Polanus, and Thomas Goodwin all spoke of the Spirit creating grace in the soul of a saint.[130] John Cotton,

---

[125]Jonathan Edwards, "Sermon on 2 Corinthians 3:18(a) (after July 1727)," in *WJE Online* 43 [L. 6r], as cited in Bombaro, *Jonathan Edwards's Vision of Reality*, 241n30.

[126]Bombaro, *Jonathan Edwards's Vision of Reality*, 241-43.

[127]Strobel, *Jonathan Edwards's Theology: A Reinterpretation*, 192.

[128]Strobel quotes WJE 21:251 (*Jonathan Edwards's Theology: A Reinterpretation*, 193n67).

[129]Strobel, *Jonathan Edwards's Theology: A Reinterpretation*, 190.

[130]Tan, *Fullness Received and Returned*, 282. See John Owen's quote in Beeke and Jones, *Puritan Theology*, 115. See also n116.

the minister of First Church in Boston, one of the founders of the church in New England, also strongly endorsed created grace. Cotton's discussion is helpful because he also explicitly engages the debate, and he argues that if grace were uncreated, then it would contradict creaturely finitude and thereby undermine the Creator-creature distinction.

> [Members of Christ's body] do not live the uncreated life of the Holy Ghost communicated to them; therefore they live by the gifts of spiritually created in them. The former Proposition (or *major*) is plain because the dis-junction is immediate: there is no middle way given, but either wee must live a created life by some gifts of spirituall grace created in us, or else we must life the uncreated life of the Holy Ghost communicated to us. The latter Proposition (or *minor*) is as plain; for no creature (if being finite) can live an increated life, which is infinite; but we are creatures, and finite, and the life of the Holy God is increated, and infinite; therefore wee cannot live his life.[131]

Created grace, then, was a key dogmatic tool the Puritans used in order to distinguish and relate Creator and creature. It allowed them to assert immediate dependence on God the Spirit, but at the same time it allowed them to avoid the problem of an infinite God self-communicating to finite creatures, and the entire question of whether God's essence is communicated or something besides God's essence. These are legitimate concerns, and they seem to have made their way into one of the key Puritan confessions of the seventeenth century. I have already mentioned the Savoy Declaration's emphasis on the soteriological implications of the Trinity. One of the other places where the Savoy Declaration adds to the Westminster is in an article titled "Of the Gospel, and the Extent of the Grace thereof." This is article XX in Savoy, and it does not appear in Westminster. Importantly, it speaks of the Holy Spirit "producing in [people] a new spiritual life."[132] The idea of the Spirit *producing* spiritual life, while stopping short of a full endorsement of created grace, points in that direction.

Here one can see Edwards modifying this aspect of his tradition. I have already shown that Edwards explicitly distances himself from created grace. However, he also appears to step judiciously around the language of Savoy.

---

[131]Cotton, *Covenant of Gods free grace*, 30-31.
[132]Savoy Declaration 20.4. See also "Confession of Faith; owned"; "Declaration of the Faith."

In the sermon "True Grace Is Divine," Edwards discusses the source and nature of true, divine, special grace. In the process, he engages the language of *production*. God *produces* grace, argues Edwards, if by that one refers to the source of grace. God is the immediate source of grace, and so it may be called a production. Yet Edwards does not rest satisfied with this language. He argues that it is preferable to speak in terms of participation and communication rather than production. "Grace is a thing supernatural and divine not only in the way it is from God, but in that 'tis a participation of God. 'Tis not only divine because of the way it is produced, but also from the nature of the thing produced, in that it is rather a communication than a production. 'Tis a participation of God, for where grace dwells, there God dwells."[133] In saying, "It is rather a communication than a production," Edwards is navigating his tradition, and he is treading carefully. He can affirm that grace is a production, in one sense. This may be read as a way of tipping his hat to the wisdom of his forbearers. But he will not concede production language (and the created-grace view implied in it) to be the best way of describing grace's nature. There communication language takes over, and communication language is well suited to uncreated grace.

So Edwards does modify at least this strain of his inherited view of grace. Yet his strong affirmation of uncreated grace, and his denial of created grace, grows directly out of his soteriological modification of the Trinity discussed above. That is, uncreated grace in Edwards is merely his doctrine of the Holy Spirit viewed from below. If the Spirit not only applies the gift of salvation but is that gift itself, then the gift of salvation (grace) must be uncreated. If the Spirit merely applies the gift, then the gift may be created. Therefore, when Edwards decided that the Spirit was relatively underhonored in the tradition, and when he decided that the best way to honor the Spirit was to affirm the Spirit as the gift of grace purchased by the Father, at the price of the Son, then he also committed himself to uncreated grace. These two modifications are really not two separate things, but one correction of the tradition, consistently applied.[134]

But it is important to note something explicitly here: this overall modification of the tradition is not something Edwards added from outside

---

[133] Edwards, "True Grace Is Divine (1738)," 357.
[134] At least in Edwards's mind it was a correction.

it. It is not that Edwards found trinitarian participation in some other tradition and transplanted it into his own. This is an insight developed from within, in critical and creative dialogue with his theological family. This leads to the final major modification in Edwards's development of soteriological participation.

Modifying creation's end. The final major modification nested in Edwards's doctrine of grace as participation in divine fullness comes in his treatment of creation's end. Yet, once again, Edwards's modification of his tradition in this area is little more than the application of his trinitarian view of uncreated grace. I noted above that Edwards's key modification is making the Holy Spirit the central gift of salvation. That move leads to a strong understanding of uncreated grace, with the attending preference of participation and communication over against production. Once Edwards is there, it simply remains for him to apply that theology to the question of creation's macro teleology. *The End for Which God Created the World* is the result of that application. Thus, Edwards's primary modification of his tradition, which occurred in his pneumatology, rolled out in his doctrines of grace and creation's teleology, with the result that all three were synchronized into a coherent unity. Grace as a communication and participation in divine fullness joins up all three spheres of theological inquiry.

Once again, in a way reminiscent of Edwards's treatment of the Trinity and the doctrine of grace, his exploration of creation's end is deeply rooted in his Reformed, and more specifically English Puritan, tradition. At the risk of stating the obvious, the Westminster Shorter Catechism's first question is, "What is the chief end of man?" The answer, equally famous, is, "The chief end of man is to glorify God and enjoy him forever." One should not underestimate the cognitive power this question exerted on anyone raised in the Puritan tradition, and its theology is clearly in view in Edwards's writing. Edwards spent his entire life wrestling with this fundamental question, broadened as it was from *humanity's* end to creation as a whole. Yet, even while Edwards broadened the question to include all creation, his answer narrowed down again to the human level. The creation's end, broadly considered, is entirely bound up with the salvation of the church. This present chapter has labored to show that when Edwards describes the communication and participation in divine fullness, it is a communication specifically aimed at the church—the saints and the angels.[135] *The End for Which God Created the World* is a treatise on grace.[136] It takes the first answer from the Westminster Shorter Catechism, and opens it up with a series of implied questions. What is a "chief end'? What is God's glory? How is God glorified in himself? How is God glorified in creation? What does it mean to enjoy God? How does the enjoyment of God relate to God's glory?[137] All of these questions grow directly out of Edwards's Puritan catechesis. This is so without Edwards citing the catechism itself. And his answer to all of these questions settles down to the same themes I have traced throughout this study: God's end in creation is to glorify himself by communicating his own internal glory, termed the divine fullness, to intelligent creatures, such that they join in the Trinity's self-delight. It is nothing more, nor less, than Edwards's trinitarianism and doctrine of grace as participation in divine fullness, applied to creation's teleology. Put differently, it is a trinitarian answer to the Shorter Catechism's first question.

What, then, is the modification Edwards brings in his consideration of creation's end? The emanation language that occurs throughout the dissertation could imply a Platonism. I have argued that Edwards does employ notions of *methexis*-participation (participation in God for being) that share similarities with Platonic understandings. Scholars have sometimes noted the apparent influence of the Cambridge Platonists on Edwards's thought. I do not dispute that they were an influence. However, Edwards's trinitarianism and soteriological orientation combine to undermine reading the dissertation as a strongly platonic work. It is a Christian, trinitarian, soteriological work before it is anything else. Stephen Holmes rightly remarks, "My contention is that a neoplatonic reading of Edwards is simply inconceivable, if my trinitarian reading is accepted. The Fathers, after all, avoided platonizing emanationisms precisely by asserting the doctrine of the Trinity."[138] Characterizing Edwards and his thought in *End of Creation* as primarily Platonic obscures more than it reveals.

Edwards did differ from some of his heroes in how he understood the notion of divine fullness. I have made clear throughout this study that the

---

[135]WJE 8:470-71.
[136]See how Edwards identifies the communication of divine fullness to the will as grace (WJE 8:529-30).
[137]These questions are addressed, respectively, in WJE 8:407, 513-18, 528, 528-29, 529-30, 531.
[138]Holmes, *God of Grace*, 59.

category of divine fullness is fundamental to his doctrine of grace. Francis Turretin and John Owen viewed christological fullness from Colossians 2:9 as incommunicable fullness.[139] Owen treated the fullness of John 1:16 as communicable in grace.[140] Edwards united the Colossians christological fullness to the John 1:16 fullness in his development of communicable grace.[141] Yet even this is a slight modification at best. They all agreed that God's essence is incommunicable, and they would all agree that the Bible sometimes refers to the divine fullness as something that is communicable (Jn 1:16 and Eph 3:19 being unambiguous examples). So their disagreement is focused on the exegesis of Colossians 1:19; 2:9. More important is that Edwards develops this notion of fullness to become a technical category over against essence, as I discussed in chapter three.

Edwards's real modification of his tradition, as I have already argued, comes in synchronizing these three major fields of discourse into one coherent whole, centered on his doctrine of the Trinity. Edwards modified Reformed pneumatology and followed the implications. He inherited a Puritan interest in showing how the Trinity is the foundation of the saints' communion with God, and showed how this is grounded in the Trinity's own internal communion. God then exports this to the creature by communicating the divine fullness such that the saint receives and returns, finitely, the divine love. This is the end for which God created the world, for in the communication and participation of divine fullness, God himself is glorified as his saints enjoy him. In Edwards, pneumatology leads to participation, which in turn yields teleology, all synchronized into a coherent whole. In every step Edwards is deeply engaged with his Reformed heritage. He is steeped in Puritan, Reformed doctrine. He pursues Reformed and Puritan interests. He justifies his key modification (pneumatology) over against Reformed convention. He studiously avoids contradicting Puritan confessions (especially Savoy), while still pressing the boundaries (preferring *participation* to *production* language), and he relates all of this to one of the most recognizably Puritan catechetical questions available (the Westminster Shorter Catechism, question 1).

---

[139]Francis Turretin, *Institutes of Elenctic Theology*, trans. George Musgrave Giger, ed. James T. Dennison Jr. (Phillipsburg, NJ: P&R, 1994), 2:328; Owen, *Works of John Owen*, 2:231.
[140]Owen, *Works of John Owen*, 3:173.
[141]*Miscellanies* 487 (WJE 13:528-29).

Conclusion

This present chapter is focused on showing how Creator and creature relate positively within this doctrine of grace. I have found them to relate teleologically. The teleological processions of the immanent Trinity repeat, finitely and temporally, in the drama of creation. That is, the same divine fullness (the Holy Spirit, or divine love) that fulfills the inner-trinitarian processions is also, in economic gift, the fulfillment of creation. This does not occur in the act of creation but in the redemption of the saints, through Jesus Christ and the Pentecostal gift of the Spirit. It is complete only in eternity. This dynamic preserves the distinction between created nature and divine grace, as well as the Creator-creature distinction, but also relates them so as to achieve the greatest possible intimacy.

McClymond calls this trinitarian participation the melody of Edwards's thought. He is right. Yet it is less helpful that this melody is presented over against the woodwinds of his Reformed and Calvinistic heritage. Edwards's melodic trinitarian participation, that is, his overall doctrine of grace as participation in divine fullness, is not added from outside his Reformed heritage. It is a modification; but it is part of the doctrinal development that has always marked the Reformed movement. Richard Muller speaks of a "confessional spectrum" within which the Reformed tradition always exhibited diversity and debate.[142] Edwards operated within this spectrum. This does not mean that his view will be uncontroversial for proponents of Reformed theology. Quite the contrary, the very fact that Edwards developed his melodic line from his own theological heritage will beg contemporary Reformed thinkers to evaluate it critically *according to their own tradition's criteria for doctrine and authority*. On the other hand, that Edwards's doctrine of grace is recognizably Reformed means that it may provide resources for contemporary engagement with soteriological participation. After all, this is not the first time the Reformed tradition has engaged these questions.

---

[142] Muller, *Post-Reformation Reformed Dogmatics*, 1:28.

5

Grace and Fulfillment

ON THE EVENING OF JULY 12, 1739, David Brainerd tasted ontological fulfillment. That is to say, the moment he gained "a new apprehension . . . of God," and the moment he saw God's "excellency and beauty," he was filled with divine fullness.[1] This divine fullness, which was ontologically distinct from anything in Brainerd's nature, was nevertheless at the same time the fulfillment of Brainerd's nature. This gift of true grace was, in Jonathan Edwards's understanding, infinitely above created nature, and yet at the same time not the divine essence. The whole reason God created the universe in the first place was in order to communicate this gift. As I argued in the previous chapter, for Edwards, being is for *koinōnia* in divine fullness. If that is true, then it follows that *koinōnia* fulfills being. Thus, when Brainerd saw God's beauty, he was tasting the beginning of his ontological fulfillment.

Yet that brings up an important question. If being is for *koinōnia* and *koinōnia* fulfills being, then in what way does *koinōnia* in divine fullness affect created nature? I have argued strenuously that Edwards resists every hint of fusing created nature and divine fullness (chap. 2), and also he avoids equating the divine fullness with the divine essence (chap. 3). All this is to protect the Creator-creature distinction. Yet in chapter four we began to see that Edwards *distinguishes* Creator and creature strongly so that he can show their *relation* in true grace. Chapter four argued for a teleological relation between created nature and divine fullness. From the beginning, and

---

[1] WJE 7:138.

Grace and Fulfillment

extending for all eternity, God intends to communicate his divine fullness to the saints; being is for *koinōnia*. Yet still, this leaves unanswered the question: If created nature is fulfilled in *koinōnia* in divine fullness, does this relation affect or transform created nature in any way?

In his *Religious Affections,* Edwards writes:

> The soul of a saint receives light from the Sun of Righteousness, in such a manner, that its nature is changed, and it becomes properly a luminous thing: not only does the sun shine in the saints, but they also become little suns, partaking of the nature of the fountain of their light. In this respect, the manner of their derivation of light, is like that of the lamps in the tabernacle, rather than that of a reflecting glass; which though they were lit up by fire from heaven, yet thereby became, themselves burning shining things.[2]

This is a startling passage: How does divine grace change the saint, and in what way does the saint become a luminous thing? If created nature and divine fullness are related *teleologically* (chap. four), then how are they related *dynamically*? How does divine fullness fulfill or transform created nature?

This is a pressing question for contemporary theology. Andrew Davison, in a wide-ranging study of participation theology, considers the distinction between participation in being (*methexis*) and soteriological participation (*koinōnia*). As I have used the terms, *methexis* describes the participation that undergirds being, and thus emphasizes ontology, whereas *koinōnia* describes the participation that undergirds saving grace and deification, and emphasizes personal and relational union. Davison acknowledges that such labels can facilitate helpful distinctions. However, Davison also issues a caution: "While the participation that belongs to redemption and theosis is indeed personal and relational, it is also fully ontological, in that it restores and elevates the creature's whole being."[3] His caution highlights the importance of this chapter's question.

In order to answer this question robustly, one must watch Edwards unpack his doctrine of Christ and the hypostatic union. It might be tempting to sidestep Christology and simply investigate directly how the saint is transformed by grace. This chapter will get there eventually, but it would distort

---

[2] WJE 2:343.
[3] Andrew Davison, *Participation in God: A Study in Christian Doctrine and Metaphysics* (Cambridge: Cambridge University Press, 2019), 297.

the picture to skip directly to the saints' transformation. The reason for prioritizing Christology follows from the previous chapters. Chapter four argued that the communication of divine fullness is the end for which God created the world, and in chapter three I noted that it is Christology that bridges the chasm between Creator and creatures. It therefore follows that Christ's human nature is the first port of call in created nature for the communication of divine fullness.[4] So it makes sense to ask the question, How does the hypostatic union impact Christ's human nature? When this is clear, I will ask how this sets the stage for the saints' transformation. After these questions, I will explore the implications for how divine grace elevates created nature.

Christ's Fulfilled Humanity

Chapter three explored how Edwards describes the hypostatic union in terms of spiritual union. That is, the divine Logos is united to the human Jesus by means of the Holy Spirit. Put differently but in terms that Edwards uses synonymously, there is a communication and participation in divine fullness between the Logos and the human Jesus, and this participation is without measure. This theory of the hypostatic union allows Edwards to achieve two objectives required by Chalcedonian orthodoxy. First, it explains how there can be a personal union between the Logos and the human Jesus; second, it explains how this personal union avoids a mixture of natures. The second point was the particular focus of chapter three. Throughout Edwards's reflections on the Trinity, Christology, and the doctrine of grace, he regularly employs two forms of participation. One form establishes essence and quiddity, and another establishes relatedness between distinct parties. When Edwards speaks of a participation in divine fullness between the Logos and the human Jesus, he is referring to the second type of participation. It is a *koinōnia* between two distinct natures, each of which receives its quiddity by another route. Still, this *koinōnia* establishes immeasurable intimacy between them, such that they become one person. The divine Logos remains unchanged in this relationship, and the human Jesus

---

[4]Christology seems to be Edwards's fulcrum in his argument in *End of Creation*. That is, Edwards reasoned from Christology regarding creation's teleology and concluded that creation is fulfilled in partaking of the divine fullness (see WJE 8:474 and n1).

retains the quiddity of his humanity.⁵ That is, Jesus' humanity remains human essence. However, this raises a key question in this present chapter. This *koinōnia* in divine fullness does not establish or modify the essence of Jesus' humanity, but does it affect it in other ways? The answer to this question is a simple yes. The humanity of Jesus is changed through the hypostatic union, but only in ways that are consistent with its nature *as human*. I will outline three ways the hypostatic union affects the humanity of Jesus, before turning to how it sets the stage for the transformation of the saints' humanity.

Christ's fulfilled humanity: Union of faculties. The hypostatic union differentiates Jesus' humanity from all other humanity by making Jesus one person with the divine Logos. The creation of Jesus' humanity and the assumption of this humanity by the eternal Logos occurred simultaneously, in *one act*, so that there was never a time in which Jesus' humanity existed apart from the Logos's assumption.⁶ This is a crucial element that makes the human Jesus different from the rest of humanity. I will show how Edwards describes this and analyze its significance.

When Edwards turned his mind to the mystery of the incarnation, one of his early instincts was to draw an analogy between the union in the Trinity and the union between the natures of Christ. In *Miscellanies* 183, Edwards writes, "Such was the love of the Son of God to the human nature, that he desired a most near and close union with it, something like the union in the persons of the Trinity, nearer than there can be between any two distinct [beings]. This moved him to make the human become one with him."⁷ This is familiar territory by now, and it is important to note how the basic grammar of Edwards's Spirit Christology is present in some of his earliest reflections. Note that the christological union is grounded on love—the love of the Son of God (Logos) for the human nature—and modeled on the trinitarian union. Both of these, as we have seen, point to the Holy Spirit. The love of the Son is the Holy Spirit, and the Holy Spirit is the bond of

---

⁵The divine Logos remains unchanged because it remains immutable. Tan, however, notes a possible exception, if one considers that the Logos becomes a subject of change in the human Jesus. See Seng-Kong Tan, *Fullness Received and Returned: Trinity and Participation in Jonathan Edwards* (Minneapolis: Fortress, 2014), 151.
⁶WJE 18:335.
⁷*Miscellanies* (WJE 13:329).

union in the Trinity. Edwards does not mention the Spirit in this early entry, but he has arranged the furniture, so to speak, for his Spirit Christology.

Yet the critical point in this early *Miscellanies* entry is that this union of love, modeled on the Trinity, is "nearer than there can be between any two distinct [beings]."[8] This, however, is a statement that brings up serious questions. Most importantly, what is it that is no longer distinct between the Logos and the human Jesus? It must not be that the essences or natures are fused and become indistinct, because this would launch Edwards well out of the boundaries of Chalcedonian orthodoxy, not to mention his own Reformed tradition. As chapter three made clear, the divine fullness, or divine love, or divine Spirit, shared between the Logos and the human Jesus does not affect such an essential fusion. The question remains, therefore, how this union is "nearer than there can be between any two distinct [beings]."

The answer comes in Edwards's charter *Miscellanies* entry on Christology: *Miscellanies* 487.[9] This is Edwards's fullest exploration of the role of the Spirit (along with his equivalent category of divine fullness) as the bond of union between the natures in Christ. Like *Miscellanies* 183 above, Edwards grounds the union between the divine Logos and the human Jesus on the love—or the Spirit—of God. God loves the human Jesus as God loves the Logos, and this establishes a communion or a sharing between the Logos and the human Jesus. This communion is a sharing in the Spirit, and it is "without measure." Then Edwards presses further, and here one sees how the Logos and the human Jesus are "nearer than there can be between any two distinct [beings]." The Logos and the human Jesus become one person "by the communion of understanding and communion of will, inclination, spirit or temper. . . . 'Tis not [just] any communion of understanding and will that makes the same person, but the communion of understanding is such that there is the same consciousness."[10] The human Jesus shares the Logos's consciousness. This is how the Logos and the human Jesus may be

---

[8] *Miscellanies* (WJE 13:329).

[9] *Miscellanies* (WJE 13:528-32). Caldwell calls *Miscellanies* 487 Edwards's "charter entry" on Christology. He also provides a helpful list of *Miscellanies* entries that fill out and expand his thinking here, including 487, 513, 624, 709, 738, 764b, 766, 1043. See Robert W. Caldwell III, *Communion in the Spirit: The Holy Spirit as the Bond of Union in the Theology of Jonathan Edwards*, Studies in Evangelical History and Thought (Milton Keynes, UK: Paternoster, 2006), 85n35.

[10] *Miscellanies* (WJE 13:529). Edwards connects the notion of "without measure" to Jn 3:34.

Grace and Fulfillment

said to be one being, or perhaps better, one subject.[11] This is one of the key elements that differentiates Jesus' humanity in the hypostatic union.

Edwards is not original in making this point, but rather it situates him in a long line of christological orthodoxy. The debates between the Nestorian account of Christ and the Cyrillian account centered on the question, Who is the subject in Christ? Is it the divine Logos, or is it the human Jesus, or is it somehow both? The (Nestorian) theology of Theodore of Mopsuestia presented Jesus as a human who was uniquely graced with the presence of the Logos. However, Jesus could still be presented as a distinct subject from the divine Son.[12] Cyril of Alexandria, on the other hand, argued vehemently that there is only one subject in Christ, and that subject is the divine Logos.[13] Cyril carried the day, and ever since the Councils of Ephesus and Chalcedon, the unity of subject in Christ has been a hallmark of orthodoxy.

Edwards lines himself up with this Cyrillian orthodoxy and explains it in terms of a communion of faculties.[14] For Edwards, a person, by definition, is something that has the faculties of understanding and will.[15] The Logos has understanding and will, and the human Jesus has understanding and will—otherwise Jesus would not be a true human person.[16] Given this state of affairs, the only way they can form one person is through a union of these faculties. Their understandings and their wills must unite such that they form one person.

---

[11]See also *Miscellanies* 738 (WJE 18:364).

[12]See Donald Fairbairn, *Grace and Christology in the Early Church*, Oxford Early Christian Studies (Oxford: Oxford University Press, 2006), 28-62, for a full rehearsal of Theodore of Mopsuestia's Christology, and especially 40-41. Owen, one of Edwards's theological influences, analyzed Nestorianism similarly. See John Owen, *The Works of John Owen*, ed. William H. Goold (Edinburgh: Banner of Truth Trust, 1976), 1:230.

[13]John Meyendorff, *Christ in Eastern Christian Thought* (Washington, DC: Corpus Books, 1969), 9.

[14]Several Edwards scholars have noted the Cyrillian or Alexandrian or sometimes Lutheran theme in Edwards. Pauw notes the Alexandrian themes. See Amy Plantinga Pauw, *The Supreme Harmony of All: The Trinitarian Theology of Jonathan Edwards* (Grand Rapids, MI: Eerdmans, 2002), 143; Robert W. Jenson, *America's Theologian: A Recommendation of Jonathan Edwards* (Oxford: Oxford University Press, 1988), 119-22. Holmes argues that Edwards incorporated Lutheran elements along with his Reformed heritage. See Stephen R. Holmes, *God of Grace and God of Glory: An Account of the Theology of Jonathan Edwards* (Edinburgh: T&T Clark, 2000), 139-42. Tan argues that Edwards's emphasis is Alexandrian, with the Antiochene themes as the lesser influence (*Fullness Received and Returned*, 158). Caldwell argues that the similarities to the Alexandrian tradition were not intentional and should not be made to contrast Edwards with his own Reformed tradition (*Communion in the Spirit*, 91-93, 96).

[15]WJE 21:133.

[16]Recall that the Logos—the divine Son—is God's understanding and has God's will (which is the Spirit) by virtue of a perichoretic communion within the Trinity (see WJE 21:133).

However, Edwards must say more. It is not enough to say that the Logos's and the human Jesus's faculties were united in a communion; he must also show how the single consciousness that results is the consciousness of the Logos. Put differently, if the Logos is the subject of the incarnate Christ, then there must be a direction of travel in the communion between the divine and human faculties.

The solution for this quandary is an Edwardsean echo of another traditional dogmatic resource. Beginning at least with John of Damascus and running right through to Edwards's theological mentors, Christian theology dealt with versions of this problem with a distinction between three categories: enypostatos, anhypostaton, and enhypostaton.[17] Enypostatos referred to things that have real existence or persons with real subsistence. Anhypostaton described things that did not have independent subsistence, and enhypostaton described a thing that derives existence or subsistence from something else. These distinctions allowed theologians to describe the direction of ontological travel in technical Christology. The aim was to guard against Nestorianism by certifying that the human nature of Jesus had no independent subsistence (personhood), but gained it by derivation from the Logos. The Logos, then, is enypostatos, in that it has real existence and subsistence. The human nature of Christ, considered in itself, is complete, but still is anhypostaton, lacking independent subsistence or personhood. However, in the assumption of the human nature, the Logos gives the human Jesus subsistence, such that the incarnate Christ is enhypostaton: real derived existence and subsistence. Thus the direction of travel: the personhood of the incarnate Christ is derived from the Logos, and therefore there is no second independent human *person*, though the humanity of Jesus is a complete human nature.

---

[17]On John of Damascus, see Jaroslav Pelikan, *The Christian Tradition: A History of the Development of Doctrine*, vol. 4, *The Reformation of Church and Dogma (1300–1700)* (Chicago: University of Chicago Press, 1984), 354-55. Both Francis Turretin and John Owen employed these categories, with their own variations. See Francis Turretin, *Institutes of Elenctic Theology*, ed. James T. Dennison Jr., trans. George Musgrave Giger (Phillipsburg, NJ: P&R, 1994), 2:311-12. Owen alludes to the thought these categories convey, even when he does not use the categories themselves. He describes the hypostatic union as "the union of the divine and human nature in the person of the Son of God, the human nature having not personality or subsistence of its own" (*Works of John Owen*, 1:228; see also 224-25 and 233-34).

Tan analyzes *Miscellanies* 709 in terms of these categories, and I am indebted to him for demonstrating the resonance between Edwards's logic and these dogmatic categories (*Fullness Received and Returned*, 144-45).

Edwards does not use these categories, but he employs the grammar, albeit modified to his own account of personhood. While Edwards could speak in traditional terms of "subsistence," he very often defined personhood in the modern terms of the faculties of understanding and will. He describes the direction of travel from the Logos to the human Jesus in terms of these faculties. *Miscellanies* 738 reads:

> The divine Logos is so united to the humanity of Christ that it . . . made use of it as its organ . . . not by an occasional communication, but a constant and everlasting union. Now 'tis manifest that the Logos, in thus acting by the humanity of Christ, did not merely make use of his body as its organ . . . but the faculties of his soul; which can be no otherwise than by such a communication with his understanding as we call identity of consciousness. If the divine Logos speaks in and by the man Christ Jesus . . . it must be by such a communication between the Logos and the human nature as to communicate consciousness.[18]

The communication of a single consciousness has a clear direction of travel: it is from the divine Logos to the human Jesus. The divine Logos makes use of the human Jesus's faculties "as its organ," such that the subject in Christ is the Logos. This is not precisely the same as the enypostatos-anhypostaton-enhypostaton distinction, but it shares strong similarities and fulfills a similar dogmatic function.[19] The faculties of Jesus do not act independently of the Logos's faculties, but rather the Logos acts through the human faculties of Jesus, and therefore they share one consciousness and form one subject, one person. This communication from the Logos to the faculties of Jesus occurs, predictably, through the activity of the Holy Spirit. The Spirit, as the bond of union between the Logos and the human Jesus, is the one who conveys the understanding and will of the Logos to the faculties of the human Jesus.[20]

This then, is the first way Jesus' humanity is differentiated from—and elevated above—the rest of humanity. Jesus is "peculiar" in that the Holy Spirit (divine fullness, divine love) dwells in him such that his faculties are

---

[18] *Miscellanies* 738 (WJE 18:364).

[19] The enypostatos-anhypostaton-enhypostaton distinction deals in a more ontological frame of reference than a psychological one. That is, it is mainly dealing with personhood as subsistence and reality of existence rather than with personhood as a psychological entity.

[20] See *Miscellanies* 766 (WJE 18:411-15, esp. 412-13).

united to the faculties of the Logos.[21] In this the Spirit conveys the Logos's understanding and will so that they animate the understanding and will of the human Jesus. This account of the hypostatic union adheres to Cyrillian orthodoxy and to the Reformed tradition Edwards inherited. He modified it by his emphasis on the Spirit as the bond of union and by his focus on personhood as understanding and will.

Christ's fulfilled humanity: Expansion of capacities. This focus on the faculties brings up the second way the hypostatic union transforms Jesus' humanity: it expands the capacity of Jesus' human faculties. The union of faculties, discussed above, differentiates Jesus' humanity from the rest of humanity, but it is not an actual change. The reason for this is that the union of faculties occurred at the moment of creation and assumption, so that there never was a time when Jesus' human faculties were not united to the Logos.[22] However, this union of faculties, beginning at the simultaneous act of creation and assumption, then subsequently brings about an expansion of the capacity of those human faculties, and this is creaturely change that happens within history. This is more than mere growth and learning. Christian theology has always grappled with the question of how Jesus can be one subject with the Logos, and yet at the same time grow and learn in the course of his life.[23] It dealt with this by reference to this growth and learning occurring in Jesus' human nature. Edwards assumes this but then makes a different move. It is not just that Jesus gains new information, but that his capacity for understanding and loving (the activity of the will) is magnified by virtue of his union with the Logos. Edwards writes:

> 'Tis probable that the faculties of the man Christ Jesus, now in his glorified state, are so enlarged that he can, with a full view and clear apprehension of mind, at the same time think on all the saints in the world, and be in the exercise of an actual and even of a passionate love (such as we experience) to all of them in particular.... This capacity of the man Jesus is so large, by reason of the personal union with the divine nature. By this means he knew the thoughts of men while on earth, and knew things acted at a distance.... What

---

[21] *Miscellanies* 487 (WJE 13:528).
[22] See *Miscellanies* 709 (WJE 18:335).
[23] This was particularly difficult for the Alexandrian-Cyrillian tradition. See Jaroslav Pelikan, *The Christian Tradition: A History of the Development of Doctrine*, vol. 1, *The Emergence of the Catholic Tradition (100–600)* (Chicago: University of Chicago Press, 1971), 251.

kind of powers are they, besides his own incommunicable attributes, that God cannot create a finite being with?[24]

Edwards did not think this was a novel idea. He felt confident that this idea of Jesus' enlarged faculties was implied throughout the tradition.[25] Nevertheless, it brings up questions as to his view of human nature. In particular, is this enlargement of Jesus' faculties a *human* thing, or some sort of "leakage" from the divine? Is this, in other words, the incarnate Christ taking up the divine attribute of omniscience? The answer to this question is important because if the answer is yes, if the humanity of Jesus takes on divine attributes (such as omniscience), then it could undermine Edwards's orthodox credentials. Chalcedon warns against mixing and mingling the natures. Reformed theology in particular was always wary of this danger and particularly rejected Lutheran accounts of the communication of majesty. In more technical language, the Reformed party rejected the realistic account of the communication of attributes (*communicatio idiomatum*) that their Lutheran contemporaries espoused. The Lutheran view came to be known as the communication of majesty (*genus maiestaticum*), and it stated that the hypostatic union in Christ allowed for divine attributes of the Son to be shared with the human nature of Christ.[26] This communication of divine attributes to the human nature of Jesus was offensive to the Reformed party, because they believed it functionally destroyed the humanity, swallowing it up in the divine nature.[27] However, there are two reasons why Edwards's view avoids

---

[24]*Miscellanies* 81 (WJE 13:247-48).

[25]"This seems to have been the universally received belief of the primitive church, which nobody ever thought of questioning" (WJE 13:248).

[26]Martin Chemnitz provides the classic statement on this doctrine. See *The Two Natures in Christ: A monograph concerning the two natures in Christ, their hypostatic union, the communication of their attributes, and related questions, recently prepared and revised on the basis of Scripture and the witness of the ancient church by Dr. Martin Chemnitz, with a preface by Dr. Nicolaus Selnecker, pastor at Leipzig*, trans. J. A. O. Preus (St. Louis: Concordia, 1971), 242-45.

[27]Bruce McCormack argues that Calvin's Christology simply does not allow—or perhaps better, specifically disallows—the foundation on which classical versions of divinization (his term) are built: "You simply cannot find the ontological ground needed for a divinization theory in Calvin's Christology." See Bruce L. McCormack, "Union with Christ in Calvin's Theology: Grounds for a Divinization Theory?," in *Tributes to John Calvin: A Celebration of His Quincentenary*, ed. David W. Hall (Philipsburg, NJ: P&R, 2010), 516. See also McCormack, "Participation in God, Yes, Deification, No: Two Modern Protestant Responses to an Ancient Question," in *Denkwürdiges Geheimnis: Beiträge zur Gotteslehre. Festschrift für Eberhard Jüngel zum 70. Geburtstag*, ed. Johannes Fischer, Hans-Peter Großhans, and Ingolf U. Dalferth (Tübingen: Mohr Siebeck, 2004), 347-74. For the other side of the Calvin-deification debate, see Carl Mosser, "The Greatest

the Lutheran communication of majesty view. These are important because one can find an answerable dynamic in the humanity of the graced saint.

The first reason to conclude that these are creaturely human capacities is his mention of finitude. Jesus' capacities in his earthly ministries were greater than other humans, and they expanded further after his exaltation. They are continuous in that they are the same powers of knowledge and love, but they are greatly enlarged in that Jesus is able to know and love each saint individually.[28] Yet these capacities remain finite. Edwards expresses wonder at the glorious power given to Christ and then exclaims, "What kind of powers are they, besides his own incommunicable attributes, that God cannot create a finite being with?"[29] He still considers Jesus to be a finite being, who has not received any incommunicable attributes. Finitude is an unmistakable mark of creatureliness. Jesus' capacities are greatly enlarged, so much so that he can know and love each saint individually, but just as his human knowledge was finite during his earthly ministry, so it is finite in his exaltation.

The second reason to conclude that these are creaturely human capacities is that the activity of the faculties is compatible with both divine and human personhood. That is, Jesus' enlarged capacities allow Jesus to do what all humans are designed to do, except that he does it more. Jesus knows and loves millions (billions?) of saints, not just corporately but individually, all at the same time. No other human can do that. However, all humans are capable of knowing and loving others in some measure, because that is part of what constitutes a person. A human person knows and loves (bearing

---

Possible Blessing: Calvin and Deification," *SJT* 55, no. 1 (2002): 36-57; Mosser, "An Exotic Flower? Calvin and the Patristic Doctrine of Deification," in *Reformation Faith: Exegesis and Theology in the Protestant Reformations*, ed. Michael Parsons (Milton Keynes, UK: Paternoster, 2014). See also responses to Mosser in Yang-ho Lee, "Calvin on Deification: A Reply to Carl Mosser and Jonathan Slater," *SJT* 63, no. 3 (2010): 272-84; Jonathan Slater, "Salvation as Participation in the Humanity of the Mediator in Calvin's *Institutes of the Christian Religion*: A Reply to Carl Mosser," *SJT* 58, no. 1 (2005): 39-58. For other Calvin scholars who link his thought with deification, see Julie Canlis, "Calvin, Osiander, and Participation in God," *IJST* 6, no. 2 (2004): 169-84; Canlis, *Calvin's Ladder: A Spiritual Theology of Ascent and Ascension* (Grand Rapids, MI: Eerdmans, 2010); J. Todd Billings, "United to God Through Christ: Assessing Calvin on the Question of Deification," *HTR* 98, no. 3 (2005): 315-34; Billings, "John Calvin: United to God Through Christ," in *Partakers of the Divine Nature: The History and Development of Deification in the Christian Traditions*, ed. Michael J. Christensen and Jeffery A. Wittung (Grand Rapids, MI: Baker Academic, 2008), 200-218; Billings, *Calvin, Participation, and Gift: The Activity of Believers in Union with Christ* (Oxford: Oxford University Press, 2007).
[28]Edwards makes this clear throughout the *Miscellanies* 81 entry (WJE 13:247-48).
[29]WJE 13:247-48.

faculties of understanding and will). Not only so, but Edwards believed all humans could think of more than one thing at a time—though probably only two or three things at any given moment. Yet if all humans can know and love, and all humans can think of more than one thing at a time, then why should one deny that Jesus, in his exaltation, can think of many more than that? The logic goes from standard human capacities to expanded ones, but the activity is the same: human knowing and human loving. This activity (knowing and loving) is compatible with both human and divine natures. God knows and loves, and this is the basis for Edwards's understanding of the Trinity. Knowing and loving is both a divine and creaturely activity, because it is the fundamental activity of personhood. This means that while Jesus' *capacities* for knowing and loving are greatly enhanced, the *activity* itself is not an incommunicable divine attribute that leaked into the human nature, but an activity always shared between Creator and creature that is operating through expanded, though still finite faculties.

Yet even if these enlarged faculties are creaturely rather than divine, this still raises an intriguing view of human nature. Edwards held an elastic view of human nature: human nature could change not simply by physical growth and learning, but also due to the participation in divine fullness. Christ's hypostatic union, with participation in the Spirit (divine fullness) that effects it, caused an enlargement of human capacities. These capacities are specific and have to do with personhood. Persons are those with understanding and will, and these are precisely the faculties that can enlarge. This will be very important for grasping the way the graced saint can grow in grace for eternity.

Christ's fulfilled humanity: The display of divine excellency. I turn now to the final way that the hypostatic union affects the humanity of Jesus: the divine excellencies of the Logos shine through the humanity of Jesus. Put differently, the infinite excellencies of the Logos become visible or revealed to the saint in and through Jesus' human nature. This is a central point in one of Edwards's key sermons on Christology: "The Excellency of Christ." Preached at a sacrament service in 1736 and later published in his *Discourses on Various Important Subjects*, the sermon aims to show the "admirable conjunction of diverse excellencies in Jesus Christ."[30] It is an exposition of

---

[30] WJE 19:565.

Revelation 5:5, a dramatic scene in which the prophet John sees Jesus presented as both a triumphant lion and a slain lamb.

Edwards seizes on this ironic portrayal and presses the idea that Jesus Christ unites apparently contradictory qualities. Jesus Christ is both infinitely high and infinite in condescension. Jesus Christ is both infinitely just and infinitely gracious. Jesus Christ is both infinite in glory and infinite in humility, exceeding in obedience and supreme in dominion, and so it goes on. In each case the incarnate Christ uniquely unites qualities, or excellencies, that would otherwise appear contradictory.[31] The reason Jesus unites these apparent contradictions is that he is God-man. That is, it is the incarnation, and more particularly the hypostatic union of the divine Logos and the human Jesus, that allows these excellencies to unite.

This point in itself is little more than one would expect from an orthodox doctrine of the incarnation. Things become more intriguing, however, later in the sermon, when Edwards describes how this uniting occurs. These excellencies, which would be contradictory in any other person, unite in Christ because the divine excellencies shine through Christ's humanity.

> [Christ's] human excellencies are but communications and reflections of his divine; and though this light, as reflected, falls infinitely short of the divine fountain of light, in its immediate glory; yet the reflection shines not without its proper advantages, as presented to our view and affection. As the glory of Christ appears in the qualifications of his human nature, it appears to us in excellencies that are of our own kind, and are exercised in our own way and manner, and so, in some respects, are peculiarly fitted to invite our acquaintance, and draw our affection. The glory of Christ as it appears in his divinity, though it be far brighter, yet doth it also more dazzle our eyes, and exceeds the strength or comprehension of our sight: but as it shines in the human excellencies of Christ, it is brought more to a level with our conceptions, and suitableness to our nature and manner, yet retaining a semblance of the same divine beauty, and a savor of the same divine sweetness.[32]

This passage is crucial for my purposes because Edwards describes a key relationship between Christ's divinity and humanity: divinity shines through humanity. It is not simply that Christ has some excellencies derived from

---
[31] WJE 19:565-72.
[32] WJE 19:590.

the divine nature and other excellencies that derive from the human nature. For instance, it would be traditional to say that Christ, in his divine nature, is omniscient, and in his human nature, learns and increases in knowledge. These are two apparently contradictory qualities of omniscience and learning, united in Christ, but still segregated between the natures. Edwards would undoubtedly agree with this line of thought, but he says something bolder in this sermon. It is not simply that Christ's two natures hold apparently contradictory qualities, but rather that divine qualities become visible through the humanity. Put differently, Edwards taught a communication of divine excellencies from the divine nature to the human nature.

As I have noted before, this raises concern as to whether Edwards has transgressed a key aspect of Reformed christological tradition. The Reformed tradition was always concerned to maintain the respective integrities of Christ's divine and human natures. Chalcedonian orthodoxy required denial of mixing of the two, or positing a sort of "third thing," and the Reformed tradition emphasized this interest with particular zeal. Does Edwards's assertion that the divine excellencies "shine through" the humanity contradict this interest? I argue that it does not. The reason that is that, for Edwards, created nature is specifically designed to display divine excellencies. In this light, Christ's humanity is not undermined by its participation in divine excellencies, but rather it fulfills its purpose *as created nature*.

Miscellanies 108 carries the same title as the sermon, "The Excellency of Christ," and provides an instructive background for Edwards's thinking. Edwards is pressing forward his thoughts concerning God's purpose in creating the universe, and in particular carries forward the insights of *Miscellanies* 104. *Miscellanies* 104 argued that God created the world in order for the Logos to communicate himself to the church.[33] Just as God inclines to communicate himself, and this inclination is satisfied in the generation of the Son, so the Son inclines to self-communication, and this inclination will be satisfied in the creation and redemption of the church. In *Miscellanies* 108 Edwards argues that this explains something of the beauty of the created world. While the self-communication of the Logos is only truly toward persons, nevertheless even the nonhuman world reflects something of the

---

[33]WJE 13:272-73.

Logos's excellencies.[34] Edwards states, "The beauties of nature are really emanations, or shadows, of the excellencies of the Son of God."[35]

This insight grows out of Edwards's theology of creation itself. As chapter two showed, all created reality depends radically on God for its being. More specifically, God creates continually through his perpetual ideation. This view of creation and ontological being connects creation very closely to the second person of the Trinity, because the Logos is God's eternal and infinite self-ideation. In this sense, all created nature is christologically mediated for Edwards. It is not surprising, then, to find that created nature reflects the excellencies of the divine person through whom it gains its being. This maps to what I dubbed common participation in chapter two. Chapter four demonstrated how common participation is teleologically oriented toward special participation. Being, and in this context *created being*, is for *koinōnia* in divine fullness. In *Miscellanies* 108 Edwards moves from this common participation to its fulfillment in special participation. While common participation allows the created world to reflect Christ's excellencies in a shadowy sort of way, it is the human soul that is particularly suited to display these excellencies. Edwards writes, "We see far the most proper image of the beauty of Christ, when we see beauty in the human soul."[36] That is, through special participation, the human soul uniquely displays the excellencies of Christ.

This means that, for Edwards, not only is created nature designed with a view to *receive* the communications of the Son of God, but also it is designed to *display* the excellencies of the Son of God. The display of divine excellencies is written into the design specifications of created nature itself, and therefore the display of the divine excellencies is a fulfillment of created nature, rather than its abrogation.

This sheds light on Edwards's sermon "The Excellency of Christ." When Edwards speaks of Christ's divine excellencies "shining" through the human nature of Christ, he does not have in mind any notion that the divinity

---

[34]See WJE 13:272, 279; see also *Miscellanies* 332 (WJE 13:410).
[35]WJE 13:279.
[36]WJE 13:280. The context in *Miscellanies* 108 makes clear that the beauty of the human soul Edwards refers to is the beauty derived from grace. Edwards points to the fall as the reason why so little of the graces of Christ's excellencies remain in the human soul, and to the future state when they will be restored. Thus it is the beauty of saving grace (special participation) that most fully displays the excellencies of Christ.

swallows up the humanity, or that there is a third thing established. The reality, at least from Edwards's perspective, is the opposite. Created nature in general is designed to display the excellencies of the Logos, and human nature in particular is designed to display them. If that is true of created nature in general and human nature specifically, then it must also be true of Christ's human nature. Indeed, Edwards believed that Christ's human nature was achieving its fullness, its end *as created nature*, precisely as it displayed the excellencies of the Son of God. Edwards states, "As the glory of Christ appears in the qualifications of his human nature, it appears to us in excellencies that are of our own kind, and are exercised in our own way and manner, and so, in some respects, are peculiarly fitted to invite our acquaintance, and draw our affection."[37] The key words here are "of our own kind," indicating that the divine excellencies that shine through Jesus' humanity are compatible with the saints' own human nature.

But what are these excellencies? What does Edwards mean by divine excellencies that can shine through humanity without abrogating that humanity? It is important to note Edwards's use of the term *excellencies*. Edwards packed a lot into his idea of excellency, and it orbits around the notions of consent, love, and holiness, and is closely related to my key theme of divine fullness. A thing is excellent in its appropriate consent to another.[38] Recall from chapter three that the Trinity *ad intra* is a bond of love, consent, fullness between the Father and the Son in the Spirit. This fullness *ad intra* is the foundation of Trinity's excellencies. When the divine fullness is shared with the human Jesus in the incarnation, the result is that human Jesus shares in the love and consent of the Trinity. This means that the human Jesus shares in the excellencies of the Trinity. Edwards's sermon emphasizes that these excellencies, grounded on the divine fullness in the hypostatic union, issue forth in virtue, because for Edwards all true virtue is founded on consent to the divine being.[39]

There is an important difference between claiming that the divine *excellencies* shine through the human Jesus and saying the divine *attributes* shine

---

[37] WJE 19:590.
[38] "One alone, without any reference to any more, cannot be excellent; for in such case there can be no manner of relation no way, and therefore, no such thing as consent.... The highest excellency, therefore, must be the consent of spirits one to another" (WJE 6:337).
[39] See the argument in *True Virtue* (WJE 8:539-40).

through the human Jesus. *Attribute* is a far more general term and can include things such as God's infinity, omniscience, omnipresence, and many other properties that Reformed theology generally viewed as incommunicable. Edwards's use of the term *excellencies* grounds the conversation in relational and personal territory. One can analyze this in terms of Edwards's distinction between real and relational attributes. As discussed briefly in chapter three, Edwards distinguished between the most fundamental (real) distinctions within the Trinity and those attributes that are really just these distinctions relative to something else.[40] The three fundamental or real distinctions in God are God, God's idea, and God's will. These three map directly to the three persons of the Trinity: the Father, the Son, and the Holy Spirit, respectively. According to Edwards, all other attributes in God (omniscience, love, power, etc.) are ways of speaking of one or more of these three real distinctions in relationship to something else. For instance, omniscience is really nothing else than God's idea (the Son) in reference to its infinite nature. God's power refers to his understanding and will, and those things that result from their operation. God's love is really simply his will, because love is simply the operation of the will, and so on and so forth. Returning to how Jesus' humanity displays the excellencies of the Logos, one can see that Jesus' humanity can participate in God's real attributes in a finite way, but this does not mean that Jesus' humanity participates in all the relative attributes. Jesus' humanity can share in the Logos's understanding (which is himself), and the Logos's will (the Holy Spirit), and thereby share an intimate communion with the Father, without thereby implying that Jesus' humanity shares in every dimension of these realities. For instance, the human Jesus may partake of the knowledge of the Logos without thereby becoming omniscient. Jesus may partake of the divine understanding and will without thereby becoming omnipotent. Edwards's distinction between the real and relative attributes allow for a finite participation in that which most defines God, without taking on every attribute, precisely because the participation remains finite.

This distinguishes Edwards's view from the Lutheran communication of majesty. Jesus' humanity displays divine excellencies not because his humanity

---

[40] WJE 21:131.

receives the divine attributes but because of the communication of divine fullness. Divine fullness is Edwards's category for the bond of the Spirit. The bond of the Spirit unites the natures of Christ such that the humanity of Christ shares in the love and consent of the Trinity. This consent and love are excellencies that shine outward through the humanity of Christ.

Summary: Christ's fulfilled humanity. The aim of this section was twofold: (1) to survey three primary ways the humanity of Jesus is affected and elevated by the hypostatic union, and (2) to argue that in each case, Jesus' humanity is uncompromised as to its creatureliness by this union. Fullness does not swallow nature but fulfills it, even in and especially in the human Jesus. I observed that in the first place Jesus' human faculties are united to the faculties of the Logos, such that they become one person. This is Edwards's way of presenting the Cyrillian tradition and represents a bulwark against Nestorian Christology. In the second place, the human Jesus' union with the divine Logos causes a progressive growth in the capacity of these faculties. This represents a progressive change in Jesus' humanity, under the influence of the hypostatic union. Still, this capacity never reaches infinity, and, at least in this respect, is a thoroughly creaturely characteristic. Third and finally, the humanity of Jesus displays the divine excellencies of the Logos. All created nature is designed with a view to some sort of a display of the excellencies of the Logos. This is partly because created nature is created through the Logos and thereby shares an echo of the beauty of the Logos. But it is also because the human soul is particularly designed with a purpose of displaying the excellencies of the Logos. The humanity of Jesus achieves this without measure.

Before I proceed, it is important to underscore that all three ways the hypostatic union affects Jesus' humanity are explained by virtue of the communication of divine fullness, or (an equivalent concept) the communication of the Holy Spirit. This is the burden of Edwards's charter *Miscellanies* entry on Christology, *Miscellanies* 487.[41] The union of faculties between the human Jesus and the divine Logos, the expansion of these faculties, and participation in the excellencies of the Logos are all derivative from the gift of divine fullness without measure to Jesus Christ. The divine fullness, or

---

[41] WJE 13:528-32. I borrow the designation "charter entry on Christology" from Caldwell, *Communion in the Spirit*, 85n35.

the Holy Spirit, or the love between the Father and the Son, is communicated without measure with the human Jesus, such that Jesus' human faculties are united to the Logos, and thereby Jesus shares in the love and consent and therefore excellency of the Trinity. It is in this dynamic that Jesus' faculties expand in his exaltation. This focus on divine fullness at the center of Edwards's Christology creates a clear bridge to the doctrine of grace in the saint.

With this in view, I will now turn to how the humanity of Jesus sets the stage for the graced saint. I will show that divine fullness affects the saints' humanity in a way that echoes the hypostatic union's impact on Jesus' humanity.

Saints' Fulfilled Humanity

Jesus' humanity is both the source and model for the transformation of the saint in grace. Chapter three showed that the hypostatic union sets the stage for the *koinōnia* between the saint and Christ. It now remains to show that this relationship transforms, or perhaps better, fulfills the humanity of the saints.

Paul taught the church to expect Jesus to "transform our lowly body to be like his glorious body" (Phil 3:21). This statement implies two very important ideas. First, Paul presents Jesus as the *source* of the transformation. It is Christ who does the transforming. But at the same time, Jesus is also the *model* for the transformation. The saints' bodies will be made like Jesus' body. These two ideas, that Christ is the source and model of saintly transformation, are crucial for the classical Christian tradition. I use the term *classical* because there have been movements that denied one or the other. Nestorian, or perhaps Theodorean, Christologies presented the human Jesus as *primarily* a model of the graced saint. The orthodox parties had to say more.[42] John Meyendorff argues that orthodox theology recognized Jesus' humanity as the source for divine life in the saint. Describing the theology that emerged in the years after the Chalcedonian debates took place, he writes:

> On the one hand, Chalcedon's legacy is perfectly preserved: the natures, even after the union, are two, because the uncreated divine essence can never as such be partaken of in any form by the created nature. . . . But, on the other hand, the humanity assumed by the Logos, hypostatised in him, deified by his energies, becomes itself the source of divine life, because it is deified not by

---

[42] See Fairbairn's overview of Theodore of Mopsuestia and Nestorius on Christ as a model of the uniquely graced saint (*Grace and Christology*, 28-62).

grace but because it is the Word's own flesh. Here is the difference between Christ and the Christians, between hypostatic possession of divine life and deification by grace and participation.[43]

Notice the two key assertions: on the one hand, Christ in his humanity is the source of divine life, and thus there are important differences between the divine life as owned by Christ in the hypostatic union and the divine life as given in grace. Yet at the same time there is a relationship or qualified similarity between the deified humanity of Christ and the "deification by grace and participation" experienced in the saints. Christ is both (unique) source and (qualified) model for the graced saint. Does Edwards teach something similar?

Christ's humanity as source and model for graced saint. Sometime in or before 1752, Edwards preached a sermon designed to show the close connection between the grace received and enjoyed by Christ, and the grace received and enjoyed by the saints.[44] This sermon provides an insight into the organic union between Christology and grace in his thinking. It is an exposition of John 1:16, "And of his fulness have all we received, and grace for grace" (KJV). Edwards begins with a set of simple exegetical observations based on the verse, and importantly draws together the key themes of christological fullness, grace toward the saint, and participation. The text teaches, states Edwards, "that we receive of his fullness. . . . We are . . . partakers with him."[45] This reaffirms what I observed in chapter three. The fullness that Christ enjoys in the incarnation, the *koinōnia* in the Spirit, is the gift shared in grace. However, Edwards presses further when he gets to the twin propositions that shape his sermon's doctrine. The first proposition asserts that Christ is the source of grace, and the second proposition asserts that Christ is the model for grace. Edwards writes:

[I] That believers do receive of Christ, of the benefits he himself hath, and do partake with him therein.

[II] That there is every grace in the heart of a believer, which there is in Jesus Christ himself.[46]

---

[43] Meyendorff, *Christ in Eastern Christian Thought*, 58.
[44] The sermon manuscript has a note at the top indicating that it was repreached in June 1752, therefore indicating that it was written sometime earlier.
[45] Jonathan Edwards, MS Sermon on John 1:16 (1730-31), no. 180, 1r. Gen Mss 151, Beinecke Rare Book and Manuscript Library, Yale University. Transcript edited by James Salladin and supplied by The Jonathan Edwards Center, Yale University.
[46] Edwards, MS Sermon, no. 180, 1r.-1v.

Consider the first proposition. It is important to see that Edwards speaks of Christ in his incarnate humanity. The saints receive of the incarnate, human Christ, and partake with him in grace. That is, Christ incarnate is the source of divine grace in Edwards's thought. This is clear from the text of John 1:16 and throughout the sermon. Early in the sermon, he asks how believers partake of Christ's excellencies, and he answers, "[By] the moral excellencies which Christ *as man* and mediator received from the Father."[47] Later he states, "None of the benefits Christ the mediator received, he received as a private person. What he did, he did not do only for himself. So what he receives, he don't receive only for himself."[48] Notice the emphasis on receiving *for someone else*. It is very standard Protestant doctrine to say that Christ *did* things for the sake of the saints' salvation. For instance, Christ died for the sins of the elect, and Christ actively obeyed the law for the sake of the elect. Edwards affirms this but says something more. Not only did Christ *do* things for the elect. Christ *received* graces for the elect. That means that Christ, in his incarnation, received grace in order to give grace. He received grace in order to become the source of grace for the saints. This creates a very close relationship between the human, incarnate Christ and the grace given to the saints.

It also sets up Edwards's second proposition above. Not only is Christ the source of grace for the saints, but he is also the model for grace. That is, there is a close relationship between the graces in the heart of the believer and the graces in Christ. Christ is the model, and believers' grace is answerable to it. "There is not one grace in Christ, but that there is not one to answer it in the saints."[49] His point here is not that they are identical, but that the grace of Christ and the grace in the saint are always answerable. The grace of Christ and the grace of the saints differ in degree—Christ received grace without measure, but the saints in far less degree—and they differ in that Christ is the head and source, and the saints are members who partake receptively.[50]

---

[47] Emphasis mine. This is Edwards's second positive answer to the question. The first way the saint partakes of Christ's excellencies is through the communicable divine excellencies. This indicates that Edwards saw both the communicable divine excellencies and the human excellencies in Christ as sources of grace. See Edwards, MS Sermon, no. 180, 2r.
[48] Edwards, MS Sermon, no. 180, 4r.
[49] Edwards, MS Sermon, no. 180, 1r.
[50] Edwards, MS Sermon, no. 180, 2r. Edwards, as was common, points to Jn 3:34 as a proof text for Christ receiving the Spirit (and therefore grace) without measure. Again, following his custom, he emphasizes that saints partake of the same grace as Christ, but to an infinitely less degree.

Still, every grace in Christ flows from the head to the members in some way, so that there is an answerable grace in the saint. As Meyendorff points out, Christ, in his humanity, is the source of divine life for the saints, but still there remain important differences. Edwards follows this pattern.

I will now turn to show how the saints' grace is answerable to that of Christ. I will explore the same three aspects of transformed humanity that I explored in reference to Jesus above, but here from the viewpoint of the graced saint.

Saints' fulfilled humanity: Union of faculties. I have already shown that the Logos and the human Jesus become one person, one consciousness, through a union of faculties. Persons, by Edwards's definition, are those who have understanding and will. The Logos's understanding and will are communicated to the human Jesus' understanding and will, such that the Logos is the subject of the human Jesus. In this way, they become one person. However, Edwards has stated that the grace received by the human Jesus always implies an answerable grace in the saint. Is there a dynamic in the graced saint that answers this union of faculties in the hypostatic union?

The answer is yes—with an important qualification. Edwards regularly describes the dynamic of grace in terms of the faculties of understanding and will. It is not difficult to find passages where he explicitly describes God's action of self-communication to the faculties of the saints. Consider this famous *Miscellanies* entry:

> God is glorified within himself these two ways: (1) by appearing or being manifested to himself in his own perfect idea, or, in his Son, who is the brightness of his glory; (2) by enjoying and delighting in himself, by flowing forth in infinite love and delight towards himself, or, in his Holy Spirit. So God glorifies himself towards the creatures also two ways: (1) by appearing to them, being manifested to their understandings; (2) in communicating himself to their hearts, and in their rejoicing and delighting in, and enjoying the manifestations which he makes of himself.[51]

This is a particularly helpful entry because he makes the connection between his trinitarianism and his doctrine of grace so explicit. God has understanding and will, and so do the saints. God's action toward the saints in

---

[51] WJE 13:495.

grace is a replication of his internal activity. This is all very consistent with Edwards's Christology as explored previously. God glorifies himself *ad intra* by self-communication of his understanding (idea or Logos) and will (love or Spirit). God assumes humanity in the incarnation by communicating his understanding (the Logos) and will (love or Spirit) to the human Jesus. God gives grace to the saints by communicating his understanding (mediated by Christ incarnate) and his will (the Spirit or divine fullness). Edwards's consistency is striking.

Edwards highlights this gracious union of faculties in many places, perhaps most famously in his sermon "A Divine and Supernatural Light."[52] His argument is that grace, or regeneration and illumination, consists in a "a real sense and apprehension of the divine excellency of things revealed in the Word of God."[53] Edwards's famous "spiritual sense" idea is grounded in his theory of the union of faculties in grace. God acts on both the faculties of understanding and will, so that the human faculties become the subject, though never the cause, of this spiritual sense.[54] One must have an idea of divine things (understanding), but one must also have a sense of its beauty (the will). Grace will always unite the two because grace is God's communication of fullness to the entire person, which consists in understanding and will. Thus, just as the hypostatic union is formed by the communication of the Logos's understanding and will to the human Jesus, such that they become one consciousness, so the mystical union with Christ is formed by the communication of God's understanding (which in Edwards's trinitarianism is the Logos) and will (which resolves to the Spirit) to the saint. The grace of the saint is answerable to the grace of the human Jesus.

Yet this is where the qualification comes into view, and it is an important qualification. It would be easy to conclude that the grace of the hypostatic union and the grace of the mystical union differ only in degree, but not in kind. That is, it would be easy to reason in the following way: it is true to say that both the hypostatic union and the union of grace include a union of human faculties. If this is the case, then we can say that if the two unions differ, they differ in degree or intensity of union, and not in kind, because

---

[52]WJE 17:408-25.
[53]WJE 17:413.
[54]WJE 17:416.

the kind of union is a union of faculties in both cases. This line of thought is tempting, but must be rejected both on the grounds of his own tradition's boundaries for orthodoxy and on the grounds of Edwards's own writing. I will take these in turn.

John Owen, a key English Reformed authority for Edwards's tradition, took up the question of whether the hypostatic union and the spiritual union of believers with Christ are analogous. He writes:

> This [spiritual union of Christ with believers] some among us do judge to be of the same kind with that of the Son of God and the man Christ Jesus. Only they say they differ in degrees. The eternal Word was so united unto the man Christ Jesus, as that thereby he was exalted inconceivably above all other man, though ever so holy, and had greater communications from God than any of them. Wherefore he was on many accounts the Son of God in a peculiar manner; and, by a communication of names, is called God also. This being the opinion of Nestorius, revived again in the days wherein we live ... whereby he constituted two distinct persons of the Son of God and the Son of man.[55]

Owen sees the specter of Nestorius, and he has good reason to do so. Donald Fairbairn argues that underlying the debates between Nestorian-Theodorean and Cyrillian Christology was always the issue of grace.[56] The Nestorian-Theodorean view presented Jesus as a uniquely graced man—graced to a greater extent than any other human, and therefore peculiar and unique—but still a man under grace's influence. This meant that the saints experienced the same sort of power and influence, though to a far less extent than did Jesus. On the other side, Cyril and his followers asserted that in Christ, the Logos had personally arrived in history. It was not that the Logos empowered and graced Jesus but rather assumed humanity and, without ceasing to be God, became human such that the subject of Jesus is the Logos. This means that Jesus Christ, and in particular the hypostatic union, must be qualitatively different from the spiritual union of grace in the saint. A Nestorian-Theodorean account could posit Jesus as the model and pioneer of the graced saint, but only a Cyrillian account could posit him as the

---

[55] Owen, *Works of John Owen*, 1:230.
[56] For an overview of how grace and Christology functioned in Nestorian-Theodorean Christology, see Fairbairn, *Grace and Christology*, 28-62. See 98-99 for a good summary of Cyril's doctrine of grace.

personal source of grace as well. Owen shares this assessment of Nestorian-Theodorean grace and Christology. If the grace of the hypostatic union and the grace of the saints' union with Christ are too continuous, then it indicates a heretical Christology.

Edwards avoids this implied Nestorianism. *Miscellanies* 487, his pivotal entry on Christology, aims at showing the close relationship between the saints' spiritual union with Christ and the hypostatic union. However, he notes that the union of the Logos with the human Jesus includes "great peculiarities." After mentioning several *similarities* between the unions in question, he finally states the thing that differentiates them:

> Only there is this difference, that God dwells in the man Christ as the head, and in us as the members, as the head is the seat of the soul after a peculiar manner; 'tis the proper seat of the soul; though the soul also dwells in the members, but 'tis by derivation from and participation with the head. So in Christ dwells all the fullness of the Godhead bodily, Colossians 2:9.[57]

The body imagery is decisive here. Christ is the head, and the saints (church) are members. This headship language implies source. This is clear when he makes the analogy of the soul. The soul dwells properly in the head, and in the members "by derivation from and participation with the head." That is, the head (Christ) is the source of grace, and the members (the saints) are receptors of grace. Using language I employed earlier, not only is Christ the *model* of the graced saint, but he is also the *source* of grace itself. This creates a qualitative difference between Christ and the saints. In Meyendorff's language, Christ, in his humanity, "becomes itself the source of divine life. . . . Here is the difference between Christ and the Christians, between hypostatic possession of divine life and deification by grace and participation."[58] All this indicates that while Edwards does stress a strong continuity between the hypostatic union and the union of grace in the saints, he does not capitulate to Nestorianism. I take it that this was his aim: to show Christ as the uniquely divine source of grace, and also the generically human model who pioneers the way for the saints.

---

[57] *Miscellanies* 487 (WJE 13:528-29).
[58] Meyendorff, *Christ in Eastern Christian Thought*, 58.

Saints' fulfilled humanity: Expansion of capacities. So far I have shown that the transformation of the humanity of Jesus by the hypostatic union delivers answerable, but not identical, dynamics in the graced saint. The Logos assumes the human Jesus through a union of faculties, so the graced saint receives the communication of divine fullness in and through its faculties. Here I had to observe an important point of discontinuity between the hypostatic union and the graced saint. Christ's hypostatic union establishes one person, and this single subject is the source of divine grace. Neither of these two dynamics occur in the graced saint. This means, importantly, that there are ways in which the hypostatic union and the union of grace differ in kind and not just in degree. Still, there is an *answerable*, but not identical, dynamic when grace operates on the human faculties of the saint. This leads to the second way the hypostatic union transforms the humanity of Jesus: the expansion of faculties. Is there an answerable dynamic in the graced saint?

As I observed earlier, Jesus' human faculties are enlarged to a great extent through the hypostatic union, and especially after his ascension and glorification. Edwards explores this idea in order to explain how it is that Jesus can be personally engaged with every single saint at the same time. The reason is that the hypostatic union, especially after the ascension and glorification, allows Jesus to think on and love each individual saint in the world (and presumably also in heaven) at the same time. This is not divine omniscience, because Jesus' humanity remains finite and changeable, but it nevertheless far exceeds normal human mental capacities. Edwards expects that something very similar occurs within the saints.

The clearest place this expansion of capacities is implied within Edwards's published corpus comes in the final pages of Edwards's celebrated *The End for Which God Created the World*. In the final pages of his work, Edwards asserts his well-known doctrine of perpetual growth. He argues that God will continue to communicate his divine fullness to intelligent creatures (he means the saints), in increasing measure, for all eternity. This will result in perpetual increase of union between God and the saints, and it will increase their happiness eternally.[59] In the larger argument of *The End of Creation*,

---

[59] WJE 8:533-36.

God's communication of divine fullness is the way in which God glorifies himself.[60] As shown, Edwards unites God's self-glorification toward the creature with communicating to their faculties.[61] While Edwards does not explicitly state it in *The End of Creation*, it would appear, if Edwards is consistent, that if God's self-communication of divine fullness to the faculties of the saints is to grow and increase perpetually, there must also be an increase of their capacities to match it.

When one investigates the unpublished *Miscellanies*, it appears that this is precisely what Edwards had in mind. Edwards states or implies the increase of the capacities of the saints in a number of *Miscellanies* entries.[62] One of the most important is *Miscellanies* 182. Here Edwards explores how the saints in heaven will be able to enjoy the beauties and the perfections of that life. In particular, he argues that "our capacities will be exceedingly enlarged, and we shall be able to apprehend, and to take in, more extended and compounded proportions." The reason the saints' capacities must enlarge is to take in the enhanced beauty. The sights of heaven will be such that their enjoyment requires enhanced capacities, and the capacities of the saints will enlarge to answer this need. The primary beauty and harmony that will require such enlarged capacities will be "the man Christ Jesus and the Deity, and among the persons of the Trinity, the supreme harmony of all."[63] Seeing and delighting in the beauty of Christ and the Trinity, along with the beauty of the saints, will require enhanced physical and mental capacities. This undergirds Edwards's doctrine of perpetual growth.

It is a grace that is answerable to the enhanced capacity of Jesus Christ. There is a elegance to the symmetry between the expansion of capacity in Christ and that of the saints. Recall that in *Miscellanies* 81 Edwards asserts that Christ must have enlarged capacities after his ascension and glorification.[64] The reason this was so important to him was to explain how Jesus, as a human, could really know and love each of the saints. The object of love (the saints) demands the enlargement of capacity. Similarly, in *Miscellanies* 182, the inverse occurs for the saints. The saints must have enlarged

---

[60]God's ultimate end is his own glory, and this can be named in various ways (see WJE 8:526).
[61]WJE 13:495.
[62]See *Miscellanies* 5, 105-6, 137, 153, 182, 198, 263, 372, 421, 430, 721 (WJE 13, 18).
[63]WJE 13:329.
[64]*Miscellanies* 81 (WJE 13:247-48).

capacities so that they can see and enjoy the beauty of Jesus Christ and the Trinity, along with the rest of the saints. The symmetry is elegant, but more importantly it demonstrates the closeness of relationship between Edwards's account of Christology and his account of grace in the life of the saint. Just as Christ's capacities enlarge, without thereby undermining his true humanity, so the saints also have an elastic capacity that will grow to match the divine discoveries and communications that await them in heaven.[65]

Saints' fulfilled humanity: Display of divine excellencies. I have already shown that Christ's humanity displays the excellencies of the eternal Logos, and this leads one to expect that the graced saint will partake of the excellencies of the divine Logos. This is precisely Edwards's argument in the sermon "Partaking of Christ's Fullness." Early in the sermon Edwards inquires how the saints partake of Christ's excellencies. He first asserts that Christ has some excellencies that derive directly from his divine nature that are incommunicable. Edwards then asserts that there are other excellencies that derive directly from his divine nature that are communicable. But then, and this is the point he develops further, he asserts that the saints partake by:

> the moral excellencies which Christ as man and mediator received from the Father. Christ received the excellencies which he had, and which he now hath in heaven, as man and mediator, from the Father. Christ received the Holy Spirit from the Father. Jn 3:34, "For he whom God hath sent speaketh the words of God: for God giveth not the Spirit by measure unto him." And as he has the Holy Spirit, so all the excellent fruits of it [are] in him.[66]

Edwards completes the picture. The divine excellencies of the eternal Son consist in his partaking of the divine fullness—the Spirit—with the Father. This gift is given without measure from the Logos to the human Jesus, establishing the hypostatic union and thereby sharing the excellencies of the Logos with the human Jesus. These excellencies shine through the human Jesus, revealing the Logos to humanity. Yet Jesus holds these excellencies not as a private person but as mediator. Therefore, they are shared with the saints, to a far lesser degree but still of the same kind. *Miscellanies* 108

---

[65] See also Edwards's discussion of varying capacities in heaven in "Heaven Is a World of Love" (WJE 8:376).
[66] Edwards, MS Sermon, no. 180, 2r.

explains that the beauty of Christ will be stamped on the saints in heaven, so that the saints will see Christ's beauty in each other.[67] This suggests that the saints' participation in the excellencies of Christ is a fulfillment of the purpose for which humanity, and indeed all nature, was designed. If one asks Edwards how this participation takes place, he gives the answer just following the quote above. Predictably, the saints receive or partake of Christ's excellencies in two ways: first, by imputation, undergirding justification; and second, by "gracious communication."[68] This communication, explains Edwards, is the gift of the Spirit, or the gift of Christ's fullness. This, of course, is the same communication, the same grace, I have called special participation throughout this study. Just in case this was not clear, Edwards explicitly explains it as, "therefore, [the saints] have the same holy and excellent temper and disposition that Christ was of, which is what is intended in II Pet. 1:4, 'they are partakers of the divine nature.'"[69]

All of this serves to confirm that the humanity of Jesus, which is transformed by the hypostatic union without taking on attributes that are incompatible with creatureliness, mediates all moral divine excellencies to the saints. This occurs through communication and participation in divine fullness, or the gift of the Spirit. In this way, Christ *as human* is both the fully graced man (the model of fulfilled humanity) and the source from which the rest of humanity gains its participation in the divine fullness.

Cosmic Fulfillment in the Divine Fullness

The key question in this chapter is, Given that created being is for *koinōnia* in divine fullness, how does this *koinōnia*, this participation in divine fullness, affect or transform created nature? Using Davison's language, how does grace elevate created nature? Another way to ask it is, What does it look like when created nature is fulfilled in participation with the divine fullness? How does grace fulfill nature? The first answer to this question comes from Christ's human nature. The hypostatic union elevates Christ's human nature such that it becomes one person with the Logos, Christ's human capacities expand, and his humanity displays the divine excellencies of the Logos. Second, the graced saint's human nature is elevated in answerable ways to

---
[67]WJE 13:280.
[68]Edwards, MS Sermon, no. 180, 2r.
[69]Edwards, MS Sermon, no. 180, 2v.

Grace and Fulfillment

that of Christ's. The saints' human faculties unite with the Logos, through the gift of the Spirit (divine fullness), such that they remain personally distinct yet bound in love that echoes the Trinity's own union. In this union, the saints' capacities enlarge through eternity so that this union strengthens perpetually. Finally, the saints' participation in divine fullness means that they display the divine excellencies to the degree of their capacities. Put differently, this is how the saint may become luminous things. Created nature and the divine fullness are never fused, but in union and *koinōnia*, there is a compatibility between them that causes the created nature to display the excellencies, or shine out with something of the divine beauty, and in so doing it fulfills its greatest purpose.

Yet shall I leave the question there? If I did so, I would leave something incomplete. Recall from chapter four that God created all things in order to communicate the divine fullness. Remember also that this communication is to the saints alone. This then raises the question about the rest of the cosmos. If only saints receive the divine fullness, and if the communication of the divine fullness is the purpose for the whole cosmos, then what role does the rest of the cosmos play in God's purpose? If only human nature is elevated, then why did God create the rest of the universe? Is it merely setting? Or does the rest of the cosmos factor into the *koinōnia* in the divine fullness? One could also ask, What role does this history of redemption play in the fulfillment of creation's purpose? Edwards spent great time and energy describing God's work of redemption. Does the unfolding of God's work in history relate to the fulfillment of created nature in the divine fullness? Finally, what role is there for community and the saints' relationship with each other? If I were to leave the discussion where I am right now, one might imagine a sort of individual vision. Each saint needs only to receive, individually, the divine fullness, and enjoy union with Christ in the Spirit. But Edwards spoke a great deal about the saints' love for each other. Is this incidental?

Edwards believed creation, history, and the saints' community with each other would all play a role the overall end for which God created the world. But in order to show this, I will need to shift the camera angle, so to speak. For most of this study, I have focused the camera on the saint receiving the divine fullness. So long as this is my focus, then one will get a picture of

God's work in the world that is very limited to the individual alone. However, I must now shift that camera angle and look at the world through the eyes of the saint herself. That is, we must imaginatively enter into the mind of the saint and consider the cosmos as *she* sees it and as it is lit up for her by divine fullness. The reason is that Edwards believed that the saint, in *koinōnia* with divine fullness, gains a new sight of the whole cosmos. The whole universe, all of history, and the community of saints become ignited with the fire of divine beauty in a way hidden from others. It is as the saint views her world and sees the beauty of God in it that the whole cosmos contributes to the fulfillment of creation's end.

Creation in marvelous light. Jonathan Edwards preached the sermon "Christians a Chosen Generation" in 1731. Based on 1 Peter 2:9 ("But ye are a chosen generation, a royal priesthood, an holy nation, a peculiar people; that ye should show forth the praises of him who hath called you out of darkness into his marvelous light," KJV), he aimed to describe the uniqueness of God's saints. Part of the uniqueness lays in this: when the sinner is converted and becomes a saint, she sees the world differently. Put in the language of this study, when the saint receives the divine fullness, she not only receives light into her soul; she sees the world in a new light.

> There is a world of new objects that is discovered, a spiritual world, a great variety of beautiful and glorious objects that were till now altogether hidden. And there is a light that shines from outward objects that before did not; the visible world has a light shining in it that before was not seen. There is a light shines from God's works of creation and providence. The face of the earth, the fields and trees, they have a spiritual light shining from them that discovers the glory of the Creator. And the sun, moon, and stars shine with a new kind of light, even spiritual light. The sun shone bright with outward light before, but it shines brighter now with discoveries of the glory of its Creator. Though this spiritual light indeed is but dim here, and often interrupted, a true saint can see this light from the Word of God or the works of God at all times.[70]

A saint sees divine beauty in the natural world in a way hidden from others. Why? Is the saint imagining a beauty that is not really there in the created world? Is the saint obsessed with God and imposing that obsession onto the

---

[70] WJE 17:323.

Grace and Fulfillment 227

rest of the natural world? Is the saint reading God's glory into a world that does not in fact bear that glory per se? No. Notice Edwards's word *hidden*. The beauty and glory of God that the saint sees are a beauty and glory that were previously hidden but present. That is, the beauty and the glory of God are somehow present in this world, but only visible to those humans who partake of the divine fullness. Why can Edwards make this claim?

The answer draws together several aspects of this study. In particular, it highlights the coordination between common participation and special participation. Recall from chapter two that all things participate in God for being (common participation). This undergirds created nature, but it is not the participation that explains true grace. Special participation is the communication and participation in the divine fullness, given only to the saints. I used this to explain how Edwards can distinguish created nature from divine grace and do so in strong terms. Yet at the same time I showed in chapter four that common participation is *for* special participation. That is, common participation is teleologically oriented toward special participation, or *being is for* koinōnia. Bring all this as background now to the saint who is viewing her beautiful world. She has received the divine fullness, and she is now united to Christ in a bond of the Spirit. This divine fullness is like a marvelous light that displays something that was always present but hidden from view.[71] Namely, she sees now how all created beauty is a reflection of the beauty of the Son of God.[72]

> When we see beautiful airs of look and gesture, we naturally think the mind that resides within is beautiful. We have all the same, and more, reason to conclude the spiritual beauty of Christ from the beauty of the world; for all the beauties of the universe do as immediately result from the efficiency of Christ, as a cast of an eye or a smile of the countenance depends on the efficiency of the human soul.[73]

Created nature and divine grace, though distinct, are not a contradiction. Rather, God created this world to display the beauties of Christ. This beauty, these "emanations . . . of the excellencies of the Son of God" are objectively

---

[71] WJE 17:323.
[72] "The beauties of nature are really emanations, or shadows, of the excellencies of the Son of God" (*Miscellanies* 108, in WJE 13:279).
[73] *Miscellanies* 185 (WJE 13:330).

present in this world.⁷⁴ Yet they remain hidden from the unregenerate, and therefore the communication of divine fullness (special participation and grace) is required to make them visible. As the saint views the excellencies of Christ in the created world around her, the created world's telos is fulfilled. In other words, not only is the communication of divine fullness pivotal for the fulfillment of the saints themselves, but through their perception, the whole created order finds its fulfillment.

Edwards lived in a world filled with natural icons of Jesus.⁷⁵ This occurred immediately upon his own spiritual renewal. Describing the season after his conversion, he writes, "God's excellency . . . seemed to appear in everything; in the sun, moon and stars; in the clouds, and blue sky; in the grass, flowers, trees; in the water, and all nature; which used greatly to fix my mind."⁷⁶ This is a spirituality of reading the "Book of Nature and Common Providence" to see the beauty of God, and especially of Christ.⁷⁷ Even the "silkworm is a remarkable type of Christ."⁷⁸ Edwards believed that this spiritual reading of the natural world was part of every saint's spirituality. Indeed, it is part of the design, purpose, and fulfillment of the cosmos.

History in marvelous light. History similarly shines with the marvelous light. "Christians a Chosen Generation" continues with Edwards pointing out how "the grace of God in the work of redemption, when it is seen in its true light discovered by divine and spiritual light to the soul, will evermore appear wonderful." Just as the saints see Christ and his excellencies in the natural world, so also they see his excellencies in the providence of God. The unfolding story of how God in Christ redeemed the world will be an object of eternal contemplation for the saints. "There is wonderfulness and glory enough in it to keep the souls of saints and angels forever in admiration and rapture."⁷⁹

This was surely part of Edwards's motivation for preaching his thirty-sermon-long series *A History of the Work of Redemption*.⁸⁰ Preached in 1739, this massive series of sermons all derived from one text: Isaiah 51:8, "my

---

⁷⁴WJE 13:279.
⁷⁵Is it mischievous to use the word *icon*? See Edwards's notebook titled "Image of Divine Things" (WJE 11:50-130).
⁷⁶WJE 16:794.
⁷⁷Subtitle of "Images of Divine Things" (WJE 11:50).
⁷⁸WJE 11:100.
⁷⁹WJE 17:324.
⁸⁰WJE 9:113-528.

righteousness shall be for ever, and my salvation from generation to generation" (KJV). The doctrine was quite straightforward and remained unchanged in all thirty sermons: "The Work of Redemption is a work that God carries on from the fall of man to the end of the world." Edwards follows the history throughout that entire time frame. He divides up history into three large sections: (1) the fall of humanity to the incarnation of Christ, (2) the life and ministry of Christ, and (3) the time from Christ's resurrection to the end of the world. The first time period prepares for redemption, the second purchases redemption, and the third achieves its success.[81] But the key point for my purposes is that Edwards believed that the saints would see something of God's beauty especially in viewing the history of redemption. He preached not only to inform, though certain he intended to so, but also because he believed the saints would see Christ's beauty uniquely through viewing his grace in history, and that this display was an anticipation of the occupation of heaven. Just as the saints view Christ's excellencies in creation, so also the saints must view Christ's excellencies in history. Of course Christ's excellencies become more explicit in the history of redemption than they are in the "book of nature."[82]

It is well known that Edwards desired to write a magnum opus that he called *A History of the Work of Redemption*. He intended to integrate the whole of divinity into this history. The reason he could envision uniting all the topics of divinity into this history was that the work of redemption is "the grand design of all God's designs, and the *summum* and *ultimum* of all the divine operations and degrees; particularly considering all parts of the grand scheme in their historical order."[83] Note the importance of *historical order*. It was typical to write divinity in a systematic and abstract doctrinal manner. One thinks of Thomas's *Summa* and Calvin's *Institutes* and Turretin's *Elenctic Theology* or Peter Van Mastricht's *Theoretical-Practical Theology*. Edwards stood in a long line of this sort of abstract doctrinal divinity. Why did Edwards want to change the method? Why change the genre?

Edwards believed that there was something in the *narrative*, the *historical order*, the *events* themselves that really mattered. God's design,

---
[81] WJE 9:116, 128.
[82] WJE 11:50.
[83] WJE 16:727.

Christ's excellencies, are set on display not only in abstract doctrine but also in the form of God's providential outworking of history. This story had to be told, because in hearing the story the saints would see a marvelous light. Providential history is part of common participation. God orchestrates the natural world toward his ends. The telic end of history is the communication of divine fullness, not only in that through history this communication happens, but also because when this communication happens, the saints look back at history and see their Lord's beauty written on its pages. Just as Edwards lived in a world full of icons of Jesus, he lived in a story that displayed Christ as well.

Saints in marvelous light. Created nature is fulfilled when saints partake of the divine fullness, and thereby see Christ's excellencies displayed in the natural world and in the history of redemption. The history of redemption displays Christ's excellencies more specifically than does the rest of the natural world. But there remains another aspect of the natural world that uniquely displays Christ's excellencies: the saints themselves.

I have already established that humanity is itself designed to display the excellencies of Christ. That is preeminently true of Christ's humanity, but it is also true of the saints. Their participation in the divine fullness causes them to become luminous things.[84] This luminosity shines from one saint to another. It is not merely that the individual saint and Christ are united in mutual affection. It is also true that the saints become united as they see Christ's excellencies shining out from one to another. Even Christ himself will enjoy the beauty of the saints; Christ will see and delight in his own beauty reflected from the saints' holiness. *Miscellanies* 108 describes the way in which Christ's excellency shines through all creation, but then moves to rejoice that these excellencies will shine out the more through the saints in heaven.

> How great a happiness will it be in heaven, for the saints to enjoy the society of each other! For if one may see so much of the loveliness of Christ in those things which are only shadows of being—with what joy are philosophers filled in beholding the aspectable world!—how sweet will it be to behold the proper images and communications of Christ's excellencies in intelligent beings, having so much of the beauty of Christ upon them as Christians shall have in heaven.[85]

---

[84] WJE 2:343.
[85] WJE 13:280.

Inanimate creation displays Christ's beauty in a shadowy way, but the saints display him as the "proper images and communications of Christ's excellencies."

A great amount of Edwards's writing was taken up with considering and meditating on Christ's excellencies *displayed through the saints*. His very first *Miscellanies* entry is on the topic of holiness. But Edwards is not just speaking of the abstract notion of holiness. His meditation is on the beauty of holiness and how it causes the saint to resemble God. "Holiness," writes Edwards, "is a most beautiful and lovely thing.... 'Tis almost too high a beauty for any creatures to be adorned with; it makes the soul a little, sweet and delightful image of the blessed Jehovah." This is not a detached theological treatise on holiness; it is one saint gazing at holiness in an imagined second saint and enjoying—even reveling—in the sight. He muses that "angels stand, with pleased, delighted and charmed eyes, and look and look, with smiles of pleasure upon their lips, upon that soul that is holy." Yet while he considers how angels enjoy the saints' luminosity, one realizes that it is in fact Edwards, in the moment of writing, who is smiling and gazing on the saint. "How doth all the world congratulate, embrace, and sing to a sanctified soul!"[86] My point in emphasizing this is to demonstrate again the spirituality Edwards cultivated and commended of meditating on Christ's excellencies and beauties through gazing at the saints. This is because the saints are filled with the divine fullness and become luminous things. Grace truly elevates nature.

Was this part of why Edwards was so inclined to narrate the lives of saints? Edwards and the Northampton revival became famous because of his *Faithful Narrative*.[87] This is a narrative of the awakening itself, and therefore something like a close-up inspection of one episode of the history of redemption. But it is interesting to note that displaying the grace poured out in Northampton triggered other awakenings. The awakened saints of Northampton became luminous things. Further, when Edwards came to explain and justify and defend the awakenings, he turned to describing his own wife's experience. Edwards had always meditated on and cherished Sarah Pierpont Edwards's holiness.[88] And in *Some Thoughts Concerning the*

---

[86]WJE 13:163.
[87]WJE 4:144-211.
[88]While rightly described as a romantic letter, Edwards's early writing about Sarah Pierpont is in actual fact a meditation on her holiness (see WJE 16:789-90).

Revival, he holds up her experience as a gold standard. Yet it is not a cool analysis, but rather Edwards takes the reader imaginatively into Sarah's own gaze on Christ's excellencies. Always keeping Sarah anonymous, Edwards details how she gained a

> clear and lively view or sense of the infinite beauty and amiableness of Christ's person, and the heavenly sweetness of his excellent and transcendent love; so that (to use the person's own expressions) the soul remained in a kind of heavenly Elysium, and did as it were swim in the rays of Christ's love, like a little mote swimming in the beams of the sun, or streams of his light that come in at a window; and the heart was swallowed up in a kind of glow of Christ's love, coming down from Christ's heart in heaven, as a constant stream of sweet light, at the same time the soul all flowing out in love to him; so that there seemed to be a constant flowing and reflowing from heart to heart.[89]

Edwards is not just reporting an episode; he is describing an experience so that the reader can gain something of a sense for it as well. Put differently, Edwards is displaying Sarah as a luminous thing. Given Edwards's view that the saints' humanity is designed to display Christ's excellencies, it is not surprising that he would adopt such a strategy for promoting and defending the revival.

The same is true, and perhaps even more strikingly so, in Edwards's *Life of David Brainerd*. David Brainerd was a missionary in New Jersey, and Edwards edited and published his diary and journal after Brainerd died. Edwards explains that, as Jesus Christ both taught doctrine and exhibited it through his virtue, so God raises up both teachers of doctrine and also eminent saints. The two work together to promote true religion and virtue.[90] The very best situation, argues Edwards, is when there is a great teacher who is also an eminent saint. In these cases the truth of doctrine is verified by the holiness of the saint. In this case the world gains a "a confirmation of the truth, efficacy, and amiableness of the religion taught, in the practice of the same persons that have most clearly and forceably taught it." These examples are most helpful when the saint walks through difficulties and trials.[91] Here again, Edwards expects the saints to display Christ's excellencies, and so he

---

[89]WJE 4:332.
[90]WJE 7:89-90.
[91]WJE 7:90.

published Brainerd's *Life of David Brainerd* because he wanted readers to watch what it looked like for the fullness of Christ to fill a man, and then lead that man through terrible trials and glorious success. Indeed, Edwards warns in his preface that Brainerd's example should only be commended to the extent it conforms to Christ.[92] Yet he believed it conformed to Christ in great measure. Edwards published Brainerd's *Life of David Brainerd* because he believed him to be a luminous thing.

This implies a theology of the communion of saints. It is not just an individual saint and Christ, as if the rest of the saints were incidental to one another. Rather, Edwards believed that all the saints are bound together at least because they all display Christ's excellencies to one another. Each receives *koinōnia* in the divine fullness, and each sees Christ's excellencies radiating from the others. As the capacities of the saints increase eternally, this dynamic will compound forever in heaven. In heaven, the saints "are all lovely, so all see each other's loveliness with answerable delight and complacence. Everyone there loves every other inhabitant of heaven whom he sees, and so he is mutually beloved by everyone."[93]

The aim of this chapter has been to describe the ways in which created nature becomes transformed through the participation in the divine fullness. If *being is for* koinōnia, then how does *koinōnia* in the divine fullness affect, or elevate, created nature? The answer begins with Christ's humanity, then extends to the saints, and eventually gathers up the cosmos. Christ's hypostatic union means that his humanity displays his excellencies perfectly. When divine grace gathers sinners and fills them with divine fullness, saints are united by the Spirit to Christ and thereby display the excellencies of Christ in limited manner. But then the whole of the cosmos and providential history gains a role in this vision. The saints come to see the divine meaning of the universe by viewing and gazing on Christ's excellencies displayed in it. This meaning, this beauty, is objectively present in the created order, but it is hidden from view to all but those who partake of the divine fullness. The saints see Christ in creation, but then even more clearly in the history of redemption, for here Christ himself is named, and his moral excellencies shine out the clearer. Finally, the saints view Christ in other saints, both now

---

[92]WJE 7:91.
[93]WJE 8:374.

in the trials of the church militant and in the glories of the church triumphant. Edwards lived in a universe designed to display Christ and saturated with his excellencies.

Conclusion: A World Designed for the Beatific Vision

Or to say it in terms specific to this study, Edwards's world was designed for *koinōnia* in the divine fullness. The world does not possess the divine fullness in itself. Created nature does not bear within itself the resources for its own fulfillment. It is a thing that needs filling. But God created in order to fill that emptiness and thus fulfill its purpose. That filling with fullness obtains in the person of Jesus Christ. His humanity is filled by the Spirit, the fullness shared between the Father and the Son, resulting in the hypostatic union between the Logos and the human Jesus. Christ then is the bridge between Creator and creature, and this union is the source and the model for the saints. The saints receive the divine fullness, the Holy Spirit, who unites them to Christ in bond of love. They retain their distinct personhoods and yet their faculties synchronize with Christ's in mutual affection. With time and throughout eternity, their capacities increase so that their mutual love in Christ never flatlines but ever increases. In and through Christ's human nature, they both see Christ's divine excellencies and shine them outward toward Christ and his people.

Yet this is not all. The saints come to see Christ's fullness everywhere around them. As they move from darkness to light, so their perception of the world moves from darkness to light. This is as God intended, for all things were created through and for Christ, and their deepest meaning is found in displaying something of Christ's excellencies. Not only does the created order declare Christ's glory, but so does the story of God in and through the created order. The history of redemption is the eternal delight of God's saints, for in this story they see the excellencies of Christ, and it is their *koinōnia* in divine fullness that makes them see it. Then, as they zoom in to the detail of God's work of redemption, the saints see their sisters and brothers, other saints walking the arduous path of following Jesus. These saints shine out with Christ's excellencies as well, for they are truly luminous things. Throughout the ages the church triumphant will continue to increase in this *koinōnia* in divine fullness, seeing the excellencies of Christ, and through him by the Spirit, seeing God himself. Being is for *koinōnia*, and *koinōnia* fulfills being.

Two implications will close this chapter. The first concerns the intimacy between created nature and divine fullness, and the second concerns the beatific vision.

Edwards's strong distinction between created nature and divine grace serves his vision of great intimacy between God and the creature. This is not always intuitive. Hans Boersma, in his book *Heavenly Participation: The Weaving of a Sacramental Tapestry*, laments the loss of what he calls a sacramental ontology. Boersma wants the church to rediscover the Platonist-Christian synthesis that created a framework for seeing how this world depended on God and pointed to God at its deepest ontology. He outlines many dynamics that have undermined this vision, but important among them is the Protestant Reformation.[94] He quotes Andrew Greely's characterization that "Catholic theologians and artists tend to emphasize the presence of God in the world, while the classic works of Protestant theologians tend to emphasize the absence of God from the world."[95] I mention this here because it is easy to read Edwards's emphasis on created nature's emptiness of the divine fullness as an iteration of this alleged theme of God's absence. This would be a mistake. Edwards's God is everywhere, and everything is made to display him. God is the ontological foundation and deepest meaning of Edwards's world. This common participation in God upholds everything, every moment, so that Paul's statement that all things were created through Christ and for Christ (Col 1:16-17) is fundamental for Edwards. But while God is not absent from creation, or even distant, the fallen human person is still empty of divine fullness. Fallen humanity, while upheld every moment by common participation, is utterly bereft of special participation in divine fullness. This is a tragedy, for it results in depravity. Created nature, in itself, does not share at all in divine fullness. Is this not absence? No, it is not. For even this emptiness is itself a teleological thing. A cup's emptiness suggests it is for being filled. So even Edwards's strong distinction between created nature and divine grace, even his absolute

---

[94]Hans Boersma, *Heavenly Participation: The Weaving of a Sacramental Tapestry* (Grand Rapids, MI: Eerdmans, 2011), 85-89.
[95]Andrew M. Greely, *The Catholic Imagination* (Berkeley: University of California Press, 2000), cited in Boersma, *Heavenly Participation*, 10.

clarity that created nature can never assume the divine fullness, ultimately points to fulfillment. Edwards's cosmos is always pointing away to God—both in its state of tragic need and also (even more so) in its fulfillment in divine fullness. Andrew Davison's point is true of Edwards: divine grace elevates created nature comprehensively, and this is so in part because of (not despite) Edwards's emphasis on natural emptiness. That created nature is empty of divine fullness in itself emphasizes both the need for special grace and the preciousness of it in fulfillment. In other words, Edwards's vision of nature and grace bears wisdom for those who desire to reweave a sacramental tapestry.[96]

The second implication relates to the beatific vision. Being is for *koinōnia*, and *koinōnia* in divine fullness fulfills being. No image unites and sums up this fulfillment in special participation more aptly than does the beatific vision. Like so many classical Christian thinkers before him, Edwards described the culmination of the cosmos in terms the saints' blessed sight of God in Christ and by the Spirit. If one were to ask Edwards, "What does it finally look like for created nature to be fulfilled in the divine fullness?" he would strain to describe "personal beatific delight."[97] Not only is this the final consummation of creation, but it is also before all time itself, for Edwards's Trinity *ad intra* is framed in terms of this beatific vision. This study has not used the imagery of beatific vision a great deal because my focus is on the Creator-creature distinction. But nevertheless I must now say what is everywhere implied: Edwards believed all created nature was designed to either enjoy the beatific vision or contribute to the beatific delight of the saints. Once filled with the divine fullness, the saints *see* Christ's excellencies in the world around them, in the history of redemption, and in the saints themselves.[98] In heaven the saints will see the divine nature through Christ

---

[96]The image of "weaving a sacramental tapestry" is Boersma's. See *Heavenly Participation*, 8. I readily note the difference between Edwards's relation of the natural and the supernatural and that of Boersma, but I also believe there are points of contact such that Edwards can be a resource in ongoing discussion of these interests.

[97]Kyle Strobel's term. See Strobel, *Jonathan Edwards's Theology: A Reinterpretation*, T&T Clark Studies in Systematic Theology (London: T&T Clark, 2013), 23-71.

[98]Even hell and the damned display something of Christ's excellencies. See *Miscellanies* 279 (WJE 13:379). See also *Miscellanies* 288 (WJE 13:381). For a sermon on how the damned fulfill their purpose in creation, see WJE 46, sermon 210 on Prov 16:4. For the saints' joy in God's glory through viewing inanimate creation, see WJE 17:323.

and by the Spirit.[99] Created nature gains its being from God's own personal beatific delight in the Trinity, and it is fulfilled in the saints' personal beatific delight gained through participation in the divine fullness.

David Brainerd, on that evening in 1739, tasted ontological fulfillment. He was filled with the divine fullness and saw something of God's glory. He became a luminous thing, and Edwards's aim in telling his story was so that Brainerd might shine such that all might see Christ's excellencies, and find their own fulfillment in him.

---

[99] See Edwards's sermon on Rom 2:10 (WJE 50, sermon 373 on Romans 2:10). See also Kyle Strobel's exposition of it in *Jonathan Edwards's Theology: A Reinterpretation*, 137-143; Hans Boersma, *Seeing God: The Beatific Vision in Christian Tradition* (Grand Rapids, MI: Eerdmans, 2018).

Conclusion

NORMAN RUSSELL SAYS that theosis is the deepest answer to the question, "Why were we born?"[1] Who among us can avoid this question? It is a strange thing to be human. The question of purpose, the question "Why?" is inescapable. There are many ways to attempt the answer. Most start with clues from below, clues in one's own experience that might suggest the larger answer. Christianity, however, charts a different course. Christianity puts the question, "Why were we born?" in second position. The story, the narrative of Christian revelation, begins by the revelation of God. "Who is God?" precedes "Why were we born?" But that is not to displace the question of humanity's purpose. Quite the contrary. Evidently, the only way to discover humanity's purpose is to look away from oneself and see the blessed Trinity. In looking at the revelation of God as Father, Son, and Holy Spirit, one discovers that God has given himself to humanity in Christ and by the Spirit. Humans were born to partake of his divine love, his divine fullness, his divine Spirit. Humans discover themselves in receiving his gift. God is his best gift, and this gift is humanity's purpose. Russell was right.

Jonathan Edwards united God and God's gift of salvation. He believed that God's self-gift and humanity's purpose met through the creature's participation in divine fullness. God communicated the fullness (enjoyed between the Father and the Son through the Spirit) to the saints so the trinitarian fullness repeated finitely and economically in a bond between Creator

---

[1] Norman Russell, "Why Does *Theosis* Fascinate Western Christians?," *Sobornost* 34, no. 1 (2012): 15.

and creature. This explains both why we were born and also how God is the fulfillment of our purpose. This study has aimed to describe what Edwards meant by these things, focusing on how he navigated the Creator-creature distinction and relation, with a view toward contributing to contemporary discussions on theosis and soteriological participation. What significance does Edwards's answer bear for us today? Six insights stand out.

1. A Reformed Theosis

I have presented Edwards's doctrine of grace as a robust doctrine of soteriological participation, *and one that grew from and reinforced his own Reformed tradition*. His doctrine of grace is not a foreign import; it is a native product. Special grace is a communication and participation in divine fullness. This divine fullness is the *ad extra* gift of the *ad intra* love between the Father and the Son. This *ad intra* love is the Holy Spirit, and the Spirit's procession is the teleological fulfillment of the Trinity's inner relation. In the economy, God created the world in order to pour this love, this Holy Spirit, out as divine fullness on intelligent creatures. This happens without measure in the incarnation, and with measure to the saints in redemption. It will continue in ever-increasing measure throughout eternity, such that God considers it an infinite intimacy between Creator and creature.

By any measure, this is a strong and robust doctrine of soteriological participation. It is no wonder that many Edwards scholars employ the term *theosis* to describe it. However, it is important to see that Edwards's doctrine is not Palamism. He probably had some access to the Greek church fathers through both Reformed Orthodox sources and the Cambridge Platonists, and he certainly had some access to the notion of theosis through the latter. However, while he learned from these sources, his doctrine of grace is deeply rooted in his own Reformed tradition. His strong distinction between created nature and divine grace, grounded on his differentiation between common and special participation, aimed to resist Arminian or synergistic accounts of grace. His distinction between the communicable divine fullness and the incommunicable divine essence differentiated him from heretical enthusiasts. He leveraged soteriological participation to pursue Reformed interests. And he developed his theory by way of synchronizing key doctrines of Reformed confessionalism: the Trinity, special grace (regeneration, effectual calling, etc.), and creation's end. All these are identifiably Reformed themes; Edwards modified them to show their soteriological harmony. This is not to say that these themes are exclusive to the Reformed tradition, but rather that Edwards engaged them with sympathetic loyalty to his own tradition. Edwards's doctrine of special grace is a native Reformed account of soteriological participation.

In presenting Edwards's doctrine of grace as a Reformed approach to soteriological participation, I am corroborating and extending the recent work of Kyle Strobel.[2] While many Edwards scholars have presented Edwards as an exponent of theosis or deification or divinization, Strobel stands out as situating his view more closely within the Reformed tradition. Strobel has recently emphasized the role of the "communicative natures," the economic answer to the perichoretic sharing of natures within the Trinity *ad intra*, as the foundation of Edwards's view of theosis (his preferred word). I have preferred Edwards's category of divine fullness rather than nature, but it is clear that these are complementary categories within Edwards's thought. I have argued that "divine fullness" is a larger category that includes the communicable natures within it. The benefit of using the category of divine fullness is that it emphasizes the single gift of grace: the Spirit given as love through the faculties of the saint that bind the saint to Christ, and thus God's self-understanding. A further benefit of the category of divine fullness is that it appears to be Edwards's preferred category when contrasting with the divine essence. Given that this study has particular focus on the Creator-creature distinction, the category of divine fullness is more appropriate, and it adds clarity for how Edwards employed the Creator-creature distinction in defending and extending Reformed interests.

Some view Edwards's approach to soteriological participation as a resource for ecumenical dialogue.[3] This is not altogether wrong. There may be points of contact between Edwards's doctrine of soteriological participation and other traditions' views on grace and salvation. However, before

---

[2] Kyle Strobel, "Jonathan Edwards's Reformed Doctrine of *Theosis*," *HTR* 109, no. 3 (2016): 371–99.
[3] See especially Michael J. McClymond, "Salvation as Divinization: Jonathan Edwards, Gregory Palamas and the Theological Uses of Platonism," in *Jonathan Edwards: Philosophical Theologian*, ed. Oliver D. Crisp and Paul Helm (Burlington, VT: Ashgate, 2003), 139–60; Michael J. McClymond and Gerald R. McDermott, "The Theme of Divinization," in *The Theology of Jonathan Edwards* (Oxford: Oxford University Press, 2012), 410–23.

one explores the similarities, one must know the differences. As Vladimir Lossky says, "If while remaining loyal to our respective dogmatic standpoints we could succeed in getting to know each other, above all in those points in which we differ, this would undoubtedly be a surer way towards unity than that which would leave differences on one side. For in the words of Karl Barth, 'the union of the Churches is not made, but we discover it.'"[4] One must read Edwards *as Reformed*, clear on the differences between his tradition and any other one, in order for one to employ his thought well in ecumenical theology. Therefore, this study is a contribution to clarity—showing how Edwards's doctrine of grace is grounded in his own tradition's interests—that in turn prepares the ground for future ecumenical work.

2. Complementary Participations

Edwards used what amounts to two different approaches to participation. The first, what I called common participation, is a sharing in being that undergirds all creation. The second, what I called special participation, is a sharing in love that undergirds special grace. These two participations provide resources for Edwards scholarship in understanding Edwards's distinctions between both nature and grace and the divine fullness and essence.

The relationship between God and creation (the Creator-creature distinction and relation) is always a big topic in Edwards studies. Edwards is sometimes called a pantheist, more defensibly a panentheist, and very often some sort of Neoplatonist. These debates grow out of a careful reading of how Edwards framed his doctrine of creation. Creation is radically dependent on God, created every moment by God's immediate action. God communicates being, and being is a participation in God. The matter is complicated further by Edwards's frequent assertions that God created the world in order to communicate his own divine fullness. This is where the critical question comes: Is this communication of divine fullness the same thing as the communication of being? If they are the same, is there any distinction between created nature and divine grace? If Edwards follows Christian Neoplatonic approaches, then one might expect divine grace to be somehow vested in created nature, albeit perhaps to a small degree. If this

---

[4]Vladimir Lossky, *The Mystical Theology of the Eastern Church* (Plymouth, UK: Latimer, Trend, 1957), 22.

is the case, what happens to gratuity? This would raise real questions about whether Edwards could remain true to Reformed confessionalism. For instance, what does depravity mean if this is the case?

This study addresses these questions by showing that the communication of being and the communication of divine fullness are two different communications. One is a *methexis* in being and quiddity; the other is a *koinōnia* in trinitarian love. Creation can have being (the first communication and participation) without *any degree* of the divine fullness. This means Edwards can distinguish created nature and divine grace in a robust way, and one that preserves space for Reformed notions of depravity and gratuity.

But how does the divine fullness differ from the divine essence? This question has troubled Edwards readers since the very beginning.[5] If the divine fullness is communicated to the creature, does this collapse the Creator-creature distinction? Edwards scholars have sometimes noted that Edwards does distinguish between the divine essence and the divine *nature* or *fullness*, but the scholarship has not adequately investigated whether it is a coherent distinction.[6] This study shows the coherence by demonstrating how Edwards employs two versions of participation theology—*methexis* in quiddity and *koinōnia* in love—from his trinitarian doctrine, through his Christology, and all the way into the doctrine of grace. This allows one to read Edwards's distinction as more than a verbal trick: it is a theological tool that allows him to maintain the Creator-creature distinction, all the while bridging it in intimate relational union.

3. The Trinity's Gift

That God is God's own best gift is everywhere in the Christian Scriptures and embedded deeply in the logic of the gospel. Regardless, Christian theology and the church's proclamation of the gospel have at times abstracted God's gifts from God himself. I am not speaking of the heresies in the church so much as the church's orthodox descriptions of soteriology. The church

---

[5]WJE 8:636-40.
[6]See especially Kyle Strobel, "Jonathan Edwards and the Polemics of Theosis," *HTR* 105, no. 3 (2012): 259-79. See also Richard B. Steele, "Transfiguring Light: The Moral Beauty of the Christian Life According to Gregory Palamas and Jonathan Edwards," *St Vladimir's Theological Quarterly* 52, nos. 3-4 (2008): 403-39. Steele distinguishes between God's internal and external glory rather than divine essence and divine fullness.

speaks of justification, sanctification, glorification, and any number of other precious benefits of Christ's salvation. These categories are crucial, and yet there is a risk that the church's description of salvation can end up sounding as if God gives Christ in order to impart these rather abstract benefits. This can result in separating theology proper from soteriology. Can one gain justification without the Trinity? Most would say no. Yet one can describe justification with only passing reference to the Trinity. God and salvation seem too separate, too often.

Edwards avoided this, and it is one of his contributions to the church. At a time when the Trinity was readily ignored and increasingly denied, Edwards swam the other direction. Not only did he insist on the doctrine of the Trinity, but he mined the doctrine for soteriological insight. Even further, Edwards integrated the doctrine of God and the doctrine of salvation so that the second became an economic corollary of the first. Salvation and redemption, for Edwards, are the Trinity's self-gift in the economy and appropriate to creaturely ontology. Indeed, not only did Edwards integrate soteriology and theology proper, but he also related the doctrine of creation to the doctrine of God. There are many dangers here. How does one show the relation between God and creation without fusing the two? Yet here again, despite the dangers, Edwards labors to demonstrate ontological and teleological relatedness between creation and the Creator, all the while guarding their difference. Edwards's doctrine of God dominated his vision of creation and redemption.

Surely there is scriptural and traditional wisdom here. The law forbids preferring God's gifts above God himself. The gospel proclaims God's self-gift in Christ and the Spirit, and calls the church to real union and fellowship with the Trinity. The creeds of the church all confess that Christ and the Spirit are not gifts other than God, but rather God himself. Edwards uses technical language and creative innovation in how he describes these realities, but his aim is to say what Christian tradition has always said: God is God's best gift.

4. Christological Creation

Edwards lived in a world animated by Jesus. It is not just that his concept of redemption was Christocentric (it was), but that the whole cosmos was

Christocentric. It was full of "shadows of divine things."[7] All things partake of God for their being, and all things are created through Christ and for Christ (Col 1:16). These presuppositions meant that he expected Christ to be the key to grasping the world's coherence. Only the saints will really be able to see this coherence, and the beauty of Christ distributed through the world, because they only are capable of seeing Christ's beauty in any regard. Nevertheless, Christ provides a coherence that is objectively present in the natural world by virtue of common participation.

Coherence is elusive today. Modern philosophy (and theology) has tended to divorce God from the investigations of the natural world, and one result is that the question of coherence is never quite answered. Yet voices such as Radical Orthodoxy, Hans Boersma, and Henri de Lubac before them press the other way. Real ontological participation in God allows bold assertions of coherence. Boersma's sacramental ontology focuses teleology and meaning on Christ.

Edwards's concept of creation and common participation supports this move, and he stands as a resource for further development of Christocentric teleology and coherent meaning in the natural world. There is also real potential for apologetics. If Christ really is the key to coherence, then the church should expect Christ and Christology to be a fruitful field for addressing the questions and anxieties of the age. If all things partake of Christ for their being, then one should not be surprised if the questions of the natural world are addressed (in ways we have not yet discovered) by that source of being.

But coherence is not enough. Not only does Christ give creation coherence, argues Edwards, but Jesus is its source of beauty. The saints will see Christ's beauty in the natural world, and in doing so they will be in closer touch with *this world* than they would have been otherwise. True, Edwards believed this world was really fulfilled in the next. But his common participation meant that he valued the natural world—both the world as it exists now and in the age to come. There are untapped implications for ethics, aesthetics, and environmental concerns, among many others. Edwards calls the church to see the beauty of Christ in and through this world he constantly upholds.

---

[7] WJE 11:51.

5. Theosis of the "Narrow Way"

Edwards is famous (notorious?) for his sermon "Sinners in the Hands of an Angry God." That this is his best-known sermon is regrettable. That it faithfully represents his view of the urgent need of salvation is indisputable. Despite all Edwards's cosmic language about creation's end in the communication of divine fullness, and despite his robust account of common participation in God for being, he still retained a frighteningly real vision of divine judgment. Edwards believed that the way to theosis was a narrow way.

This belief will disturb many. Theologies that emphasize cosmic participation in God for being can tend toward (at least an implied) universalism. Edwards took a different path, and did so decisively. He pressed against universalism by distinguishing special grace from common grace in strong terms. Created nature assumes common participation, but it cannot assume special participation in divine fullness. This means created nature, especially human nature, without special grace, is truly empty of the divine goodness, the divine fullness. Empty of the fullness of divine love, the sinner loves only self, and all other things for the sake of self. Self-love, unrestrained by divine love, will drive the sinner further into sin, and without divine intervention it will drive the sinner to hell. Theosis requires a divine inbreaking of something infinitely above created nature. Theosis is a narrow path.

This theosis of the narrow way is unfashionable, but that may be part of its value. Contemporary theology has many strengths. Can one say that a strong account of evil and sin is one of them? The world is increasingly shocked by violence and scandal and moral failure. Why is the reality of evil so surprising? It may be that there are better ways to account for evil than Edwards's. Yet even if that is true, ontologies of participation and theologies of theosis that fail to account for evil and sin risk ringing hollow. More importantly, one risks ignoring the very source of theosis, who says, "The gate is wide and the way is easy that leads to destruction, and those who enter by it are many" (Mt 7:13).

6. Lament unto Repentance

And yet how shall we speak of theosis of the narrow way without stopping in our tracks to lament and to repent?

In 1736, a woman named Leah became a full communicant member of the Northampton Church. She was a convert from the first "surprising work of God" just a short time earlier. As we have seen, to say that she was converted meant a great deal in Edwards's view of things. It meant that she bore the natural image of God, that she was uniquely designed to receive a supernatural and uncreated divine fullness that characterized the Holy Trinity. And not only that, but Leah demonstrated signs that a divine and supernatural light had, in fact, shone into her soul, giving her a sense of the sweetness of God himself. Her conversion meant that she had begun, in small measure and in a manner appropriate to a creature, to know the bond of union in the Spirit that the Son enjoys with the Father. And in this participation in the divine fullness, Leah's humanity was being fulfilled. She bore in her soul a dignity beyond all nature.

And yet, despite this supernatural dignity, she remained enslaved by her pastor, Jonathan Edwards.[8] How can we pass by this contradiction? We must not ignore it; we dare not minimize it. We must lament it. Edwards's own son, Jonathan Edwards Jr. gives us words when he preached:

> Let such inquire how it is possible, that our fathers ... universally reputed righteous, should hold Negro slaves, and yet be subjects of real piety? ... To hold a man in a state of slavery, who has a right to his liberty, is to be every day guilty of robbing him of his liberty, or of manstealing. The consequence is inevitable, that other things being the same, to hold a Negro slave, unless he has forfeited his liberty, is a greater sin in the sight of God, than concubinage or fornication.[9]

Surely the man who preached this also lamented his own father's "manstealing." So must we. And as we lament, we must also seek the gift of real repentance. This book addresses the wider theosis conversation, and I put forward two questions in hopes of promoting such repentance.

The first question is this: How might theosis theology learn from people like Leah? Theosis and deification and participation theology is often written

---

[8]See Marsden, *Jonathan Edwards: A Life* (New Haven, CT: Yale University Press, 2003), 255-58, esp. 258.

[9]Jonthan Edwards Jr. (1745–1801), *The Injustice and Impolicy of the Slave Trade and of the Slavery of the Africans: Illustrated in a Sermon preached before the Connecticut Society for the Promotion of Freedom, and the Relief of Persons Unlawfully Holden in Bondage, At their Annual Meeting in New-Haven, Sept 15, 1791* (Boston: Wells and Lilly, Court-Street, 1822), 29.

by highly educated and generally privileged people. But surely we must remember that the God who communicates his divine fullness is the same God who "brought down the mighty from their thrones and exalted those of humble estate" (Lk 1:52). And indeed he placed those words in the mouth of a young woman of nearly no worldly status. If we want to describe the divine nature of a humble God, then we must both embrace humility ourselves and eagerly listen to the wisdom of those whom God exalts, that is, "those of humble estate."

There is precedent for this. Saint Athanasius told the story of an illiterate orphan to show what his view of deification looked like in practice. We know his story as *The Life of St. Anthony*.[10] Saint Gregory Nyssa did something similar with his sister Saint Macrina.[11] We must be humble enough to learn from the masters at this point, masters like Macrina and Anthony, and others who are easy to ignore.

The second question is this: How might theosis theology serve people like Leah? Theosis scholarship is often abstract and obscure, even speculative. This book is an example. Abstract theology has value, but there is also a need to make connections into concrete life. What implications might theosis scholarship bear for a world full of injustice, oppression and so many reasons to grieve? Howard Thurman, in his classic *Jesus and the Disinherited* asked, "Is there any help to be found for the disinherited in the religion of Jesus?"[12] He points to the Christian identity of being children of God. He describes how this identity was transformative for the African American enslaved peoples: "This established for them the ground of personal dignity, so that a profound sense of personal worth could absorb the fear reaction. This alone is not enough, but without it, nothing else is of value."[13] If adoption in Christ, a constituent part of any Christian concept of theosis, bore such power for oppressed African Americans, then surely there are other gifts within theosis that can be given to a church wrestling with injustice.

The only safe way to read Edwards is to read him with a heart and mind quick to lament, and even quicker to repentance.

---

[10] Athanasius, *The Life of Antony*, trans. Tim Vivian and Apostoos N. Athanassakis with Rowan A. Greer (Kalamazoo, MI: Cistercian Publications, 2003).

[11] Gregory of Nyssa, *The Life of St. Macrina*, trans. Kevin Corrigan (Eugene, OR: Wipf & Stock Publishers, 2001).

[12] Howard Thurman, *Jesus and the Disinherited* (Boston, MA: Beacon Press, 1976), 36.

[13] Howard Thurman, *Jesus and the Disinherited*, 40.

7. The Sweetness of Theosis

And as we lament for sin, we also attend the sweetness of Christ's divine grace. When Edwards described true grace as a *koinōnia* in the divine fullness, he was using technical language to describe a profound intimacy between the saint and Christ. Throughout all his technical arguing, all his detailed reasoning, all his finely tuned language, he drives to this experiential intimacy. Edwards describes theosis, or partaking of the divine fullness, in technical language, and this technical language aims at precision. But his precision is always aimed at lived reality. One can hear it in the urgency of his preaching and in the way his logic lifts to heights of wonder in his descriptions of the saints' union with the Godhead. If his language is technical and precise, it is not cold.

Edwards's theology of theosis allures the reader toward its reality. C. S. Lewis distinguishes between *looking at* something and *looking along* something. *Looking at* something is the detached analysis of an observer. *Looking along* something is the experiential perspective of a participant. "The mathematician sits thinking, and to him it seems that he is contemplating timeless and spaceless truths about quantity. But the cerebral physiologist, if he could look inside the mathematician's head, would find nothing timeless and spaceless there—only tiny movements in the grey matter."[14] The mathematician is *looking along*, and the physiologist is *looking at*. Lewis argues both are required, and especially that *looking at* must not be crowned superior.

Edwards does both, and he does both nearly all the time. Great theologians, and especially great preachers, always do both. Why did Edwards analyze true grace and labor to describe it as a participation of divine fullness? That is, why was Edwards so motivated to *look at* true grace and find it a form of divine participation? He *looked at* divine fullness, because he *looked along* it as well. "I have sometimes had a sense of the excellent fullness of Christ," he writes, and on one particular occasion he describes his desire "to be totally wrapt up in the fullness of Christ; and to be perfectly sanctified and made pure, with a divine and heavenly purity."[15] No one who reads Edwards, even his technical descriptions of divine grace, will doubt

---

[14] C. S. Lewis, "Meditation in a Toolshed," in *God in the Dock*, ed. Walter Hooper (Grand Rapids, MI: Eerdmans, 1970), 212-15.
[15] WJE 16:801.

that his aim was to bring his reader (hearer) to *look at* so as to *look along* with him. Indeed, "there is a difference between having a rational judgment that honey is sweet, and having a sense of its sweetness."[16]

Edwards challenges contemporary theology to remember its task of both *looking at* and *looking along*. This union may be easier maintained in the church than the academy, but if church is to recover a doctrine of *theosis*, then it must become a thing the church *tastes*. Athanasius explored the dogmatic and polemical aspects of soteriological participation in *On the Incarnation*, but then popularized its spirituality in *The Life of Anthony*.[17] Similarly, Edwards emphasizes the mechanics of special grace in his sermons and treatises, but he asks readers to *look along* in *The Life and Diary of David Brainerd*. Like the greatest theosis teachers before him, he enticed the church "to taste and see that the LORD is good" (Ps 34:8). As the church seeks, in this current day, to pursue the vision of theosis, it will do well to learn, with critical care and repentant lamentation, from the pen of Northampton's most famous pastor.

---

[16] WJE 17:414.
[17] Saint Athanasius of Alexandria, *St. Athanasius on the Incarnation: The Treatise De Incarnatione Verbi Dei*, trans. A Religious of C.S.M.V. (London: Mowbray, 1953); Athanasius, *The Life of Antony*.

Bibliography

Alston, Wallace M., Jr., and Michael Welker, eds. *Reformed Theology: Identity and Ecumenicity.* Grand Rapids, MI: Eerdmans, 2003.
Athanasius. *The Life of Antony.* Translated by Tim Vivian and Apostoos N. Athanassakis with Rowan A. Greer. Kalamazoo, MI: Cistercian Publications, 2003.
———. *St. Athanasius on the Incarnation: The Treatise De Incarnatione Verbi Dei.* Translated by A Religious of C.S.M.V. London: Mowbray, 1953.
Beeke, Joel R., and Mark Jones. *A Puritan Theology.* Grand Rapids, MI: Reformation Heritage Books, 2012.
Bezzant, Rhys. *Jonathan Edwards and the Church.* Oxford: Oxford University Press, 2014.
Billings, J. Todd. *Calvin, Participation, and Gift: The Activity of Believers in Union with Christ.* Oxford: Oxford University Press, 2007.
———. "John Calvin: United to God Through Christ." In *Partakers of the Divine Nature: The History and Development of Deification in the Christian Traditions*, edited by Michael J. Christensen and Jeffery A. Wittung, 200-218. Grand Rapids, MI: Baker Academic, 2008.
———. "United to God Through Christ: Assessing Calvin on the Question of Deification." *HTR* 98, no. 3 (2005): 315-34.
Boersma, Hans. *Heavenly Participation: The Weaving of a Sacramental Tapestry.* Grand Rapids, MI: Eerdmans, 2011.
———. "Sacramental Ontology: Nature and the Supernatural in the Ecclesiology of Henri De Lubac." *New Blackfriars* 88 (2007): 242-73.
———. *Seeing God: The Beatific Vision in Christian Tradition.* Grand Rapids, MI: Eerdmans, 2018.
Bombaro, John J. *Jonathan Edwards's Vision of Reality: The Relationship of God to the World, Redemption History, and the Reprobate.* Eugene, OR: Pickwick, 2012.
———. "Jonathan Edwards's Vision of Salvation." *Westminster Theological Journal* 65 (2003): 45-67.
Braaten, Carl E. "The Finnish Breakthrough in Luther Research." *Pro Ecclesia* 5, no. 2 (1996): 141-43.
Braaten, Carl E., and Robert W. Jenson. *Union with Christ: The New Finnish Interpretation of Luther.* Grand Rapids, MI: Eerdmans, 1998.
Busch, Eberhard. "Reformed Strength in Its Denominational Weakness." In *Reformed Theology: Identity and Ecumenicity*, edited by Wallace M. Alston Jr. and Michael Welker, 20-33. Grand Rapids, MI: Eerdmans, 2003.
Caldwell, Robert W., III. *Communion in the Spirit: The Holy Spirit as the Bond of Union in the Theology of Jonathan Edwards*, Studies in Evangelical History and Thought. Milton Keynes, UK: Paternoster, 2006.
———. "The Holy Spirit as the Bond of Union in the Theology of Jonathan Edwards." *Refor-*

mation & Revival 12, no. 3 (2003): 43-58.

Calvin, John. *Institutes of the Christian Religion*. Edited by John T. McNeill. Vol. 2. Library of Christian Classics. Louisville, KY: Westminster John Knox, 1960.

Canlis, Julie. "Calvin, Osiander, and Participation in God." *IJST* 6, no. 2 (2004): 169-84.

———. *Calvin's Ladder: A Spiritual Theology of Ascent and Ascension*. Grand Rapids, MI: Eerdmans, 2010.

Carpenter, James A. *Nature and Grace: Toward an Integral Perspective*. New York: Crossroad, 1988.

Chemnitz, Martin. *The Two Natures in Christ: A monograph concerning the two natures in Christ, their hypostatic union, the communication of their attributes, and related questions, recently prepared and revised on the basis of Scripture and the witness of the ancient church by Dr. Martin Chemnitz, with a preface by Dr. Nicolaus Selnecker, pastor at Leipzig*. Translated by J. A. O. Preus. St. Louis: Concordia, 1971.

Cherry, Conrad. *The Theology of Jonathan Edwards: A Reappraisal*. Garden City, NY: Anchor Books, 1966.

Christensen, Michael J. "John Wesley: Christian Perfection as Faith Filled with the Energy of Love." In *Partakers of the Divine Nature*, edited by Michael J. Christensen and Jeffery A. Wittung, 219-29. Grand Rapids, MI: Baker Academic, 2008.

———. "Theosis and Sanctification : John Wesley's Reformulation of a Patristic Doctrine." *Wesleyan Theological Journal* 31, no. 1 (1996): 71-94.

"A Confession of Faith; Owned, and Consented to by the Elders and Messengers of the Churches, Assembled at Boston in New-England, May 12. 1680. Being the Second Session of That Synod." In *Magnalia Christi Americana: Or, the Ecclesiastical History of New-England from Its First Planting in the Year 1620, Unto the Year of Our Lord, 1698. In Seven Books*, edited by Cotton Mather, 5-19. London: Printed for Thomas Parkhurst, at the Bible and Crown in Cheapside, 1702.

Cooper, Adam G. *Naturally Human, Supernaturally God: Deification in Pre-conciliar Catholicism*. Minneapolis: Fortress, 2014.

Cotton, John. *The covenant of Gods free grace, most sweetly unfolded and comfortably applied to a disquieted soul. Whereunto is added, a profession of faith, made by J. Davenport*. Edited by Thomas A. Schafer. London: John Hancock, 1645.

Crisp, Oliver D. "Jonathan Edwards, Idealism, and Christology." In *Idealism and Christian Theology*, edited by Joshua R. Farris and S. Mark Hamilton, 145-75. New York: Bloomsbury, 2016.

———. *Jonathan Edwards Among the Theologians*. Grand Rapids, MI: Eerdmans, 2015.

———. *Jonathan Edwards and the Metaphysics of Sin*. Aldershot, UK: Ashgate, 2005.

———. "Jonathan Edwards on Divine Simplicity." *Religious Studies* 39, no. 1 (2003): 23-41.

———. *Jonathan Edwards on God and Creation*. Oxford: Oxford University Press, 2012.

———. "Jonathan Edwards on the Divine Nature." *Journal of Reformed Theology* 3, no. 2 (2009): 175-201.

———. "Jonathan Edwards's Ontology: A Critique of Sang Hyun Lee's Dispositional Account of Edwardsian Metaphysics." *Religious Studies* 46, no. 1 (2010): 1-20.

———. *Revisioning Christology*. Surrey, UK: Ashgate, 2011.

Cunnington, Ralph. "A Critical Examination of Jonathan Edwards's Doctrine of the Trinity." *Themelios* 39, no. 2 (2014): 224-40.

Danaher, W. J., Jr. *The Trinitarian Ethics of Jonathan Edwards*. Louisville, KY: Westminster John Knox, 2004.

Davison, Andrew. *Participation in God: A Study in Christian Doctrine and Metaphysics*. Cambridge: Cambridge University Press, 2019.

"A Declaration of the Faith and Order Owned and Practiced in the Congregational Churches in England; Agreed Upon and Consented Unto by Their Elders and Messengers in Their Meeting at the Savoy, Octob. 12, 1658." Printed for D.L. and are to be sold in Paul's Churchyard, Fleet-Street, and Westminster-Hall, 1659. http://www.creeds.net/congregational/savoy/.

Downing, Lisa. "George Berkeley." In *The Stanford Encyclopedia of Philosophy*, edited by N. Zalta Edward. 2013 ed. https://plato.stanford.edu/archives/spr2013/entries/berkeley.

Edwards, Jonathan. *Apocalyptic Writings*. Edited by Stephen Stein. WJE 5.

———. *The "Blank Bible."* Edited by Stephen J. Stein. WJE 24.

———. *Catalogues of Books*. Edited by Peter J. Thuesen. WJE 26.

———. *Ecclesiastical Writings*. Edited by David D. Hall. WJE 12.

———. *Ethical Writings*. Edited by Paul Ramsey. WJE 8.

———. *Freedom of the Will*. Edited by Paul Ramsey. WJE 1.

———. *The Great Awakening*. Edited by Clarence Curtis Goen. WJE 4.

———. *A History of the Work of Redemption*. Edited by John F. Wilson. WJE 9.

———. *Letters and Personal Writings*. Edited by Georg S. Claghorn. WJE 16.

———. *The Life of David Brainerd*. WJE 7.

———. *The Miscellanies*. Edited by Thomas A. Schafer. WJE 13.

———. *The "Miscellanies," Entry Nos. 501–832*. Edited by Ava Chamberlain. WJE 18.

———. *The "Miscellanies" 833–1152*. Edited by Amy Plantinga Pauw. WJE 20.

———. *The "Miscellanies," 1153–1360*. Edited by Douglas A. Sweeney. WJE 23.

———. MS Sermon on John 1:16 (1730-31), no. 180, Gen Mss 151, Beinecke Rare Book and Manuscript Library, Yale University. Transcript edited by James Salladin and supplied by The Jonathan Edwards Center, Yale University.

———. *Notes on Scripture*. Edited by Stephen J. Stein. WJE 15.

———. *Original Sin*. Edited by Clyde A. Holbrook. WJE 3.

———. *Religious Affections*. Edited by John E. Smith. WJE 2.

———. *Scientific and Philosophical Writings*. Edited by Wallace Earl Anderson. WJE 6.

———. "Sermon 321. Hebrews 1:3." In *Sermon Series II, 1729–1731*. WJE Online vol. 45.

———. *Sermons, Series II, 1738, and Undated, 1734–1738*. WJE Online 53.

———. *Sermons and Discourses, 1720–1723*. Edited by Wilson H. Kimnach. WJE 10.

———. *Sermons and Discourses, 1723–1729*. Edited by Kenneth P. Minkema. WJE 14.

———. *Sermons and Discourses, 1730–1733*. Edited by Mark Valeri. WJE 17.

———. *Sermons and Discourses, 1734–1738*. Edited by M. X. Lesser. WJE 19.

———. *Sermons and Discourses, 1739–1742*. Edited by Harry S. Stout. WJE 22.

———. *Sermons and Discourses 1743–1758*. Edited by Wilson H. Kimnach. WJE 25.

———. "True Grace Is Divine (1738)." In *Jonathan Edwards: Spiritual Writings*, ed. Adriaan C. Neele, Kyle C. Strobel, and Kenneth P. Minkema, 350-62. Classics of Western Spirituality. New York: Paulist Press, 2019.

———. *Typological Writings*. Edited by Wallace Earl Anderson. WJE 11.

———. *Writings on the Trinity, Grace, and Faith*. Edited by Sang Hyun Lee. WJE 21.

Fabro, Cornelio. "The Intensive Hermeneutics of Thomistic Philosophy: The Notion of Participation." *The Review of Metaphysics* (1974): 449-91.

Fairbairn, Donald. *Grace and Christology in the Early Church*. Oxford Early Christian Studies. Oxford: Oxford University Press, 2006.

Fantino, Jacques. "Circumincession." In *Encyclopedia of Christian Theology*, edited by Jean-

Yves Lacoste, 315-16. New York: Routledge, 2005.

Fiering, Norman. *Jonathan Edwards's Moral Thought and Its British Context*. Chapel Hill: University of North Carolina Press, 1981.

Gavrilyuk, Paul. "The Retrieval of Deification: How a Once-Despised Archaism Became an Ecumenical Desideratum." *Modern Theology* 25, no. 4 (2009): 647-59.

Greely, Andrew M. *The Catholic Imagination*. Berkeley: University of California Press, 2000.

Habets, Myk. "'Reformed Theosis?' A Response to Gannon Murphy." *ThTo* 65, no. 4 (2009): 489-98.

———. *Theosis in the Theology of Thomas Torrance*. Burlington, VT: Ashgate, 2009.

Hallonsten, Gosta. "Theosis in Recent Research." In *Partakers of the Divine Nature: The History and Development of Deification in the Christian Traditions*, edited by Michael J. Christensen and Jeffery Wittung, 281-93. Grand Rapids, MI: Baker Academic, 2008.

Hamilton, S. Mark. "Jonathan Edwards, Hypostasis, Impeccability, and Immaterialism." *Neue Zeitschrift für Systematische Theologie und Religionsphilosophie* 58, no. 1 (2016): 206-28.

Hammond, William Andrew, ed. *The Definitions of Faith and Canons of Discipline of the Six Oecumenical Councils with the Remaining Canons of the Code of the Universal Church. Translated with Notes Together with the Apostolical Canons*. New York: James A. Sparks, 1844.

Hastings, W. Ross. *Jonathan Edwards and the Life of God: Toward an Evangelical Theology of Participation*. Minneapolis: Fortress, 2015.

Haynes, Daniel. "The Metaphysics of Christian Ethics: Radical Orthodoxy and Theosis." *Heythrop Journal* 52 (2011): 659-71.

Hobbs, Thomas. *Leviathan, or the Matter, Forme, & Power of a Common-Wealth Ecclesiastical and Civill*. London: Printed for Andrew Crooke, at the Green Dragon in St. Paul's Churchyard, 1651.

Holmes, Stephen R. "Does Jonathan Edwards Use a Dispositional Ontology? A Response to Sang Hyun Lee." In *Jonathan Edwards: Philosophical Theologian*, edited by Oliver D. Crisp and Paul Helm, 99-114. Burlington, VT: Ashgate, 2003.

———. *God of Grace and God of Glory: An Account of the Theology of Jonathan Edwards*. Edinburgh: T&T Clark, 2000.

———. *The Holy Trinity: Understanding God's Life*. Milton Keynes, UK: Paternoster, 2012.

———. "Reformed Varieties of the Communicatio Idiomatum." In *The Person of Christ*, edited by Stephen R. Holmes and Murray A. Rae, 70-86. London: T&T Clark, 2005.

Hooker, Richard. *The Lawes of Ecclesiastical Polity*. Vol. 2. Edited by John Keble. Oxford: Clarendon, 1888.

Hunsinger, George. "Baptism and the Soteriology of Forgiveness." *IJST* 2, no. 3 (November 2000): 247-69.

Jenson, Robert W. *America's Theologian: A Recommendation of Jonathan Edwards*. Oxford: Oxford University Press, 1988.

———. "Christ in the Trinity: Communicatio Idiomatum." In *The Person of Christ*, edited by Stephen R. Holmes and Murray A. Rae, 61-69. London: T&T Clark, 2005.

Jones, Cheslyn, Geoffrey Wainwright, and Edward Yarnold, SJ, eds. *The Study of Spirituality*. London: SPCK, 1986.

Keating, Daniel A. "Typologies of Deification." *IJST* 17, no. 3 (2015): 267-83.

Kerr, Fergus. "A Catholic Response to the Programme of Radical Orthodoxy." In *Radical Orthodoxy? A Catholic Enquiry*, edited by Laurence Paul Hemming, 46-60. Aldershot, UK: Ashgate, 2000.

Knight, Janice. *Orthodoxies in Massachusetts: Rereading American Puritanism*. Cambridge,

MA: Harvard University Press, 1994.
Lee, Sang Hyun. "Editor's Introduction." In *Writings on the Trinity, Grace, and Faith*, edited by Sang Hyun Lee, WJE 21, 38-62.
———. "Jonathan Edwards's Dispositional Conception of the Trinity: A Resource for Contemporary Reformed Theology." In *Toward the Future of Reformed Theology: Tasks, Topics, Traditions*, edited by E. David Willis, Michael Welker, and Matthias Gockel, 444-55. Grand Rapids, MI: Eerdmans, 1999.
———. *The Philosophical Theology of Jonathan Edwards*. Princeton, NJ: Princeton University Press, 1988.
Lee, Yang-ho. "Calvin on Deification: A Reply to Carl Mosser and Jonathan Slater." *SJT* 63, no. 3 (2010): 272-84.
Leigh, Edward. *A Systeme or Body of Divinity*. London: Printed by A.M. for William Lee at the Signe of the Turks-head in Fleet Street over against Fetter-lane, 1662.
Letham, Robert. "Reformed Theology." In *New Dictionary of Theology: Historical and Systematic*, edited by Tim Grass Martin Davie, Stephen R. Holmes, John McDowell, and T. A. Noble, 747-50. Downers Grove, IL: InterVarsity Press, 2016.
Lewis, C. S. "Meditation in a Toolshed." In *God in the Dock*, edited by Walter Hooper, 212-15. Grand Rapids, MI: Eerdmans, 1970.
Lewis, Thomas. *The Scourge: In Vindication of the Church of England; to Which Is Added, I. The Danger of the Church-Establishment of England, from the Insolence of Protestant Dissenters; Occasion'd by a Presentment of the Forty Second Paper of the Scourge at the King's Bench Bar, by the Grand Jury of the Hundred of Ossulston; II. The Anatomy of the Heretical Synod of Dissenters at Salters-Hall*. London, 1720.
Lim, Paul C. H. *Mystery Unveiled: The Crisis of the Trinity in Early Modern England*. Oxford: Oxford University Press, 2012.
Linman, Jonathan. "Little Christs for the World: Faith and Sacraments as Means to Theosis." In *Partakers of the Divine Nature: The History and Development of Deification in the Christian Traditions*, edited by Michael J. Christensen and Jeffery A. Wittung, 189-99. Grand Rapids, MI: Baker Academic, 2008.
Lossky, Vladimir. *The Mystical Theology of the Eastern Church*. Plymouth, UK: Latimer, Trend, 1957.
Louth, Andrew. "The Place of Theosis in Orthodox Theology." In *Partakers of the Divine Nature: The History and Development of Deification in the Christian Traditions*, edited by Michael J. Christensen and Jeffery A. Wittung, 32-44. Grand Rapids, MI: Baker Academic, 2008.
Lubac, Henri de. *Catholicism: Christ and the Common Destiny of Man*. San Francisco: Ignatius, 1950.
Mander, William. "Pantheism." *Stanford Encyclopedia of Philosophy*. 2013 ed. http://plato.stanford.edu/archives/sum2013/entries/pantheism/.
Mantzaridis, George. *The Deification of Man*. Crestwood, NY: St. Vladimir's Seminary Press, 1984.
Marsden, George M. *Jonathan Edwards: A Life*. New Haven, CT: Yale University Press, 2003.
McClenahan, Michael. *Jonathan Edwards and Justification by Faith*. Burlington, VT: Ashgate, 2012.
McClymond, Michael J. *Encounters with God: An Approach to the Theology of Jonathan Edwards*. Religion in America. New York: Oxford University Press, 1998.
———. "Hearing the Symphony: A Critique of Some Critics of Sang Lee's and Amy Pauw's Accounts of Jonathan Edwards' View of God." In *Jonathan Edwards as Contemporary: Essays in Honor of Sang Hyun Lee*, edited by Don Schweitzer, 67-92. New York: Peter Lang, 2010.
———. "Salvation as Divinization: Jonathan Edwards, Gregory Palamas and the Theological Uses of Platonism." In *Jonathan Edwards: Philosophical Theologian*, edited by Oliver D. Crisp and Paul Helm, 139-60. Burlington, VT: Ashgate, 2003.
McClymond, Michael J., and Gerald R. McDermott. "The Theme of Divinization." In *The

Theology of Jonathan Edwards, 410-23. Oxford: Oxford University Press, 2012.

———. *The Theology of Jonathan Edwards*. New York: Oxford University Press, 2012.

McCormack, Bruce L. "Participation in God, Yes, Deification, No: Two Modern Protestant Responses to an Ancient Question." In *Denkwürdiges Geheimnis: Beiträge Zur Gotteslehre. Festschrift Für Eberhard Jüngel Zum 70. Geburtstag*, edited by Johannes Fischer, Hans-Peter Großhans, and Ingolf U. Dalferth, 347-74. Tübingen: Mohr Siebeck, 2004.

———. "Union with Christ in Calvin's Theology: Grounds for a Divinization Theory?" In *Tributes to John Calvin: A Celebration of His Quincentenary*, edited by David W. Hall, 504-29. Philipsburg, NJ: P&R, 2010.

McDermott, Gerald. "Jonathan Edwards and God's Inner Life: A Response to Kyle Strobel." *Themelios* 39, no. 2 (2014): 241-50.

Meyendorff, John. *Christ in Eastern Christian Thought*. Washington, DC: Corpus Books, 1969.

———. "Doctrine of Grace in St Gregory Palamas." *St Vladimir's Seminary Quarterly* 2, no. 2 (1954): 17-26.

———. *A Study of Gregory Palamas*. London: Faith Press, 1964.

Milbank, John. "Postmodern Critical Augustinianism: A Short Summa in Forty-Two Responses to Unasked Questions." In *The Radical Orthodoxy Reader*, edited by John Milbank and Simon Oliver, 3-27. New York: Routledge, 2009.

Milbank, John, Catherine Pickstock, and Graham Ward, eds. *Radical Orthodoxy*. New York: Routledge, 1999.

Moeller, Charles, and G. Philips. *The Theology of Grace and the Oecumenical Movement*. Translated by A. Wilson. London: Mowbray, 1961.

More, Henry. *Enthusiasmus Triumphatus, or, a Discourse of the Nature, Causes, Kinds, and Cure of Enthusiasme*. London, 1656.

Morimoto, Anri. *Jonathan Edwards and the Catholic Vision of Salvation*. University Park: Pennsylvania State University Press, 1995.

Morris, Thomas V. *Our Idea of God: An Introduction to Philosophical Theology*. Vancouver, BC: Regent College Publishing, 1991.

Mosser, Carl. "The Earliest Patristic Interpretations of Psalm 82, Jewish Antecedents, and the Origin of Christian Deification." *Journal of Theological Studies* 56, no. 1 (2005): 30-74.

———. "An Exotic Flower? Calvin and the Patristic Doctrine of Deification." In *Reformation Faith: Exegesis and Theology in the Protestant Reformations*, edited by Michael Parsons, 38-56. Milton Keynes, UK: Paternoster, 2014.

———. "The Greatest Possible Blessing: Calvin and Deification." *SJT* 55, no. 1 (2002): 36-57.

Muller, Richard A. *Post-Reformation Reformed Dogmatics*. Vol. 4, *The Trinuity of God*. Grand Rapids, MI: Baker, 2003.

———. *Post-Reformation Reformed Dogmatics: The Rise and Development of Reformed Orthodoxy, ca. 1520 to ca. 1725*. Vol. 1, *Prolegomena to Theology*. 2nd ed. Grand Rapids, MI: Baker Academic, 2003.

Murphy, Gannon. "Reformed Theosis?" *ThTo* 65, no. 2 (2008): 191-212.

Oliver, Simon. "Henri De Lubac and Radical Orthodoxy." In *T&T Clark Companion to Henri De Lubac*, edited by Jordon Hillebert, 393-417. New York: Bloomsbury, 2017.

———. "What Is Radical Orthodoxy?" In *The Radical Orthodoxy Reader*, edited by John Milbank and Simon Oliver, 3-27. New York: Routledge, 2009.

Olsen, Roger. "Deification in Contemporary Theology." *ThTo* 64 (2007): 186-200.

Ortiz, Jared, ed. *Deification in the Latin Patristic Tradition*. Washington, DC: Catholic University of America Press, 2019.

Owen, John. *Communion with God: Of Communion with God the Father, Son, and Holy Ghost,*

Each Person Distinctly, in Love, Grace, and Consolation; or, the Saints' Fellowship with the Father, Son, and Holy Ghost Unfolded. Oxford: Benediction Classics, 2017.

———. *A Vindication of Some Passages in a Discourse concerning Communion with God.* London, 1674.

———. *The Works of John Owen.* 3 vols. Edinburgh: Banner of Truth Trust, 1976–1981.

Owen, John, et al. *Proposals for the Furtherance and Propagation of the Gospel in This Nation. As the Same Were Humbly Presented to the Honourable Committee of Parliament by Divers Ministers of The Gospell, and Others, as Also, Some Principles of Christian Religion, without the Beliefe of Which, the Scriptures Doe Plainly and Clearly Affirme, Salvation Is Not to Be Obtained, Which Were Also Presented in the Explanation of One of The Said Proposals.* London: R. Ibbitson, 1653.

Patrides, C. A., ed. *The Cambridge Platonists.* Cambridge: Cambridge University Press, 1969.

Pauw, Amy Plantinga. "A Response from Amy Plantinga Pauw." *SJT* 57, no. 4 (2004): 486-89.

———. *The Supreme Harmony of All: The Trinitarian Theology of Jonathan Edwards.* Grand Rapids, MI: Eerdmans, 2002.

Pelikan, Jaroslav. *The Christian Tradition: A History of the Development of Doctrine.* Vol. 1, *The Emergence of the Catholic Tradition (100–600).* Chicago: University of Chicago Press, 1971.

———. *The Christian Tradition: A History of the Development of Doctrine.* Vol. 4, *The Reformation of Church and Dogma (1300–1700).* Chicago: University of Chicago Press, 1984.

———. *The Christian Tradition: A History of the Development of Doctrine.* Vol. 5, *Christian Doctrine and Modern Culture (Since 1700).* Chicago: University of Chicago Press, 1989.

Rohls, Jan. "Reformed Theology—Past and Present." In *Reformed Theology: Identity and Ecumenicity,* edited by Wallace M. Alston Jr. and Michael Welker. Grand Rapids, MI: Eerdmans, 2003.

Russell, Norman. *The Doctrine of Deification in the Greek Patristic Tradition.* Oxford Early Christian Studies. Oxford: Oxford University Press, 2006.

———. "Theosis and Gregory Palamas: Continuity or Doctrinal Change?" *St Vladimir's Theological Quarterly* 50, no. 4 (2006): 357-79.

———. "Why Does *Theosis* Fascinate Western Christians?" *Sobornost* 34, no. 1 (2012): 5-15.

Rutherford, Samuel. *A Survey of the Spiritual Antichrist.* London: J. D. & R. for Andrew Cooke, 1648.

Salladin, James. "Essence and Fullness: Evaluating the Creator-Creature Distinction in Jonathan Edwards." *SJT* 70, no. 4 (2017): 427-44.

———. "Nature and Grace: Two Participations in the Thought of Jonathan Edwards." *IJST* 18, no. 3 (2016): 290-303.

———. "Theosis." In *The Jonathan Edwards Encyclopedia,* edited by Kenneth P. Minkema, Harry S. Stout, and Adriaan C. Neele, 563-64. Grand Rapids, MI: Eerdmans, 2017.

Schweitzer, William M. *God Is a Communicative Being: Divine Communicativeness and Harmony in the Theology of Jonathan Edwards.* London: Bloomsbury T&T Clark, 2012.

Slater, Jonathan. "Salvation as Participation in the Humanity of the Mediator in Calvin's Institutes of the Christian Religion: A Reply to Carl Mosser." *SJT* 58, no. 1 (2005): 39-58.

Smith, James K. A. *Introducing Radical Orthodoxy: Mapping a Post-secular Theology.* Grand Rapids, MI: Baker Academic, 2004.

Steele, Richard B. "Transfiguring Light: The Moral Beauty of the Christian Life According to Gregory Palamas and Jonathan Edwards." *St Vladimir's Theological Quarterly* 52, nos. 3-4 (2008): 403-39.

Strobel, Kyle. "By Word and Spirit: Jonathan Edwards on Redemption, Justification, and Regeneration." In *Jonathan Edwards and Justification*, edited by Josh Moody, 45-69. Wheaton, IL: Crossway, 2012.

———. "Jonathan Edwards and the Polemics of Theosis." *HTR* 105, no. 3 (2012): 259-79.

———. "Jonathan Edwards's Reformed Doctrine of *Theosis*." *HTR* 109, no. 3 (2016): 371-99.

———. *Jonathan Edwards's Theology: A Reinterpretation*. T&T Clark Studies in Systematic Theology. London: T&T Clark, 2013.

Studebaker, Steven. "Jonathan Edwards's Social Augustinian Trinitarianism: An Alternative to a Recent Trend." *SJT* 56, no. 3 (2003): 268-85.

———. "The Supreme Harmony of All: The Trinitarian Theology of Jonathan Edwards." *Fides et historia* 36, no. 1 (2004): 156-57.

———. "Supreme Harmony or Supreme Disharmony? An Analysis of Amy Plantinga Pauw's *The Supreme Harmony of All: The Trinitarian Theology of Jonathan Edwards*." *SJT* 57, no. 4 (2004): 479-85.

Studebaker, Steven, and Robert W. Caldwell. *The Trinitarian Theology of Jonathan Edwards: Text, Context, and Application*. Surrey, UK: Ashgate, 2012.

Tan, Seng-Kong. *Fullness Received and Returned: Trinity and Participation in Jonathan Edwards*. Minneapolis: Fortress, 2014.

Te Velde, Rudi A. "General Introduction." In *Participation and Substantiality in Thomas Aquinas*, ix-xiv. New York: Brill, 1995.

Thuesen, Peter J. "Introduction." In *Catalogues of Books*, edited by Peter J. Thuesen, 1-114. WJE 26.

Torrance, T. F. *Theology in Reconstruction*. London: SCM Press, 1965.

Turner, John. *A Phisico-Theological Discourse*. London: Printed by F.C. for Timothy Childe at the White Hart at the West End of St. Paul's Church-yard, 1698.

Turretin, Francis. *Institutes of Elenctic Theology*. Vol. 2. Translated by George Musgrave Giger. Edited by James T. Dennison Jr. Phillipsburg, NJ: P&R, 1994.

Webster, John. *Holiness*. London: SCM Press, 2003.

Williams, A. N. *The Ground of Union: Deification in Aquinas and Palamas*. New York: Oxford University Press, 1999.

Williams, N. P. *The Grace of God*. London: Longmans, Green, 1930.

Wilson, Stephen A. *Virtue Reformed: Rereading Jonathan Edwards's Ethics*. Leiden: Brill, 2005.

Wisse, Maarten. *Trinitarian Theology Beyond Participation*. Edited by Ian A. McFarland, John Webster, and Ivor Davidson. T&T Clark Studies in Systematic Theology. London: T&T Clark, 2011.

Withrow, Brandon G. *Becoming Divine: Jonathan Edwards's Incarnational Spirituality Within the Christian Tradition*. Eugene, OR: Cascade Books, 2011.

Yarnold, Edward, SJ. *The Second Gift: A Study of Grace*. Slough, UK: Society of St. Paul, 1974.

Zerwick, Max, and Mary Grosvenor. *A Grammatical Analysis of the Greek New Testament*. 5th ed. Rome: Editrice Pontificio Istituto Biblico, 1996.

Name Index

Ames, William, 50
Anthony, Saint, 247, 249
Arminius, Jacob, 52
Athanasius, Saint, 118, 247, 249
Augustine, Saint, 78
Barth, Karl, 241
Baxter, Richard, 50
Beeke, Joel, 185
Berkeley, George, 72
Beza, Theodore, 50
Billings, J. Todd, 10
Boersma, Hans, 5, 88, 235, 244
Bombaro, John, 14, 17, 176-78, 180, 188-89
Brainerd, David, 20-22, 62-63, 196, 232-33, 237, 249
Breck, Robert, 25, 53
Bullinger, Heinrich, 50
Caldwell, Robert, 42
Calvin, John, 11, 43, 50
Canlis, Julie, 43, 67-68, 74
Cassian, John, 77
Chauncey, Charles, 60
Chemnitz, Martin, 205
Cheynell, Francis, 183-84
Cotton, John, 55, 179, 189-90
Crisp, Oliver, 14, 72, 173
Cyril of Alexandria, Saint, 201
Davison, Andrew, 197, 224, 236
de Lubac, Henri, 5, 86, 88, 146, 244
Edwards, Jonathan, 2, 7-18
Fabro, Cornelio, 74-75
Fairbairn, Donald, 219
Fiering, Norman, 69

Gavrilyuk, Paul, 66-67, 76, 84, 87, 94, 169
Goodwin, Thomas, 189
Greeley, Andrew, 235
Gregory of Nyssa, Saint, 247
Habets, Myk, 97-98, 100, 136-37, 139
Hallonston, Gosta, 8
Hastings, W. Ross, 43
Hawley, Joseph, Sr., 25
Haynes, Daniel, 85-87
Hobbes, Thomas, 70-71
Holmes, Stephen, 14, 17, 70, 172-77, 193
Hunsinger, George, 44, 46-47
Jenson, Robert, 52, 94
John of Damascus, Saint, 202
Jones, Mark, 185
Lee, Sang Hyun, 13, 17, 101, 148, 164-69, 171-75, 177-79, 188
Leigh, Edward, 59-60
Lewis, C. S., 248
Lim, Paul, 57
Lossky, Vladimir, 4, 241
Louth, Andrew, 8
Macrina, Saint, 247
Maximus the Confessor, Saint, 97
McClenahan, Michael, 188-89
McClymond, Michael, 17, 22, 174-81, 195
McCormack, Bruce, 8, 97-98, 100, 136-37, 143
McDermott, George, 17, 22

Meyendorf, John, 4, 214, 217, 220
More, Henry, 59-60
Morimoto, Anri, 17, 188-89
Mosser, Carl, 11
Muller, Richard, 184, 195
Nicolas, Henry, 57
Oliver, Simon, 86-87, 146
Owen, John, 46, 50, 58, 183, 189, 194, 219
Palamas, Gregory, 9, 97
Pauw, Amy Plantinga, 174, 183
Perkins, William, 50
Polanus, Amandus, 189
Russell, Norman, 138
Rutherford, Samuel, 57, 60
Scotus, Duns, 85, 88-89
Smith, John (Cambridge Platonist), 82-84
Strobel, Kyle, 14, 17, 39-40, 109, 140, 160, 176, 189, 240
Studebaker, Steve, 176
Tan, Seng-Kong, 115
Theodore of Mopsuestia, 201
Thomas Aquinas, Saint, 8, 71, 79, 84
Thurman, Howard, 247
Torrance, T. F., 5-7, 9-10, 118-19, 122, 135
Turner, John, 59-60
Turretin, Francis, 50, 194
Van Mastricht, Peter, 50, 229
Williams, A. N., 77
Wisse, Maarten, 66, 84, 95
Yarnold, Edward, 77-79, 82
Zwingli, Huldrych, 50

Subject Index

A History of the Work of Redemption, 25, 228-29
A Treatise Concerning the Religious Affections, 56, 60, 76, 99-100, 187-88, 197, 230
agape, 35, 38, 185
Anabaptist theology, 50
angels, 30, 35, 54, 67, 93, 157, 193, 228, 231
anhypostaton, 202-3
Arminianism, Arminian, 15-16, 20-25, 50, 52-54, 56, 63, 84, 87, 95, 148, 239
aseity, 71
asymptotic union, 134, 167
attribute, 29, 37, 105-9, 159, 185, 205-6, 211-13, 224
 divine, 105-9, 185-86, 205, 207, 211-13
 incommunicable, 205-6
 real, 106, 159, 185, 212
 relational, 212
Augustinian tradition, 64, 81, 186
autonomy, autonomous, 20-21, 54, 70, 72, 75, 85, 88-89, 94, 121, 132-33, 146, 174
beatific vision, 86, 88, 234-36
beauty, 20, 28, 53, 61, 63, 99, 147, 189, 196, 208-10, 213, 218, 222-33, 244
being in general, 76, 161-62, 164, 180
Body (of Christ), 60-61, 132, 190, 203, 214, 220
bond
 of love, 35-36, 62-63, 114, 131, 211, 234
 of union, 32, 63, 200, 203-4, 246
Boston Synod of 1680, 184
Calvinism, 22, 53
Cambridge Platonists, 86, 170, 193, 239
Canons of Dort, 50
causality, 177-78
Chalcedon(ian), 46-47, 117-27, 135, 198, 200-201, 205, 209, 214
Charity and its Fruits, 25, 151
Christian life, 3, 18
Christology, 17, 37, 41, 58, 100-101, 117-20, 123, 126, 129, 130-32, 134, 138-39, 144, 157-58, 171, 182, 197-200, 202, 207, 213-15, 218-20, 223, 242, 244
Church of England (Anglican), 50, 53, 60
circumincession. *See* perichoresis
communication
 of attributes (*communicatio idiomatum*), 205
 of being, 167, 241-42
 of divine fullness, 2, 61-62, 148, 154, 157, 163, 165, 178, 198, 213, 221-22, 228, 230, 241, 242, 245
 of majesty (*genus maiestaticum*), 204-6, 212
 and participation, 2, 7, 12, 22, 28, 32-33, 41-42, 47, 63, 67, 91, 153, 159, 178-82, 192, 194, 198, 224, 227, 239, 242
 See also participation and communion
communicative natures, 39, 240
communion, 16, 36, 40-42, 44, 47-48, 60-63, 68, 92-95, 113-16, 118, 123-28, 138, 162, 168, 183-84, 186, 194, 201, 202, 212, 233
confessional, 50-51, 195, 242
consent, 107, 211, 213, 214
consubstantiality, 43, 113
continuous creation, 71-72, 74, 92, 121, 173-74
conversion, 20-21, 62, 228, 246
corruption, 54-55, 79-81, 170
Council of Ephesus, 201
creation, 2, 5-7, 14, 18, 26-31, 37-43, 52, 54, 68, 70-79, 82, 86-87, 91-92, 94, 101, 104, 111, 121-22, 126-29, 139, 148-49, 152-82, 192-93, 195, 199, 204, 209-10, 221-22, 225-26, 229-31, 233, 235-36, 240-45
Creator-creature
 distinction, 2-3, 7, 14-18, 20-22, 24, 30, 32, 52, 58, 60-61, 64, 94, 97, 129, 133, 136, 146, 172, 189, 190, 195-96, 236, 239-42
 relation, 138, 145-46
Cyrillian orthodoxy, 201, 204
deification (divinization, theosis), 2-12, 15-17, 21-23, 27, 49, 58-59, 66-67, 76,

Subject Index 261

80, 85-86, 94, 97, 118, 124, 128, 136, 181, 197, 215, 220, 238-49
deism, deists, 54, 70-71
deity, 36, 45, 71, 94, 105-7, 114, 117, 131, 137, 140-41, 222
delight, 35, 38, 46, 61, 63, 92, 102-3, 105, 111-12, 140-41, 147, 193, 217, 222, 230-31, 233-34, 236-37
differentiation, 30, 43-46, 95, 97, 100-101, 112, 114, 128-29, 139, 239
Discourse on the Trinity, 38, 104, 109, 159, 183
Display of the Spiritual Antichrist, 60
disposition, dispositionalism, dispositional ontology, 17, 20, 60, 103, 105, 111, 115, 165-68, 171-80, 187-89, 224
divine
 essence, 2, 7, 15-17, 21-22, 24-25, 27-28, 33, 35, 44-45, 56, 61, 98-101, 105, 108-17, 122-23, 126, 129, 137-38, 141-44, 145, 149, 168, 171-72, 196, 214, 239, 240, 242
 love, 34-35, 40-41, 79-81, 90, 110, 113, 115, 117, 137, 149, 150, 160, 170, 187, 194-95, 200, 203, 238, 245
 mind, 73
 nature, 3, 41, 58, 61, 81-82, 90, 105, 118-19, 131, 136, 141, 143, 170, 204-7, 209, 223-24, 236, 242, 247

divinity, 24, 26-27, 29, 65, 82, 94, 139, 208, 210, 229
divinization. *See* deification
doctrines of grace, 19, 90, 130, 192
Eastern Orthodoxy, 4, 5, 8-9, 11, 18, 22, 27, 97-98, 128, 143, 181
ecumenical theology, 7, 9-10, 12, 18, 240-41
Edwards scholarship, 13, 148, 164, 241
effectual calling, 56, 62, 240
elect, 6-7, 67, 151, 175, 216
emanation, 37, 154, 158-60, 167, 169-70, 193, 210, 227
enhypostaton, 202-3
ens entium, being of beings, 71, 76, 121, 128, 177, 180
enthusiasm, enthusiasts, 15, 20-21, 22, 24, 52, 56-63, 75, 148, 239
enypostatos, 202-3
essence. *See* divine essence and human essence
essence-energies distinction, 17, 97-98, 100, 128, 136-37, 139, 143, 215
eternity, 2, 18, 63, 90, 122, 162, 167, 169, 195, 197, 207, 221, 225, 234, 239
ethics, 103, 149, 244
ex nihilo, 31, 70, 72
excellency, 20, 28, 107, 124, 135, 189, 196, 207-14, 218, 228, 230
excellencies of Christ, 208, 210, 224, 228, 230, 233-34
extrinicism, 88, 145-46

fall of humanity, 54, 80, 82-83, 89, 90, 95, 170, 229, 235
Familists, 57-58, 60
finitum non capax infiniti, 125, 133
fullness-essence distinction, 17, 96-144
gift, 1-2, 6-7, 10, 15, 21, 28, 31-32, 35, 37, 39-41, 53, 55, 70, 82, 85-87, 92, 95, 96, 116, 128, 135, 141, 143, 145, 153, 155, 160, 168-69, 171, 179, 185-87, 190-92, 195, 196, 213, 215, 223-25, 238-40, 242-43, 246-47
glorification, 6, 221-22, 243
glory, 1-2, 19-20, 27, 37, 63, 82, 140, 150, 158-60, 175-76, 186, 193, 208, 211, 217, 226-28, 234, 237
Godhead, 31, 37-39, 104-5, 116, 118, 120, 126, 129, 131, 141, 150, 176, 185, 220, 248
gospel, 1, 109-10, 124, 131, 184, 190, 242-43
grace
 common, created, 31, 98, 143, 186-91
 doctrine of, 3-4, 8-10, 12, 14-16, 18, 22-24, 29, 33-34, 40, 47-49, 51-53, 56, 61, 63, 82, 96, 110, 114, 116-17, 120, 130, 135, 141-42, 146, 148, 168, 180-82, 185, 189, 192-95, 198, 214, 217, 239-42
 efficacious, 55-56
 infused, 187
 saving, 26, 35, 41, 68, 87, 89, 128-29, 163, 187, 197

special, 2-3, 6-9, 14-16, 18, 21, 24, 27, 31, 34-35, 37, 39, 41, 44-48, 54-56, 61-62, 65, 67-68, 77, 87, 91-92, 96, 129, 137, 138-39, 143, 145, 159, 152, 154-55, 158-63, 168-69, 178-80, 182-83, 191, 236, 239-41, 245, 249
true, 2, 22, 24-26, 30, 32, 33-34, 36, 41, 44, 53, 60, 79, 80, 84, 87-88, 147, 153, 168-69, 196, 227, 248
uncreated, 180, 186-92
gratuity, 30, 56, 65, 86-87, 146, 242
habit, habitus, habitual, 165-66, 178-80, 189, 233
happiness, 28, 35-36, 38, 54, 62, 92, 99, 102-6, 111-12, 114-16, 120, 124, 126, 132, 137, 147, 150, 159, 175, 221, 230
Heidelberg Catechism, 50
holiness, 6-7, 22, 30, 32, 36, 38, 61, 77, 79, 81, 107, 114, 116, 137, 147, 159, 211, 230-32
Holy Spirit, 1, 7, 16, 35-41, 47-48, 56, 59, 63, 92-93, 105, 108, 111, 113-16, 119, 123-24, 131-32, 136-37, 140-43, 145, 147, 149-50, 159, 168, 171, 176, 185-88, 190-92, 195, 198, 199, 203, 212-14, 217, 223, 234, 238-39
homoousion, 117, 120, 139, 142-43
human essence, 117, 123, 126, 138, 169, 171, 178, 199

hypostatic union, 59, 119, 123, 129-30, 132, 134, 142, 197-99, 201, 204-5, 207-8, 211, 213-15, 217-21, 223-24, 233-34
idealism, idealist, 72, 104-5, 120-21, 123, 128-29, 173-74
immediate, immediacy, 14, 30-31, 33, 36, 44-45, 47, 55-56, 62, 68-73, 78-81 91, 93, 95, 121, 157, 167, 170, 173-74, 176-78, 190-91, 208, 227-28, 241
incarnation, 6, 47, 95, 177, 120, 122-25, 128, 138, 145-46, 199, 208, 211, 215-16, 218, 229, 239, 249
intermediary, 45, 139, 143
intimacy, 15-18, 21, 32, 43, 45-46, 57, 61-62, 95-96, 100-101, 112, 114, 126, 131-32, 134-36, 139, 143-47, 157, 169, 195, 198, 235, 239, 248
Jesus Christ
   and creation, 121-22, 127, 199
   human and divine natures, 117-26, 129, 138, 198-214
   See also Christology
justification, 6, 182, 224, 243
knowledge (divine and human), 38-40, 82-83, 92, 159-60, 206, 209, 212
koinōnia, 12-13, 16, 43-48, 60, 62-63, 67-68, 93, 96-97, 100-101, 110, 112, 114-20, 123-24, 126-29, 135, 139, 142, 147-53, 155, 160-62, 164, 168, 171, 180,

196-99, 210, 214-15, 224-27, 233-36, 242, 248
law(s), 70, 165-66, 177, 216, 243
Logos, 35, 38, 104, 120, 123-34, 138, 142, 146, 185, 198-204, 207-14, 217-21, 223-25, 234
love
   between the Father and the Son, 35-37, 41, 63, 92, 112, 114, 135, 150, 178, 214, 239
   divine, 34-35, 40-41, 79-81, 90, 110, 113, 115, 117, 137, 149-50, 160, 170, 187, 194-95, 200, 203, 238, 245
   trinitarian, 93, 104-5, 242
   self-love, 55, 80, 89, 161-64, 170, 178, 245
   uncreated, 16
Lutheran theology, 50, 52, 205-6, 212
Mary, 128
mediation, 36-37, 40, 46
metaphysics, 5, 69, 71, 73, 166,
   participatory, 5-6, 67, 76, 79-81, 84, 95
methexis, 12-13, 16, 43-44, 48, 67, 70, 74-75, 85, 91, 93, 95, 100-101, 110-14, 116-18, 120-23, 126-29, 139, 142, 147, 149-54, 161, 193, 197, 242
Miscellanies, 61, 111, 123-24, 127, 130, 134, 147, 165, 179, 199-200, 209-10, 213, 217, 220, 222-23, 230-31
modification, 15, 18, 51-52, 110, 140, 171, 176, 180-95

monergism, monergistic, 23
mystical union, 59, 125,
  129, 142, 218
natural, 65-95
  appetite, 170
  autonomy, 21, 70, 75,
    88-89, 94, 146
  being, 89, 177
  capacity, 21, 55, 80
  causes, 31, 45
  dependence on God,
    70, 74, 76, 87, 94
  desire, 86, 88, 90
  development, 29
  effort, 21-22
  emptiness, 79, 90, 236
  end, 20
  endowment, 20
  faculties, 93
  gifts, 28
  goodness, 55
  humanity of Jesus, 120
  icons, 228
  image of God, 76, 246
  influence of the Spirit,
    76
  humanity, 19, 163, 169
  need, 55
  ontology, 122
  principles, 77, 80-81, 89,
    95
  reality, 121
  reason, 82
  substance, 121-22
  and the supernatural, 90
  world, 69-72, 74, 96,
    226-28, 230, 244
naturalization of God, 21
nature
  book of, 228-29
  Christ's human and
    divine, 117-26, 129,
    138, 198-214

created, 2, 7, 12, 14-17, 22,
  24, 32-34, 44-45, 53, 56,
  63, 65-67, 79-80, 85-90,
  94, 129, 138, 145-49,
  152-55, 158, 168-69, 171,
  173, 177-78, 180, 187,
  189, 195-98, 209-11,
  213-14, 224-25, 227,
  230, 233-37, 239,
  241-42, 245
communicative,
  communicable,
  39-40, 160, 240
and grace, 52, 65-95, 96,
  101, 145-46, 169-70,
  178, 196-237, 241, 246
human, 3, 53, 55, 60, 81,
  88, 90, 118, 121-23,
  126-27, 130, 136, 169,
  170, 198-99, 202-11,
  224-25, 234, 245
See also divine nature
Nestorianism (Nestorian),
  127, 201, 202, 213-14,
  219-20
Newtonian physics, 71
Northampton,
  Massachusetts, 25, 140,
  144, 231, 246, 249
Notes on Scripture, 78, 80
ontology, ontological, 3-6,
  16-17, 29-30, 33, 44-45, 48,
  63, 65-66, 69-70, 73, 85,
  88, 116, 122, 148, 154-55,
  158, 165-67, 172-88, 188,
  197, 235, 243-44
  created, 16, 166-67
  differentiation, 45
  essential, 30
  sacramental, 5, 88, 235,
    244
See also dispositional
  ontology

Palamas, Palamism,
  Palamite, 9, 11-12, 17,
  97-98, 101, 128, 136-37,
  139, 143-44, 239
panentheism,
  panentheistic, 148, 241
pantheism, pantheistic, 71,
  122, 143
partake, partaker. *See*
  participation
participation, 2-8, 41-48, 197
  common, 16, 67-77,
    79-81, 85, 87-95, 121,
    127, 146-49, 154,
    158-59, 161-64, 177-78,
    210, 227, 230, 235, 241,
    244, 245
  in being, 73, 129,
    163-64, 197
  in God, 5, 55, 66, 75-76,
    78-79, 82, 83, 85, 89,
    94-95, 97, 121, 127,
    158-59, 163, 180, 193,
    235, 241, 244, 245
  koinōnia participation
    (see *koinōnia*)
  methexis participation
    (see *methexis*)
  ontological, 5, 12, 16,
    44, 48, 67, 85-86, 88,
    91, 244
  soteriological, 7, 9-12,
    14-18, 22-24, 37, 49,
    56, 59, 64, 67, 84-88,
    181-82, 192, 195, 197,
    239-40, 249
  soteriology, 3, 7-8, 14
  special, 67, 68, 89-95,
    147-49, 152, 161-64,
    178, 210, 224, 227-28,
    235-36, 239, 241, 245
  theology, 9, 12-13, 15,
    22, 49, 64, 65, 67, 68,
    85, 95, 197, 242, 246

Pelagian, Pelagianism, Pelagians, 54, 65, 77
perichoresis, perichoretic, perichoretically (circumincession), 108-9, 240
perpetual growth/progress, 2, 134, 157, 221-22, 225
personal faculties, 123-25
personhood, 205-9, 111, 120, 202-7, 234
philosophy, 13, 70, 75, 149, 164, 244
Platonism, platonic, Neoplatonism, 43, 48, 57, 59, 60, 67-68, 74-76, 81-89, 91, 93, 95, 100, 170, 193, 235, 239, 241
pneumatology, 17, 123, 192, 194
polemical, polemics, 8, 15-18, 22, 24-25, 48-62, 65, 84-85, 95, 97, 107, 115, 249
process theology, 6
providence, providential, 6, 96, 156, 177, 226, 228, 230, 233
pure act, 38, 105, 113, 140, 142
pure nature, 89-90
Puritan, 19-21, 26, 50-63, 149, 183-94
quiddity, 16, 43, 44-45, 48, 110, 113-14, 116-17, 126-27, 139, 144, 150, 161, 171, 198-99, 242
Radical Orthodoxy, 5, 43, 85-88, 146, 244
Ranters, 57
reason, 82-83, 155-56, 161, 170
Reformation, 10, 23, 57, 182, 235

Reformed Orthodoxy, 17, 24, 52, 61, 176, 182, 184, 239
Reformed tradition/theology, 3, 5-10, 13, 17, 21, 23, 48-62, 64, 84, 100, 118-19, 133, 136, 148, 159, 163, 176, 180-82, 195, 200, 204-5, 209, 212, 239, 240
relational, relationality, 13, 15-17, 32, 42-44, 46, 48, 61, 68, 93-95, 96, 110, 112, 114-16, 127-28, 138-44, 150, 161-62, 166, 168, 171-72, 197, 212, 242
religion, religious, 19, 21, 52, 56, 60, 62, 82, 99, 140, 145, 160, 197, 232, 247
revival, 25, 60, 231-32
Roman Catholic tradition, 5, 10, 50, 52, 57, 146
Russian diaspora, 4-5
Salter's Hall Synod of 1719, 183
sanctification, 6, 243
Savoy Declaration, 56, 184, 190, 194
Scripture, 2, 22, 28, 36, 56-59, 78, 80-81, 90, 99, 109, 156, 163, 183, 242
self-worship, 19, 21
semi-Pelagianism, 52, 77, 179
Sermons
 "Christians a Chosen Generation," 226, 228
 "A Divine and Supernatural Light," 69, 91, 99, 218
 "The Excellency of Christ," 135, 207, 209, 210

 "MS Sermon on John" 1:16, no. 180,
 "Partaking of Christ," 39, 131, 215-16, 223-24
 "True Grace is Divine," 24-34, 36, 44, 53, 60, 79-80, 84, 169, 191
Socinianism, 57
soteriology, soteriological, 3, 5-7, 14, 16-17, 35, 41, 47, 58, 65, 66, 86, 95, 110, 117-18, 135-36, 140, 149, 155, 157-58, 171, 174-75, 179-80, 182-86, 190-91, 193, 240, 242-43
sovereignty, 19, 63, 84, 168, 175
spiritual sense, 218
substance, 13, 43, 44, 71-76, 91-92, 94, 100, 104-5, 112-14, 120-23, 126, 129, 139, 150, 161, 165-66, 172-74, 177
supernatural, 19, 27-31, 62, 69, 77-92, 95, 191, 218, 246
 principles, 77-92, 95, 170
 end, 21-22, 86, 146
synergistic, synergism, 15, 52, 95, 239
teleology, 18, 79, 90, 147-58, 167, 192-94, 244
terminology, 12-13
The End for which God created the World, 37, 39, 40, 111, 148, 152-67, 179, 193, 221-22
The Great Doctrine of Original Sin Defended (Original Sin), 80, 84, 89, 170
The Nature of True Virtue, 162, 211

The Philosophical Theology of Jonathan Edwards, 164-80
The Religious Affections. See *A Treatise Concerning the Religious Affections*
Theologica Germanica, 59
theosis. *See* deification
total depravity, 79, 84
Treatise on Grace, 34, 38-39, 44, 46, 77, 84, 92, 160, 169, 193
trinitarian, trinitarianism, 35-38, 40-42, 47, 49, 67-68, 91, 93, 96-144, 147, 150-53, 159, 162, 165-66, 171, 175-76, 178-85, 192-93, 195, 199, 217-18, 238, 242
Trinity, 96-144
   ad extra, 37, 39, 41, 117-28, 135, 140, 150-53, 155, 161-62, 165, 168, 239
   ad intra, 35, 37, 39, 41, 110, 111, 115-17, 121, 124-26, 135, 138, 140, 149-52, 155, 160-62, 165, 168, 211, 218, 236, 239, 240
   economic, 3, 62, 63, 92, 97, 100-101, 125-26, 135, 137, 139-41, 151, 164, 195, 238, 240, 243
   immanent, 41, 97, 100-101, 119, 125, 137, 139-42, 195
   social model of, 108
   typology, typological, 27, 100-101
understanding
   divine, 39, 160, 212
   human (of Jesus), 125
   and will, 39-40, 108, 124-25, 134, 160, 200-201, 203-4, 207, 212, 217-18
Unitarianism, 183
   See also Socinianism
univocity of being, 89
virtue (ethical), 25-26, 34, 81, 83, 159, 162-63, 211, 232
Western (theology or tradition), 4-5, 8-12, 27, 43, 65, 98, 143, 149, 181, 186
Westminster Confession and Catechism, 50, 158, 184, 190, 192-94
will
   divine, 38-39, 160
   human, 54
   understanding and, 39-40, 108, 124-25, 134, 160, 200-201, 203-4, 207, 212, 217-18
work of redemption, 25-26, 155, 168, 225, 228-29, 234

Scripture Index

OLD TESTAMENT

Genesis
1:2, *78*

Psalms
34:8, *249*
82, *11*

Proverbs
16:4, *147, 236*

Isaiah
51:8, *228*

NEW TESTAMENT

Matthew
7:13, *245*

Luke
1:52, *247*

John
1:16, *37, 39, 99, 131, 194, 215, 216*
3:32, *133*
3:34, *37, 131, 133, 200, 216, 223*
17:5, *125*
17:13, *134*
17:26, *1*

Acts
17:28, *86, 87*

Romans
2:10, *237*

1 Corinthians
13, *25*

2 Corinthians
3:18, *189*
13:14, *47, 48, 114, 124*

Ephesians
3:14-19, *1*
3:17-19, *99*
3:19, *25, 37, 78, 117, 131, 194*

Philippians
3:21, *214*

Colossians
1:16, *244*
1:16-17, *235*
1:19, *117, 194*
2:6, *61*
2:9, *37, 131, 194, 220*

Hebrews
1:3, *112*

1 Peter
2:9, *226*

2 Peter
1:4, *47, 58, 61, 131*

1 John
1:3, *92*
4:12, *26, 34*

Revelation
5:5, *208*

New Explorations in Theology

Theology is flourishing in dynamic and unexpected ways in the twenty-first century. Scholars are increasingly recognizing the global character of the church, freely crossing old academic boundaries and challenging previously entrenched interpretations. Despite living in a culture of uncertainty, both young and senior scholars today are engaged in hopeful and creative work in the areas of systematic, historical, practical and philosophical theology. New Explorations in Theology provides a platform for cutting-edge research in these fields.

In an age of media proliferation and academic oversaturation, there is a need to single out the best new monographs. IVP Academic is committed to publishing constructive works that advance key theological conversations. We look for projects that investigate new areas of research, stimulate fruitful dialogue, and attend to the diverse array of contexts and audiences in our increasingly pluralistic world. IVP Academic is excited to make this work available to scholars, students and general readers who are seeking fresh new insights for the future of Christian theology.

NET ADVISORY BOARD:

Daniel Castelo, *Duke Divinity School*
Tom Greggs, *University of Aberdeen*
Kristen Johnson, *Western Theological Seminary*
Beth Felker Jones, *Northern Seminary*
Veli-Matti Karkkainen, *Fuller Theological Seminary*
Tom McCall, *Asbury Theological Seminary*
Kyle Strobel, *Biola University*

VOLUMES INCLUDE:

- *Chrysostom's Devil: Demons, the Will, and Virtue in Patristic Soteriology*, Samantha L. Miller
- *Reading Scripture as the Church: Dietrich Bonhoeffer's Hermeneutic of Discipleship*, Derek W. Taylor
- *T. F. Torrance as Missional Theologian: the Ascended Christ and the Ministry of the Church*, Joseph H. Sherrard
- *The Making of Stanley Hauerwas: Bridging Barth and Postliberalism*, David B. Hunsicker